Introduction to
JavaScript Programming

The "Nothing but a Browser" Approach

Eric S. Roberts
Stanford University and Reed College

 **Pearson**

221 River Street, Hoboken NJ 07030

Senior Vice President Courseware Portfolio Management: Engineering, Computer Science, Mathematics, Statistics, and Global Editions: *Marcia J. Horton*
Director, Portfolio Management: Engineering, Computer Science, and Global Editions: *Julian Partridge*
Executive Portfolio Manager: *Tracy Johnson*
Portfolio Management Assistant: *Meghan Jacoby*
Managing Producer, ECS and Mathematics: *Scott Disanno*
Senior Content Producer: *Erin Ault*
Manager, Rights and Permissions: *Ben Ferrini*
Operations Specialist: *Maura Zaldivar-Garcia*

Inventory Manager: *Bruce Boundy*
Product Marketing Manager: Yvonne Vannatta
Field Marketing Manager: *Demetrius Hall*
Marketing Assistant: *Jon Bryant*
Cover Design: *Black Horse Designs*
Cover Image: *philipp igumonov/Getty*
Composition: *Eric S. Roberts*
Cover Printer: *Phoenix Color*
Printer/Binder: *Lake Side Communications, Inc. (LSC)*
Typeface: *Times New Roman*

Library of Congress Cataloging-in-Publication Data
Names: Roberts, Eric, author.
Title: Introduction to JavaScript Programming / Eric S. Roberts, Stanford University.
Description: First edition. | Pearson Education, Inc., [2020] | Includes index.
Identifiers: LCCN 2018054226 | ISBN 9780135245859 | ISBN 0135245850
Subjects: LCSH: JavaScript (Computer program language)
Classification: LCC QA76.73.J39 R59 2019 | DDC 005.2/762--dc23
LC record available at https://lccn.loc.gov/2018054226

1 19

 Pearson

ISBN 10:   0-13-524585-0
ISBN 13:   978-0-13-524585-9

To Lauren, with love

To the Student

Welcome! By picking up this book, you have taken a step into the world of computer science. Twenty-five centuries ago, the Chinese philosopher Lao-tzu observed that the longest journey begins with a single step. This book can be your beginning.

Computing is a profoundly empowering technology. Jobs are plentiful, salaries are high, and there are far too few people with the necessary skills to fill those jobs. Computation, moreover, is transforming almost every discipline, not just in science and engineering but also across the entire university curriculum. No matter what field of study you choose, understanding how to use computing effectively will be of enormous value.

To get you started on your journey into the wonders of computer science, this book teaches you how to write programs in a language called JavaScript, which is a central technology for web-based applications. The programs you create as you go through this book will run in any web browser, including the browser on your phone. More importantly, however, the book will teach you the fundamental principles of programming. While it uses JavaScript to illustrate these principles, they will carry over into any other language that you learn.

As with any skill that is worth knowing, programming will not necessarily come easily. Many students find computers overwhelming and imagine that computer science is beyond their reach. Learning the basics of programming, however, does not require advanced mathematics or a detailed understanding of electronics. What matters is whether you can progress from the statement of a problem to its solution.

To do so, you must be able to think logically and to express your logic in a form that the computer can understand. Perhaps most importantly, you must be able to see the task through to its completion without getting discouraged by difficulties and setbacks. If you stick with the process, you will discover that reaching the solution is so exhilarating that it more than makes up for any frustrations along the way.

I wish you an exciting and empowering journey.

Eric Roberts
Stanford University
January 2019

To the Instructor

This book is designed for use in the first programming course in a typical college or university curriculum. It covers the material in a traditional first course in computer science, generically referred to as CS1. The book assumes no prior programming experience and is appropriate both for prospective computer science majors and for students in other disciplines who are interested in learning the fundamentals of programming.

The book uses a programming language called *JavaScript,* which is one of the most widely used languages in industry and has become the standard language for writing interactive web applications. Because of its popularity, JavaScript is built into every major web browser, which means that any device with a browser can run JavaScript programs without any additional software. The focus of this text, however, is on the fundamental concepts of programming rather than the language. It does not cover all of JavaScript and avoids several aspects of the language that students are likely to misuse. The subset of JavaScript employed in this book provides students with more than enough power to write exciting programs that run in any web browser.

The case for using JavaScript in CS1

As a discipline, computing is always changing. These changes can be profoundly exciting, particularly for students who have grown up in the digital world. For educators, the breakneck pace of development creates challenges that invariably extend even into the earliest levels of the curriculum. As languages, tools, and paradigms shift, teaching strategies must evolve to remain current.

Two decades ago, the Java programming language, with its support for applets, looked like the wave of the future and seemed likely to become the standard for web-based programming. That didn't happen. By the early 2000s, Java applets had been abandoned in favor of the ubiquitous blend of JavaScript, HTML, and CSS that serves as the foundation for web applications today.

Once it was clear that JavaScript had triumphed in the race to become the language of the web, several of my colleagues and I began to think about using it in Stanford's introductory programming course. Much of our original motivation for choosing JavaScript came from our excitement about a "Nothing but a Browser" model in which students—even those with no access to computers other than a smart phone—could work entirely in the web environment. When we began teaching the JavaScript version of our introductory course, we found that the browser-based model worked exactly as we envisioned. Students no longer have to install and use a separate development environment. All they need is a web browser, which every student has. They are also able to add JavaScript content to their own web pages, which increases the students' incentive to learn the material and encourages them to show off their work.

Beyond the advantages of the web-based model, we were delighted to discover just how well JavaScript works as a teaching language. Students can master the essentials of JavaScript much more quickly than their predecessors learned Java. As Douglas Crockford, who developed the widely used JavaScript Object Notation described in Chapter 9, observes, JavaScript is "a beautiful, elegant, highly expressive language," even though it is often used in the context of other web technologies that share little of that elegance. If you focus on the JavaScript language itself, its beauty and elegance make teaching JavaScript much simpler than teaching other languages, with far fewer confusing details to explain.

The relative simplicity of JavaScript is reflected in the length of this textbook, which is 30 percent shorter than my Java book for the same course. Despite being shorter, the JavaScript version covers at least 25 percent *more* material. In part, the economy of presentation reflects the fact that JavaScript programs are shorter than the same programs written in Java. Of even greater importance, however, is the fact that the parts of those programs that disappear in the transition from Java to JavaScript are precisely the parts that would have required the most explanation.

Pedagogical approach

Introduction to JavaScript Programming relies on three proven strategies to maximize students' understanding. First, it introduces the concepts of programming using a JavaScript version of Rich Pattis's wonderful Karel the Robot microworld, which has gently welcomed Stanford students to the world of programming for almost 40 years. Although it is possible to skip the Karel chapter, we have found that the increased conceptual understanding students derive from that introduction more than repays the time. Second, the book adopts the programming guidelines recommended by Douglas Crockford in *JavaScript: The Good Parts,* which outlines how to write elegant, well-structured programs in JavaScript. Third, the book presents topics in an order that defers the most challenging topics until students have the necessary background. For example, the detailed discussion of how JavaScript works together with other web technologies like HTML and CSS appears in Chapter 12, after students have already completed chapters on data structures and inheritance.

Pedagogical features

The text uses the following features to enhance student learning:

- *Chapter openers.* Every chapter begins with a photograph and short biography of someone who has had a major impact on computing. These biographies, and the diverse backgrounds of the people included, emphasize the human side of computing.

- *Key terms.* Each new term in the text appears in boldface italic and is followed immediately by a definition.

- *Syntax boxes.* Each new syntactic form is summarized in a highlighted box that appears in the margin of that page.

- *Syntax coloring.* The major program examples appear in numbered figures that use syntax coloring to ensure that students can easily differentiate comments, keywords, and string constants from the rest of the code.

- *Source code.* The source code for all the sample programs is available on the web site for the book. The programs, moreover, all run in any browser.

- *Chapter summary.* Each chapter includes an extensive summary that lists the key ideas introduced in the chapter.

- *Review questions.* Each chapter summary is followed by review questions that provide a self-test of student understanding. Answers to the review questions appear on the web site.

- *Programming exercises.* Each chapter ends with an extensive set of exercises that test whether students understand the chapter material while giving them opportunities to create exciting applications.

Resources for the instructor

The following resources are available to instructors who adopt this textbook on the Pearson Instructor Resource Center (http://www.pearsonhighered.com/irc):

- *Guide to the instructor.* Teachers who adopt the text receive an instructor's guide that includes additional examples, recommendations for projects and programming assignments, hints on pedagogical strategy, and suggestions for possible variations in the order of presentation.

- *Lecture slides.* The web-based repository for the book includes a set of slides in Microsoft® PowerPoint for each of the 12 chapters. These slides illustrate the key points in each chapter and include detailed animations of the program examples.

- *Solutions to the exercises.* Adopters have access to a repository containing solutions to the programming exercises.

Resources for students

The following resources are available at www.pearsonhighered.com/cs-resources:

- *Program sources.* The web site includes the source code for all sample programs presented in the text. The web pages for those programs also allow students to run the programs directly in the browser.

- *Program animations.* For several of the most important sample programs, the web site makes it possible for students to step through the execution of the program so they can see it in operation.

- *Answers to the review questions.* The review questions serve as a self-test that allows students to check their understanding. The answers to these review questions are available on the web site.

System requirements

The most important advantage of using JavaScript in an introductory course is that programs run in any browser that implements HTML 5 and ECMA 6—both of which are supported by all major browsers today. None of the JavaScript programs require features from more recent versions of JavaScript and in fact use only ECMA 6 extensions that are typically supported even in older browsers.

Although it is possible to use the interactive applications on the web site to write simple programs without using any other tools, many students will find it easier to use a more powerful text editor to write and edit their programs. Many excellent editors are freely available on the web, and we have found it best to let students choose an editor that fits their own needs rather than to impose a particular choice.

Acknowledgments

Many people contributed in different ways to the development of this book. I am especially indebted to Douglas Crockford, whose book *JavaScript: The Good Parts* proved that it is possible to write "beautiful, elegant, highly expressive" programs in JavaScript and showed his readers how to do so.

I also want to thank colleagues at Stanford who have helped make this book possible. I am profoundly grateful to Jerry Cain, with whom I taught a pilot version of a JavaScript-based introductory course in the spring of 2016-17. We learned a great deal from that exercise and have integrated those insights and understandings into the final version of this book. In addition to being a wonderful co-teacher, Jerry has been a tireless reader of this text through many drafts. His amazingly thorough comments have made it much stronger. I owe considerable thanks as well to my colleagues Chris Piech, Keith Schwarz, and Marty Stepp for their extensive contributions to the book. And I also need to thank several generations of section leaders and the students in the pilot versions of the course, all of whom have helped make it so exciting to teach this material.

I am grateful to Tracy Johnson, Marcia Horton, Erin Ault, Meghan Jacoby, and the other members of the team at Pearson for their support on this book as well as its predecessors over the years. In addition, I deeply appreciate the comments from reviewers Paul Fodor, Ian Utting, Kristine Christensen, and Zerksis Umrigar, who offered excellent feedback and suggestions.

As always, my greatest thanks are due to my wife Lauren Rusk, who has again worked her magic as my developmental editor. Lauren's expertise has added considerable clarity and polish to the text. Without her, nothing would ever come out as well as it should.

Contents

CHAPTER 1
A Gentle Introduction

In many schools today . . . the computer is being used to program the child. In my vision, the child programs the computer and, in doing so, both acquires a sense of mastery over a piece of the most modern and powerful technology and establishes an intimate contact with some of the deepest ideas from science, from mathematics, and from the art of intellectual model-building.

— Seymour Papert, *Mindstorms,* 1980

(Rick Friedman/Corbis Entertainment/Getty Images)

Seymour Papert (1928–2016)

In the 1960s, Professor Seymour Papert at MIT used a language called LOGO to teach programming to schoolchildren in the Boston area, who wrote programs to control a robotic turtle. The turtle could move forward or backward, rotate a specified number of degrees around its center, and draw pictures on large sheets of paper with a pen mounted on its underside. The LOGO turtle thereby became the first programming microworld, designed to teach the basics of computation in a simplified environment.

Computer science is one of the most dynamic and vibrant fields of study in today's world. Most students recognize that obtaining a degree in computer science provides outstanding career options. Fewer, however, realize that computer science offers extraordinary opportunities for creativity, intellectual challenge, and finding solutions to important problems facing the world.

Unlocking the power of computing requires you to master the discipline of **_programming,_** which is the process of transforming a strategy for solving a problem into a precise formulation that can be executed by a computer. Programming is not, however, something you can learn simply by reading a book. Like almost any skill worth learning, computing requires practice. This book provides the tools you need to begin that practice by writing programs that solve interesting problems.

At the same time, it would be hard to learn programming through the metaphorical equivalent of jumping in at the deep end of the pool. You have to approach the subject gradually. Modern programming languages involve so many details that their complexity gets in the way of understanding the bigger picture.

To avoid overwhelming you with the intricacies inherent in those languages, this book introduces programming in the context of a simplified environment called a **_microworld._** By design, microworlds are easy to understand and make it possible for you to start programming right away. In the process, you will learn the fundamental concepts of programming without having to master a lot of extraneous details.

Many different microworlds have flourished over the years, including the Project LOGO Turtle described briefly on the title page of this chapter. This book begins by introducing a microworld called Karel that we have used with great success at Stanford University for more than 30 years. Working with Karel enables you to solve challenging problems from the very beginning. And because Karel encourages imagination and creativity, you can have fun along the way.

1.1 Introducing Karel

In the 1970s, a Stanford graduate student named Richard Pattis decided that it would be easier to teach the fundamentals of programming if people could learn those concepts in an environment free from the complexities that characterize most programming languages. Drawing inspiration from the success of the LOGO project, Pattis designed a microworld in which students teach a virtual robot to solve simple problems. Pattis called his robot **_Karel_** after the Czech playwright Karel Čapek whose 1923 play *R.U.R.* (*Rossum's Universal Robots*) gave the word *robot* to the English language. Karel was an immediate success and soon spread to universities all over the world.

(Courtesy of Richard Pattis)

Richard Pattis

Programming in Karel

Karel is a very simple robot living in an equally simple world. By giving Karel a set of instructions, you can direct it to perform certain tasks within its world. Those instructions constitute a *program*. Generically, the text that makes up a program is called *code*. When you write a Karel program, you must do so in a precise way so that Karel can correctly interpret the instructions. Every program you write must obey a set of syntactic rules that define whether that program is legal.

The rules of Karel's programming language are similar to those of other, more sophisticated languages. The difference is that Karel's programming language is tiny—so small, in fact, that you can learn everything there is to know about the Karel language in less than an hour. Even so, you will discover that solving a problem in Karel's world can be quite challenging. Solving problems is the essence of programming. By learning the rules, you unlock the power of problem-solving.

Karel's world

Karel's world is defined by *streets* running from west to east and *avenues* running from south to north. The intersection of a street and an avenue is called a *corner*. Karel can only be positioned on a corner and must be facing in one of the four standard compass directions (north, east, south, and west). In the following sample world, Karel is facing east at the corner of 1st Street and 1st Avenue:

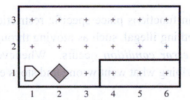

Several other components of Karel's world can be seen in this example. The gray, diamond-shaped object in front of Karel is a *beeper*. Rich Pattis describes beepers as "plastic cones which emit a quiet beeping noise." These noises are audible only if Karel and the beeper are on the same corner. For example, Karel is unaware of the beeper in the diagram as it appears and will discover the beeper only if Karel moves forward to the next corner. The solid lines in the diagram are *walls*. Karel's world always has walls along the edges and may also contain internal walls.

Karel's world is used to tell stories in which the geometry of the world can be interpreted in different ways. In some cases, it is appropriate to view the world as streets and avenues in a two-dimensional plane. In others, you need to forget about streets and avenues and think about Karel's world in a different way. In the diagram shown in the example, it is easiest to imagine that you are seeing the world from the side. Karel is standing on the ground, and the interior walls form a ledge

FIGURE 1-1 Karel's built-in functions

`move()`	Karel moves forward one block. Karel cannot move forward if there is a wall blocking the way.
`turnLeft()`	Karel rotates 90 degrees to the left (counterclockwise).
`pickBeeper()`	Karel picks up one beeper from the current corner and stores that beeper in its beeper bag, which can hold an infinite number of beepers. Karel can execute the `pickBeeper` function only if there is a beeper on that corner.
`putBeeper()`	Karel puts a beeper from its bag down on the current corner. Karel can execute the `putBeeper` function only if there are any beepers in its beeper bag.

that Karel must surmount. Beepers, moreover, are used to represent any objects that appear in the story. You just need to use your imagination.

Karel's built-in functions

The operations that Karel performs as it executes a program are called *functions.* When Karel is shipped from the factory, it knows how to execute only the four functions shown in Figure 1-1. The parentheses that appear in each of these examples are part of Karel's syntax and specify that you want to perform that operation, which in programming terminology is known as *calling the function.*

Several of the built-in functions place specific restrictions on Karel's activities. If Karel tries to do something illegal, such as moving through a wall or picking up a nonexistent beeper, an *error condition* occurs. Whenever an error arises, Karel displays a message describing what went wrong and stops executing the program.

■ 1.2 Teaching Karel to solve problems

For the most part, learning to program in Karel is a matter of figuring out how to use Karel's limited set of operations to solve a specified problem. As a simple example, suppose that you want Karel to move the beeper from its initial position on 2nd Avenue and 1st Street to the center of the ledge at 5th Avenue and 2nd Street. Thus, your goal is to write a Karel program that accomplishes the task illustrated in the following before-and-after diagram:

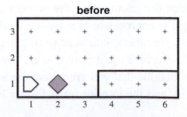

before

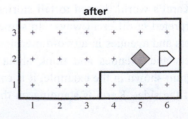

after

Getting started

The first few steps in solving this problem are simple enough. You need to tell Karel to move forward, pick up the beeper, and then move forward again to reach the base of the ledge. The Karel simulator allows you to execute instructions by typing them into an interactive window called the *Karel console.* The first three steps in the program therefore look like this:

```
                        Karel Console
> move()
> pickBeeper()
> move()
>
```

Executing these function calls leaves Karel in the following position:

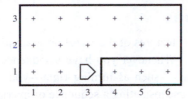

From here, Karel's next step is to turn left to begin climbing the ledge. That operation is also easy, because Karel's set of built-in functions includes `turnLeft`. Calling `turnLeft` at the end of the preceding program leaves Karel facing north on the corner of 3rd Avenue and 1st Street. If you then call the `move` instruction, Karel will move north to reach the following position:

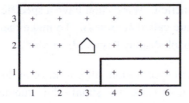

The next thing you need to do is get Karel to turn right so that it is again facing east. While this operation is conceptually as easy as getting Karel to turn left, there is a slight problem: Karel's language includes a `turnLeft` instruction, but no `turnRight` instruction. It's as if you bought the economy model only to discover that it is missing an important feature.

At this point, you have your first opportunity to begin thinking like a programmer. You have access to a set of Karel functions, but not exactly the set you need. What can you do? Can you accomplish the effect of a `turnRight` function using only the capabilities you have? The answer, of course, is yes. You can turn right by turning left three times. After three left turns, Karel will be facing in the desired direction. The next three steps in the program might therefore be

```
turnLeft()
turnLeft()
turnLeft()
```

Although turning left three times has the desired effect, it is hardly an elegant solution. What you as the programmer want to say is

```
turnRight()
```

The only difficulty is that Karel doesn't yet have a definition for the `turnRight` function. To include `turnRight` in a program, you first have to teach Karel what `turnRight` means.

Defining functions

One of the most powerful features of the Karel programming language is the ability to define new functions. Whenever you have a sequence of Karel operations that performs some useful task—such as turning right—you can give that sequence a name. The operation of encapsulating a sequence of instructions under a new name is called *defining a function.* The format for defining a function looks like this:

```
function name() {
      statements that make up the body of the function
}
```

The first word in this pattern is `function`, which is used in both Karel and JavaScript to define a function. Words that have a specific, predefined meaning in a programming language are called *keywords.* To make them easier to recognize, the program listings in this book display keywords in blue.

To complete the function definition, all you have to do is substitute `turnRight` for the italicized placeholder *name* and supply the statements needed to implement the function, as follows:

```
function turnRight() {
    turnLeft();
    turnLeft();
    turnLeft();
}
```

Once you have defined a function like `turnRight`, you can think of it as a new built-in function, just like `move` or `turnLeft`. In a sense, defining a function is like buying an upgrade for your robot that includes the missing operations.

Completing the program

After you have gotten Karel to turn right toward the top of the ledge, the rest of the program is easy. All you have to do is move forward twice, put down the beeper, and then move forward to reach the desired final state. The complete sequence of steps you need to solve the program from beginning to end looks like this:

```
                     Karel Console
> move()
> pickBeeper()
> move()
> turnLeft()
> move()
> turnRight()
> move()
> move()
> putBeeper()
> move()
>
```

Instead of typing each instruction into the console, it makes sense to define a new function that contains this sequence of instructions. You can then call that function with a single name. In this book, functions that represent complete programs begin with an uppercase letter and have names that describe their purpose as clearly as possible. Figure 1-2 at the top of the next page defines a program-level function named **MoveBeeperToLedge** together with the function **turnRight**.

In addition to the definitions of **MoveBeeperToLedge** and **turnRight**, Figure 1-2 includes two examples of an important programming feature called a *comment*, which consists of text designed to explain the operation of the program to human readers. In Karel, comments begin with the characters **/*** and end with the characters ***/**. The first comment describes the operation of the program as a whole; the second describes the **turnRight** function. In a program this short, such comments are probably unnecessary. As programs become more complicated, however, comments quickly become essential tools to document the program design and make it easier for other programmers to understand.

Figure 1-2 also illustrates the technique of *syntax coloring,* which is the practice of using different colors in a program listing to make it easy to recognize different components of the program. In the program listings that appear as separate figures, this book uses green to identify comments, blue to identify language keywords like **function**, cyan for quoted strings, and black for the rest of the program text. Depending on what editor you use to write your programs, the colors chosen for the various program components may be different from the ones used in Figure 1-2. Many editors will use additional colors to make further distinctions. For you as a programmer, the primary value of syntax coloring is that it allows you to see immediately where each program component starts and ends.

FIGURE 1-2   **Program to move the beeper up to the ledge**

```
/*
 * File: MoveBeeperToLedge.k
 * ---------------------------
 * This program solves the problem of moving a beeper to a ledge.
 */

function MoveBeeperToLedge() {
    move();
    pickBeeper();
    move();
    turnLeft();
    move();
    turnRight();
    move();
    putBeeper();
    move();
}

/*
 * Turns Karel right 90 degrees.
 */

function turnRight() {
    turnLeft();
    turnLeft();
    turnLeft();
}
```

Using library functions

Although the code in Figure 1-2 explicitly includes the definition of **turnRight**, it is tedious to have to copy that code into every program that needs that function. For the most common operations, it makes sense to store them in a way that makes it easy to reuse them in other programs. In computer science, collections of useful functions and other program components are called *libraries.* For example, the **turnRight** function and the equally useful **turnAround** function are both included in a special Karel library called **turns,** which you can use simply by including the following line at the beginning of your program:

> **"use turns";**

This statement asks Karel to use the **turns** library, which includes definitions for the functions **turnRight** and **turnAround.** All the Karel examples in the rest of this chapter use the **turns** library.

Decomposition

Whenever you begin to solve a programming problem—no matter whether that program is written in Karel or a more advanced programming language—your first task is to figure out how to divide the complete problem into smaller pieces called *subproblems*, each of which can be implemented as a separate function. That process is called *decomposition.* Decomposition is one of the most powerful strategies that programmers use to manage complexity, and you will see it again and again throughout this book.

To get a sense of how decomposition works in the context of a very simple problem, imagine that Karel is standing on a "road" as shown on the left side of the following before-and-after diagram:

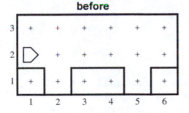 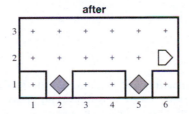

Karel's job is to fill each of the two potholes—the one on 2nd Avenue and the one on 5th Avenue—with a beeper and then continue on to the next corner, ending up in the position shown on the right.

Although you could solve this problem using the four predefined instructions, you can use functions to improve the structure of your program. If nothing else, you can use `turnAround` and `turnRight` to shorten the program and make its intent clearer. More importantly, you can use decomposition to break the problem down into subproblems and then solve those problems independently. You can, for example, divide the problem of filling the pothole into the following subproblems:

1. Move one block forward to reach the first pothole on 2nd Avenue.
2. Fill the pothole by dropping a beeper into it.
3. Move three blocks forward to reach the second pothole on 5th Avenue.
4. Fill the pothole by dropping a beeper into it.
5. Move one block forward to reach the desired final position.

If you think about the problem in this way, you can use functions to ensure that the program reflects your conception of the problem structure, as shown in Figure 1-3.

As with any programming problem, there are other decomposition strategies you might have tried. Some strategies make the program easier to read, while others

FIGURE 1-3   Karel program to fill two potholes

```
/*
 * File: FillTwoPotholes.k
 * ------------------------
 * This program instructs Karel to fill two potholes, which must be on
 * 2nd and 5th Avenues.
 */

"use turns";

function FillTwoPotholes() {
   move();
   fillPothole();
   move();
   move();
   move();
   fillPothole();
   move();
}

/*
 * Fills a pothole immediately underneath Karel.  When you call
 * this function, Karel must be standing just above the pothole,
 * facing east.  When the function returns, Karel will be in its
 * original position above the repaired pothole.
 */

function fillPothole() {
   turnRight();
   move();
   putBeeper();
   turnAround();
   move();
   turnRight();
}
```

only make the meaning more opaque. As your programming problems become more complex, decomposition will turn out to be one of the most important aspects of the design process.

Choosing an effective decomposition is much more of an art than a science, although you will find that you get better with practice. Section 1.4 presents some general guidelines that will help you in that process.

1.3 Control statements

As useful as it is, the ability to define new functions does not actually enable Karel to solve any new problems. The name of a function is merely shorthand for a specific set of instructions. It is therefore always possible to expand a program written as a series of function calls into a single function that accomplishes the same task, although the resulting code is likely to be long and difficult to read. The instructions are still executed in a fixed order that does not depend on the state of Karel's world. Before you can solve more interesting problems, you must be able to write programs that transcend this strictly linear, step-by-step operation. To do so, you need to learn several new statements in Karel's programming language that enable Karel to examine its world and change its execution pattern accordingly.

Statements that affect the order in which a program executes instructions are called *control statements.* Control statements fall into the following two classes:

1. *Conditional statements.* Conditional statements specify that certain statements in a program should be executed only if a particular condition holds. In Karel, you specify conditional execution using an `if` statement.

2. *Iterative statements.* Iterative statements specify that certain statements in a program should be executed repeatedly, forming what programmers call a *loop.* Karel supports two iterative statements: a `repeat` statement that allows you to repeat a set of instructions a fixed number of times, and a `while` statement that allows you to repeat a set of instructions as long as some condition holds.

Conditional statements

To give you a sense of where conditional statements might come in handy, let's go back to the pothole-filling program presented at the end of section 1.2. Before filling the pothole in the `fillPothole` function, Karel might want to check whether some other repair crew has already filled the hole on that corner with a beeper. If so, Karel does not need to put down a second one. To represent such checks in the context of a program, you need to use the `if` statement, which has one of the following two forms:

```
if (conditional test) {
    statements to be executed only if the condition is true
}
```

or

```
if (conditional test) {
    statements to be executed if the condition is true
} else {
    statements to be executed if the condition is false
}
```

The first form of the **if** statement is useful when you want to perform an action only under certain conditions. The second is appropriate when you need to choose between two alternative courses of action.

The conditional test shown in the first line of these patterns must be replaced by one of the tests Karel can perform on its environment, listed in Figure 1-4. Like function calls, tests include an empty set of parentheses, which are part of the Karel syntax. Every test in the list is paired with a second test that checks the opposite condition. For example, you can use the **frontIsClear** condition to check whether the path ahead of Karel is clear or the **frontIsBlocked** condition to see whether a wall is blocking the way. Choosing the right condition requires you to think about the logic of the problem and see which condition is easiest to test.

You can use the **if** statement to modify the definition of the **fillPothole** function so that Karel puts down a beeper only if there is not already a beeper on that corner. The new definition of **fillPothole** looks like this:

```
function fillPothole() {
    turnRight();
    move();
    if (noBeepersPresent()) {
        putBeeper();
    }
    turnAround();
    move();
    turnRight();
}
```

FIGURE 1-4 **Conditions that Karel can test**

frontIsClear()	frontIsBlocked()	Is there a wall in front of Karel?
leftIsClear()	leftIsBlocked()	Is there a wall to Karel's left?
rightIsClear()	rightIsBlocked()	Is there a wall to Karel's right?
beepersPresent()	noBeepersPresent()	Are there any beepers on this corner?
beepersInBag()	noBeepersInBag()	Are there any beepers in Karel's bag?
facingNorth()	notFacingNorth()	Is Karel facing north?
facingEast()	notFacingEast()	Is Karel facing east?
facingSouth()	notFacingSouth()	Is Karel facing south?
facingWest()	notFacingWest()	Is Karel facing west?

The `if` statement in this example illustrates several features common to all control statements in Karel. The control statement begins with a ***header,*** which indicates the type of control statement along with any additional information to control the program flow. In this case, the header is

```
if (noBeepersPresent())
```

which shows that the statements enclosed within the braces should be executed only if the `noBeepersPresent` test is true. The statements enclosed in braces represent the ***body*** of the control statement.

It often makes sense to include `if` statements in a function that check whether it is appropriate to apply that function in the current state of the world. For example, calling the `fillPothole` function works correctly only if Karel is facing east directly above a hole. You can use the `rightIsClear` test to determine whether there is a hole to the south, which is the direction to the right of the one that Karel is facing. The following implementation of `fillPothole` includes this test along with the `noBeepersPresent` test you have already seen:

```
function fillPothole() {
    if (rightIsClear()) {
        turnRight();
        move();
        if (noBeepersPresent()) {
            putBeeper();
        }
        turnAround();
        move();
        turnRight();
    }
}
```

As you can see from the spacing used in this example, the body of each control statement is indented with respect to the statements that enclose it. The indentation makes it much easier to see exactly which statements will be affected by the control statement. Such indentation is particularly important when the body of a control statement contains other control statements. Control statements that occur inside other control statements are said to be ***nested.***

Iterative statements

In solving Karel problems, you will often find that repetition is a necessary part of your solution. If you were really going to program a robot to fill potholes, it would hardly be worthwhile to have it fill just one. The value of having a robot perform

such a task comes from the fact that the robot could repeatedly execute its program
to fill one pothole after another.

To see how repetition can be used in the context of a programming problem,
consider the following stylized roadway in which the potholes are evenly spaced
along 1st Street at every even-numbered avenue:

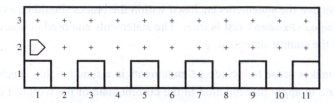

Your mission is to write a program that instructs Karel to fill all the holes in this
road. Note that the road reaches a dead end after 11th Avenue, which means that
you have exactly five holes to fill.

Because you know from this example that there are exactly five holes to fill, the
control statement that you need is a **repeat** statement, which specifies that you
want to repeat some operation a predetermined number of times. The **repeat**
statement looks like this:

>   repeat (*number of repetitions*) {
>   *statements to be repeated*
>   }

For example, if you want to change the **FillTwoPotholes.k** program so that it
solves the more complex problem of filling five evenly-spaced holes, all you have
to do is write the following code:

```
function FillFivePotholes() {
    repeat (5) {
        move();
        fillPothole();
        move();
    }
}
```

The **repeat** statement is useful only when you know in advance the number of
repetitions you need to perform. In most applications, the number of repetitions is
controlled by the specific nature of the problem. For example, it seems unlikely that
a pothole-filling robot could always count on there being exactly five potholes. It
would be much better if Karel could continue to fill holes until it encountered some
condition that caused it to stop, such as reaching the end of the street. Such a
program would be more general in its application and would work correctly in

either of the following worlds as well as any other world in which the potholes were spaced exactly two corners apart:

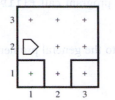 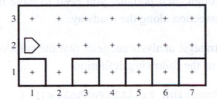

To write a general program that works with any of these worlds, you need to use a **while** statement. In Karel, a **while** statement has the following general form:

> **while** (*conditional test*) {
>   *statements to be repeated*
> }

The conditional test is chosen from the set of conditions listed in Figure 1-4.

To solve the pothole-filling problem, Karel needs to check whether the path in front is clear by invoking the condition **frontIsClear**. If you use the **frontIsClear** condition in a **while** loop, Karel will repeatedly execute the loop until it hits a wall. The **while** statement therefore makes it possible to solve the somewhat more general problem of repairing a roadway, as long as the potholes appear at every even-numbered corner and the end of the roadway is marked by a wall. The following definition of the function **FillRegularPotholes** accomplishes this task:

```
function FillRegularPotholes() {
    while (frontIsClear()) {
        move();
        fillPothole();
        move();
    }
}
```

Solving general problems

So far, the various pothole-filling programs have not been very realistic, because they rely on specific conditions—such as evenly spaced potholes—that are unlikely to be true in the real world. If you want to write a more general program to fill potholes, it should be able to work with fewer constraints. In particular, it does not really make sense to assume that the potholes occur on every other corner. Ideally, there should be no limits on the number of potholes or any restrictions on their spacing. A pothole is simply an opening in the wall representing the road surface.

To change the program so that it solves this more general problem requires you to think about the overall strategy in a different way. Instead of having a loop that cycles through each pothole, you need to have the program call `fillPothole` at every intersection along the roadway.

This strategic analysis suggests that the solution to the general problem might be as simple as the following definition:

```
function FillAllPotholes() {
    while (frontIsClear()) {
        fillPothole();
        move();
    }
}
```

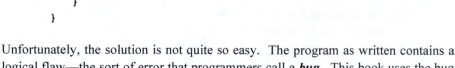

Unfortunately, the solution is not quite so easy. The program as written contains a logical flaw—the sort of error that programmers call a *bug.* This book uses the bug symbol on the right to mark functions that contain errors, to ensure that you don't accidentally use those examples as models for your own code.

The bug in this example turns out to be relatively subtle. It would be easy to miss, even if you thought you had tested the program thoroughly. In particular, the program works correctly on all the pothole-filling worlds you've seen so far and on many that you haven't. It fails only if there is a pothole in the very last avenue on the street, as illustrated by the following before-and-after diagram:

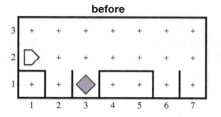
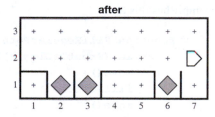

In this example, Karel stops without filling the last pothole. In fact, if you watch the execution carefully, you'll see that Karel never even goes down into that last pothole to check whether it needs filling. What's the problem here?

Following through the logic of the program carefully, you'll discover that the bug lies in the structure of the loop in `FillAllPotholes`, which looks like this:

```
while (frontIsClear()) {
    fillPothole();
    move();
}
```

As soon as Karel finishes filling the pothole on 6th Avenue, it executes the **move** instruction and returns to the top of the **while** loop. At that point, Karel is standing at the corner of 7th Avenue and 2nd street, up against the boundary wall. Because the **frontIsClear** test now fails, the **while** loop exits without checking the last segment of the roadway.

The bug in this program is an example of a programming problem called a *fencepost error.* The name comes from the fact that it takes one more fence post than you might think to fence off a particular distance. How many fence posts, for example, do you need to build a 100-foot fence if the posts are always positioned 10 feet apart? The answer is 11, as illustrated by the following diagram:

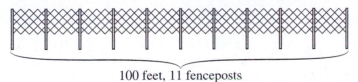

100 feet, 11 fenceposts

The situation in Karel's world has much the same structure. In order to fill potholes in a street that is seven corners long, Karel has to check for seven potholes but only has to move six times. Because Karel starts and finishes at an end of the roadway, it needs to execute one fewer **move** instruction than the number of corners it checks.

Once you discover this bug, fixing it is actually quite easy. Before Karel stops at the end of the roadway, all the program has to do is make a special-case check for a pothole at the final intersection, as follows:

```
function FillAllPotholes() {
    while (frontIsClear()) {
        fillPothole();
        move();
    }
    fillPothole();
}
```

The complete program appears in Figure 1-5 at the top of the next page.

 ## 1.4 Stepwise refinement

When you are faced with a complex programming problem, figuring out how to decompose the problem into pieces is usually one of your most important tasks. One of the most productive strategies is called *stepwise refinement,* which consists of solving problems by starting with the problem as a whole. You break the whole problem down into pieces, and then solve each piece, breaking those down further if necessary.

FIGURE 1-5 Karel program to fill any number of potholes

```
/*
 * File: FillAllPotholes.k
 * -----------------------
 * This program fills an arbitrary number of potholes in a road.
 */

"use turns";

function FillAllPotholes() {
    while (frontIsClear()) {
        fillPothole();
        move();
    }
    fillPothole();
}

/*
 * Fills a pothole immediately underneath Karel, if one exists.
 * When you call this function, Karel must be standing just above
 * the pothole, facing east.  When the function returns, Karel
 * will be in its original position above the repaired pothole.
 */

function fillPothole() {
    if (rightIsClear()) {
        turnRight();
        move();
        if (noBeepersPresent()) {
            putBeeper();
        }
        turnAround();
        move();
        turnRight();
    }
}
```

An exercise in stepwise refinement

Suppose that Karel is initially facing east at the corner of 1st Street and 1st Avenue in a world in which each avenue may contain a vertical tower of beepers of an unknown height, although some avenues may also be empty. Karel's job is to collect the beepers in each of these towers, put them all back down on the easternmost corner of 1st Street, and then return to its starting position. Figure 1-6 illustrates the operation of this program for one possible world.

The key to solving this problem is to decompose the program in the right way. This task is more complex than the others you have seen, which makes choosing appropriate subproblems more important to obtaining a successful solution.

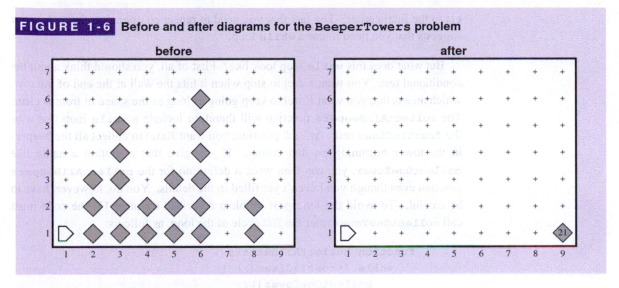

FIGURE 1-6 Before and after diagrams for the `BeeperTowers` problem

The principle of top-down design

The central idea in stepwise refinement is that you should start the design of your program from the top, which refers to the level of the program that is conceptually highest and most abstract. At this level, the beeper tower problem is clearly divided into three independent phases. First, Karel has to collect all the beepers. Second, Karel has to deposit them on the last intersection. Third, Karel has to return to its home position. This outline suggests the following decomposition of the problem:

```
function CollectBeeperTowers() {
    collectAllBeepers();
    dropAllBeepers();
    returnHome();
}
```

At this level, the problem is easy to understand. Even though you have not written the code for the functions in the body of **CollectBeeperTowers**, it is important to convince yourself that, as long as you believe that the functions you are about to write will solve the subproblems correctly, you will have a solution to the problem as a whole.

Refining the first subproblem

Now that you have defined the structure for the program as a whole, it is time to move on to the first subproblem, which consists of collecting all the beepers. This task is itself more complicated than the problems you have seen so far. Collecting all the beepers means that you have to pick up the beepers in every tower until you get to the final corner. The fact that you need to repeat an operation for each tower suggests that you need to use a `while` loop.

But what does this `while` loop look like? First of all, you should think about the conditional test. You want Karel to stop when it hits the wall at the end of the row, which means that you want Karel to keep going as long as the space in front is clear. The `collectAllBeepers` function will therefore include a `while` loop that uses the `frontIsClear` test. At each position, you want Karel to collect all the beepers in the tower beginning on that corner. If you give that operation a name like `collectOneTower`, you can then write a definition for the `collectAllBeepers` function even though you haven't yet filled in the details. You do, however, have to be careful. To avoid the fencepost problem described on page 17, the code must call `collectOneTower` after the last cycle of the loop, as follows:

```
function collectAllBeepers {
   while (frontIsClear()) {
      collectOneTower();
      move();
   }
   collectOneTower();
}
```

As you can see, this function has the same structure as the `FillAllPotholes` function in Figure 1-5. The only difference is that `collectAllBeepers` calls `collectOneTower` where the earlier one called `fillPothole`. These two programs are each examples of a general strategy that looks like this:

```
while (frontIsClear()) {
   Perform some operation.
   move();
}
Perform the same operation for the final corner.
```

You can use this strategy whenever you need to perform an operation on every corner as you move along a path that ends at a wall. If you remember the general strategy, you can quickly write the code whenever you encounter a problem of a similar form. Reusable strategies of this sort come up frequently in programming and are referred to as ***programming idioms,*** or ***patterns.*** The more patterns you know, the easier it will be for you to find one that fits a particular type of problem.

Coding the next level

Even though the code for `collectAllBeepers` is complete, you can't run the program until you implement `collectOneTower`. When `collectOneTower` is called, Karel is standing either at the base of a tower or on an empty corner. In the former case, you need to collect the beepers in the tower. In the latter case, you can simply move on. This situation at first suggests that you need an `if` statement in which you call **beepersPresent** to see whether a tower exists.

Before you add such a statement to the code, it is worth giving some thought to whether you need to make this test. Often, programs can be made much simpler by observing that cases that at first seem special can be treated in precisely the same way as the more general situation. With the current problem, you might decide that there is a tower of beepers on *every* avenue but that some of those towers are zero beepers high. Making use of this insight simplifies the program because you no longer have to test whether there is a tower on a particular avenue.

The **collectOneTower** function is still complex enough that an additional level of decomposition makes sense. To collect all the beepers in a tower, Karel has to climb the tower to collect each beeper, turn around, and then return to the wall that marks the southern boundary of the world. These steps suggest the following code:

```
function collectOneTower() {
    turnLeft();
    collectLineOfBeepers();
    turnAround();
    moveToWall();
    turnLeft();
}
```

The **turnLeft** instructions at the beginning and end of the **collectOneTower** function are critical to the correctness of this program. When **collectOneTower** is called, Karel is always somewhere on 1st Street facing east. When it has completed its operation, the program works correctly only if Karel is once again facing east. Conditions that must be true prior to a function call are *preconditions;* conditions that must apply after the function finishes are *postconditions.*

Finishing up

Although the hard work has been done, a few loose ends still need to be resolved because several functions are as yet unwritten. Fortunately, each of these functions can easily be coded without any further decomposition. The function **moveToWall,** for example, looks like this:

```
function moveToWall() {
    while (frontIsClear()) {
        move();
    }
}
```

The complete implementation of **BeeperTowers** appears in Figure 1-7.

FIGURE 1-7 Karel program to collect all the beepers in a set of towers

```
/*
 * File: BeeperTowers.k
 * ---------------------
 * This program collects all the beepers in a series of towers, deposits
 * them at the easternmost corner on 1st Street, and then returns home.
 */

function BeeperTowers() {
   collectAllBeepers();
   dropAllBeepers();
   returnHome();
}

/*
 * Collects the beepers from every tower along 1st Street.
 */

function collectAllBeepers() {
   while (frontIsClear()) {
      collectOneTower();
      move();
   }
   collectOneTower();
}

/*
 * Collects the beepers in a single tower.
 */

function collectOneTower() {
   turnLeft();
   collectLineOfBeepers();
   turnAround();
   moveToWall();
   turnLeft();
}

/*
 * Collects a consecutive line of beepers.
 */

function collectLineOfBeepers() {
   while (beepersPresent()) {
      pickBeeper();
      if (frontIsClear()) {
         move();
      }
   }
}
```

FIGURE 1-7   Karel program to collect all the beepers in a set of towers (continued)

```
/*
 * Drops all the beepers from Karel's bag onto the current corner.
 */
function dropAllBeepers() {
   while (beepersInBag()) {
      putBeeper();
   }
}

/*
 * Returns Karel to the corner of 1st Avenue and 1st Street, facing east.
 */
function returnHome() {
   turnAround();
   moveToWall();
   turnAround();
}

/*
 * Moves Karel forward until it is blocked by a wall.
 */
function moveToWall() {
   while (frontIsClear()) {
      move();
   }
}
```

1.5 Algorithms in Karel's world

Although top-down design is a critical strategy for programming, you can't apply it mechanically without thinking about problem-solving strategies. Figuring out how to solve a particular problem generally requires considerable creativity. The process of designing a solution strategy is traditionally called *algorithmic design.*

The word *algorithm* comes from the name of a ninth-century Persian mathematician, Muhammad ibn Mūsā al-Khwārizmī, who developed the first systematic treatment of algebra. You will have more of a chance to learn about algorithms and al-Khwārizmī in Chapter 3.

Even before you have a chance to study algorithms in more detail, it is useful to consider a simple algorithm in Karel's domain. Suppose, for example, that you want to teach Karel to escape from any maze that contains no loops. In Karel's world, a maze might look like this:

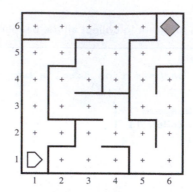

Karel's job is to navigate the corridors of the maze until it finds the beeper marking the exit. The program, however, must be general enough to solve any loop-free maze, not just the one pictured here.

For any loop-free maze (and in fact for any maze in which no loop surrounds Karel's initial position), you can use a simple strategy called the *right-hand rule,* in which you start by putting your right hand on the wall and then go through the maze without ever taking your hand off the wall. Another way to express this strategy is to proceed through the maze one step at a time, always taking the rightmost available path. The program that implements the right-hand rule turns out to be easy to implement in Karel and fits in a single function:

```
function SolveMaze() {
   while (noBeepersPresent()) {
      turnRight();
      while (frontIsBlocked()) {
         turnLeft();
      }
      move();
   }
}
```

At the beginning of the outer `while` loop, Karel turns right to check whether that path is available. The inner `while` loop then turns left until an opening appears. When that happens, Karel moves forward, and the entire process continues until Karel reaches the beeper marking the end of the maze.

Summary

In this chapter, you've had a chance to meet Karel, a very simple robot living in a very simple world. Starting off with Karel makes it possible to learn the fundamentals of programming without having to master the many complexities that come with a full-scale programming language. The important points in this chapter include the following:

- Karel the Robot is a *programming microworld* developed in the 1970s by Rich Pattis, who was then a computer science graduate student at Stanford.

- Karel lives in a rectangular world defined by *streets* running from west to east and *avenues* running from south to north. Karel is always positioned on a *corner* marking the intersection of a street and an avenue and must be facing in one of the four standard compass directions (north, east, south, and west).

- Karel's world is surrounded by *walls* around the border and may also contain additional interior walls that block Karel's passage between two corners.

- Karel's world can also contain *beepers,* which Rich Pattis describes as "plastic cones which emit a quiet beeping noise." Beepers exist either on corners or in Karel's beeper bag, both of which can contain any number of beepers.

- When Karel is shipped from the factory, it knows how to execute only four operations—**move**, **turnLeft**, **putBeeper**, and **pickBeeper**—which are defined in detail in Figure 1-1 on page 4.

- You can extend Karel's repertoire of operations by defining *functions,* which are sequences of operations that have been collected together and given a name. For example, the following function definition gives Karel the power to turn right by executing three consecutive left turns:

```
function turnRight() {
    turnLeft();
    turnLeft();
    turnLeft();
}
```

- The functions **turnRight** and **turnAround** are included in a library called **turns**, which you can use by including the following line in your program:

```
"use turns";
```

- The best strategy for solving a large problem is to divide it into successively smaller subproblems, each of which is implemented as a separate function. This process is called *decomposition* or *stepwise refinement.*

- The Karel programming language includes control statements that fall into two classes. *Conditional statements* allow you to execute other statements only if a particular condition holds. *Iterative statements* allow you to repeat a sequence of statements, either a specified number of times or as long as a condition holds.

- The syntactic rules for each of Karel's control statements appear in the boxes to the right.

The if statement

```
if (condition) {
    statements
}
```

The if–else statement

```
if (condition) {
    statements
} else {
    statements
}
```

The repeat statement

```
repeat (count) {
    statements
}
```

The while statement

```
while (condition) {
    statements
}
```

- The conditions that Karel can test appear in Figure 1-4 on page 12.

- When you are using iterative statements, it is important to avoid the *fencepost error,* which consists of failing to recognize that the number of **move** instructions necessary to cover a distance is one fewer than the number of corners.

- In computer science, an *algorithm* is a solution strategy. Algorithms are one of the most important topics in the field.

Review questions

1. In your own words, explain the meaning and purpose of a *programming microworld.*

2. Who created the Karel microworld?

3. What is the etymology of the name *Karel?*

4. Define each of the following aspects of Karel's world: *street, avenue, corner, wall,* and *beeper.*

5. What are the four predefined Karel functions?

6. What are the two functions included in the Karel library named **turns**?

7. What is the meant by the strategy of *stepwise refinement?*

8. What control statement do you use to execute statements only if some condition applies? What are the two forms of this statement?

9. What two statements does Karel offer for repeating a group of statements?

10. What condition would you use to test whether Karel can move forward from its current position? What condition would you use to test whether there are any beepers on the current corner?

11. What is a *fencepost error?*

12. What are *preconditions* and *postconditions?*

13. The **collectLineOfBeepers** function in Figure 1-7 includes an **if** statement that checks the **frontIsClear** condition before moving. Why is it important to make this test?

Exercises

1. Only one of the two functions in the **turns** library is defined explicitly in this chapter. Write a Karel function that implements the other.

2. Suppose that Karel has settled into its house, which is the square area in the center of the following diagram:

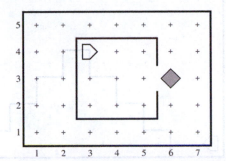

Karel starts off in the northwest corner of its house as shown in the diagram. The problem is to program Karel to collect the newspaper—represented by a beeper—from outside the doorway and then to return to its initial position.

This exercise is extremely simple and is intended mostly to get you started. You can assume that every part of the world looks just as it does in the diagram. The house is exactly this size, the door is always in the position shown, and the beeper is just outside the door. Thus, all you have to do is write the sequence of statements necessary to have Karel perform the following tasks:

1. Move to the newspaper.
2. Pick it up.
3. Return to Karel's original starting point.

Even though the program requires just a few lines, it is still worth getting at least a little practice in decomposition. In your solution, decompose the program so that it includes a function for each step shown in the outline.

3. Implement a Karel function named **backup** that has the effect of moving Karel backward one square but leaves it facing in the same direction. For example, the following before-and-after diagram shows the effect of calling **backup** if Karel is facing east at the corner of 1st Street and 2nd Avenue:

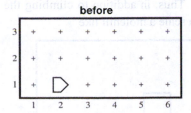
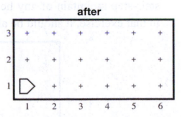

If Karel's back is against a wall, the **backup** function should fail when Karel tries to execute the **move** instruction that is part of the implementation.

4.   Write a program that teaches Karel to climb a mountain exactly like this:

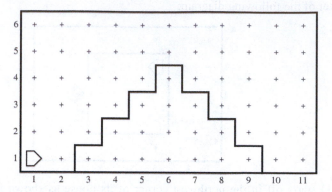

The steps involved are to

1.   Move up to the mountain.
2.   Climb each of the four stair steps to reach the summit.
3.   Plant a flag (represented by a beeper, of course) at the top of the mountain.
4.   Climb down each of the four stair steps on the opposite side.
5.   Move forward to the east end of the world.

The final state of the world should look like this:

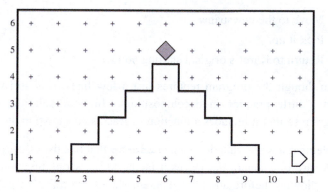

5.   Generalize the program you wrote in exercise 3 so that Karel is able to climb a stair-step mountain of any height. Thus, in addition to climbing the mountain in that exercise, it should be able to scale a molehill like

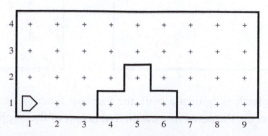

or an Everest-sized peak like

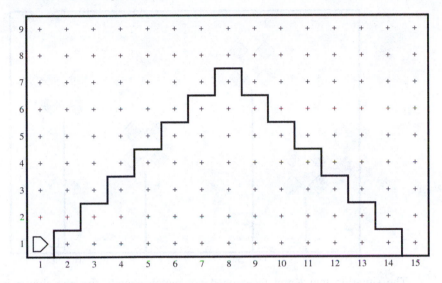

6. For those who live in colder climates, winter can be a bitter time. The trees have lost their leaves and stand as monuments to the ravages of the season, as shown in the following sample world:

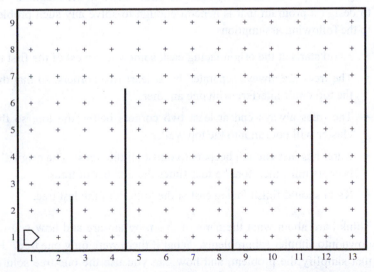

In this sample world, the vertical wall sections represent barren tree trunks. Karel's job is to climb each of the trunks and adorn the top of each tree with a cluster of four leaves arranged in a square like this:

Thus, when Karel is done, the scene will look like this:

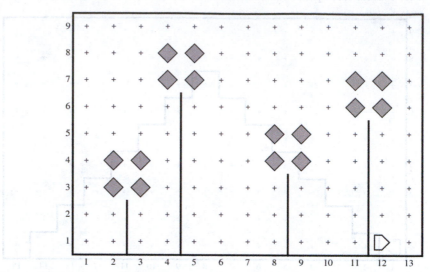

The situation that Karel faces need not match exactly the one shown in the diagram. There may be more trees; Karel simply continues the process until there are no beepers left in the beeper bag. The trees may also be of different heights or spaced differently than the ones shown in the diagram. Your task is to design a program that is general enough to solve any such problem, subject to the following assumptions:

- Karel starts at the origin facing east, somewhere west of the first tree.

- The trees are always separated by at least two corners, so that the leaves at the top don't interfere with one another.

- The trees always end at least two corners below the top, so that the leaf cluster will not run into the top wall.

- Karel has just enough beepers to outfit all the trees. The original number of beepers must therefore be four times the number of trees.

- Karel should finish facing east at the bottom of the last tree.

Think hard about what the parts of this program are and how you can break it down into simpler subproblems. What if there were only one tree? How would that simplify the problem, and how can you use the one-tree solution to help solve the more general case?

7. Suppose that it's Halloween and Karel is going trick-or-treating. Karel starts off at the west end of a dead-end street that contains houses on both sides of street, such as the one pictured in the following diagram:

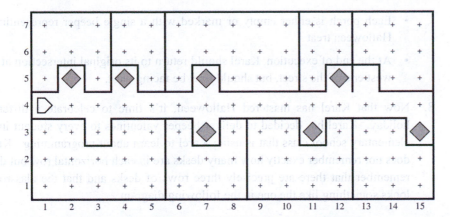

Each house has a front porch at some point along its front side. Karel's mission is to go to each house, step into the porch area, and see if the porch contains a treat, represented by a beeper. If it does, Karel should pick up the treat. If not, Karel should move on to the next house. Karel must check every porch on both sides of the street and should end up at the original intersection, facing in the opposite direction. Thus, after executing your program in the world shown above, Karel should finish in the following position:

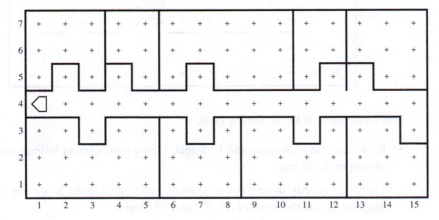

Karel can count on the following facts about the world:

- Karel starts at the west end of a street, facing east, with an empty beeper bag.
- The houses on the street are packed closely together, with no space between adjacent houses.
- There may be any number of houses, which typically vary in size.
- The side of each house facing the street is a solid wall except for a small porch, which is always one intersection wide. The porch can appear at any point in the front wall.

- Each porch is either empty or marked with a single beeper representing a Halloween treat.

- At the end of execution, Karel should return to its original intersection at the west end of the street, but should now be facing west.

8. Now that Karel has mastered Halloween, it's time to celebrate a different holiday. Karel has decided to deliver beeper valentines to every student in an elementary school class that is using Karel to learn about programming. Karel does not remember exactly how many desks are in each horizontal row but does remember that there are precisely three rows of desks and that the classroom looks something like the one in the following diagram:

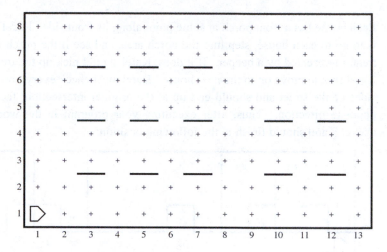

Karel can count on the following facts:

- Karel starts at 1st Avenue and 1st Street, facing east, with an infinite number of beepers in its bag.

- There are exactly three rows of student desks, positioned as shown in the diagram, just to the south of 3rd, 5th, and 7th Streets.

- Karel does not know how many desks are in each row (which may differ), how many blank spaces there are between the desks, or how many spaces exist between the desks at the ends of each row and the walls of the classroom. What Karel does know is that each of the desks is exactly one unit wide and that there are no desks right up against the wall.

When Karel is finished, all the desks in the room should have a valentine, as shown in the following diagram:

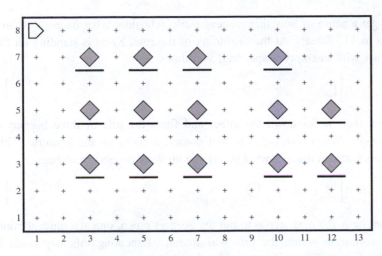

9. Having heard that programming is at least as much an art as a science (and being totally clueless about the nature of art), Karel has decided to enroll in a paint-by-numbers class. In this class, Karel is presented with a "canvas" containing piles of beepers, such as those shown in the following diagram:

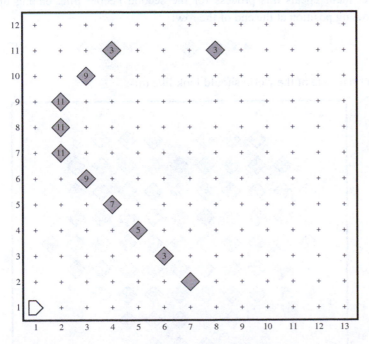

To complete the paint-by-numbers task, all Karel has to do is walk from left to right across each street, pick up each pile of beepers, and then redistribute the beepers from that pile, one at a time, on each successive corner.

To get a sense of how this process works, consider what happens when Karel gets to 11th Street. At the beginning of the row, Karel is standing on the first corner with an empty beeper bag, as follows:

Karel then walks down the street and finds the pile of three beepers on 4th Avenue. When Karel gets to that corner, it picks up the beepers. This step leaves Karel in the following position with three beepers in its bag:

From here, the next step is to put the beepers down, one at a time, starting with the corner in which the pile was found. Executing this step leads to the following configuration, where Karel again has an empty beeper bag:

Karel then repeats this process for the second beeper pile, ending up in the following position at the end of the row:

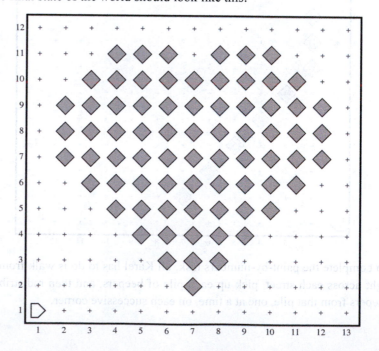

The final state of the world should look like this:

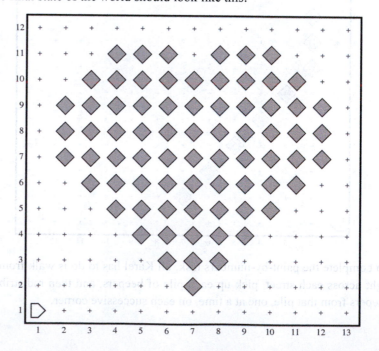

Your job is to write the program that converts a paint-by-number picture of this sort into the corresponding completed masterpiece. In writing the program, Karel can count on the following facts about the world:

- The world contains an arbitrary number of beeper piles but no interior walls.

- The beeper piles never have so many beepers that they cause Karel to run into a wall or another beeper pile.

- Karel always starts facing east in the southwest corner (1st Street and 1st Avenue) with an empty beeper bag.

- Karel must finish execution facing east at the northeast corner of the world.

10. More than a decade after Hurricane Katrina, considerable damage remains along the Gulf Coast, and some communities have yet to rebuild. As part of its plans to improve the nation's infrastructure, the government has established a program named Katrina Automated RELief (or KAREL) to send house-building robots to repair the damaged area. Your job is to program those robots.

Each robot begins at the west end of a street that might look like this:

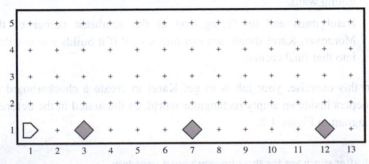

Each beeper in the figure represents a pile of debris where a house once stood. Karel's job is to walk along the street and build a new house in the place marked by each beeper. Those houses, moreover, need to be raised on stilts to avoid damage from the next storm. Each house should look exactly like this:

The new house should be centered where the bit of debris was left, which means that the first house in the diagram above would be constructed with its left edge along 2nd Avenue.

At the end of the run, Karel should be at the east end of the street, having created a set of houses that look like this for the initial conditions shown:

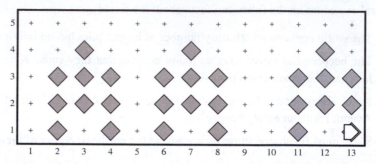

In solving this problem, you can count on the following facts about the world:

- Karel starts off facing east at the corner of 1st Street and 1st Avenue with an infinite number of beepers in its beeper bag.

- The beepers indicating the positions at which houses should be built will be spaced so there's room to build the houses without overlapping them or hitting walls.

- Karel must end up facing east at the southeast corner of the world. Moreover, Karel should not run into a wall if it builds a house that extends into that final corner.

11. In this exercise, your job is to get Karel to create a checkerboard pattern of beepers inside an empty rectangular world, as illustrated in the before-and-after diagram in Figure 1-8.

FIGURE 1-8 Before-and-after diagram for the checkerboard problem

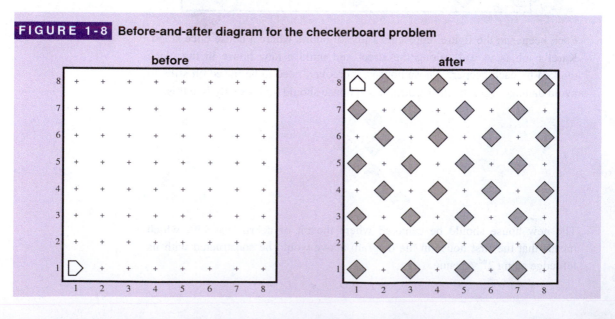

This problem has a nice decomposition structure along with some interesting algorithmic issues. As you think about how you will solve the problem, you should make sure your solution works with checkerboards that are different in size from the standard 8×8 checkerboard shown in the example. Odd-sized checkerboards are tricky, and you should make sure that your program generates the following pattern in a 5×3 world:

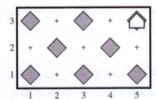

Another special case you need to consider is that of a world that is only one column wide or one row high.

12. Program Karel to place a single beeper at the center of 1st Street. For example, if Karel starts in the world

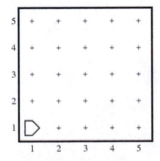

the program should finish its execution with Karel standing on a beeper in the following position:

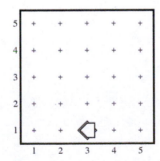

Note that the final configuration of the world should have only a single beeper at the midpoint of 1st Street. Along the way, Karel is allowed to place additional beepers wherever it wants to, but must pick them all up again before it finishes.

In solving this problem, you may count on the following:

- Karel starts at 1st Avenue and 1st Street, facing east, with an infinite number of beepers in its bag.

- The initial state of the world includes no interior walls or beepers.

- The world need not be square, but you may assume that it is at least as tall as it is wide.

- If the width of the world is odd, Karel must put the beeper in the center square. If the width is even, Karel may drop the beeper on either of the two center squares.

- It does not matter which direction Karel is facing at the end of the run.

There are many different algorithms you can use to solve this problem. The interesting challenge is to come up with a strategy that works.

CHAPTER 2
Introducing JavaScript

Computer programs are the most complex things that humans make.

— Douglas Crockford, *JavaScript: The Good Parts,* 2008

Douglas Crockford (1955–)

(Jagadeesh Nv/EPA/Shutterstock)

Douglas Crockford has written extensively about JavaScript and has for many years championed the virtues of a language that acquired, particularly in its early years, a largely undeserved negative reputation. In his 2008 book *JavaScript: The Good Parts,* Crockford maintains that "in JavaScript, there is a beautiful, elegant, highly expressive language" as long as you look past its largely superficial and entirely avoidable shortcomings. As we have discovered by using JavaScript in Stanford's introductory programming course, it is not at all difficult to write programs that reflect its beauty, elegance, and expressiveness simply by focusing on the good parts of the language. The purpose of this book is to teach you how JavaScript can support the creation of highly readable, well-structured programs.

The Karel microworld from Chapter 1 offers a gentle introduction to the idea of programming, but it is missing at least one critically important concept. Although beepers make it possible for Karel to manipulate the contents of its world, Karel offers no effective mechanism for working with data. In computing, the word *data* is usually synonymous with *information*. Computers derive most of their power from their ability to manipulate information in great quantity and at high speed. In much of Europe, computer science is commonly referred to as **informatics,** which emphasizes the central role that information plays.

Before you can appreciate the power of computing, you need to learn at least the basics of a programming language that makes it possible to work with data. The programs in this book use a programming language called **JavaScript,** which has become the standard language for writing interactive web applications. The first version of JavaScript appeared in 1995, reportedly written by a single programmer at the Netscape Communications Corporation in just ten days. Because of its popularity, JavaScript is built into every major web browser, which means that any device with a browser can run JavaScript programs without any additional software.

The focus of this book, however, is not on the JavaScript language itself but rather on the programs that you write using that language. This book does not cover all of JavaScript and deliberately avoids those aspects of the language that are easy to misuse. Even so, the subset of JavaScript you will learn with this book gives you the tools you need to write exciting applications that use the best features of the JavaScript language.

 ## 2.1 Data and types

For much of their history, computing machines—even before the age of modern computing—have worked primarily with numeric data. The computers built in the mid-1960s were so closely tied to processing numeric data that they earned the nickname **number crunchers** as a result. Information, however, comes in many forms, and computers are increasingly good at working with data of many different types. When you write programs that count or add things up, you are working with **numeric data.** When you write programs that manipulate characters—typically assembled into larger units such as words, sentences, and paragraphs—you are working with **string data.** You will learn about these and many other data types as you progress through this book.

In computer science, a data type is defined by two properties: a domain and a set of operations. The **domain** is simply the set of values that are elements of that type. For numeric data, the domain consists of numbers like 0, 42, –273, and 3.14159265. For string data, the domain comprises sequences of characters that appear on the keyboard or that can be displayed on the screen. The **set of operations** is the toolbox that allows you to manipulate values of that type. For numeric data, the set of operations includes addition, subtraction, multiplication, and division, along with a variety of more sophisticated functions. For string data, however, it is hard to imagine what an operation like multiplication might mean. Using string data requires a different set of operations such as combining two strings to form a longer one or comparing two strings to see if they are in alphabetic order. The general rule is that the set of operations must be appropriate to the elements of the domain. The two components together—the domain and the operations—define a ***data type.***

◼ 2.2 Numeric data

Computers today store data in so many exciting forms that numbers may seem a bit boring. Even so, numbers are a good starting point for talking about data, mostly because they are both simple and familiar. You've been using numbers, after all, ever since you learned to count. Moreover, as you'll discover in Chapter 7, all information is represented inside the computer in numeric form.

Representing numbers in JavaScript

One of the important design principles of modern programming languages is that concepts that are familiar to human readers should be expressed in an easily recognizable form. Like most languages, JavaScript adopts that principle for numeric representation, which means that you can write numbers in a JavaScript program in much the same way you would write them anywhere else. Most languages, however, separate numbers into two classes: ***integers,*** which represent whole numbers, and ***floating-point*** numbers, which are numbers that contain a decimal point. By contrast, JavaScript defines a single numeric type, which consists of a sequence of digits, optionally containing a decimal point. Negative numbers are preceded by a minus sign. Thus, the following examples are all legal numbers in JavaScript:

```
0     42     -273     3.14159265     -0.5     1000000
```

Note that large numbers, such as the value of one million shown in the last example, are written without using commas to separate the digits into groups of three.

Numbers can also be written in a variant of scientific notation, in which the value is represented as a number multiplied by a power of 10. To express a value in scientific notation, you write a number in standard decimal notation, followed immediately by the letter **E** and an integer exponent, optionally preceded by a + or − sign. For example, the speed of light in meters per second is approximately

$$2.9979 \times 10^8$$

which can be written in JavaScript as

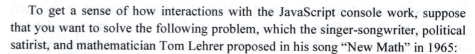

2.9979E+8

In JavaScript's scientific notation, the letter **E** stands for the words *times 10 to the power*.

Arithmetic expressions

The real power of numeric data comes from the fact that JavaScript allows you to perform computation by applying mathematical operations, ranging in complexity from addition and subtraction up to highly sophisticated mathematical functions. As in mathematics, JavaScript allows you to express those calculations through the use of operators, such as + and – for addition and subtraction.

As you are learning how JavaScript works, it is useful to have access to some application that allows you to enter JavaScript expressions and see what values they produce. The website associated with this textbook includes an application that does precisely that, and there are similar facilities available in other JavaScript environments. The examples in this book illustrate interactions with JavaScript in the context of a window called the *JavaScript console,* but those examples should be easy to follow even if you are using a different environment.

To get a sense of how interactions with the JavaScript console work, suppose that you want to solve the following problem, which the singer-songwriter, political satirist, and mathematician Tom Lehrer proposed in his song "New Math" in 1965:

$$
\begin{array}{r}
3\,4\,2 \\
-\,1\,7\,3 \\
\hline
\end{array}
$$

To find the answer, all you have to do is enter the subtraction into the JavaScript console, as follows:

Tom Lehrer

(MixPix/Alamy Stock Photo)

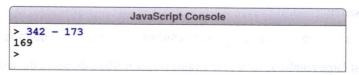

JavaScript Console
> 342 − 173
169
>

This computation is an example of an *arithmetic expression,* which consists of a sequence of values called *terms* combined using symbols called *operators,* most of which are familiar from elementary-school arithmetic. The arithmetic operators in JavaScript include the following:

+	Addition
–	Subtraction (or negation, if written with no value to its left)
*	Multiplication
/	Division
%	Remainder

The only operator that may seem unfamiliar is %, which computes the remainder of one value divided by another. For example, 7 % 3 has the value 1, because 7 divided by 3 leaves a remainder of 1. If one number is evenly divisible by another, there is no remainder, so that, for example, 12 % 4 has the value 0. In this book, the % operator is used only with positive integers for which its meaning is easy to understand.

Following the conventions of standard mathematics, multiplication, division, and remainder are performed before addition and subtraction, although you can use parentheses to change the evaluation order. For example, if you want to average the numbers 4 and 7, you can enter the following expression on the console:

```
JavaScript Console
> (4 + 7) / 2
5.5
>
```

If you leave out the parentheses, JavaScript first divides 7 by 2 and then adds 4 and 3.5 to produce the value 7.5, as follows:

```
JavaScript Console
> 4 + 7 / 2
7.5
>
```

If JavaScript is your first programming language, the calculation in this example will seem perfectly natural because it follows the usual conventions of arithmetic. If you have used other languages before, however, JavaScript's treatment of numbers may require you to think about arithmetic expressions in a different way. As noted earlier in the chapter, many programming languages define two different numeric types: one for whole numbers and one for numbers with fractional parts. JavaScript has just one numeric type, which makes arithmetic a bit simpler.

Precedence

The order in which JavaScript evaluates the operators in an expression is governed by their *precedence,* which is a measure of how tightly each operator binds to the expressions on either side, which are called its *operands*. If two operators compete for the same operand, the one with higher precedence is applied first. If two operators have the same precedence, they are applied in the order specified by their *associativity,* which indicates whether that operator groups to the left or to the right. Most operators in JavaScript are *left-associative,* which means that the leftmost operator is evaluated first; a few, however, are *right-associative* and group from right to left, as you can see in Figure 2-1 at the top of the next page.

FIGURE 2-1 Complete precedence table for the JavaScript operators

Operators in decreasing order of precedence	Associativity
() [] .	*left*
unary operators: − ++ −− ! ~ typeof new	*right*
* / %	*left*
+ −	*left*
<< >> >>>	*left*
< <= > >= instanceof in	*left*
=== !== == !=	*left*
&	*left*
^	*left*
		left
&&	*left*
||	*left*
?:	*right*
= *op=*	*right*

Figure 2-1 shows a complete precedence table for the JavaScript operators, many of which you will have little or no occasion to use. As additional operators are introduced later in this book, you can look them up in this table to see where they fit in the precedence hierarchy. Since the purpose of the precedence rules is to ensure that JavaScript expressions obey the same rules as their mathematical counterparts, you can usually rely on your intuition. Moreover, if you are ever in any doubt, you can always include parentheses to make the order of operations explicit.

2.3 Variables

When you write a program that works with data values, it is often convenient to use names to refer to a value that can change as the program runs. In programming, names that refer to values are called **variables.**

Every variable in JavaScript has two attributes: a *name* and a *value*. To understand the relationship of these attributes, it is best to think of a variable as a box with a label attached to the outside, like this:

The name of the variable appears on the label and is used to tell different boxes apart. If you have three variables in a program, each variable will have a different name. The value corresponds to the contents of the box. The name of the box is fixed, but you can change the value as often as you like.

Declaring variables

If you need to create a new variable in JavaScript, the standard approach in modern versions of JavaScript is to include a line in your program that begins with the keyword `let` followed by the name of the variable, an equal sign, the initial value for that variable, and finally a semicolon. A program line that introduces a new variable is called a ***declaration.*** The following declaration, for example, introduces a variable named `r` and assigns it the value 10:

```
let r = 10;
```

Conceptually, this declaration creates a box inside the computer's memory, gives it the name `r`, and stores the value 10 in the box, like this:

r
┌──────────────┐
│   10   │
└──────────────┘

Assignment

Once you have declared a variable, you can change its value by using an ***assignment statement,*** which looks just like a declaration, but without the `let` keyword at the beginning. For example, if you execute the assignment statement

```
r = 2.5;
```

the value in the box will change as follows:

r
┌──────────────┐
│   2.5   │
└──────────────┘

The value that appears to the right of the equal sign in either a declaration or an assignment statement can be any JavaScript expression. For example, you can compute the average of the numbers 3, 4, and 5 using the following declaration:

```
let average = (3 + 4 + 5) / 3;
```

Assignment statements are often used to modify the current value of a variable. For example, you can add the value of `deposit` to `balance` using the statement

```
balance = balance + deposit;
```

which takes the current value of `balance`, adds the value of `deposit`, and then stores the result back in `balance`. Assignment statements of this form are so common that JavaScript allows you to use the following shorthand:

```
balance += deposit;
```

Similarly, you can subtract the value of **surcharge** from **balance** by writing

```
balance -= surcharge;
```

More generally, the JavaScript statement

variable *op*= *expression*;

is equivalent to

variable = *variable* *op* (*expression*);

The parentheses are included in this pattern to emphasize that the expression is evaluated before *op* is applied. Such statements are called ***shorthand assignments***.

Increment and decrement operators

Beyond the shorthand assignment operators, JavaScript offers a further level of abbreviation for the particularly common operations of adding or subtracting 1 from a variable. Adding 1 to a variable is called ***incrementing*** it; subtracting 1 is called ***decrementing*** it. JavaScript makes it possible to express these operations in an extremely compact form. The expression **x++** increments the variable **x**, and the expression **x--** decrements it.

These operators, however, are not quite as simple as the preceding paragraph suggests. The **++** and **--** operators can each be written in two different ways. The operator can come *after* the operand to which it applies, as in the expression **x++**, or *before* the operand, as in **++x**. The first form, in which the operator follows the operand, is called the ***suffix*** form; the second, in which the operator precedes the operand, is called the ***prefix*** form.

If all you do is execute the **++** or **--** operator in isolation, the prefix and suffix operators have precisely the same effect. You notice the difference only if you use these operators as part of a larger expression. Then, like all operators, the increment and decrement operators produce a value, but the value depends on where the operator is written relative to the operand. The two cases are as follows:

x++   Calculates the value of **x** first, and then increments it. The value of the expression is the original value *before* the increment occurs.

++x   Increments the value of **x** first, and then uses the new value as the value of the **++** operation as a whole.

The **--** operator behaves similarly, except that the value is decremented rather than incremented.

At first glance, this feature may seem esoteric and unnecessary, and in some ways it is. The ++ and -- operators are certainly not essential. Moreover, there are few circumstances in which embedding these operators in a larger expression leads to programs that are demonstrably better than those that separate the process of using the value and incrementing the value. On the other hand, ++ and -- are firmly entrenched in the historical tradition shared by the languages C, C++, Java, and JavaScript. Programmers use them so frequently that they have become standard idioms in these languages. In light of their widespread use in programs, you need to understand these operators so that you can make sense of existing code.

Naming conventions

The names used for variables, constants, functions, and so forth are collectively known as *identifiers*. In JavaScript, the rules for identifier formation are

1. The identifier must start with a letter, an underscore (_), or a dollar sign ($).

2. All other characters must be letters, digits, underscores, or dollar signs. This book uses underscores only as separators in constant names and makes no use at all of the dollar sign, which is typically reserved for JavaScript libraries.

3. The identifier must not be one of the reserved keywords listed in Figure 2-2.

Uppercase and lowercase letters appearing in an identifier are considered to be different. Thus, the identifier **ABC** is not the same as the identifier **abc**.

You can make your programs more readable by using variable names that immediately suggest the meaning of that variable. If **r**, for example, refers to the radius of a circle, that name makes sense because it follows standard mathematical convention. In most cases, however, it is better to use longer names that make it clear to anyone reading your program exactly what value a variable contains. For example, if you need a variable to keep track of the number of pages in a document, it is better to use a name like **numberOfPages** than an abbreviated form like **np**.

FIGURE 2-2 **Reserved words in JavaScript**

abstract	default	for	new	throw
arguments	delete	function	null	throws
await	do	goto	package	transient
boolean	double	if	private	true
break	else	implements	protected	try
byte	enum	import	public	typeof
case	eval	in	return	var
catch	export	instanceof	short	void
char	extends	int	static	volatile
class	false	interface	super	while
const	final	let	switch	with
continue	finally	long	synchronized	yield
debugger	float	native	this	

The variable name `numberOfPages` may at first look a little odd because of the capital letters that appear in the middle of the name. That name, however, follows what has become a widely accepted standard for naming variables. By convention, variable names in JavaScript begin with a lowercase letter but include uppercase letters at the beginning of each new word. This convention is called *camel case* because it creates uppercase "humps" in the middle of the variable name.

Constants

You can also make your programs more readable by giving names to values that do not change as a program runs. Such values are called ***constants.*** Modern versions of JavaScript support the declaration of constants simply by replacing the keyword `let` in the declaration with the keyword `const`. For example, if you are writing a program that needs to undertake geometrical calculations involving circles, it is useful to have a constant named `PI` whose value is a reasonable approximation of the mathematical constant π. Although you will discover later in this chapter that the constant `PI` is already defined in one of the standard libraries, you could always define it yourself by writing the following declaration:

```
const PI = 3.14159265;
```

By convention, constant names are written entirely in uppercase using underscores to indicate word boundaries.

Although constants do not change their values while a program is running, it often makes sense to use constants for values that you, as the programmer, might want to change over the development cycle of an application. The value of using constants for this purpose is discussed in more detail in section 2.8.

Sequential calculations

The ability to define variables and constants makes arithmetic calculations easier to follow, even in the console window. The following sequence of statements, for example, calculates the area of a circle of radius 10:

```
                    JavaScript Console
> const PI = 3.14159265;
> let r = 10;
> let area = PI * r * r;
> area
314.159265
>
```

JavaScript does not include an operator for raising a number to a power, so the easiest way to express the computation of r^2 is simply to multiply r by itself.

2.4 Functions

As you discovered when you wrote simple Karel programs in Chapter 1, you don't need to enter all your computational operations in the console window but can instead store those steps as a function. The big difference between functions in Karel and JavaScript is that functions can use information supplied by their callers and then give back information in return. The caller sends information to the function by specifying values inside the parentheses that indicate a function call. These values are called **arguments.** Inside the function, each of these arguments is assigned to a variable called a **parameter.** The function uses these parameters to compute a result, which is delivered back to the caller. This process is called **returning a result.**

In the context of a programming language like JavaScript, the term *function* is intended to evoke the similar concept in mathematics. A mathematical function like

$$f(x) = x^2 - 5$$

expresses a relationship between the value of x and the value of the function. This relationship is depicted in the graph to the right, which shows how the value of the function changes with respect to the value of x.

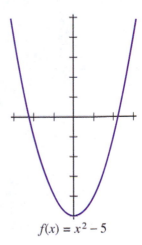

$$f(x) = x^2 - 5$$

Implementing functions in JavaScript

The process of writing functions is best introduced by example. The mathematical function $f(x) = x^2 - 5$ has the following implementation in JavaScript:

```
function f(x) {
   return x * x - 5;
}
```

In this definition, **x** is the parameter variable, which is set by the argument passed by the caller. For example, if you were to call **f(2)**, the variable **x** would be set to the value 2. The **return** statement specifies the computation needed to calculate the result. Multiplying **x** by itself gives the value 4; subtracting 5 gives the final result of −1, which is passed back to the caller.

Once you have defined the function **f**, you can call it from the console like this:

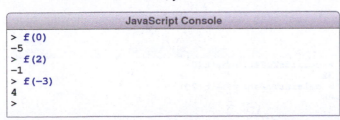

Parameter variables and variables introduced in a `let` statement are accessible only in the context—which for now is always a function—in which they appear. For this reason, those variables are called *local variables.* By contrast, variables declared outside of a function are *global variables,* which can be used anywhere in the program. As programs get larger, using global variables makes those programs more difficult to read and maintain. The programs in this book therefore avoid using any global variables except for constants. Thus, declaring `PI` as a global variable is acceptable, but variables whose values might change are always local.

Assuming that you have defined the constant `PI` as shown on page 48, you can use the following function to calculate the area of a circle:

```
function circleArea(r) {
    return PI * r * r;
}
```

To call the `circleArea` function, all you need to do is specify a value for the radius. For example, given these definitions of `PI` and `circleArea`, you can then execute the following commands in the console window:

JavaScript Console
> `circleArea(1)` 3.141592653 > `circleArea(10)` 314.1592653 >

You can use functions to compute values that come up in practical situations that are largely outside of traditional mathematics. For example, if you travel outside the United States, you will discover that the rest of the world measures temperatures in Celsius rather than Fahrenheit. The formula to convert a Celsius temperature to its Fahrenheit equivalent is

$$F = \frac{9}{5}C + 32$$

which you can easily translate into the following JavaScript function:

```
function celsiusToFahrenheit(c) {
    return 9 / 5 * c + 32;
}
```

The use of `celsiusTofahrenheit` is illustrated in the following sample run:

JavaScript Console
> `celsiusToFahrenheit(0)` 32 > `celsiusToFahrenheit(20)` 68 >

Functions can take more than one argument, in which case both the parameter names in the definition and the argument values in the call are separated by commas. For example, the function

```
const INCHES_PER_FOOT = 12;
const CENTIMETERS_PER_INCH = 2.54;

function feetAndInchesToCentimeters(feet, inches) {
   let totalInches = feet * INCHES_PER_FOOT + inches;
   return totalInches * CENTIMETERS_PER_INCH;
}
```

converts a length specified in feet and inches to the equivalent length in centimeters.

When you call the function `feetAndInchesToCentimeters`, you must supply the arguments in the order specified by the parameter list. The first argument specifies the number of feet, and the second specifies the number of inches. The following sample run shows three calls to `feetAndInchesToCentimeters`, one showing that one inch is 2.54 centimeters, a second showing that a foot is 30.48 (12×2.54) centimeters, and a third showing that eight feet and four inches (a total of 100 inches) corresponds to a length of 254 centimeters:

```
JavaScript Console
> feetAndInchesToCentimeters(0, 1)
2.54
> feetAndInchesToCentimeters(1, 0)
30.48
> feetAndInchesToCentimeters(8, 4)
254
>
```

Even though a JavaScript function can take more than one argument, a function can return only one result. It is therefore impossible to write a JavaScript function that converts a length in centimeters into two independent values, one of which represents the whole number of feet and one that represents the number of extra inches left over. As you will see later in this chapter and again in Chapter 9, there are several strategies that will allow you to come close to achieving this goal.

Library functions

Like all modern languages, JavaScript predefines certain collections of functions and other useful definitions and makes those collections available to programmers as *libraries*. One of the most useful libraries in JavaScript is the `Math` library, which includes several mathematical definitions that come up often when you are writing programs, even when those programs don't seem particularly mathematical.

Like most built-in libraries in JavaScript, the `Math` library is implemented as part of a *class,* which for the moment you can think of simply as a structure that unifies a related set of definitions. Figure 2-3 lists several constants and functions available in the `Math` library.

In JavaScript, you can use the facilities available in a class by writing the class name, a dot, and the name of the constant or function you want to use. For example, the expression `Math.PI` represents the constant named `PI` in the `Math`

FIGURE 2-3 Selected constants and functions from the JavaScript `Math` library

Mathematical constants

`Math.PI`	The mathematical constant π.
`Math.E`	The mathematical constant e, which is the base for natural logarithms.

General mathematical functions

`Math.abs` (*x*)	Returns the absolute value of x.
`Math.max` (*x*, *y*, ...)	Returns the largest of the arguments.
`Math.min` (*x*, *y*, ...)	Returns the smallest of the arguments.
`Math.sqrt` (*x*)	Returns the square root of x.
`Math.round` (*x*)	Returns the closest integer to x.
`Math.floor` (*x*)	Returns the largest integer less than or equal to x.
`Math.ceil` (*x*)	Returns the smallest integer greater than or equal to x.

Logarithmic and exponential functions

`Math.exp` (*x*)	Returns the exponential function of x (e^x).
`Math.log` (*x*)	Returns the natural logarithm (base e) of x.
`Math.log10` (*x*)	Returns the common logarithm (base 10) of x.
`Math.pow` (*x*, *y*)	Returns x^y.

Trigonometric functions

`Math.cos` (*theta*)	Returns the cosine of the radian angle *theta*.
`Math.sin` (*theta*)	Returns the sine of the radian angle *theta*.
`Math.tan` (*theta*)	Returns the tangent of the radian angle *theta*.
`Math.atan` (*x*)	Returns the principal arctangent of x, which lies between $-\pi/2$ and $+\pi/2$.
`Math.atan2` (*y*, *x*)	Returns the angle between the x-axis and the line from the origin to (x, y).

Random number generator

`Math.random` ()	Returns a random number that is at least 0 but strictly less than 1.

class, which is defined to be as close an approximation as possible to the mathematical constant π. Similarly, the function call `Math.sqrt(2)` returns the best possible approximation of the square root of 2.

You can use the functions from the `Math` class in writing your own functions. The following function uses the Pythagorean theorem to compute the distance from the origin to the point (x, y):

```
function distance(x, y) {
    return Math.sqrt(x * x + y * y);
}
```

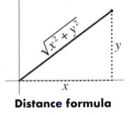

Distance formula

2.5 String data

So far, the programming examples in this chapter have worked only with numeric data. These days, computers work less with numeric data than with string data, which is a generic term for information composed of individual characters. The ability of modern computers to process string data has led to the development of text messaging, electronic mail, word processing systems, social networking, and a wide variety of other useful applications.

Conceptually, a *string* is a sequence of characters taken together as a unit. As in most modern languages, JavaScript includes strings as a built-in type, indicated in a program by enclosing the sequence of characters in quotation marks. For example, the string `"JavaScript"` is a sequence of ten characters including two uppercase letters and eight lowercase letters. The string `"To be, or not to be"` from Hamlet's soliloquy is a sequence of 19 characters including 13 letters, five spaces, and a comma.

JavaScript allows you to use either single or double quotation marks to specify a string, but it is good practice to pick a style and then use it consistently. The programs in this book use double quotation marks, mostly because that convention is common across a wide range of programming languages. The only exception is when the string itself contains a double quotation mark, as in `'"'`, which specifies a one-character string consisting of a double quotation mark. You can also include a quotation mark in a string by preceding it with a backslash character (\). Thus, you can also write the one-character string containing a double quotation mark as `"\""`.

For the most part, you can use strings as a JavaScript data type in much the same way that you use numbers. You can, for example, declare string variables and assign them values, just as you would with numeric variables. For example, the declaration

```
let name = "Eric";
```

declares a variable called **name** and initializes it to the four-character string **"Eric"**. As with the code used earlier in the chapter to declare numeric variables, the easiest way to represent a string-valued variable is to draw a box with the name on the outside and the value on the inside, like this:

name

> "Eric"

The quotation marks are not part of the string but are nonetheless included in box diagrams to make it easier to see where the string begins and ends.

Similarly, you can declare string constants, as in the following example:

```
const ALPHABET = "ABCDEFGHIJKLMNOPQRSTUVWXYZ";
```

This declaration defines the constant **ALPHABET** to be a string consisting of the 26 uppercase letters, as illustrated by the following box diagram:

ALPHABET

> "ABCDEFGHIJKLMNOPQRSTUVWXYZ"

String operations

In section 2.1, you learned that data types are defined by two properties: a *domain* and a *set of operations*. For strings, the domain is the set of all sequences of characters. In JavaScript, most string operations are defined as part of the **String** class, which is covered in detail in Chapter 7. For the moment, it is sufficient to learn just two string operations:

1.   Determining the length of a string.

2.   Joining two strings together end to end, which is called ***concatenation.***

In JavaScript, you can determine the length of a string by adding **.length** to the end of the string expression. For example, **ALPHABET.length** has the value 26.

JavaScript specifies concatenation using the **+** operator, which is also used to indicate addition for numbers. When JavaScript evaluates the **+** operator, it first checks the types of the operands. If both operands are numeric, JavaScript interprets the **+** operator as addition. If either or both of the operands are strings, JavaScript interprets the **+** operator as concatenation. For example, the expression

```
2 + 2
```

has the value 4, because both of the operands to + are numbers. Conversely,

```
"abc" + "def"
```

produces the six-character string **"abcdef"**.

In this example, it is important to observe that the concatenation operator does not introduce a space character or any other separator between the words. If you want to combine two strings into a single string that represents two distinct words, you have to include the space explicitly. For example, assuming that the variable **greeting** contains the string **"Hello"** and the variable **name** contains the string **"Eric"**, the expression

```
greeting + " " + name
```

produces the ten-character string **"Hello Eric"**.

The concatenation operator also allows you to combine string data with other data types. If one of the operands to **+** is a string but the other is some other value, JavaScript automatically converts that value to a string before performing the concatenation. For example, the expression

```
"Fahrenheit " + 451
```

produces the string **"Fahrenheit 451"** because JavaScript converts the numeric value 451 to the string **"451"** before combining the strings together.

Writing simple string functions

Although you will need the additional operations from Chapter 7 to write anything more than the simplest string functions, it is worth looking at a few examples that use only the concatenation operator.

The following function

```
function doubleString(str) {
   return str + str;
}
```

returns two copies of the supplied string joined together. This function enables the following sample run:

```
JavaScript Console
> doubleString("a")
aa
> doubleString("boo")
booboo
> doubleString("hots")
hotshots
>
```

Similarly, you can use the function that follows to add the string **"s"** to the end of a word to create a simple plural form:

```
function simplePlural(word) {
    return word + "s";
}
```

This function does not work for all English words, many of which require adding `"es"` instead of `"s"` depending on the final consonants. You will have a chance to solve that more sophisticated problem in Chapter 7.

You can also use concatenation to provide a partial solution to the problem raised earlier in the chapter of converting a distance in centimeters to the equivalent distance in feet and inches. Although JavaScript does not allow you to return two separate values from a function, you can display the correct answer by returning a string that contains both of the desired values, as illustrated by the following function, which makes use of the same constants introduced earlier in the chapter:

```
function centimetersToFeetAndInches(cm) {
    let totalInches = cm / CENTIMETERS_PER_INCH;
    let feet = Math.floor(totalInches / INCHES_PER_FOOT);
    let inches = totalInches % INCHES_PER_FOOT;
    return feet + "ft " + inches + "in";
}
```

The following console log shows three calls to `centimetersToFeetAndInches`, one for each of the values produced earlier by `feetAndInchesToCentimeters`:

```
JavaScript Console
> centimetersToFeetAndInches(2.54)
0ft 1in
> centimetersToFeetAndInches(30.48)
1ft 0in
> centimetersToFeetAndInches(254)
8ft 4in
>
```

2.6 Running JavaScript in the browser

Although the JavaScript console used in the earlier examples allows you to see how JavaScript evaluates expressions and simple functions, it does not give you a sense of how JavaScript runs a complete program. JavaScript was designed to be the programming language for the *World Wide Web*—more commonly referred to simply as the *web*—the vast constellation of interconnected documents accessible on the computer networks that span the globe. JavaScript programs typically run under the control of a web browser. When you visit a page that contains JavaScript content, your browser executes the JavaScript program to display its output on the screen. The sections that follow show you how to embed simple JavaScript programs into a web page.

The "Hello World" program

As is usually the case when you are studying programming, the best way to learn how JavaScript programs work is to look at an example. Although many examples might serve, the cultural history of computer science suggests a program that is appropriate as a first example in any language. That programming problem first appeared in *The C Programming Language* by Brian Kernighan and Dennis Ritchie, who offer the following advice on the first page of Chapter 1:

> The only way to learn a new programming language is by writing programs in it. The first program to write is the same for all languages:
>
> *Print the words*
>   `hello, world`
>
> This is the big hurdle; to leap over it you have to be able to create the program text somewhere, compile it successfully, load it, run it, and find out where the output went. With these mechanical details mastered, everything else is comparatively easy.

That advice was followed by the four-line text of the "Hello World" program, which became part of the heritage shared by all C programmers.

Although JavaScript is one of many languages derived from C, the "Hello World" program does not look exactly the same in the two languages. Even so, Kernighan and Ritchie's advice remains sound: the first program you write should be as simple as possible so that you can focus your attention on the mechanics of the programming process. Your mission—and you *should* definitely decide to accept it—is to get the JavaScript version of "Hello World" running in the browser. The JavaScript version of the program, complete with explanatory comments that acknowledge the debt to the original authors, appears in Figure 2-4.

FIGURE 2-4 The "Hello World" program in JavaScript

```
/*
 * File: HelloWorld.js
 * --------------------
 * This program displays "hello, world" on the console.  It is inspired
 * by the first program in Brian Kernighan and Dennis Ritchie's classic
 * book, The C Programming Language.
 */

function HelloWorld() {
   console.log("hello, world");
}
```

Outside of the commentary, the program itself consists of a single function definition whose body is one line long, as follows:

```
function HelloWorld() {
    console.log("hello, world");
}
```

The body of the `HelloWorld` function calls the built-in function `console.log` and asks it to display the string `"hello world"` on the JavaScript console.

So far, everything seems reasonably straightforward. As Kernighan and Ritchie suggest, however, the hard parts lie in figuring out how "to create the program text somewhere, compile it successfully, load it, run it, and find out where the output went." Those operations—which would no longer involve exactly the same steps as in the time Kernighan and Ritchie were writing—differ depending on what programming tools you happen to be using.

You will need at least two applications to get started. First, you need a *text editor,* which will allow you to create JavaScript program files. All modern computers come with some kind of text editor, but you will find it easier to write your programs if the editor you use understands the structure of JavaScript well enough to catch simple typographical errors and help you understand the different programming constructs by displaying them in colors that indicate their function. Second, you need a *web browser* that can read and display web pages. It doesn't matter which browser you use as long as it is modern enough to interpret JavaScript Version 6, which was released in 2015. If you are using a browser that is older than that, you should update your browser to the current version.

The first thing you need to do is use your editor to type in the `HelloWorld.js` program exactly as it appears in Figure 2-4 and then save it in a new folder on your computer. That step, however, only gets you part of the way toward running the program in the browser. To complete the task, you need to learn more about the structure of the web and how to embed JavaScript programs within a web page.

JavaScript and the Web

Every page on the World Wide Web is identified by a *uniform resource locator* or *URL* that serves as its address. Most web pages contain embedded references to other pages on related topics. These references are called *hyperlinks* and give the web its interconnected structure. When you enter an explicit URL into your browser or click on a hyperlink containing an embedded URL, the browser fetches the contents of the web page at that address. For most web pages, the browser uses an interaction scheme called the *Hypertext Transfer Protocol*—indicated by the prefix `http:` or its secure counterpart `https:` at the beginning of a URL—to read the contents of the page. The browser then interprets the content of the page and displays it on the screen.

Modern web pages use three distinct but interrelated technologies to define the contents of the page:

1. The structure and contents of the page are defined using a file written using the *Hypertext Markup Language* or *HTML.*

2. The visual appearance of the page is specified using *Cascading Style Sheets* or *CSS.*

3. Any interactive behavior of the page is represented using one or more files, which are conventionally written in JavaScript.

If you want to create professional-quality web pages, you need to learn something about these technologies. Because this book focuses on programming in JavaScript, the early chapters present only enough about HTML and CSS to let you run JavaScript programs. Chapter 12 covers these technologies in more detail.

An HTML template for JavaScript programs

Every web page is associated with an HTML file—which, by convention, is usually named `index.html`—that describes the contents of the page. In particular, the `index.html` file is organized into a series of sections marked by keywords enclosed in angle brackets, which are called *tags* in HTML. As you will see in the examples later in this section, some tags include additional information before the closing angle bracket. These additional fields are called *attributes.*

The `index.html` file begins with a special tag that marks the file as a standard HTML index:

```
<!DOCTYPE html>
```

After the `<!DOCTYPE>` tag, HTML tags usually occur in pairs. The first tag opens a section of the HTML file. The second tag, which uses the same keyword preceded by a slash character, closes that section. For example, the entire HTML text in the `index.html` file begins with a tag named `<html>` and ends with the corresponding closing tag `</html>`. To make it clear to the reader exactly what parts of the HTML file are included within each pair of tags, the lines between the opening and closing tag are typically indented.

A standard HTML file includes two sections between the `<html>` and `</html>` markers. The first of these is the `<head>` section, which defines features of the page as a whole; the second is the `<body>` section, which defines the page contents.

As with other paired tags, the `<head>` and `<body>` sections end with the tags `</head>` and `</body>`, respectively.

For simple JavaScript-based web pages, the `<head>` section contains two types of interior tags. The first of these is the `<title>` section, which defines the title that appears at the top of the web page. The `<title>` section has the form

<code><title>whatever title you want to use</title></code>

where you can replace the italicized text with whatever text you want to use as the title. By convention, the web programs in this book use the name of the program file as the title, so that the `<title>` section for the `HelloWorld.js` program would be

```
<title>HelloWorld</title>
```

The other component of the `<head>` section is one or more `<script>` tags that specify the names of the JavaScript files to load. Each of these `<script>` tags has the following form:

<code><script src="<i>filename</i>"></script></code>

In this pattern, you need to replace the *filename* marker with the actual name of the file. To load `HelloWorld.js`, for example, you would use the following tag:

```
<script src="HelloWorld.js"></script>
```

As your programs become larger and more sophisticated, they will often require more that one JavaScript file. In some cases, those additional JavaScript files will be general-purpose libraries, but there will also be cases in which it makes sense to subdivide a complex application into several JavaScript files, each of which is responsible for some part of the complete program. In either of these cases, you need to include additional `<script>` tags in the `<head>` section to load any JavaScript libraries or program components that your application requires.

Although the "Hello World" program does not technically require any libraries, it turns out that adding a library to the `<head>` section will make your life as a programmer much easier. Remember that one of your tasks in Kernighan and Ritchie's checklist is to "find out where the output went." Most browsers make the console log hard to find, mostly to minimize confusion for the average web user, who could easily be distracted by messages appearing in the console log. To make console output easier to find, the `index.html` files used in this book include the following `<script>` tag to load a library called `JSConsole.js`, which displays the console log as part of the web page itself:

```
<script src="JSConsole.js"></script>
```

FIGURE 2-5 The `index.html` file for "Hello World"

```html
<!DOCTYPE html>
<html>
  <head>
    <title>HelloWorld</title>
    <script src="JSConsole.js"></script>
    <script src="HelloWorld.js"></script>
  </head>
  <body onload="HelloWorld()"></body>
</html>
```

For simple JavaScript-based web pages that contain no other content, the `<body>` section will be empty, with nothing between the opening and closing tags. The `<body>` tag, however, must specify an `onload` attribute to get the program started. The value of the `onload` attribute is a JavaScript expression, which is ordinarily a function call. For example, to trigger a call to the `HelloWorld` function when the page has finished loading all the necessary JavaScript code, the `onload` attribute would have the value `"HelloWorld()"`.

The complete contents of the `index.html` file for the "Hello World" program appear in Figure 2-5. You can use this file as a template for the `index.html` files you need to implement other JavaScript-based web pages.

2.7 Testing and debugging

Although you may sometimes get lucky with extremely simple programs, one of the truths you'll soon have to accept as a programmer is that very few of your programs will run correctly the first time around. Most of the time, you will need to spend a considerable fraction of your time testing the program to see whether it works, discovering that it doesn't, and then settling into the process of *debugging,* in which you find and fix the errors in your code.

Perhaps the most compelling description of the centrality of debugging to the programming process comes from the British computing pioneer Maurice Wilkes (1913–2010), who in 1979 offered the following reflection from his early years in the field:

> As soon as we started programming, we found to our surprise that it wasn't as easy to get programs right as we had thought. We had to discover debugging. I can remember the exact instant when I realized that a large part of my life from then on was going to be spent in finding mistakes in my own programs.

Maurice Wilkes

(Science and Society Picture Library/Getty Images)

Programming defensively

Even though it is impossible to avoid bugs altogether, you can reduce the number of bugs by being careful during the programming process. Just as it's important to drive defensively in your car, it makes sense to program defensively as you write your code. The most important aspect of defensive programming is looking over your programs to ensure that they do what you intend them to do. You will also find that taking the time to make your code as clear and readable as possible will help avoid problems down the road.

You can, however, get JavaScript to help you out. The original versions of JavaScript were overly permissive in the sense that they failed to check for common programming errors, such as forgetting to declare a variable. In standard JavaScript, forgetting to declare a variable does not generate an error message; what happens instead is that JavaScript automatically creates that variable as part of the entire web document, which is usually not what the programmer intended.

Modern versions of JavaScript allow you to enable more stringent checking by including the line

```
"use strict";
```

at the beginning of a JavaScript file. Doing so makes it possible for the JavaScript interpreter to do a much better job of identifying potential problems in your code. From here on, all the programs in this text will use this feature.

Becoming a good debugger

Debugging is one of the most creative and intellectually challenging aspects of programming. It can, however, also be one of the most frustrating. If you are just beginning your study of programming, it is likely that the frustrating aspects of debugging will loom much larger than the excitement of meeting an interesting intellectual challenge. That fact in itself is by no means surprising. Debugging, after all, is a skill that takes time to learn. Before you have developed the necessary experience and expertise, your forays into the world of debugging will often leave you facing a completely mysterious problem that you have no idea how to solve. And when your assignment is due the next day and you can make no progress until you somehow solve that mystery, frustration is probably the most natural reaction.

To a surprising extent, the challenges that people face while debugging are not so much technical as they are psychological. To become a successful debugger, the most important thing is to start thinking in new ways that get you beyond the psychological barriers that stand in your way. There is no magical, step-by-step approach to finding the problems, which are usually of your own making. What you need is logic, creativity, patience, and a considerable amount of practice.

The phases of the programming process

When you are developing a program, the actual process of writing the code is only one piece of a more complex intellectual activity. Before you sit down to write the code, it is always wise to spend some time thinking about the program design. As you discovered when you were working with Karel in Chapter 1, there are usually many ways to decompose a large problem into more manageable pieces. Putting some thought into the design of that decomposition before you start writing the individual functions is almost certain to reduce the total amount of time—and frustration—involved in the project as a whole. After you've written the code, you need to test whether it works and, in all probability, spend some time ferreting out the bugs that prevent the program from doing what you want.

These four activities—designing, coding, testing, and debugging—constitute the principal components of the programming process. And although there are certainly some constraints on order (you can't debug code that you haven't yet written, for example), it is a mistake to think of these phases as rigidly sequential. The biggest problem that students have comes from thinking that it makes sense to design and code the entire program and then try to get it working as a whole. Professional programmers never work that way. They develop a preliminary design, write some pieces of the code, test those pieces to see if they work as intended, and then fix the bugs that the testing uncovers. Only when that individual piece is working do professional programmers return to code, test, and debug the next section of the program. From time to time, they go back and revisit the design as they learn from the experience of seeing how well the original design works in practice. You must learn to work in much the same way.

It is equally important to recognize that each phase in the programming process requires a fundamentally different approach. As you move back and forth among the various phases, you need to adopt different ways of thinking. In my experience, the best way to illustrate how these approaches differ is to associate each phase with a profession that depends on much the same skills and modes of thought.

During the design phase, you have to think like an *architect*. You need to have a sense not only of the problem that must be solved but also an understanding of the underlying aesthetics of different solution strategies. Those aesthetic judgments are not entirely free from constraints. You know what's needed, you recognize what's possible, and you choose the best design that lies within those constraints.

When you move to the coding phase, your role shifts to that of the *engineer*. Now your job is to apply your understanding of programming to transform a theoretical design into an actual implementation. This phase is by no means mechanical and requires a significant amount of creativity, but your goal is to produce a program that you believe implements the design.

Phases and roles in the programming process

Design	= Architect
Coding	= Engineer
Testing	= Vandal
Debugging	= Detective

In many respects, the testing phase is the most difficult aspect of the process to understand. When you act as a tester, your role is not to establish that the program works, but just the opposite. Your job is to break it. A tester therefore needs to assume the role of a *vandal*. You need to search deliberately for anything that might go wrong and take real joy in finding any flaws. It is in this phase of the programming process that the most difficult psychological barriers arise. As the coder, you want the program to work; as the tester, you want it to fail. Many people have trouble shifting focus in this way. After all, it's hard to be overjoyed at pointing out the stupid mistakes the coder made when you also happen to be that coder. Even so, you need to make this shift.

Finally, your job in the debugging phase is that of a *detective*. The testing process reveals the existence of errors but does not necessarily reveal why they occur. Your job during the debugging phase is to sort through all the available evidence, create a hypothesis about what is going wrong, check that hypothesis through additional testing, and then make the necessary corrections.

As with testing, the debugging phase is full of psychological pitfalls when you act in the detective role. When you were writing the code in your role as engineer, you believed that it worked correctly when you designed it in your role as architect. You now have to discover why it doesn't, which means that you have to discard any preconceptions you've retained from those earlier phases and approach the problem with a fresh perspective. Making that shift successfully is always a difficult challenge. Code that looked correct to you once is likely to look just as good when you come back to it a second time.

What you need to keep in mind is that the testing phase has determined that the program is not working correctly. There must be a problem somewhere. It's not the browser or JavaScript that's misbehaving or some unfortunate conjunction of the planets. As Cassius reminds Brutus in Shakespeare's *Julius Caesar,* "the fault, dear Brutus, is not in our stars, but in ourselves." You introduced the error when you wrote the code, and it is your job to find it.

This book will offer additional suggestions about debugging as you learn how to write more complex programs, but the following principle will serve you better than any specific debugging strategy or technique:

> *When you are trying to find a bug, it is more important to understand what your program is doing than to understand what it isn't doing.*

Most people who come upon a problem in their code go back to the original problem and try to figure out why their program isn't doing what they wanted. Although such an approach can be helpful in some cases, it is far more likely that this kind of thinking will make you blind to the real problem. If you make an unwarranted assumption the first time around, you are likely to make it again, and be left not seeing any reason why your program isn't doing the right thing. You need instead to gather information about what your program is in fact doing and then try to work out where it goes wrong.

Although many modern browsers come equipped with sophisticated JavaScript debuggers, you are likely to get the most mileage out of the `console.log` function. If you discover that your program isn't working, add a few calls to `console.log` at places where you think your program might be going down the wrong path. In some cases, it's sufficient to include a line like

```
console.log("I got here");
```

to the program. If the message `"I got here"` appears on the console, you know that the program got to that point in the code. It is often even more helpful to have the call to `console.log` display the value of an important variable. If, for example, you expect the variable `n` to have the value 100 at some point in the code, you can add the line

```
console.log("n = " + n);
```

If running the program shows that `n` has the value 0 instead, you know that something has gone wrong prior to this point. Narrowing down the region of the program in which the problem might be located puts you in a much better position to find and correct the error.

Because the process of debugging is similar to the art of detection, it seems appropriate to offer some of the more relevant bits of debugging wisdom I've encountered in detective fiction, which appear in Figure 2-6 at the top of the next page. I also strongly recommend Robert Pirsig's critically acclaimed novel *Zen and the Art of Motorcycle Maintenance: An Inquiry into Values* (Bantam, 1974), which stands as the best exposition of the art and psychology of debugging ever written. The most relevant section is the discussion of "gumption traps" in Chapter 26.

An example of a psychological barrier

Although most testing and debugging challenges involve a level of programming sophistication beyond the scope of this chapter, there is a very simple program that illustrates just how easy it is to let your assumptions blind you not only to the cause of an error but even to its very existence. Throughout the many years I've taught computer science, one of my favorite problems to assign at the beginning of the term is to write a function that solves the quadratic equation

$$ax^2 + bx + c = 0$$

FIGURE 2-6 Debugging advice from detective fiction

Regard with distrust all circumstances which seem to favor our secret desires.
—Émile Gaboriau, *Monsieur Lecoq*, 1868

There is nothing like first-hand evidence.
—Sir Arthur Conan Doyle, *A Study in Scarlet*, 1888

It is a capital mistake to theorise before one has data. Insensibly one begins to twist facts to suit theories, instead of theories to suit facts.
—Sir Arthur Conan Doyle, *A Scandal in Bohemia*, 1892

It is of the highest importance in the art of detection to be able to recognize out of a number of facts which are incidental and which vital. Otherwise your energy and attention must be dissipated instead of being concentrated.
—Sir Arthur Conan Doyle, *The Adventure of the Reigate Squires*, 1892

With method and logic one can accomplish anything.
—Agatha Christie, *Poirot Investigates*, 1924

Detection requires a patient persistence which amounts to obstinacy.
—P. D. James, *An Unsuitable Job for a Woman*, 1972

It was always more difficult than you thought it would be.
—Alexander McCall Smith, *The No. 1 Ladies' Detective Agency*, 1998

As you know from secondary school, this equation has two solutions given by the formula

$$x = \frac{-b \pm \sqrt{b^2 - 4ac}}{2a}$$

The first solution is obtained by using + in place of the ± symbol; the second is obtained by using – instead. The problem I give students is to write a function that takes *a*, *b*, and *c* as parameters and displays the two resulting solutions for *x*.

Although the majority can solve this problem correctly, there are always a number of students—as much as 20 percent of a large class—who turn in functions that look something like this:

```
function quadratic(a, b, c) {
    let root = Math.sqrt(b*b - 4*a*c);
    let x1 = (-b + root) / 2*a;
    let x2 = (-b - root) / 2*a;
    console.log("x1 = " + x1);
    console.log("x2 = " + x2);
}
```

As the bug symbol indicates, this implementation of `quadratic` is incorrect, although the problem is subtle. It *looks* as if the expression `2*a` is in the denominator of the fraction, when in fact it isn't. In JavaScript, operators in the same precedence class, such as the `/` and `*` in the lines defining `x1` and `x2`, are evaluated in left-to-right order. The parenthesized value in these expressions is therefore first divided by 2 and then multiplied by `a`. The quadratic formula requires the denominator to be the quantity `(2*a)`, which means that the parentheses are necessary.

The real lesson in this example, however, lies in the fact that many students compound their mistake by failing to discover it. Most of the students who make this error fail to test their programs for any values of the coefficient *a* other than 1, since those are the easiest answers to compute by hand. If *a* is 1, it doesn't matter whether you multiply or divide by *a* because the answer will be the same. Worse still, students who test their program for other values of *a* often fail to notice that their programs give incorrect answers. I often get sample runs that look like this:

```
JavaScript Console
> quadratic(8, -6, 1)
x1 = 32
x2 = 16
>
```

This sample run asserts that $x = 32$ and $x = 16$ are solutions to the equation

$$8x^2 - 6x + 1 = 0$$

but it is easy to check that neither of these values in fact satisfy the equation. Even so, students happily submit programs that generate this sample run without noticing that the answers are wrong.

Writing effective test programs

Whenever you write a function, it is a good idea to write a companion function to check that your implementation works for a large set of cases. Figure 2-7 on the next page shows how a test program for the `quadratic` function can be included in the program file along with the function definition. Each of the sample programs supplied with this book contains a test function of this sort, and it is good practice for you to adopt this approach in your own code. Thinking about testing as you write the program will make it much easier to find the bugs that will inevitably show up in your code from time to time.

The `TestQuadratic` function generates several test runs of the `quadratic` functions with a range of parameters. Moreover, to make sure that anyone running the program doesn't simply believe the answers generated by the computer, the

FIGURE 2-7 Implementation of the `quadratic` function and an associated test program

```
/*
 * File: Quadratic.js
 * --------------------
 * This file defines the quadratic function, which solves the quadratic
 * equation given the coefficients a, b, and c.
 */

"use strict";

function quadratic(a, b, c) {
   let root = Math.sqrt(b*b - 4*a*c);
   let x1 = (-b + root) / (2*a);
   let x2 = (-b - root) / (2*a);
   console.log("x1 = " + x1);
   console.log("x2 = " + x2);
}

/* Test program */

function TestQuadratic() {
   console.log("x^2 + 5x + 6 = 0 (roots should be -2 and -3):");
   quadratic(1, 5, 6);
   console.log("");
   console.log("x^2 + x - 12 = 0 (roots should be 3 and -4):");
   quadratic(1, 1, -12);
   console.log("");
   console.log("x^2 - 10x + 25 = 0 (roots should be 5 and 5):");
   quadratic(1, -10, 25);
   console.log("");
   console.log("8x^2 - 6x + 1 = 0 (roots should be 0.5 and 0.25):");
   quadratic(8, -6, 1);
}
```

program indicates exactly what the correct answers should be. A complete sample run of the `TestQuadratic` program looks like this:

```
                        Quadratic
> TestQuadratic()
x^2 + 5x + 6 = 0 (roots should be -2 and -3):
x1 = -2
x2 = -3

x^2 + x - 12 = 0 (roots should be 3 and -4):
x1 = 3
x2 = -4

x^2 - 10x + 25 = 0 (roots should be 5 and 5):
x1 = 5
x2 = 5

8x^2 - 6x + 1 = 0 (roots should be 0.5 and 0.25):
x1 = 0.5
x2 = 0.25
>
```

Although it is impossible to test all inputs for a function, it is usually possible to identify a set of test cases that check for the most likely sources of error. For the `quadratic` function, for example, you should make sure your test function checks a range of values for the coefficients $a, b,$ and c. It is also important, as the example in the preceding section demonstrates, to know what the answers ought to be.

2.8 Software maintenance

One of the more surprising aspects of software development is that programs require maintenance. In fact, studies of software development indicate that, for commercial applications, paying programmers to maintain the software after it has been released constitutes between 80 and 90 percent of the total cost. In the context of software, however, it is a little hard to imagine precisely what maintenance means. At first hearing, the idea sounds rather bizarre. If you think in terms of a car or a bridge, maintenance occurs when something has broken—some of the metal has rusted away, a piece of some mechanical linkage has worn out from overuse, or something has gotten smashed up in an accident. None of these situations apply to software. The code itself doesn't rust. Using the same program over and over again does not in any way diminish its functioning. Accidental misuse can certainly have dangerous consequences but does not usually damage the program itself; even if it does, the program can often be restored from a backup copy. What does maintenance mean in such an environment?

Software requires maintenance for two principal reasons. First, even after considerable testing and, in some cases, years of field use, bugs can still survive in the original code. Then, when some unanticipated situation arises, the bug, previously dormant, causes the program to fail. Thus, debugging is an essential part of program maintenance. It is not, however, the most important part. Far more consequential, especially in terms of the impact on the overall cost of program maintenance, is that programs need to change in response to changing requirements. Users often want new features in their applications, and software developers try to provide those features to maintain customer loyalty. In either case—whether one wants to repair a bug or add a feature—someone has to look at the program, figure out what's going on, make the necessary changes, verify that those changes work, and then release a new version. This process is difficult, time-consuming, expensive, and prone to error.

Program maintenance is especially difficult because many programmers do not write their programs for the long haul. To them it seems sufficient to get the program working and then move on to something else. The discipline of writing programs so that they can be understood and maintained by others is called *software engineering.* In this text, you are encouraged to write programs that demonstrate effective software engineering techniques.

Many novice programmers are disturbed to learn that there is no precise set of rules you can follow to ensure good programming style. Software engineering is not a cookbook sort of process. Instead it is a skill blended with more than a little bit of artistry. Practice is critical. One learns to write well-structured programs by writing them, and by reading others, much as one learns to be a novelist. Becoming an effective programmer requires discipline—the discipline not to cut corners or to forget, in the rush to complete a project, about that future maintainer. Good programming practice also requires developing an aesthetic sense of what it means for a program to be readable and well presented.

Although there are no hard-and-fast rules for writing maintainable programs, there are certainly some important principles, including the following:

- Write both your code and your comments with future maintainers in mind.
- Choose names for variables, constants, and functions that convey their purpose.
- Use indentation to highlight the hierarchical structure of your programs.
- Design your programs so that they are easy to modify as requirements change.

The last point in this list deserves additional discussion. Given that programs will inevitably change over their lifetimes, it is good programming practice to help future maintainers make the necessary changes. A useful strategy to support ongoing maintenance is to use constant definitions for values that you expect might change at some point down the road.

The value of using constant definitions is perhaps easiest to illustrate in the context of a historical example. Imagine for the moment that you are a programmer in the late 1960s working on the initial design of the *ARPANET,* which is the forerunner of today's Internet. Because resources were highly constrained at that time, the designers of the ARPANET placed a limit on the number of computers (which were called *hosts* in the ARPANET days) that could be connected to the network. In the early years of the ARPANET, that limit was 127 hosts. If JavaScript had existed in 1969, you might have declared a constant like this:

```
const MAXIMUM_NUMBER_OF_HOSTS = 127;
```

At some later point, however, the explosive growth of networking would force you to raise this bound.

Making that change would be easy if you had defined a constant but hard if you had instead written the number 127. In that case, you would need to change all instances of 127 that refer to the number of hosts. Some instances of 127 might refer to things other than the limit on the number of hosts, and it would be just as important not to change any of those values. In the likely event that you had made a mistake in that process, you would have a very hard time tracking down the bug.

Summary

In this chapter, you have started your journey toward programming in JavaScript by considering several example programs that make use of two different data types: numbers and strings. Important points introduced in the chapter include:

- The primary focus of this book is not the JavaScript language itself but rather the principles you need to understand the fundamentals of programming. To reduce the number of language details you need to master, this text relies on the features that Douglas Crockford, whose contributions are described at the beginning of the chapter, identifies as the "good parts" of JavaScript.

- Data values come in many different types, each of which is defined by a *domain* and a *set of operations*.

- Numbers in JavaScript are written in conventional decimal notation. JavaScript also allows you to write numbers in scientific notation by adding the letter **E** and an exponent indicating the power of 10 by which the number is multiplied.

- Expressions consist of individual *terms* connected by *operators*. The subexpressions to which an operator applies are called its *operands*.

- The order of operations is determined by rules of *precedence*. The complete table of operators and their precedence appears in Figure 2-1 on page 44.

- *Variables* in JavaScript have two attributes: a name and a value. Variables used in a JavaScript program are *declared* using a line of the form

      let *identifier* = *expression*;

  which establishes the name and initial value of the variable.

- *Constants* are used to specify values that do not change within a program. You can declare constants in JavaScript by replacing the keyword **let** with the keyword **const** in a declaration. By convention, you write the names of constants entirely in upper case, using the underscore to mark word boundaries.

- You can change the value of variables through the use of *assignment statements*. When you assign a new value to a variable, any previous value is lost.

- JavaScript includes an abbreviated form of assignment in which the statement

      variable op= *expression*;

  acts as a shorthand for the longer expression

      variable = *variable op* (*expression*) ;

- JavaScript includes the operators ++ and --, which add and subtract 1 from a variable, respectively. These operators may appear either before or after their operand. The placement determines whether the operation occurs before or after the value is retrieved.

- A *function* is a block of code that has been organized into a separate unit and given a name. Other parts of the program can then *call* that function, possibly passing it *arguments* and receiving a result *returned* by that function.

- Variables declared inside the body of a function are called *local variables* and are visible only inside that function. Variables declared outside of any function are *global variables,* which can be used anywhere in the program. This book avoids using global variables, because they make programs harder to maintain.

- A function that returns a value must have a **return** statement that specifies the result. Functions may return values of any type.

- JavaScript's **Math** library defines a variety of functions that implement such standard mathematical functions as **sqrt**, **sin**, and **cos**. A list of the more common mathematical functions appears in Figure 2-3 on page 52.

- A *string* is a sequence of characters taken together as a unit. In JavaScript, you write a string by enclosing its characters in quotation marks. JavaScript accepts either single or double quotation marks for this purpose.

- Although strings support many additional operations that will be presented in Chapter 7, the examples in this chapter and the next few chapters use only the **length** field and the + operator. If both operands to + are numeric, the values are added; if either operand is a string, both operands are converted to strings and *concatenated* end to end.

- In the defining document for the programming language C, Brian Kernighan and Dennis Ritchie suggest that the first program written in any language should be one that prints the string **"hello, world"**. This book follows their advice.

- JavaScript was designed for use in conjunction with the World Wide Web. JavaScript programs typically run in the context of a web browser.

- Modern web pages use three distinct technologies to define the contents of a web page. The structure and contents of the page are defined using *HTML* (*Hypertext Markup Language*), the visual appearance is specified using *CSS* (*Cascading Style Sheets*), and the interactive behavior is defined using *JavaScript.*

- Every JavaScript program that runs in a browser must include an **index.html** file, which defines the overall structure of the page, loads the necessary JavaScript programs and libraries, and specifies a JavaScript expression to be evaluated when the page is loaded. These **index.html** files have a conventional form, which appears in Figure 2-5.

- JavaScript files are loaded into the browser by means of **<script>** tags in the **index.html** file, each of which has the following form:

```
<script src="filename"></script>
```

- The four phases of the programming process are *design, coding, testing,* and *debugging,* although it is best to view these phases as interrelated rather than sequential. Professional programmers typically code one piece of a program, test it, debug it, and then go back and work on the next piece.

- Each phase in the programming process requires you to behave in a different way. During the design phase, you act as an *architect.* When you are coding, you function as an *engineer.* During testing, you must act like a *vandal,* striving to break the program, not to prove that it works. When debugging, you need to think like a *detective* employing all the cleverness and insight of a Sherlock Holmes.

- When you are trying to find a bug, it is more important to understand what your program *is* doing than to understand what it *isn't* doing.

- In seeking to understand what your program is doing, your most helpful resource is the `console.log` function.

- The most serious problems programmers face during the testing and debugging phases are psychological rather than technical. It is extremely easy to let your assumptions and desires get in the way of understanding where the problems lie.

- It is good programming practice to include test programs along with the definitions of any functions that you write.

- Programs require maintenance over their life cycles both to correct bugs and to add new features as user requirements change.

Review questions

1. What are the two attributes that define a data type?

2. Identify which of the following are legal numbers in JavaScript:

   a) `42`
   b) `-17`
   c) `2+3`
   d) `-2.3`
   e) `20`
   f) `2.0`
   g) `1,000,000`
   h) `3.1415926`
   i) `123456789`
   j) `0.000001`
   k) `1.1E+11`
   l) `1.1X+11`

3. Rewrite the following numbers using JavaScript's form for scientific notation:

   a) 6.02252×10^{23}
   b) 29979250000.0
   c) 0.00000000529167
   d) 3.1415926535

By the way, each of these values is an approximation of an important scientific or mathematical constant: (a) Avogadro's number, which is the number of molecules in one mole of a chemical substance; (b) the speed of light in centimeters per second; (c) the Bohr radius in centimeters, which is the average radius of an electron's orbit around a hydrogen atom in its lowest-energy state; and (d) the mathematical constant π. In the case of π, there is no advantage in using the scientific notation form, but it is certainly legal to do so.

4. Indicate which of the following are legal variable names in JavaScript:

a) `x`
b) `formula1`
c) `average_rainfall`
d) `%correct`
e) `short`
f) `tiny`
g) `total output`
h) `aReasonablyLongVariableName`
i) `12MonthTotal`
j) `marginal-cost`
k) `b4hand`
l) `_stk_depth`

5. What does the `%` operator signify in JavaScript?

6. True or false: The `-` operator has the same precedence when it is used before an operand to indicate negation as it does when it is used to indicate subtraction.

7. By applying the appropriate precedence rules, calculate the result of each of the following expressions:

a) `6 + 5 / 4 - 3`
b) `2 + 2 * (2 * 2 - 2) % 2 / 2`
c) `10 + 9 * ((8 + 7) % 6) + 5 * 4 % 3 * 2 + 1`
d) `1 + 2 + (3 + 4) * ((5 * 6 % 7 * 8) - 9) - 10`

8. What shorthand assignment statement would you use to multiply the value of the variable **salary** by 2?

9. What is the most common way in JavaScript to write a statement that has the same effect as the statement

```
x = x + 1;
```

10. In your own words, explain the difference between the prefix and suffix forms of the increment and decrement operators.

11. What is the value of each of the following expressions:

a) `Math.round(5.99)`
b) `Math.floor(5.99)`
c) `Math.ceil(5.99)`
d) `Math.floor(-5.99)`
e) `Math.sqrt(Math.pow(3, 2) + Math.pow(4, 2))`

12. What is the possible range of values returned by the function **Math.random**?

13. How do you specify a string value in JavaScript?

14. If a string is stored in the variable **str**, how would you determine its length?

15. What is meant by the term *concatenation?*

16. How does JavaScript decide whether to interpret the + operator as addition or concatenation?

17. Given the definition of the **doubleString** function on page 55, what value does JavaScript produce if you call **doubleString(2)**?   In light of this behavior, would it be reasonable to shorten the name of the function to **double**? Why or why not?

18. Evaluate each of the following expressions:

    a)   **123 + 456**

    b)   **123 + "456"**

    c)   **"Catch-" + 2 + 2**

    d)   **"Citizen" + 2 * 2**

19. What did Brian Kernighan and Dennis Ritchie suggest should be the first program you write in any language? What reasons did they offer for starting with a program that simple?

20. What are the three technologies used to specify a web page? What aspects of the web page do each of these technologies control?

21. What is the conventional name of the HTML file that defines a web page?

22. What is the syntax of the HTML tag used to load JavaScript files into the browser?

23. What is the name of the JavaScript library used in this chapter to implement programs that write output to the console? What reasons does the chapter give for using this library to replace the standard system console?

24. How can you enable rigorous error checking in a JavaScript program?

25. What are the four phases of the programming process identified in this chapter? For each of those phases, what professional role does the chapter offer as a model for how to perform that phase?

26. True or false: Professional programmers work through the four phases of the programming process in order, finishing each one before moving on to the next.

27. True or false: When you are testing your program, your primary goal is to show that it works.

28. What piece of advice does the chapter offer to help you think effectively about debugging?

29. What built-in function does the text identify as the most useful debugging tool?

30. In your own words, explain what is meant by *program maintenance*.

31. What guidelines does this chapter offer to improve your programming style?

███ Exercises

1. How would you implement the following mathematical function in JavaScript:

$$f(x) = x^2 - 5x + 6$$

2. Write a function **quotient** that takes two numbers, **x** and **y** (which you may assume are both positive integers), and returns the integral quotient of **x / y**, discarding any remainder. For example, calling **quotient(9, 4)** should return 2 because four goes into nine twice with a remainder of one left over. This function is easy to write if you use the **Math.floor** function; the challenge in this exercise is to write **quotient** using only the standard arithmetic operators.

3. According to mathematical historians, the German mathematician Carl Friedrich Gauss (1777–1855) began to show his mathematical talent at a very early age. When he was in primary school, Gauss was asked by his teacher to compute the sum of the first 100 integers. Gauss is said to have produced the answer instantly by working out that the sum of the first N integers is given by the formula

$$\frac{N \times (N + 1)}{2}$$

Write a function **sumFirstNIntegers** that takes the value of N as its argument and returns the sum of those integers, as illustrated in the following sample run:

(Georgios Kollidas/Alamy Stock Photo)

Carl Friedrich Gauss

JavaScript Console
> **sumFirstNIntegers(3)**
6
> **sumFirstNIntegers(100)**
5050
>

4. Using the `celsiusToFahrenheit` function on page 50 as a model, write a function `fahrenheitToCelsius` that converts a temperature value in the opposite direction. The conversion formula is

    $$C = \frac{5}{9}(F - 32)$$

5. Write a function that computes the area of a triangle given values for its base and its height, which are defined as shown in the following diagram:

    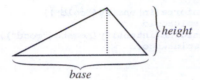

    Given any triangle, the area is always one half of the base times the height.

6. Write a function `quote` that takes a string value and adds double quotation marks at both the beginning and the end. Your function definition should allow you to replicate the following console session:

    ```
    JavaScript Console
    > quote("hello")
    "hello"
    > quote("Fahrenheit " + 11 * 41)
    "Fahrenheit 451"
    > " "

    > quote("   ")
    "   "
    >
    ```

    As the lines at the end of this example indicate, the `quote` function can make it easier to see where a string begins and ends, particularly if the string contains spaces.

7. *It is a beautiful thing, the destruction of words.*
    —Syme in George Orwell's *1984*

    In Orwell's novel, Syme and his colleagues at the Ministry of Truth are engaged in simplifying English into a more regular language called *Newspeak*. As Orwell describes in his appendix entitled "The Principles of Newspeak," words can take a variety of prefixes to eliminate the need for the massive number of words we have in English. For example, Orwell writes,

    > Any word—this again applied in principle to every word in the language—could be negatived by adding the affix *un-*, or could be strengthened by the affix *plus-*, or, for still greater emphasis, *doubleplus-*. Thus, for example, *uncold* meant "warm," while *pluscold* and *doublepluscold* meant, respectively, "very cold" and "superlatively cold."

Define three functions—`negate`, `intensify`, and `reinforce`—that take a string and add the prefixes `"un"`, `"plus"`, and `"double"` to that string, respectively. Your function definitions should allow you to generate the following console session:

```
                        JavaScript Console
> negate("cold")
uncold
> intensify("cold")
pluscold
> reinforce(intensify("cold"))
doublepluscold
> reinforce(intensify(negate("good")))
doubleplusungood
>
```

8. Use an editor to create the program `HelloWorld.js` and the file `index.html` exactly as they appear in Figures 2-4 and 2-5. Use your browser to open the `index.html` file to show that you can get JavaScript programs working.

9. For each of exercises 3 through 7, write a test program that displays some representative values of the functions along the lines of the `TestQuadratic` function in Figure 2-7. Create an `index.html` file that loads a JavaScript file containing both the function definition and the test program, and then show that your program works by reading the `index.html` file into your browser.

CHAPTER 3
Control Statements

I had a running compiler and nobody would touch it. . . . They carefully told me, computers could only do arithmetic; they could not do programs.

— Grace Murray Hopper, as quoted in Charlene Billings, *Grace Hopper: Navy Admiral and Computing Pioneer,* 1989

Grace Murray Hopper (1906–1992)

(Bettmann/Getty Images)

Grace Murray Hopper studied mathematics and physics at Vassar College and went on to earn her Ph.D. in mathematics at Yale. During the Second World War, Hopper joined the United States Navy and was posted to the Bureau of Ordinance Computation at Harvard University, where she worked with computing pioneer Howard Aiken. Hopper became one of the first programmers of the Mark I digital computer, which was one of the first machines capable of performing complex calculations. Hopper made several contributions to computing in its early years and was one of the major contributors to the development of the language COBOL, which continues to have widespread use in business programming applications. In 1985, Hopper became the first woman promoted to the rank of admiral. During her life, Grace Murray Hopper served as the most visible example of a successful woman in computer science. In recognition of that contribution, there is now a biennial Celebration of Women in Computing, named in her honor.

In Chapter 2, you saw several examples of simple JavaScript functions. In each of those examples, execution of the function started with the first statement in its body and then continued through the remaining statements in order, possibly calling other functions along the way. Before you can write more interesting applications, you need to learn how to control the operation of your program in more sophisticated ways, much as you did with the Karel programs in Chapter 1.

Like their counterparts in Karel, functions in JavaScript often include control statements to specify the order of operation. The `if` and the `while` statements are essentially the same in both languages, but JavaScript uses a more flexible statement called `for` to achieve the effect of the `repeat` statement in Karel. In addition, JavaScript includes a conditional statement called `switch` that makes it easier to write code that needs to choose among several possible execution paths. This chapter covers these control statements in JavaScript and, in the process, extends the set of tools you have for solving problems.

Students often believe that there must be some rule that determines when they need to use each of the various control statements a programming language provides. That's not how programming works. Control statements are tools for solving problems. Before you can determine what control statement makes sense in a particular context, you have to give serious thought to the problem you are trying to solve and the strategy you should choose to solve it. You write the code for a program *after* you have decided how to solve the underlying problem. There is nothing automatic about the programming process.

The fact that there are no magic rules that turn a problem statement into a working program is what makes programming such a valuable skill. If it *were* possible to carry out the programming process according to some well-defined algorithm, it would be easy to automate the process and eliminate the need for programmers entirely. Programming consists of solving problems, many of which are extremely complex and require considerable ingenuity and creativity to solve. Solving such problems is what makes computer programming hard; it is also what makes programming interesting and fun.

3.1 Boolean data

The major difference between control statements in the two languages lies in the conditions you can check. Karel's conditional expressions, which have names like `frontIsClear` and `facingNorth`, make sense only in Karel's world. In JavaScript, you express conditions by constructing expressions whose values are either true or false. Such expressions are called ***Boolean expressions,*** after the English mathematician George Boole, who developed an algebraic approach for

(Pictorial Press Ltd./Alamy Stock Photo)

George Boole

working with data of this type. Boolean values are represented in JavaScript using a built-in type whose domain consists of exactly two values: `true` and `false`.

JavaScript defines several operators that work with Boolean values. These operators fall into two classes—relational operators and logical operators—which the next two sections discuss.

Relational operators

The simplest questions you can ask in JavaScript are those that compare two data values. You might want, for example, to determine whether two values are equal or whether one is greater than or smaller than another. Traditional mathematics uses the operators =, ≠, <, >, ≤, and ≥ to signify the relationships *equal to, not equal to, less than, greater than, less than or equal to,* and *greater than or equal to,* respectively. Unfortunately, because several of these symbols don't appear on a standard keyboard, JavaScript represents these operators in a slightly different form, which uses the following character combinations in place of the usual mathematical symbols:

`===`	Equal to
`!==`	Not equal to
`<`	Less than
`>`	Greater than
`<=`	Less than or equal to
`>=`	Greater than or equal to

Collectively, these operators are called *relational operators* because they test the relationship between two values. Like the arithmetic operators introduced in Chapter 2, relational operators appear between the two values to which they apply. For example, if you need to check whether the value of **x** is less than 0, you can use the expression **x < 0**.

At first glance, the relational operators `===` and `!==` probably seem a bit strange. Because the single equal sign had already been reserved to indicate assignment, the designers of the C programming language from which JavaScript is derived introduced a new operator consisting of two adjacent equal signs to specify equality. The designers of JavaScript retained the `==` operator, but defined it in such a confusing way that it is hard for anyone—novices and experienced programmers alike—to use it correctly. In JavaScript, the operators that check for exact equality and exact inequality are `===` and `!==`, and you will save yourself a great deal of confusion if you use these operators in preference to the shorter forms.

Logical operators

In addition to the relational operators, which take values of any type and produce Boolean results, JavaScript defines three operators that take Boolean operands and combine them to form other Boolean values:

!	Logical not (**true** if the following operand is **false**)
&&	Logical and (**true** if both operands are **true**)
||	Logical or (**true** if either or both operands are **true**)

These operators are called *logical operators* and are listed in decreasing order of precedence.

Although the operators **&&**, **||**, and **!** correspond to the English words *and, or,* and *not,* it is important to remember that English is somewhat imprecise when it comes to logic. To avoid that imprecision, it helps to think of these operators in a more formal, mathematical way. Logicians define these operators using *truth tables,* which show how the value of a Boolean expression changes as the values of its operands change. For example, the truth table for the **&&** operator, given Boolean values **p** and **q**, is

p	q	p && q
false	false	false
false	true	false
true	false	false
true	true	true

The last column of the table indicates the value of the Boolean expression **p && q**, given the individual values of the Boolean variables **p** and **q** shown in the first two columns. Thus, the first line in the truth table shows that when **p** is **false** and **q** is **false**, the value of the expression **p && q** is also **false**.

The truth table for **||** is

p	q	p || q
false	false	false
false	true	true
true	false	true
true	true	true

Even though the **||** operator corresponds to the English word *or,* it does not indicate *one or the other,* as it often does in English, but instead indicates *either or both,* which is its mathematical meaning.

The ! operator has the following simple truth table:

p	!p
false	true
true	false

If you need to determine how a more complex logical expression operates, you can break it down into these primitive operations and build up a truth table for the individual pieces of the expression.

In most cases, logical expressions are not so complicated that you need a truth table to figure them out. The only case that often causes confusion is when the ! operator comes up in conjunction with && or ||. When English speakers talk about situations that are not true (as is the case when you work with the ! operator), a statement whose meaning is clear to human listeners is often at odds with mathematical logic. Whenever you find that you need to express a condition involving the word *not,* you should use extra care to avoid errors.

As an example, suppose you wanted to express the idea "x is not equal to either 2 or 3" as part of a program. Just reading from the English version of this conditional test, new programmers are likely to code this expression as follows:

```
x !== 2 || x !== 3
```

As noted in Chapter 1, this book uses the bug symbol to mark sections of code that contain deliberate errors. In this case, the problem is that an informal English translation of the code does not correspond to its interpretation in JavaScript. If you look at this conditional test from a mathematical point of view, you can see that the expression is **true** if either (a) **x** is not equal to 2 or (b) **x** is not equal to 3. No matter what value **x** has, one of the statements must be **true**, since, if **x** is 2, it cannot also be equal to 3, and vice versa. To fix this problem, you need to refine your understanding of the English expression so that it states the condition more precisely. That is, you want the condition to be **true** whenever "it is not the case that either **x** is 2 or **x** is 3." You could translate this expression directly to JavaScript by writing

```
!(x === 2 || x === 3)
```

but the resulting expression would be a bit ungainly. The question you really want to ask is whether *both* of the following conditions are **true**:

- **x** is not equal to 2, *and*
- **x** is not equal to 3.

If you think about the question in this form, you can write the test as

```
x !== 2 && x !== 3
```

This simplification is a specific illustration of the following more general relationship from mathematical logic:

$$! (p \mid\mid q) \quad \textit{is equivalent to} \quad !p \ \&\& \ !q$$

for any logical expressions *p* and *q*. This transformation rule and its symmetric counterpart

$$! (p \ \&\& \ q) \quad \textit{is equivalent to} \quad !p \mid\mid !q$$

Augustus De Morgan

(The History Collection/Alamy Stock Photo)

are called **De Morgan's laws** after the British mathematician Augustus De Morgan. Forgetting to apply these rules and relying instead on the English style of logic is a common source of programming errors.

Short-circuit evaluation

JavaScript interprets the `&&` and `||` operators in a way that differs from the interpretation used in many other programming languages. In the programming language Pascal, for example, evaluating these operators (which are written as AND and OR) requires evaluating both halves of the condition, even when the result can be determined partway through the process.

The designers of JavaScript (or, more accurately, the designers of the languages on which JavaScript is based) took a different approach that is usually more convenient for programmers. Whenever JavaScript evaluates an expression of the form

exp_1 **&&** exp_2

or

exp_1 **||** exp_2

the individual subexpressions are always evaluated from left to right, and evaluation ends as soon as the answer can be determined. For example, if exp_1 is **false** in the expression involving `&&`, there is no need to evaluate exp_2 because the final answer will always be **false**. Similarly, in the example using `||`, there is no need to evaluate the second operand if the first operand is **true**. This style of evaluation, which stops as soon as the answer is known, is called **short-circuit evaluation.**

A primary advantage of short-circuit evaluation is that it allows one condition to control the execution of a second one. In many situations, the second part of a compound condition is meaningful only if the first part comes out a certain way. For example, suppose you want to express the combined condition that (1) the value of the integer **x** is nonzero and (2) **x** divides evenly into **y**. You can express this conditional test in JavaScript as

```
(x !== 0) && (y % x === 0)
```

because the expression **y % x** is evaluated only if x is nonzero. The corresponding expression in Pascal fails to generate the desired result, because both parts of the Pascal condition will always be evaluated. Thus, if **x** is 0, a Pascal program containing this expression will end up dividing by 0 even though it appears to have a conditional test to check for that case. Conditions that protect against evaluation errors in subsequent parts of a compound condition, such as the conditional test

```
(x !== 0)
```

in the preceding example, are called *guards.*

3.2 The `if` statement

The simplest way to express conditional execution in JavaScript is by using the **if** statement, which comes in the same two forms that you saw in Karel, as shown in the syntax boxes on the right. The *condition* component of these templates is a Boolean expression, as defined in the preceding section. In the simple form of the **if** statement, JavaScript executes the block of statements only if the conditional test evaluates to **true**. If the conditional test is **false**, JavaScript skips the body of the **if** statement entirely. In the form that includes the **else** keyword, JavaScript executes the first block of statements if the condition is **true** and the second if the condition is **false**. In both of these forms, the code that JavaScript executes when the conditional expression is **true** is called the *then clause.* In the if-else form, the code executed when the condition is **false** is called the *else clause.*

You can use the **if** statement to implement several of the simplest functions in JavaScript's **Math** class. For example, you can implement **abs** as follows:

```
function abs(x) {
   if (x < 0) {
      return -x;
   } else {
      return x;
   }
}
```

```
if (condition) {
   statements
}
```

```
if (condition) {
   statements
} else {
   statements
}
```

Similarly, you can implement **max**—at least for two arguments—like this:

```
function max(x, y) {
    if (x > y) {
        return x;
    } else {
        return y;
    }
}
```

As you almost certainly realized during your study of Karel, the choice of whether to use the `if` or the `if-else` form depends on the structure of the problem. You use the simple `if` statement when your problem requires code to be executed only if a particular condition applies. You use the `if-else` form for situations in which the program must choose between two independent sets of actions. You can often make this decision based on how you would describe the problem in English. If that description contains the word *otherwise* or some similar expression, there is a good chance that you'll need the `if-else` form. If the English description conveys no such notion, the simple form of the `if` statement is probably sufficient.

Additional formats for the `if` statement

If either of the clauses associated with the `if` consists of a single statement, JavaScript allows you to eliminate the curly braces that surround it. However, as a general rule, it is good practice to include these braces because doing so makes it easier for someone reading the code to determine which statements are included in the body. Requiring the braces also makes programs easier to maintain, by making it harder for someone to imagine that two consecutive statements are governed by a single `if` statement. For example, it is easy to misread the lines

```
if (condition)
    statement₁;
    statement₂;
```

and think that the `if` statement controls the execution of both statements. Without the braces, *statement₂* is outside the range of the `if` and will always be executed.

There are two situations in which the programs in this book relax the rule that every clause in an `if` statement requires curly braces. The first of these is when an `if` statement fits on a single line and has no `else` clause. The second is when the `else` clause consists of another test to check for some additional condition. Such statements are called ***cascading `if` statements*** and may involve any number of `else if` lines. For example, the following function implements the `sign` function from the `Math` class, which returns −1, 0, or +1 depending on whether the value of `x` is positive, zero, or negative:

```
if (condition) statement
```

```
if (condition₁) {
    statements
} else if (condition₂) {
    statements
} else if (condition₃) {
    statements
} else {
    statements
}
```

```
function sign(x) {
   if (x < 0) {
      return -1;
   } else if (x === 0) {
      return 0;
   } else {
      return 1;
   }
}
```

Note that there is no need to check explicitly for the $x > 0$ condition. If the program reaches that last **else** clause, there is no other possibility (assuming that **x** is a number), since the earlier tests have eliminated the negative and zero cases.

In many situations, it makes more sense to use the **switch** statement to choose among a set of independent cases than to adopt the cascading **if** form. The **switch** statement is described in section 3.3.

The **?:** operator

The JavaScript programming language provides another, more compact mechanism for expressing conditional execution that can be extremely useful in certain situations: the **?:** operator. (This operator is referred to as *question-mark colon*, even though the two characters do not actually appear adjacent to each other in the code.) Unlike any other operator in JavaScript, **?:** requires three operands. The general form of the operation is

$$condition \; ? \; expression_1 \; : \; expression_2$$

When JavaScript encounters the **?:** operator, it first evaluates the condition. If the condition turns out to be **true**, *expression₁* is evaluated and used as the value of the entire expression; if the condition is **false**, the value is the result of evaluating *expression₂*. The **?:** operator is therefore a space-efficient form of the statement

```
if (condition) {
      Use the value of expression₁
} else {
      Use the value of expression₂
}
```

implemented in the context of an expression.

For example, you can use the **?:** operator to implement the function **max** in the following streamlined form:

```
function max(x, y) {
    return (x > y) ? x : y;
}
```

The parentheses around the condition are not technically required, but many JavaScript programmers include them in this context to enhance the readability of the code.

3.3 The switch statement

The **if** statement is ideal for applications in which the program logic calls for a two-way decision point: some condition is either **true** or **false**, and the program acts accordingly. Some applications, however, call for more complicated decision structures involving more than two choices, where those choices can be divided into a set of mutually exclusive cases: in one case, the program should do x; in another case, it should do y; in a third, it should do z; and so forth. In many applications, the most appropriate statement to use for such situations is the **switch** statement, which is outlined in the syntax box on the left.

The header line of the **switch** statement is

```
switch (e)
```

where e is an expression. In the context of the **switch** statement, this expression is called the *control expression.* The body of the **switch** statement is divided into individual groups of statements introduced with one of two keywords: **case** or **default**. A **case** line and all the statements that follow it up to the next instance of either of these keywords are called a *case clause.* The **default** line and its associated statements are called the *default clause.* For example, in the template shown in the syntax box, the range of statements

```
case c₁:
    statements
    break;
```

constitutes the first **case** clause.

When the program executes a **switch** statement, the control expression e is evaluated and compared against the values c_1, c_2, and so forth, each of which must be a constant. If one of the constants matches the value of the control expression, the statements in the associated **case** clause are executed. When the program reaches the **break** statement at the end of the clause, the operations specified by that clause are complete, and the program continues with the statement following

---

```
switch (expression) {
  case c₁:
    statements
    break;
  case c₂:
    statements
    break;
  case c₃:
    statements
    break;
  default:
    statements
    break;
}
```

the entire `switch` statement. If none of the case constants match the value of the control expression, the statements in the `default` clause are executed.

The template shown in the syntax box deliberately suggests that the `break` statements are a required part of the syntax. I encourage you to think of the `switch` syntax in precisely that form. JavaScript is defined so that if the `break` statement is missing, the program starts executing statements from the next clause after it finishes the selected one. While this design can be useful in a few unusual situations, it tends to cause more problems than it solves. To reinforce the importance of remembering to include the `break` statement, every `case` clause in this text ends with an explicit `break` or a `return` statement.

The one exception to this rule is that multiple `case` lines specifying different constants can appear together, one after another, before the same statement group. For example, a `switch` statement might include the following code:

```
case 1:
case 2:
    statements
    break;
```

which indicates that the specified statements should be executed if the `switch` expression is either 1 or 2. The JavaScript interpreter treats this construction as two `case` clauses, the first of which is empty. Because the empty clause contains no `break` statement, a program that selects that path simply continues on with the second clause. From a conceptual point of view, however, you are probably better off thinking of this construction as a single `case` clause that represents two possibilities.

The `default` clause is optional in the `switch` statement. If none of the cases match and there is no `default` clause, the program simply continues on with the next statement after the `switch` statement without taking any action at all. To avoid the possibility that the program might ignore an unexpected case, it is good programming practice to include a `default` clause in every `switch` statement unless you are certain that you've enumerated all the possibilities.

Because `switch` statements can be rather long, programs are easier to read if the `case` clauses themselves are short. If there is room to do so, it also helps to put the `case` identifier, the statements forming the body of the clause, and the `break` or `return` statement all together on the same line. This style is illustrated in the `monthName` function in Figure 3-1, which uses a `switch` statement to translate a numeric month into its name.

FIGURE 3-1 Function to convert a numeric month to its name

```
/*
 * Converts a numeric month in the range 1 to 12 into its name.
 */
function monthName(month) {
   switch (month) {
     case  1: return "January";
     case  2: return "February";
     case  3: return "March";
     case  4: return "April";
     case  5: return "May";
     case  6: return "June";
     case  7: return "July";
     case  8: return "August";
     case  9: return "September";
     case 10: return "October";
     case 11: return "November";
     case 12: return "December";
     default: return undefined;
   }
}
```

The **default** clause in Figure 3-1 deserves special mention. If the **month** parameter is not one of the legal values between 1 and 12, the **monthName** function returns the predefined JavaScript constant **undefined**, which is often used as a marker to indicate that no meaningful result exists.

▩ **3.4 The while statement**

```
while (condition) {
   statements
}
```

The simplest iterative construct is the **while** statement, which repeatedly executes a simple statement or block until the conditional expression becomes **false**. The template for the **while** statement appears in the syntax box on the left. The entire statement, including both the **while** control line itself and the statements enclosed within the body, constitutes a *while loop.* When the program executes a **while** statement, it first evaluates the conditional expression to see if it is **true** or **false**. If the condition is **false**, the loop *terminates* and the program continues with the next statement after the entire loop. If the condition is **true**, the entire body is executed, after which the program goes back to the top to check the condition again. A single pass through the statements in the body constitutes a *cycle* of the loop.

There are two important principles to observe about the operation of a **while** loop:

1. The conditional test is performed before every cycle of the loop, including the first. If the test is **false** initially, the body of the loop is not executed at all.

2. The conditional test is performed only at the *beginning* of a loop cycle. If that condition happens to become `false` at some point during the loop, the program doesn't notice that fact until it has executed a complete cycle. At that point, the program evaluates the test condition again. If it is still `false`, the loop terminates.

Learning how to use the `while` loop effectively usually requires looking at several examples in which a `while` loop appears in the solution strategy. One application that has particular historical significance is that of finding the largest proper divisor of an integer, which is one of the first programs run on the Small-Scale Experimental Machine at Manchester University—the first computer to implement the stored-program architecture that is used in essentially all computers today. The author of the program was Tom Kilburn, the lead engineer on the team that built the machine, which its inventors nicknamed the "Baby."

Because the Baby had extremely limited capabilities, Kilburn's algorithm had to be almost absurdly simple. Given a number N, the program simply counted down from $N - 1$ until it found a number that divided evenly into N. Taking at least some advantage of JavaScript's extended set of operations, Kilburn's algorithm might look like this:

```
function largestFactor(n) {
   let factor = n - 1;
   while (n % factor !== 0) {
      factor--;
   }
   return factor;
}
```

Two sample calculations using `largestFactor` appear in the following console log:

```
                        LargestFactor
> largestFactor(63)
21
> largestFactor(262144)
131072
>
```

When the second of these calculations was run on the Manchester Baby on June 21, 1948, the program took 52 minutes to compute the answer. In the process, it demonstrated both the efficacy and the reliability of the Baby's architecture.

As a second example, suppose that you have been asked to write a function `digitSum` that adds up the digits in a positive integer. Calling `digitSum(1729)` should therefore produce the result 19, which is $1 + 7 + 2 + 9$. How would you go about implementing such a function?

The first thing that your function needs to do is keep track of a running total. The usual strategy for doing so is to declare a variable called **sum**, initialize it to 0, add each digit to **sum** one at a time, and finally return the value of **sum**. That much of the structure, with the rest of the problem written in English, appears below:

```
function digitSum(n) {
    let sum = 0;
    For each digit in the number, add that digit to sum.
    return sum;
}
```

Programs that are written partly in a programming language and partly in English are called *pseudocode*.

The sentence

>*For each digit in the number, add that digit to* **sum***.*

clearly specifies a loop structure of some sort, because there is an operation that needs to be repeated for each digit in the number. If it were easy to determine how many digits a number contained, you might choose to use the **for** loop described later in this chapter to run through precisely that many cycles. As it happens, finding out how many digits there are in a number is just as hard as adding them up in the first place. The best way to write this program is just to keep adding in digits until you discover that you have added the last one. Loops that run until some condition occurs are most often coded using the **while** statement.

The essence of this problem lies in determining how to break up a number into its component digits. The last digit of an integer **n** is simply the remainder left over when **n** is divided by 10, which is the result of the expression **n % 10**. The rest of the number—the integer that consists of all digits *except* the last one—is given by **Math.floor(n / 10)**, which is denoted in mathematics as $\lfloor n / 10 \rfloor$. For example, if **n** has the value 1729, you can use these two expressions to break that number into two parts, 172 and 9, as shown in the following diagram:

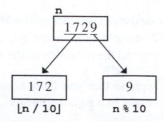

Thus, in order to add up the digits in the number, all you need to do is add the value n % 10 to the variable sum on each cycle of the loop and then replace the value of n by Math.floor(n / 10). The next cycle will add in the second-to-last digit from the original number, and so on, until all the digits have been processed.

But how do you know when to stop? As you compute Math.floor(n / 10) in each cycle, you will eventually reach the point at which n becomes 0. At that point, you've processed all the digits in the number and can exit from the loop. Thus, the while loop needed for the problem is

```
while (n > 0) {
    sum += n % 10;
    n = Math.floor(n / 10);
}
```

The full implementation of the digitSum function appears in Figure 3-2.

As a final example of the use of while, it is useful to be able to add spaces to a string in order to ensure that strings of different lengths still line up correctly when displayed in a fixed-width font of the sort used in the JavaScript console. For example, columns of numbers are conventionally aligned on the right, which means that it is necessary to add spaces at the beginning of a number until it fills the entire width of the column. You can achieve this goal with the following function, which takes a value (which can be of any type) and a field width:

```
function alignRight(value, width) {
    let str = "" + value;
    while (str.length < width) {
        str = " " + str;
    }
    return str;
}
```

FIGURE 3-2   Function to add up the digits in a number

```
/*
 * Returns the sum of the digits in n, which must be a nonnegative integer.
 */

function digitSum(n) {
    let sum = 0;
    while (n > 0) {
        sum += n % 10;
        n = Math.floor(n / 10);
    }
    return sum;
}
```

The function returns a string in which **value** appears at the right edge of a field that is **width** characters wide. The first line of the function uses the concatenation operator to convert **value** to a string and then adds it to the end of a string that contains no characters at all, which is called the ***empty string***. The effect is therefore to initialize the variable **str** so that it contains the string representation of **value**. From here, the function uses concatenation to add spaces to the beginning of **str** until it has attained the desired length and then returns the padded string to the caller. You will have a chance to see **alignRight** in action in the following section.

3.5 The **for** statement

One of the most important control statements in JavaScript is the **for** statement, which is most often used in situations in which you want to repeat an operation a particular number of times. The general form of the **for** statement is shown in the syntax box on the left.

```
for (init; test; step) {
    statements
}
```

The operation of the **for** loop is determined by the three italicized expressions on the **for** control line: *init*, *test*, and *step*. The *init* expression indicates how the **for** loop should be initialized and typically consists of a variable declaration specifying an initial value. In a **for** loop, this variable is called the ***index variable***. The *test* expression is a conditional test written exactly like the test in a **while** statement. As long as the test expression is **true**, the loop continues. The *step* expression indicates how the index variable changes at the end of each cycle.

The interpretation of the *init*, *test*, and *step* expressions is easiest to illustrate by example. The most common **for** loop uses the following header line:

```
for (let i = 0; i < n; i++)
```

The loop begins by declaring the index variable **i** and initializing it to 0. The loop increments the value of **n** at the end of each cycle and continues as long as **i** is less than **n**. The loop therefore runs for a total of **n** cycles, with **i** taking on the values 0, 1, 2, and so forth, up to the final value **n − 1**.

More generally, the **for** loop idiom

```
for (let i = start; i <= finish; i++)
```

starts by setting the value of **i** to *start* and then continues as long as the value of **i** is less than or equal to *finish*. This loop therefore uses the variable **i** to count from *start* to *finish*.

You can use this form of the **for** loop idiom to define a function called **fact** that takes an integer **n** and returns its ***factorial***, which is defined as the product of the integers between 1 and **n** and is traditionally written as $n!$ in mathematics. The first several factorials are shown in the following table:

$$
\begin{array}{rcrcl}
0! &=& 1 && \text{(by definition)} \\
1! &=& 1 &=& 1 \\
2! &=& 2 &=& 1 \times 2 \\
3! &=& 6 &=& 1 \times 2 \times 3 \\
4! &=& 24 &=& 1 \times 2 \times 3 \times 4 \\
5! &=& 120 &=& 1 \times 2 \times 3 \times 4 \times 5 \\
6! &=& 720 &=& 1 \times 2 \times 3 \times 4 \times 5 \times 6 \\
7! &=& 5040 &=& 1 \times 2 \times 3 \times 4 \times 5 \times 6 \times 7 \\
8! &=& 40320 &=& 1 \times 2 \times 3 \times 4 \times 5 \times 6 \times 7 \times 8 \\
9! &=& 362880 &=& 1 \times 2 \times 3 \times 4 \times 5 \times 6 \times 7 \times 8 \times 9 \\
10! &=& 3628800 &=& 1 \times 2 \times 3 \times 4 \times 5 \times 6 \times 7 \times 8 \times 9 \times 10
\end{array}
$$

Factorials have extensive applications in statistics, combinatorial mathematics, and computer science. A function to compute factorials is therefore a useful tool for solving problems in those domains.

As a programming problem, computing a factorial has some similarities to the problem of adding a series of numbers, which appears in the implementation of the **digitSum** function in Figure 3-2. That function uses a variable called **sum** to keep track of a running total of the digits. For the factorial function, the situation is much the same, except that you have to keep track of a product rather than a sum. Keeping track of a running product uses similar code; the only significant difference—other than replacing the **+** with the ***** operator—is that you have to initialize the running product to 1 instead of 0. The complete implementation of the **fact** function therefore looks like this:

```
function fact(n) {
   let result = 1;
   for (let i = 1; i <= n; i++) {
      result *= i;
   }
   return result;
}
```

In its current form, you can use the **fact** function in the console window or in other functions. It would, however, also be useful if you could generate a table of factorials such as the one shown above. To do so, the simplest approach would be to use the JavaScript console to display the output by calling the function **console.log**, which displays its argument on the console and then moves the cursor to the beginning of the next line. The **FactorialTable.js** program in Figure 3-3 displays a list of factorials that extends through the range given by the constants `LOWER_LIMIT` and `UPPER_LIMIT`, as illustrated by the following sample run:

```
                           FactorialTable
> FactorialTable();
  0! =        1
  1! =        1
  2! =        2
  3! =        6
  4! =       24
  5! =      120
  6! =      720
  7! =     5040
  8! =    40320
  9! =   362880
 10! = 3628800
>
```

Note that the `FactorialTable` program uses `alignRight` to display the values in fixed-width columns.

Although the *step* component of the `for` loop usually increments the index variable, that is not the only possibility. You can, for example, count by twos by replacing `i++` with `i += 2` or count backwards using `i--`. As an illustration of counting in the reverse direction, the following function counts down from an initial value until it reaches 0:

```
function countdown(start) {
   for (let t = start; t >= 0; t--) {
      console.log(t);
   }
}
```

Calling `countdown(10)` produces the following output on the console:

```
                              Countdown
10
9
8
7
6
5
4
3
2
1
0
```

The `Countdown` program demonstrates that any variable can be used as an index variable. In this case, the variable is called `t`, presumably because that is the traditional variable for a rocket countdown, as in the phrase "T minus 10 seconds and counting."

FIGURE 3-3   Program to display a list of factorials on the console

```
/*
 * File: FactorialTable.js
 * ------------------------
 * This program defines the function FactorialTable, which prints a table
 * of factorials in a specified range.
 */

"use strict";

/* Constants */

const LOWER_LIMIT = 0;
const UPPER_LIMIT = 10;
const NUMBER_WIDTH = 2;
const FACTORIAL_WIDTH = 7;

/*
 * Displays a table of factorials between LOWER_LIMIT and UPPER_LIMIT.
 */

function FactorialTable() {
   for (let i = LOWER_LIMIT; i <= UPPER_LIMIT; i++) {
      console.log(alignRight(i, NUMBER_WIDTH) + "! = " +
                  alignRight(fact(i), FACTORIAL_WIDTH));
   }
}

/*
 * Returns the factorial of n.  The factorial is simply the product of
 * the integers between 1 and n, inclusive.
 */

function fact(n) {
   let result = 1;
   for (let i = 1; i <= n; i++) {
      result *= i;
   }
   return result;
}

/*
 * Returns a string in which value appears at the right edge of a field
 * that is at least the specified width.  If the value does not fit in
 * that field, the returned string will be longer than the specified width.
 */

function alignRight(value, width) {
   let str = "" + value;
   while (str.length < width) {
      str = " " + str;
   }
   return str;
}
```

The expressions *init*, *test*, and *step* in the **for** loop pattern are optional, but the semicolons must appear. If *init* is missing, no initialization is performed. If *test* is missing, it is assumed to be **true**. If *step* is missing, no action occurs at the end of the loop cycle.

The relationship between for and while

The **for** statement

```
for (init; test; step) {
    statements
}
```

is similar in operation to the **while** statement

```
init;
while (test) {
    statements
    step;
}
```

Even though you can rewrite a **for** statement using **while**, there are advantages to using the **for** statement whenever you can. With a **for** statement, all the information you need in order to know how many cycles will be executed is contained in the header line of the statement. For example, if you see the statement

```
for (let i = 0; i < 10; i++) {
    ... body ...
}
```

in a program, you know that the body of the loop will be executed 10 times, once for each of the values of **i** between 0 and 9. In the corresponding **while** loop

```
let i = 0;
while (i < 10) {
    ... body ...
    i++;
}
```

the increment operation at the bottom can easily get lost if the body is large.

Although the code fragments using **for** and **while** are similar, they are not identical. The primary difference lies in the treatment of the declaration of the index variable. In the most recent **for** loop example, the variable **i** is defined only inside the body of the loop and undefined outside of it. The region in which a variable is defined is called its *scope.* The scope of the index variable in a **for** loop, for example, is the code inside the curly braces that surround the loop body.

Nested `for` statements

In many applications, you will discover that you need to write one `for` loop inside another so that the statements in the innermost loop are executed for every possible combination of values of the `for` loop indices. Suppose, for example, that you want to display a multiplication table showing the product of every pair of numbers in the range 1 to 10. You would like the output of the program to look like this:

MultiplicationTable									
1	2	3	4	5	6	7	8	9	10
2	4	6	8	10	12	14	16	18	20
3	6	9	12	15	18	21	24	27	30
4	8	12	16	20	24	28	32	36	40
5	10	15	20	25	30	35	40	45	50
6	12	18	24	30	36	42	48	54	60
7	14	21	28	35	42	49	56	63	70
8	16	24	32	40	48	56	64	72	80
9	18	27	36	45	54	63	72	81	90
10	20	30	40	50	60	70	80	90	100

The code to draw this multiplication table appears in Figure 3-4. To create the individual entries, you need a pair of nested `for` loops: an outer loop that runs through each of the rows and an inner loop that runs through each of the entries in

FIGURE 3-4   Program to display a multiplication table

```
/*
 * File: MultiplicationTable.js
 * ---------------------------------
 * This program uses nested loops to create a multiplication table.
 */

"use strict";

/* Constants */

const TABLE_SIZE = 10;
const FIELD_WIDTH = 4;

/*
 * Draws a multiplication table on the console.
 */

function MultiplicationTable() {
   for (let i = 1; i <= TABLE_SIZE; i++) {
      let line = "";
      for (let j = 1; j <= TABLE_SIZE ; j++) {
         line += alignRight(i * j, FIELD_WIDTH);
      }
      console.log(line);
   }
}
```

each row. The code inside the inner `for` loop will be executed once for every row and column, for a total of 100 individual entries in the table.

The outer loop runs through each value of `i` from 1 to 10 and is responsible for displaying one row of the table on each cycle. To do so, the code first declares the variable `line` and initializes it to be the empty string. The inner loop then runs through the values of `j` from 1 to 10 and concatenates the product of `i` and `j` to the end of `line`, once again using the `alignRight` function to ensure that the columns have the same width. When the inner loop is complete, the program calls `console.log` to display the completed line of the multiplication table.

A useful way to get some practice using nested `for` loops is to write programs that draw patterns on the console by displaying lines of characters. As a simple example, the following function draws a triangle in which the number of stars increases by one in each row:

```
function drawConsoleTriangle(size) {
    for (let i = 1; i <= size; i++) {
        let line = "";
        for (let j = 0; j < i; j++) {
            line += "*";
        }
        console.log(line);
    }
}
```

Calling `drawConsoleTriangle(10)`, for example, produces the following output on the console:

ConsoleTriangle
`*`
`**`
`***`
`****`
`*****`
`******`
`*******`
`********`
`*********`
`**********`

You will have a chance to create several similar displays in the exercises.

 ## 3.6 Algorithmic programming

The concept of an algorithm is fundamental to computer science. As you know from Chapter 1, the word *algorithm* comes from the name of the 9th-century Persian

FIGURE 3-5 Statue of al-Khwārizmī outside the gates of Khiva, Uzbekistan

mathematician Muhammad ibn Mūsā al-Khwārizmī, whose work had significant impact on modern mathematics. Figure 3-5 contains a photograph of a statue of al-Khwārizmī near his birthplace in what is now Uzbekistan.

Although it is usually sufficient to think of an algorithm as a strategy for solving a problem, modern computer science formalizes that definition so that ***algorithm*** refers to a solution strategy that is

- *Clear and unambiguous,* in the sense that the description is understandable.
- *Effective,* in the sense that it is possible to carry out the steps in the strategy.
- *Finite,* in the sense that the strategy terminates after some number of steps.

The next few sections offer several examples of how control statements can be used to implement several historically important algorithms.

An early square-root algorithm

The use of algorithms extends much further back in history than al-Khwārizmī's time. Almost 4000 years ago, Babylonian mathematicians used an algorithmic process to calculate square roots. The primary evidence of the existence of an algorithmic process comes from cuneiform tablets such as the one shown in Figure 3-6, which shows an approximation of the square root of 2 that is far more accurate than anyone could possibly derive through measurement alone. And although the precise details of how Babylonian mathematicians performed the necessary calculations have been lost, historians believe that their technique was similar to the algorithm described by the 1st-century Greek mathematician Hero of Alexandria. The algorithm Hero described is usually called the **Babylonian method** after its most likely origin.

The Babylonian method for calculating square roots is an example of a general technique called **successive approximation,** in which you begin by making a rough guess at the answer and then improve that guess through a series of refinements that get closer and closer to the exact answer. For example, if you want to find the square root of some number *n,* you start by choosing some smaller number *g* as your first guess. At every point in the process, your guess *g* will be smaller or larger than

---

FIGURE 3-6 **Babylonian cuneiform tablet showing an approximation of the square root of 2**

(Yale Peabody Museum of Natural History)

The cuneiform fragment on the left dates from the First Babylonian Dynasty, which ran from the 19th century to the 16th century BCE. The diagram consists of a square and its diagonals together with three numbers written using Babylonian numerals. Those numerals are barely visible in the photograph but are reproduced in the stylized diagram at the bottom of the figure.

The numerals across the horizontal diagonal have the following values:

1　24　51　10

Babylonian arithmetic uses a base-60 system, which means that each digit counts for one-sixtieth of the digit position to its left. This sequence of digits therefore corresponds to the following calculation:

$$1 + \frac{24}{60} + \frac{51}{60 \times 60} + \frac{10}{60 \times 60 \times 60} \approx 1.414213$$

This value is the closest possible representation of the square root of 2 in four base-60 digits.

The two other numbers on the tablet illustrate the relationship between the length of the side and the diagonal. If the length of the side is 30 (the ⫷⫷⫷ in the upper left), the length of the diagonal is approximately

42　25　35

$$= 42 + \frac{25}{60} + \frac{35}{60 \times 60} \approx 42.4264$$

the actual square root. In either case, if you divide n by g, the result will inevitably lie on the opposite side of the desired value. For example, if g is too small, n divided by g will be too large, and vice versa. Averaging the two values will always give a better approximation. At each step, you simply replace your previous guess g with the result of the following formula, which averages g and n divided by g:

$$\frac{g + \frac{n}{g}}{2}$$

You then continue to apply this formula to each new guess until the answer is as close to the actual value as you need it to be.

To get more of a sense of how the Babylonian method works, it helps to consider a simple example. Suppose that you want to calculate, as the scribes who incised the cuneiform tablet did, the square root of 2. One possible first guess for g is 1, which is half the value of n. The first approximation step therefore computes the following average:

$$\frac{1 + \frac{2}{1}}{2} = \frac{3}{2} = 1.5$$

The value 1.5 is closer to the actual square root of 2—which is approximately 1.4142136—so the process is on the right track.

To calculate the next approximation, all you need to do is plug $\frac{3}{2}$ into the formula as the next value of g, and calculate the new average, as follows:

$$\frac{\frac{3}{2} + \frac{2}{\frac{3}{2}}}{2} = \frac{17}{12} \approx 1.4166667$$

From this point, you simply repeat the calculation with $\frac{17}{12}$ as the new value of g:

$$\frac{\frac{17}{12} + \frac{2}{\frac{17}{12}}}{2} = \frac{577}{408} \approx 1.4142157$$

Applying successive approximation one more time gives you

$$\frac{\frac{577}{408} + \frac{2}{\frac{577}{408}}}{2} = \frac{665857}{470832} \approx 1.4142136$$

After just four cycles, the Babylonian method has produced an approximation to the square root of 2 that is correct to eight decimal digits. Moreover, because each step generates an approximation that is closer to the exact value, you can repeat the process to produce an approximation with any desired level of accuracy.

FIGURE 3-7 JavaScript program to compute square roots using the Babylonian algorithm

```
/*
 * File: BabylonianSquareRoot.js
 * -----------------------------
 * This file implements a function sqrt that calculates square roots
 * using the Babylonian method.
 */

"use strict";

/* Define a constant specifying how close the value needs to be */

const TOLERANCE = 0.000000000000001;

/*
 * Calculates the square root of n using the Babylonian method, which
 * operates as follows:
 *
 * 1. Choose a guess g (any value will do; this code uses n / 2).
 * 2. Compute a new guess by averaging g and n / g.
 * 3. Repeat step 2 until the error is less than the desired tolerance.
 */

function sqrt(n) {
   let g = n / 2;
   while (Math.abs(n - g * g) > TOLERANCE) {
      g = (g + n / g) / 2;
   }
   return g;
}
```

Figure 3-7 shows the definition of a `sqrt` function that uses the Babylonian method to approximate the square root of its argument. The function uses a `while` loop to continue the process until the approximation reaches the desired level of precision. In this implementation, the `while` loop continues until the difference between the square of the current approximation and the original number is no larger than the value of the constant `TOLERANCE`.

Finding the greatest common divisor

Although you have seen a few simple algorithms implemented in the context of the programming examples, you have had little chance to focus on the nature of the algorithmic process itself. Most of the programming problems you have seen so far are simple enough that the appropriate solution strategy springs immediately to mind. As problems become more complex, however, their solutions require more thought, and you will need to consider more than one strategy before writing the final program.

As an illustration of how algorithmic strategies take shape, the sections that follow consider two solutions to another problem from classical mathematics, which is to find the greatest common divisor of two integers. Given two integers x and y, the **greatest common divisor** (or **gcd** for short) is the largest integer that divides evenly into both. For example, the gcd of 49 and 35 is 7, the gcd of 6 and 18 is 6, and the gcd of 32 and 33 is 1.

Suppose that you have been asked to write a function that accepts two positive integers x and y as input and returns their greatest common divisor. From the caller's point of view, what you want is a function `gcd(x, y)` that takes the two integers as arguments and returns another integer that is their greatest common divisor. The header line for this function is therefore

```
function gcd(x, y)
```

In many ways, the most obvious approach to calculating the gcd is simply to try every possibility. To start, you simply "guess" that `gcd(x, y)` is the smaller of `x` and `y`, because any larger value could not possibly divide evenly into a smaller number. You then proceed by dividing `x` and `y` by your guess and seeing if it divides evenly into both. If it does, you have the answer; if not, you subtract 1 from your guess and try again. A strategy that tries every possibility is often called a **brute-force approach.**

The brute-force approach to calculating the `gcd` function looks like this in JavaScript:

```
function gcd(x, y) {
    let guess = Math.min(x, y);
    while (x % guess !== 0 || y % guess !== 0) {
        guess--;
    }
    return guess;
}
```

Before you decide that this implementation is in fact a valid algorithm for computing the `gcd` function, you need to ask yourself several questions about the code. Will the brute-force implementation of `gcd` always give the correct answer? Will it always terminate, or might the function continue forever?

To determine whether the program gives the correct answer, you need to look at the condition in the `while` loop

```
x % guess !== 0 || y % guess !== 0
```

As always, the `while` condition indicates under what circumstances the loop will continue. To find out what condition causes the loop to terminate, you have to negate the `while` condition. Negating a condition involving `&&` or `||` can be tricky unless you remember how to apply De Morgan's laws, which were introduced in the section on "Logical operators" earlier in this chapter. De Morgan's laws indicate that the following condition must hold when the `while` loop exits:

```
x % guess === 0 && y % guess === 0
```

From this condition, you can see immediately that the final value of `guess` is certainly a common divisor. To recognize that it is in fact the greatest common divisor, you have to think about the strategy embodied in the `while` loop. The critical factor to notice in the strategy is that the program counts *backward* through all the possibilities. The greatest common divisor can never be larger than `x` or `y`, and the brute-force search therefore begins with the smaller of these two values. If the program ever gets out of the `while` loop, it must have already tried each value between the starting point and the current value of `guess`. Thus, if there were a larger value that divided evenly into both `x` and `y`, the program would already have found it in an earlier iteration of the `while` loop.

In recognizing that the function terminates, the key insight is that the value of `guess` must eventually reach 1, unless a larger common divisor is found. At this point, the `while` loop will surely terminate, because 1 will divide evenly into both `x` and `y`, no matter what values those variables have.

Euclid's algorithm

Brute force is not, however, the only effective strategy. Although brute-force algorithms have their place in other contexts, they are a poor choice for the `gcd` function if you are concerned about efficiency. For example, if you call

```
gcd(1000005, 1000000)
```

the brute-force algorithm will run through the body of the `while` loop almost a million times before it comes up with the answer 5, even though you can instantly arrive at that result just by thinking about the two numbers.

What you need to find is an algorithm that is guaranteed to terminate with the correct answer but that requires fewer steps than the brute-force approach. This is where cleverness and a clear understanding of the problem pay off. Fortunately, the necessary creative insight was described sometime around 300 BCE by the Greek mathematician Euclid, whose *Elements* (book 7, proposition II) contains an elegant solution to this problem. In modern English, Euclid's algorithm can be described as follows:

1.   Divide **x** by **y** and compute the remainder; call that remainder **r**.

2.   If **r** is zero, the procedure is complete, and the answer is **y**.

3.   If **r** is not zero, set **x** equal to the old value of **y**, set **y** equal to **r**, and repeat the entire process.

You can easily translate this algorithmic description into the following code:

```
function gcd(x, y) {
    let r = x % y;
    while (r !== 0) {
        x = y;
        y = r;
        r = x % y;
    }
    return y;
}
```

This implementation of the **gcd** function also correctly finds the greatest common divisor of two integers. It differs from the brute-force implementation in two respects. On the one hand, it computes the result much more quickly. On the other, it is more difficult to prove correct.

Although a formal proof of correctness for Euclid's algorithm is beyond the scope of this book, you can easily get a feel for how the algorithm works by adopting the mental model of mathematics the Greeks used. In Greek mathematics, geometry held center stage, and numbers were thought of as distances. For example, when Euclid set out to find the greatest common divisor of two whole numbers, such as 51 and 15, he framed the problem as one of finding the longest measuring stick that could be used to mark off each of the two distances involved. Thus, you can visualize the specific problem by starting out with two sticks, one 51 units long and one 15 units long, as follows:

The problem is to find a new measuring stick that you can lay end to end on top of each of these sticks so that it precisely covers each of the distances **x** and **y**.

Euclid's algorithm begins by marking off the large stick in units of the shorter one, like this:

Unless the smaller number is an exact divisor of the larger one, there is some remainder, as indicated by the shaded section of the lower stick. In this case, 15 goes into 51 three times with 6 left over, which means that the shaded region is 6 units long. The fundamental insight that Euclid had is that the greatest common divisor for the original two distances must also be the greatest common divisor of the length of the shorter stick and the length of the shaded region in the diagram.

Given this observation, you can solve the original problem by reducing it to a simpler problem involving smaller numbers. Here, the new numbers are 15 and 6, and you can find their greatest common divisor by reapplying Euclid's algorithm. You start by representing the new values, x' and y', as measuring sticks of the appropriate length. You then mark off the larger stick in units of the smaller one.

x'	15	
y'	6	6	3

Once again, this process results in a leftover region, which this time has length 3. If you then repeat the process one more time, you discover that the shaded region of length 3 is itself the common divisor of x' and y' and, therefore, by Euclid's proposition, of the original numbers x and y. That 3 is indeed a common divisor of the original numbers is demonstrated by the following diagram:

x	3	3	3	3	3	3	3	3	3	3	3	3	3	3	3	3	3
y	3	3	3	3	3

Euclid supplies a complete proof of his proposition in the *Elements*. If you are intrigued by how mathematicians thought about such problems more than 2000 years ago, you may find it interesting to look up translations of the original Greek source.

Although Euclid's algorithm and the brute-force algorithm correctly compute the greatest common divisor of two integers, there is an enormous difference in the efficiency between the two algorithmic strategies. Suppose once again that you call

    gcd(1000005, 1000000)

The brute-force algorithm requires on the order of a million steps to find the answer; Euclid's algorithm requires only two. At the beginning of Euclid's algorithm, `x` is `1000005`, `y` is `1000000`, and `r` is set to `5` during the first cycle of the loop. Because the value of `r` is not 0, the program sets `x` to `1000000`, sets `y` to `5`, and starts again. On the second cycle, the new value of `r` is `0`, so the program exits from the `while` loop and reports that the answer is 5.

The two strategies for computing greatest common divisors presented in this chapter offer a clear demonstration that the choice of algorithm can have a profound effect on the efficiency of the solution. If you continue your study of computer science beyond what is covered in this book, you will learn how to quantify such differences in performance along with several general approaches for improving algorithmic efficiency.

3.7 Avoiding fuzzy standards of truth

In the programs included in this book, every conditional test produces a Boolean value, which means that it will always be either **true** or **false**. Unfortunately, the JavaScript language is much less disciplined on this point. JavaScript defines the following values (a couple of which you have not yet seen) to be *falsy,* presumably to imply that they are like the legitimate Boolean value **false**:

> **false**, 0, **""**, **undefined**, **null**, and **NaN**

Conversely, JavaScript defines any other value to be *truthy.* In any conditional context, any "falsy" value is treated as if it were the value **false**; any "truthy" value is treated as if it were the value **true**.

If you want to write programs that are easy to read and maintain, you should absolutely avoid relying on these fuzzy definitions of truth and falsity and make sure—as this book does—that every test produces a legitimate Boolean value. In his book, *JavaScript: The Good Parts,* Douglas Crockford lists the "surprisingly large number of falsy values" in his appendix on JavaScript's "awful parts." But you might also take the following advice from an even older source:

> Let what you say be simply "Yes" or "No"; anything more than this comes from evil.
>
> —Matthew 5:37, *The New English Bible*

Summary

The purpose of this chapter is to introduce the most common control statements available in JavaScript and give you various examples of their use. The important points include:

- One of the most useful types in any modern programming language is *Boolean data,* for which the domain consists of just two values: **true** and **false**.

- You can generate Boolean values using the *relational operators* (**<**, **<=**, **>**, **>=**, **===**, and **!==**), and you can combine Boolean values using the *logical operators* (**&&**, **||**, and **!**).

- The logical operators `&&` and `||` are evaluated in left-to-right order in such a way that the evaluation stops as soon as the program can determine the result. This behavior is called *short-circuit evaluation*.

- Control statements fall into two classes: *conditional* and *iterative*.

- The `if` statement specifies conditional execution when a section of code should be executed only if certain conditions apply.

- The `switch` statement specifies conditional execution when a problem has the following structure: in case 1, do this; in case 2, do that; and so forth.

- The `while` statement specifies repetition as long as some condition is met.

- The `for` statement specifies repetition in which some action is needed on each cycle in order to update the value of an index variable. The general form of the `for` statement header is

      for (*init*; *test*; *step*)

  where *init* typically declares and initializes an index variable, *test* specifies the conditions under which the loop continues, and *step* determines what operations are performed at the end of each cycle.

- An algorithm is a strategy that is *clear and unambiguous, effective,* and *finite*.

- There are usually many different algorithms for solving a particular problem. Algorithms often vary dramatically in their efficiency. Choosing the algorithm that best fits the application is an important part of your task as a programmer.

- JavaScript does not insist that conditional tests have the values `true` or `false`, but instead allows programmers to slip into using a fuzzier standard of truth. If you want to write programs that are easy to read and maintain, you should avoid writing any code that relies on this unfortunate feature of the language.

Review questions

1. What are the JavaScript keywords for the two Boolean values?

2. How would you write a Boolean expression to test whether the value of the integer variable `n` was in the range 0 to 9, inclusive?

3. Describe in English what the following conditional expression means:

       (x !== 4) || (x !== 17)

   For what values of `x` is this condition `true`?

4. What is meant by the term *short-circuit evaluation?*

5. What are the two classes of control statements?

6. What does it mean to say that two control statements are *nested?*

7. Describe in English the general operation of the `switch` statement.

8. What rule does this chapter suggest with respect to the final statement in any `case` or `default` clause?

9. What special value is used in the `monthName` function in Figure 3-1 to indicate an illegal numeric month?

10. What was the nickname of the Small-Scale Experimental Machine developed at Manchester University that was the forerunner of modern digital computers?

11. Suppose the body of a `while` loop contains a statement that, when executed, causes the condition for that `while` loop to become `false`. Does the loop terminate immediately at that point or does it complete the current cycle?

12. What term do computer scientists use to refer to an incomplete program written partly in a programming language and partly in English?

13. Why is it important for the comments preceding the `digitSum` function shown in Figure 3-2 to require that the argument value be positive? What would happen if the argument were negative?

14. What is the *empty string* and how do you write it in JavaScript?

15. What is the purpose of each of the three expressions that appear in the control line of a `for` statement?

16. What `for` loop control line would you use in each of the following situations:
    a) Counting from 1 to 100.
    b) Counting by sevens starting at 0 until the number has more than two digits.
    c) Counting backward by twos from 100 to 0.

17. What conditions must a solution strategy meet in order to be an algorithm?

18. Use Euclid's algorithm to compute the greatest common divisor of 7735 and 4185. What values does the local variable `r` take on during the calculation?

19. In the examples of Euclid's algorithm to calculate `gcd(x, y)` that appear in this chapter, `x` is always larger than `y`. What happens if `x` is smaller than `y`?

20. What do the terms *falsy* and *truthy* signify in JavaScript? What strategy does this book suggest for avoiding the ambiguity associated with these terms?

Exercises

1. Using the two definitions of the `max` function—one with an `if` statement and one with the `?:` operator—as examples, write corresponding implementations of the `min` function, which returns the smaller of its two arguments.

2. Write a function `max3` that returns the largest of its three arguments.

3. As a way to pass the time on long bus trips, young people growing up in the United States have been known to sing the following rather repetitive song:

> 99 bottles of beer on the wall.
> 99 bottles of beer.
> You take one down, pass it around.
> 98 bottles of beer on the wall.
>
> 98 bottles of beer on the wall. . . .

Anyway, you get the idea. Write a JavaScript program to display the lyrics of this song using `console.log`. In testing your program, it would make sense to use some constant other than 99 as the initial number of bottles.

4. While we're on the subject of silly songs, another old standby is "This Old Man," for which the first verse is

> This old man, he played 1.
> He played knick-knack on my thumb.
> With a knick-knack, paddy-whack,
> Give your dog a bone.
> This old man came rolling home.

Each subsequent verse is the same, except for the number and the rhyming word at the end of the second line, which get replaced as follows:

2—shoe	5—hive	8—pate
3—knee	6—sticks	9—spine
4—door	7—heaven	10—shin

Write a program to display all 10 verses of this song.

5. Write a function that takes a positive integer N and then calculates and displays the sum of the first N odd integers. For example, if N is 4, your function should display the value 16, which is $1 + 3 + 5 + 7$.

6.
> *Why is everything either at sixes or at sevens?*
> —Gilbert and Sullivan, *H.M.S. Pinafore,* 1878

Write a program that displays the integers between 1 and 100 that are divisible by either 6 or 7 but not both.

7. Using the `digitSum` function as a model, define a function that takes a number and returns a number that contains the same digits in the reverse order, as illustrated by the following sample run:

> | JavaScript Console |
> | :--- |
> | > **reverseDigits(1729)** |
> | 9271 |
> | > **reverseDigits(123456789)** |
> | 987654321 |
> | > |

    The idea in this exercise is not to take the integer apart character by character, which you will not learn how to do until Chapter 7. Instead, you need to use arithmetic to compute the reversed integer as you go. For example, in the call to `reverseDigits(1729)`, the new integer will be 9 after the first cycle of the loop, 92 after the second, 927 after the third, and 9271 after the fourth.

8. The *digital root* of an integer *n* is defined as the result of summing the digits repeatedly until only a single digit remains. For example, the digital root of 1729 can be calculated using the following steps:

Step 1:	$1 + 7 + 2 + 9$	→	19
Step 2:	$1 + 9$	→	10
Step 3:	$1 + 0$	→	1

    Because the total at the end of step 3 is the single digit 1, that value is the digital root. Write a function `digitalRoot` that returns this value.

9. Rewrite the `countdown` function on page 96 so that it uses a `while` loop instead of a `for` loop.

10. Write a function `drawConsoleBox(width, height)` that draws a box on the console with the specified dimensions. The corners of the box should be represented using a plus sign (+), the top and bottom borders using a minus sign (-), and the left and right borders using a vertical bar (|). For example, calling `drawConsoleBox(52, 6)` should produce the following diagram:

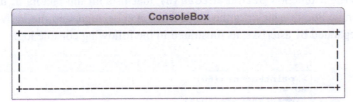

11. Write a function `drawConsoleArrow(width)` that draws a triangular arrow pointing to the right in which the center line has the specified width. For example, calling `drawConsoleArrow(6)` should create the following output:

```
                    ConsoleArrow
*
**
***
****
*****
******
*****
****
***
**
*
```

This program is easy to write if you simply add a second loop that counts backwards at the end of the code from `drawConsoleTriangle`. You can get a better sense of the flexibility of the `for` statement in JavaScript if you instead use a single outer loop that changes direction when it reaches the desired width.

12. Write a function `drawConsolePyramid(height)` that draws a pyramid of the specified height in which the width of each row increases by two as you move downward on the console. Each of the rows should be centered with respect to the others, and the bottom line should begin at the left margin. Thus, calling `drawConsolePyramid(8)` should produce the following figure:

```
                   ConsolePyramid
       *
      ***
     *****
    *******
   *********
  ***********
 *************
***************
```

13. The first program written for the Manchester Baby found the largest factor of a number. A more interesting problem is to find the complete set of factors. Write a function `printFactors(n)` that lists all the factors in the form of a single line that includes the number n, an equal sign, and the individual factors separated by asterisks, as illustrated in the following console log:

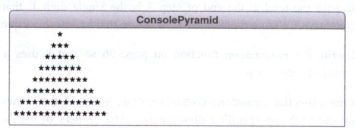

```
                    PrintFactors
> printFactors(60)
60 = 2 * 2 * 3 * 5
> printFactors(1024)
1024 = 2 * 2 * 2 * 2 * 2 * 2 * 2 * 2 * 2 * 2
> printFactors(1789)
1789 = 1789
>
```

14. The German mathematician Gottfried Wilhelm von Leibniz discovered the rather remarkable fact that the mathematical constant π can be computed using the following mathematical relationship:

$$\frac{\pi}{4} = 1 - \frac{1}{3} + \frac{1}{5} - \frac{1}{7} + \frac{1}{9} - \cdots$$

The formula to the right of the equal sign represents an infinite series; each fraction represents a term in that series. If you start with 1, subtract one-third, add one-fifth, and so on, for each of the odd integers, you get a number that gets closer and closer to the value of $\pi/4$ as you go along.

Write a program that calculates an approximation of π consisting of the first 10,000 terms in Leibniz's series.

15. An integer greater than 1 is said to be *prime* if it has no divisors other than itself and one. The number 17, for example, is prime because it has no factors other than 1 and 17. The number 91, however, is not prime because it is divisible by 7 and 13. Write a predicate function `isPrime(n)` that returns `true` if the integer `n` is prime, and `false` otherwise. As an initial strategy, implement `isPrime` using a brute-force algorithm that simply tests every possible divisor. Once you have that version working, try to come up with improvements to your algorithm that increase its efficiency without affecting its correctness.

16. Greek mathematicians took a special interest in numbers that are equal to the sum of their proper divisors (a proper divisor of *n* is any divisor less than *n* itself). They called such numbers *perfect numbers.* For example, 6 is a perfect number because it is the sum of 1, 2, and 3, which are the integers less than 6 that divide evenly into 6. Similarly, 28 is a perfect number because it is the sum of 1, 2, 4, 7, and 14.

Write a predicate function `isPerfect(n)` that returns `true` if the integer `n` is perfect, and `false` otherwise. Test your implementation by writing a program that uses the `isPerfect` function to check for perfect numbers in the range 1 to 9999 by testing each number in turn. Whenever your program identifies a perfect number, it should display that number on the screen. The first two lines of output should be 6 and 28. Your program should find two other perfect numbers in that range as well.

17. Although Euclid's algorithm for calculating the greatest common divisor is one of the oldest to be dignified with that term, there are other algorithms that date back many centuries. In the Middle Ages, one of the problems that required sophisticated algorithmic thinking was determining the date of Easter, which falls on the first Sunday after the first full moon following the vernal equinox.

Given this definition, the calculation involves interacting cycles of the day of the week, the orbit of the moon, and the passage of the sun through the zodiac. Early algorithms for solving this problem date back to the third century and are described in the writings of the eighth-century scholar known as the Venerable Bede. In 1800, the German mathematician Carl Friedrich Gauss published an algorithm for determining the date of Easter that was purely computational in the sense that it relied on arithmetic rather than looking up values in tables. His algorithm—translated from the German—appears in Figure 3-8.

Write a JavaScript function `findEaster(year)` that returns a string showing the date of Easter in the specified year. For example, calling `findEaster(1800)` returns the string `"April 13"` because that is the date of Easter in the year that Gauss published his algorithm.

Unfortunately, the algorithm in Figure 3-8 works only for years in the 18th and 19th centuries. It is easy, however, to search the web for extensions that work for all years. Once you have completed your implementation of Gauss's algorithm, undertake the necessary research to implement a more general approach.

FIGURE 3-8   **Gauss's algorithm for computing the date of Easter**

I.   Divide the number of the year for which one wishes to calculate Easter by 19, by 4, and by 7, and call the remainders of these divisions a, b, and c, respectively. If the division is even, set the remainder to 0; the quotients are not taken into account. Precisely the same is true of the following divisions.

II. Divide the value $19a + 23$ by 30 and call the remainder d.

III. Finally, divide $2b + 4c + 6d + 3$, or $2b + 4c + 6d + 4$, choosing the former for years between 1700 and 1799 and the latter for years between 1800 and 1899, by 7 and call the remainder e.

Then Easter falls on March $22 + d + e$, or when $d + e$ is greater than 9, on April $d + e - 9$.

Translated from Karl Friedrich Gauss, "Berechnung des Osterfestes," August 1800
http://gdz.sub.uni-goettingen.de/no_cache/dms/load/img/?IDDOC=137484

CHAPTER 4
Simple Graphics

A display connected to a digital computer gives us a chance to gain familiarity with concepts not realizable in the physical world. It is a looking glass into a mathematical wonderland.

— Ivan Sutherland, "The Ultimate Display," 1965

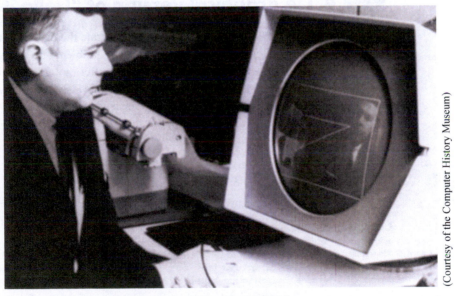

(Courtesy of the Computer History Museum)

Ivan Sutherland (1938–)

Ivan Sutherland was born in Nebraska and developed a passion for computers while still in high school, when a family friend gave him the opportunity to program a tiny relay-based machine called SIMON. Because computer science was not yet an academic discipline, Sutherland majored in electrical engineering at Pittsburgh's Carnegie Institute of Technology (now Carnegie Mellon University) and then went on to get a master's degree at Caltech and a Ph.D. from MIT. His doctoral thesis, "Sketchpad: A Man-Machine Graphical Communications System," became one of the cornerstones of computer graphics and introduced the idea of the graphical user interface, which has become an essential feature of modern software. After completing his degree, Sutherland held faculty positions at Harvard, the University of Utah, and Caltech before leaving academia to found a computer-graphics company. Sutherland received the ACM Turing Award in 1988.

Although it is possible to learn the fundamentals of programming using only the numeric and string types you saw in Chapter 2, numbers and strings are not as exciting as they were in the early years of computing. For students who have grown up in the 21st century, much of the excitement surrounding computers comes from their ability to work with other more interesting types of data, including images and interactive graphical objects. JavaScript is ideal for working with graphical data. Introducing just a few graphical types will enable you to create applications that are much more engaging and give you a greater incentive to master the material.

This chapter introduces you to the facilities in the *Portable Graphics Library,* a collection of tools for writing simple graphical applications. The discussion in this chapter provides enough information to get you started; more advanced features of the graphics library will be introduced as they are needed.

4.1 A graphical version of "Hello World"

Just as **HelloWorld.js** is a useful program to illustrate the use of JavaScript with a web-based console, it makes sense to use the same problem as a starting point for graphical programs in JavaScript. The code for a graphically oriented **GraphicsHelloWorld.js** program appears in Figure 4-1. The new goal is no longer to print the words "hello, world" but instead to display those words in a graphics window embedded in the web page.

FIGURE 4-1 A graphical version of the "Hello World" program

```
/*
 * File: GraphicsHelloWorld.js
 * ----------------------------
 * This program displays the string "hello, world" at location (50, 100)
 * on the graphics window.  The inspiration for this program comes from
 * Brian Kernighan and Dennis Ritchie's book, The C Programming Language.
 */

"use strict";

/* Constants */

const GWINDOW_WIDTH = 500;
const GWINDOW_HEIGHT = 200;

/* Main program */

function GraphicsHelloWorld() {
   let gw = GWindow(GWINDOW_WIDTH, GWINDOW_HEIGHT);
   let msg = GLabel("hello, world", 50, 100);
   gw.add(msg);
}
```

FIGURE 4-2 The `index.html` file for `GraphicsHelloWorld.js`

```
<!DOCTYPE html>
<html>
  <head>
    <title>GraphicsHelloWorld</title>
    <script src="JSGraphics.js"></script>
    <script src="GraphicsHelloWorld.js"></script>
  </head>
  <body onload="GraphicsHelloWorld()"></body>
</html>
```

Like the `HelloWorld.js` program in Figure 2-4, `GraphicsHelloWorld.js` is designed to run in the browser and therefore needs to have an `index.html` file that defines the structure of the web page, which appears in Figure 4-2. This file is almost exactly the same as the one for `HelloWorld.js`. The only difference is that this program needs to load the graphics library instead of the console library. The corresponding `<script>` tag looks like this:

```
<script src="JSGraphics.js"></script>
```

The main function for the `GraphicsHelloWorld.js` program looks like this:

```
function GraphicsHelloWorld() {
    let gw = GWindow(GWINDOW_WIDTH, GWINDOW_HEIGHT);
    let msg = GLabel("hello, world", 50, 100);
    gw.add(msg);
}
```

The body of `GraphicsHelloWorld` begins with two variable declarations—one for the variable `gw`, which stands for "graphics window," and one for the variable `msg`, which refers to the message on the screen. The declarations themselves have the same form as the ones you have seen earlier. Each declares a variable and initializes it to a value. What's different are the types of these values.

4.2 Classes, objects, and methods

One of the most important things to notice about the `GraphicsHelloWorld.js` program in Figure 4-1 is that the values stored in the variables `gw` and `msg` are more complex than the values you've worked with so far, even though the underlying principles are the same. So far, the values you have stored in variables have been numbers or strings. In the `GraphicsHelloWorld.js` program, the values stored in each of these variables is an *object,* which is the term computer science uses to refer to a conceptually integrated entity that ties together the information that defines the state of the object and the operations that affect that state.

Each of these objects is also a representative of a *class,* which is easiest to imagine as a template that defines the attributes and operations shared by all objects of a particular type. A single class can give rise to many different objects; each such object is said to be an *instance* of that class.

Creating objects

The `GraphicsHelloWorld.js` program includes two declarations that create objects:

```
let gw = GWindow(GWINDOW_WIDTH, GWINDOW_HEIGHT);
let msg = GLabel("hello, world", 50, 100);
```

The functions `GWindow` and `GLabel` are part of the `JSGraphics.js` library and create new objects of those classes. The `GWindow` class represents a graphical window on the screen, and the `GLabel` class represents a string that can appear in that window. Functions that create new objects are called *factory methods* and typically start with an uppercase letter.

The declaration

```
let gw = GWindow(GWINDOW_WIDTH, GWINDOW_HEIGHT);
```

uses the `GWindow` factory method to create an object whose class is `GWindow`. The parameters `GWINDOW_WIDTH` and `GWINDOW_HEIGHT` specify the window size in units called *pixels,* which are the tiny dots that cover the face of the display. The call to `GWindow` therefore creates a new `GWindow` object that is 500 pixels wide and 200 pixels high. That object is then assigned to a variable named `gw`, which makes it possible for the program to refer to the window in the rest of the code.

Even though the declarations of the variables `gw` and `msg` create the necessary objects, these lines alone do not cause the `GLabel` to appear in the `GWindow`. To get the message to appear, the program has to tell the `GWindow` object stored in `gw` to add the `GLabel` stored in `msg` to its internal list of graphical objects to display on the window. This step in the process is the responsibility of the last line in the `GraphicsHelloWorld.js` program, which looks like this:

```
gw.add(msg);
```

Understanding how this statement works requires you to learn a little more about the way that JavaScript works with objects.

Sending messages to objects

When you are programming in a language that supports objects, it is useful to adopt at least some of the ideas and terminology of the *object-oriented paradigm,* a conceptual model of programming that focuses on objects and their interactions rather than on the more traditional model in which data and operations are seen as separate. In object-oriented programming, the generic term for anything that triggers a particular behavior in an object is called a ***message.*** In JavaScript, the object-oriented idea of sending a message to an object is implemented by calling a function associated with that object. Functions that are associated with an object are called ***methods,*** and the object on which the method is invoked is called the ***receiver.***

In JavaScript, method calls use the following syntax:

> *receiver* . *name* (*arguments*)

In the method call `gw.add(msg)`, the graphics window stored in `gw` is the receiver, and `add` is the name of the method that responds to the message. The argument `msg` lets the implementation of the `GWindow` class know what graphical object to add, which in this case is the `GLabel` stored in the `msg` variable. The `GWindow` responds by displaying the message at the specified coordinates on the screen, which creates the following image:

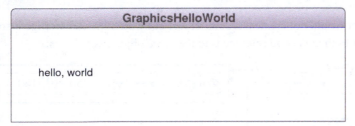

As you can see from the screen image, the desired message is there. Although it's not very large or exciting, you'll have a chance to spice it up later in the chapter.

References

In JavaScript, the value stored in a variable like `gw` is not the entire object but instead a ***reference,*** which is a value internal to the computer that serves as a link to the data in the actual object. In the `GraphicsHelloWorld.js` program, the declaration

```
let gw = GWindow(GWINDOW_WIDTH, GWINDOW_HEIGHT);
```

initializes the variable `gw` to contain a reference to a region of the browser window capable of displaying graphical objects, as illustrated by the following diagram:

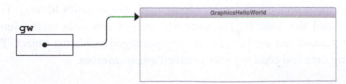

As the arrow suggests, the reference stored in **gw** points to a larger value that represents the graphics window on the screen.

The declaration

```
let msg = GLabel("hello, world", 50, 100);
```

operates in a similar fashion. This line creates a **GLabel** object and assigns a reference to that object to the variable **msg**, as follows:

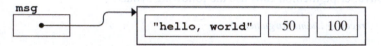

Although it is often possible to ignore the distinction between a reference and its associated object, it is important to understand that assigning an object value to a variable does not copy the entire object but instead copies only the reference. For example, if you were to write the declaration

```
let msg2 = msg;
```

JavaScript would not create a second object but would instead arrange it so that **msg** and **msg2** both contained references to the *same* object, as follows:

If you need to create a second **GLabel**—even one that has the same contents—you need to call the **GLabel** factory method.

Understanding how JavaScript uses references as links to larger data structures will be particularly important when you learn about arrays and objects in Chapters **8** through 11.

Encapsulation

The diagrams for the **GLabel** objects in the preceding section show only the data values that are stored inside those objects. In addition to these values, objects also contain the methods that apply to objects of that class, even though you won't see the code for those methods unless you look inside the graphics library. The internal data values and the code for the methods are not available to the function that creates the **GLabel** but are instead securely packaged inside the object. This model of packaging data and code together is called *encapsulation.*

4.3 Graphical objects

The **GLabel** class introduced in the preceding section is only one of several classes in the graphics library that represent an object you can display on the screen. This section introduces three other classes—**GRect**, **GOval**, and **GLine**—that, together with **GLabel** and **GWindow**, provide a useful "starter kit" for creating graphical applications. You will have a chance to learn about other classes later in this book.

The GRect class

The **GRect** class allows you to create rectangles and add them to the graphics window. For example, the program in Figure 4-3 creates a graphics window and then adds a rectangle to the window, solidly filled using the color blue, like this:

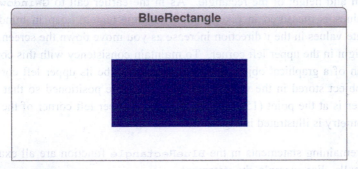

FIGURE 4-3 **Program to draw a blue rectangle on the graphics window**

```
/*
 * File: BlueRectangle.js
 * -----------------------
 * This program draws a blue rectangle on the graphics window.
 */

"use strict";

/* Constants */

const GWINDOW_WIDTH = 500;
const GWINDOW_HEIGHT = 200;

/* Main program */

function BlueRectangle() {
   let gw = GWindow(GWINDOW_WIDTH, GWINDOW_HEIGHT);
   let rect = GRect(150, 50, 200, 100);
   rect.setColor("Blue");
   rect.setFilled(true);
   gw.add(rect);
}
```

For the most part, the **BlueRectangle.js** program looks much the same as the **GraphicsHelloWorld.js** program from Figure 4-1. It includes—as every graphics programs in this book does—constant definitions indicating the size of the graphics window and a main program that begins by creating a **GWindow** with the specified dimensions and assigning it to the variable **gw**.

The next statement in the **BlueRectangle** function is

```
let rect = GRect(150, 50, 200, 100);
```

which creates a **GRect** object used to display the rectangle in the window. In this call, the first two arguments, 150 and 50, indicate the *x* and *y* coordinates at which the rectangle should be positioned; the second two arguments, 200 and 100, specify the width and height of the rectangle. As in the earlier call to **GWindow**, each of these values is measured in pixels, but it is important to keep in mind that the coordinate values in the *y* direction increase as you move down the screen, with the (0, 0) origin in the upper left corner. To maintain consistency with this convention, the origin of a graphical object is usually defined to be its upper left corner. The **GRect** object stored in the variable **rect** is therefore positioned so that its upper left corner is at the point (150, 50) relative to the upper left corner of the window. This geometry is illustrated in Figure 4-4.

The remaining statements in the **BlueRectangle** function are all examples of method calls. For example, the statement

```
rect.setColor("Blue");
```

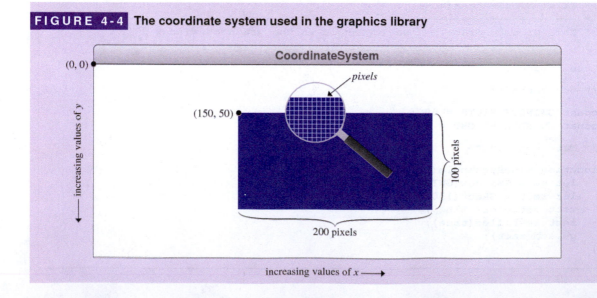

FIGURE 4-4 **The coordinate system used in the graphics library**

sends the rectangle object a `setColor` message asking it to change its color. The argument to `setColor` is a string representing one of the many color names that JavaScript defines, which are listed in Figure 4-5. In this case, the `setColor` call tells the rectangle to set its color to blue.

If the 140 standard web colors listed in Figure 4-5 are not enough for you, JavaScript allows you to specify 16,777,216 different colors by indicating the proportion of the three primary colors of light: red, green, and blue. To do so, all you need to do is specify the color as a string in the form `"#rrggbb"`, where *rr* indicates the red value, *gg* indicates the green value, and *bb* indicates the blue value. Each of these values is expressed as a two-digit number written in **hexadecimal,** or base 16. You may already be familiar with this form of color specification from designing web pages. If not, you will have a chance to learn more about hexadecimal notation in Chapter 7.

FIGURE 4-5 Predefined color names in JavaScript

AliceBlue	DarkSlateGrey	LightPink	PaleVioletRed
AntiqueWhite	DarkTurquoise	LightSalmon	PapayaWhip
Aqua	DarkViolet	LightSeaGreen	PeachPuff
Aquamarine	DeepPink	LightSkyBlue	Peru
Azure	DeepSkyBlue	LightSlateGray	Pink
Beige	DimGray	LightSlateGrey	Plum
Bisque	DimGrey	LightSteelBlue	PowderBlue
Black	DodgerBlue	LightYellow	Purple
BlanchedAlmond	FireBrick	Lime	RebeccaPurple
Blue	FloralWhite	LimeGreen	Red
BlueViolet	ForestGreen	Linen	RosyBrown
Brown	Fuchsia	Magenta	RoyalBlue
BurlyWood	Gainsboro	Maroon	SaddleBrown
CadetBlue	GhostWhite	MediumAquamarine	Salmon
Chartreuse	Gold	MediumBlue	SandyBrown
Chocolate	Goldenrod	MediumOrchid	SeaGreen
Coral	Gray	MediumPurple	Seashell
CornflowerBlue	Grey	MediumSeaGreen	Sienna
Cornsilk	Green	MediumSlateBlue	Silver
Crimson	GreenYellow	MediumSpringGreen	SkyBlue
Cyan	Honeydew	MediumTurquoise	SlateBlue
DarkBlue	HotPink	MediumVioletRed	SlateGray
DarkCyan	IndianRed	MidnightBlue	SlateGrey
DarkGoldenrod	Indigo	MintCream	Snow
DarkGray	Ivory	MistyRose	SpringGreen
DarkGrey	Khaki	Moccasin	SteelBlue
DarkGreen	Lavender	NavajoWhite	Tan
DarkKhaki	LavenderBlush	Navy	Teal
DarkMagenta	LawnGreen	OldLace	Thistle
DarkOliveGreen	LemonChiffon	Olive	Tomato
DarkOrange	LightBlue	OliveDrab	Turquoise
DarkOrchid	LightCoral	Orange	Violet
DarkRed	LightCyan	OrangeRed	Wheat
DarkSalmon	LightGoldenrodYellow	Orchid	White
DarkSeaGreen	LightGray	PaleGoldenrod	WhiteSmoke
DarkSlateBlue	LightGrey	PaleGreen	Yellow
DarkSlateGray	LightGreen	PaleTurquoise	YellowGreen

The next line in the **BlueRectangle** function is the method call

```
rect.setFilled(true);
```

which sends a **setFilled** message to the rectangle. The argument to **setFilled** is a Boolean value, which specifies whether the rectangle is filled or outlined. Calling **rect.setFilled(true)** indicates that the interior of the rectangle should be filled. Conversely, calling **rect.setFilled(false)** indicates that it should not be, which leaves only the outline.

The final line in the **BlueRectangle** function is the method call

```
gw.add(rect);
```

which sends an **add** message to the graphics window, asking it to add the graphical object stored in **rect** to the contents of the window. Adding the rectangle produces the final contents of the display.

By default, the **GRect** function creates rectangles that are unfilled. Thus, if you left this statement out of **BlueRectangle.js**, the result would look like this:

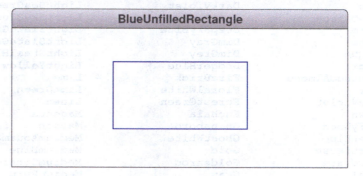

For filled shapes, you can set the color of the interior by calling **setFillColor** with any of the color names from Figure 4-5. For example, if you replace the call to **setColor("Blue")** in Figure 4-3 with a call to **setFilledColor("Cyan")**, the rectangle would be filled in cyan but outlined in black, like this:

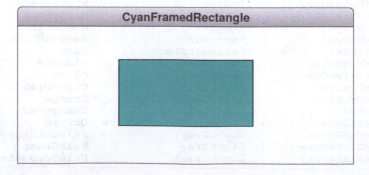

The GOval **class**

As its name suggests, the GOval class is used to display an oval-shaped figure in a graphics window. Structurally, the GOval class is similar to the GRect class: the GOval function itself takes the same arguments as the GRect function, and the two classes respond to the same set of methods. The difference lies in the figures those classes produce on the screen. The GRect class displays a rectangle whose location and size are determined by the argument values *x, y, width,* and *height.* The GOval class displays the oval whose edges just touch the boundaries of that rectangle.

The relationship between the GRect and the GOval classes is most easily illustrated by example. The following function definition takes the code from the earlier **BlueRectangle.js** program and extends it by adding a GOval with the same coordinates and dimensions:

```
function GRectPlusGOval() {
    let gw = GWindow(GWINDOW_WIDTH, GWINDOW_HEIGHT);
    let rect = GRect(150, 50, 200, 100);
    rect.setFilled(true);
    rect.setColor("Blue");
    gw.add(rect);
    let oval = GOval(150, 50, 200, 100);
    oval.setFilled(true);
    oval.setColor("Red");
    gw.add(oval);
}
```

The resulting output looks like this:

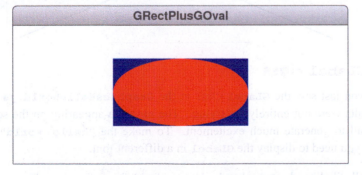

There are two important things to notice in this example. First, the red GOval extends so that its edges touch the boundary of the rectangle. Second, the GOval, which was added after the GRect, hides the portions of the rectangle that lie underneath the oval. If you were to add these figures in the opposite order, all you would see is the blue GRect, because the entire GOval would be within the boundaries of the GRect.

The GLine class

The **GLine** class is used to display line segments on the graphics window. The **GLine** function takes four arguments, which are the x and y coordinates of the two endpoints. For example, the function call

```
GLine(0, 0, GWINDOW_WIDTH, GWINDOW_HEIGHT)
```

creates a **GLine** object running from the point $(0, 0)$ in the upper left corner of the graphics window to the point at the opposite corner in the lower right.

The following function uses the **GLine** class to draw the two diagonals across the graphics window:

```
function DrawDiagonals() {
   let gw = GWindow(GWINDOW_WIDTH, GWINDOW_HEIGHT);
   gw.add(GLine(0, 0, GWINDOW_WIDTH, GWINDOW_HEIGHT));
   gw.add(GLine(0, GWINDOW_HEIGHT, GWINDOW_WIDTH, 0));
}
```

Loading this program in the browser generates the following display:

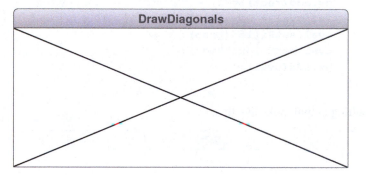

The GLabel class

When you last saw the **GLabel** class in the **GraphicsHelloWorld.js** program, the results were not entirely satisfying. The message appearing on the screen was too small to generate much excitement. To make the **"hello, world"** message bigger, you need to display the **GLabel** in a different font.

In all likelihood, you already know about fonts from working with other computer applications and have an intuitive sense that fonts determine the style in which characters appear. More formally, a *font* is an encoding that maps characters into images that appear on the screen. To change the font of the **GLabel**, you need to send it a **setFont** message, which might look like this:

```
msg.setFont("36px 'Times New Roman'");
```

This call to the `setFont` method tells the `GLabel` stored in `msg` to change its font to one in which the height of a text line is 36 pixels and the font family is Times New Roman, used by *The New York Times*. If you include the `setFont` call in the program, the graphics window will look like this:

```
BiggerHelloWorld

    hello, world
```

The string passed as the argument to `setFont` is written using CSS, which, as noted in Chapter 2, is the technology the web uses to specify the visual appearance of the page. This string specifies several properties of the font, which appear in the following order:

- The *font style*, which can be used to indicate an alternative form of the font. This specification is ordinarily omitted from the font string to indicate a normal font but may appear as `italic` or `oblique` to indicate an italic variant or a slanted one.

- The *font weight*, which specifies how dark the font should be. This specification is omitted for normal fonts but may appear as `bold` to specify a boldface one.

- The *font size*, which specifies how tall the characters should be by indicating the distance between two successive lines of text. In CSS, the font size is usually specified in pixel units as a number followed by the suffix `px`, as in the `36px` specification used in the most recent call to `setFont`.

- The *font family*, which specifies the name associated with the font. If the name of the font contains spaces, it must be quoted, usually using single quotation marks because the font specification appears inside a double-quoted string. Setting the text in Times New Roman, for example, therefore requires the font string to include `'Times New Roman'`. Because different computers support different fonts, CSS allows a font specification to include several family names separated by commas. The browser will then use the first font family that is available.

CSS defines several *generic family names,* which do not identify a specific font but instead describe a type of font that is always available in some form. The most common generic family names appear in Figure 4-6. It is good practice to end the list of preferred font families with one of these generic names to ensure that your program will run on the widest possible set of browsers.

FIGURE 4-6	Generic font families available in CSS and JavaScript
`Serif`	A traditional newspaper-style font in which the characters have short lines at the top and bottom, called *serifs,* that lead the eye to read words as single units. The most common example of a serif font is `'Times New Roman'`.
`Sans-Serif`	An unadorned font style lacking serifs. Common examples of sans-serif fonts include `'Arial'` and `'Helvetica Neue'`.
`Monospaced`	A typewriter-style font in which all characters have the same width. The most common monospaced fonts are `'Monaco'` and `'Courier New'`.

As you probably know from using your word processor, it can be fun to experiment with different fonts. On most Macintosh systems, for example, there is a font called Lucida Blackletter, which produces a script reminiscent of the style of illuminated manuscripts of medieval times. To set the message in this font, you could change the `setFont` call in this program to

```
msg.setFont("24px 'Lucida Blackletter',Serif");
```

Note that the font string includes the generic family name `Serif` as an alternative. If the browser displaying the page could not find a font called Lucida Blackletter, it could then substitute one of the standard serif fonts, such as Times New Roman. If, however, it were able to load the Lucida Blackletter font successfully, the output would look something like this:

FancyHelloWorld

hello, world

The `GLabel` class uses its own geometric model, which is similar to the ones that typesetters have used over the centuries since Gutenberg's invention of the printing press. The notion of a font, of course, originally comes from printing. Printers would load different sizes and styles of type into their presses to control the way in which characters appeared on a page. The terminology that the graphics library uses to describe both fonts and labels also derives from the typesetting world. You will find it easier to understand the behavior of the `GLabel` class if you learn the following terms:

- The *baseline* is the imaginary line on which characters sit.

- The *origin* is the point at which the text of a label begins. In languages that read left to right, the origin is the point on the baseline at the left edge of the first character. In languages that read right to left, the origin is the point at the right edge of the first character, at the right end of the line.

- The *height* is the distance between successive baselines in multiline text.

- The *ascent* is the maximum distance that characters extend above the baseline.

- The *descent* is the maximum distance that characters extend below the baseline.

The interpretation of these terms in the context of the **GLabel** class is illustrated in Figure 4-7.

The **GLabel** class includes methods that allow you to determine these properties. For example, the **GLabel** class includes a method called **getAscent** to determine the ascent of the font in which the label appears. In addition, it includes a method called **getWidth**, which determines the horizontal extent of the **GLabel**.

These methods make it possible to center a label in the window, although they raise an interesting question. The only function you've seen to create a **GLabel** takes its initial coordinates as parameters. If you want to center a label, you won't know those coordinates until after you have created the label. To solve this problem, the function that creates a **GLabel** comes in two forms. The first takes the string for the label along with the x and y coordinates of the origin. The second leaves out the origin point, setting the origin to the default value of $(0, 0)$.

Suppose, for example, that you want to center the string **"hello, world"** in the graphics window. To do so, you first need to create the **GLabel**, then change its font so the label has the appearance you want, and finally determine the dimensions of the label to calculate the correct initial position. You can then supply those

FIGURE 4-7   **The geometry of the GLabel class**

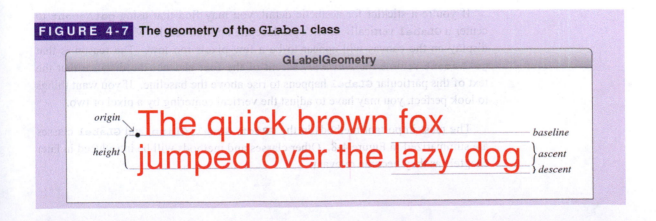

coordinates in the **add** method, which takes optional *x* and *y* parameters to set the location of the object when you add it to the **GWindow**. The following program implements this strategy:

```
function CenteredHelloWorld() {
    let gw = GWindow(GWINDOW_WIDTH, GWINDOW_HEIGHT);
    let msg = GLabel("hello, world");
    msg.setFont("36px 'Sans-Serif'");
    let x = (gw.getWidth() - msg.getWidth()) / 2;
    let y = (gw.getHeight() + msg.getAscent()) / 2;
    gw.add(msg, x, y);
}
```

The calculations necessary to center the **GLabel** occur in the declarations of the variables **x** and **y**, which specify the origin point for the centered label. To compute the *x* coordinate of the label, you need to shift the origin left by half the width of the label from the center of the window. Centering the label in the vertical dimension is a bit trickier. You can get pretty close by defining the *y* coordinate to be half the font ascent below the centerline. These declarations also introduce the fact that the **GWindow** object implements the **getWidth** and **getHeight** methods, so you can use these method calls to determine the width and height of the window.

Running the **CenteredHelloWorld** function produces the following image on the graphics window:

If you're a stickler for aesthetic detail, you may find that using **getAscent** to center a **GLabel** vertically doesn't produce the optimal result. Most labels that you display on the canvas will appear to be a few pixels too low. The reason is that **getAscent** returns the *maximum* ascent of the font and not the distance that the text of this particular **GLabel** happens to rise above the baseline. If you want things to look perfect, you may have to adjust the vertical centering by a pixel or two.

The most important methods in the **GRect**, **GOval**, **GLine**, and **GLabel** classes are summarized in Figure 4-8. Other classes and methods will be introduced in later chapters as they become relevant.

FIGURE 4-8 Summary of methods that apply to graphical objects

Factory methods to create graphical objects

GRect (*x*, *y*, *width*, *height*)	Creates a GRect object with the specified dimensions.
GRect (*width*, *height*)	Creates a GRect object of the specified size with its origin at (0, 0).
GOval (*x*, *y*, *width*, *height*)	Creates a GOval that fits inside the corresponding rectangle.
GOval (*width*, *height*)	Creates a GOval object in which the oval fits inside a rectangle of the specified size. The origin of the GOval is (0, 0).
GLine (x_1, y_1, x_2, y_2)	Creates a GLine object connecting (x_1, y_1) and (x_2, y_2).
GLabel (*str*, *x*, *y*)	Creates a GLabel object containing the specified string with its baseline origin at the point (*x*, *y*).
GLabel (*str*)	Creates a GLabel object containing the specified string with its baseline origin at the point (0, 0).

Methods common to all graphical objects

object.getX ()	Returns the *x* coordinate of the object.
object.getY ()	Returns the *y* coordinate of the object.
object.getWidth ()	Returns the width of the graphical object.
object.getHeight ()	Returns the height of the graphical object.
object.setColor (*color*)	Sets the color of the object to *color*.

Methods available only for the GRect and GOval classes

object.setFilled (*flag*)	Sets whether this object is filled.
object.setFillColor (*color*)	Sets the color used to fill the interior of the object.

Methods available only for the GLabel class

object.setFont (*str*)	Sets the font for the label. The format of the font specification is a CSS string as described in the text.
object.getAscent ()	Gets the *ascent* (maximum distance above the baseline) for the font.
object.getDescent ()	Gets the *descent* (maximum distance below the baseline) for the font.

 ## 4.4 The graphics window

Although it is essential for any program that uses the graphics library, the GWindow class is conceptually different from the other classes in the library. Classes like GRect and GLabel represent objects that you can display in a graphics window. The GWindow class represents the graphics window itself.

The **GWindow** object is conventionally initialized by the line

```
let gw = GWindow(GWINDOW_WIDTH, GWINDOW_HEIGHT);
```

which appears at the beginning of every program that uses the graphics library. This statement creates the graphics window and installs it in the web page so that it is visible to the user. It also serves to implement the conceptual framework for displaying graphical objects. The conceptual framework implemented by a library package is called its *model.* The model gives you a sense of how you should think about working with that package.

One of the most important roles of a model is to establish what analogies and metaphors are appropriate for the package. Many real-world metaphors are possible for computer graphics, just as there are many different ways to create visual art. One possible metaphor is that of painting, in which the artist selects a paintbrush and a color and then draws images by moving the brush across a screen that represents a virtual canvas.

For consistency with the principles of object-oriented design, the Portable Graphics Library uses the metaphor of a *collage.* A collage artist works by taking various objects and assembling them on a background canvas. In the real world, those objects might be, for example, geometrical shapes, words clipped from newspapers, lines formed from bits of string, or images taken from magazines. The graphics library offers counterparts for all these objects.

The fact that the graphics window uses the collage model has implications for the way you describe the process of creating a design. If you were using the metaphor of painting, you might talk about making a brush stroke in a particular position or filling an area with paint. With the collage model, the key operations are adding and removing objects, along with repositioning them on the background canvas.

Collages also have the property that some objects can be positioned on top of other objects, obscuring whatever is behind them. Removing those objects reveals whatever used to be underneath. In this book, the back-to-front ordering of objects in the collage is called the *stacking order,* although you will sometimes see it referred to as *z-ordering* in more formal writing. The name *z-ordering* comes from the fact that the stacking order occurs along the axis that comes out of the two-dimensional plane formed by the x and y axes. In mathematics, the axis coming out of the plane is called the *z-axis.*

The methods exported by the **GWindow** class appear in Figure 4-9. For now, your most important methods are **add**, **getWidth**, and **getHeight**. The other methods will be described in more detail when they are needed for an application.

FIGURE 4-9 Methods in the GWindow class

GWindow (*width*, *height*)	Creates a new GWindow object of the specified size.
gw.getWidth()	Returns the width of the graphics window.
gw.getHeight()	Returns the height of the graphics window.
gw.add(*obj*)	Adds the object to the graphics window.
gw.add(*obj*, *x*, *y*)	Repositions the object at (*x*, *y*) and adds it to the window.
gw.remove(*obj*)	Removes the object from the graphics window.
gw.getElementCount()	Returns the number of objects displayed in the window.
gw.getElement(*k*)	Returns the object at index *k*, numbering from back to front.
gw.getElementAt(*x*, *y*)	Returns the topmost graphical object that covers the point (*x*, *y*). If no such object exists getElementAt returns null.
gw.addEventListener(*type*, *fn*)	Primes the window to respond to events of the specified type by calling *fn*. Event listeners are discussed in Chapter 6.

 ## 4.5 Creating graphical applications

Once you have access to the graphics library, you can create graphical displays composed of instances of the GRect, GOval, GLine, and GLabel classes. The next few sections work through several examples that illustrate how to use these classes in your programs.

Specifying coordinates and sizes

To get a sense of how you might design a graphics program that places a few different shapes in the positions necessary to create a complete picture, suppose that you wanted to display a red balloon marked with an upbeat message, as follows:

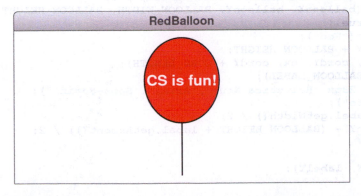

This program, which appears in Figure 4-10, displays three graphical objects:

1. A **GOval** representing the balloon itself, outlined in black and filled in red

2. A **GLine** representing the string attached to the balloon. In the code, the word *cord* is used instead of *string* to avoid any possible confusion with the message, which is a JavaScript string.

3. A **GLabel** displaying the string **"CS is fun!"** drawn in white.

FIGURE 4-10 Program to draw a red balloon on a string

```
/*
 * File: RedBalloon.js
 * --------------------
 * This program draws a red balloon emblazoned with the message
 * "CS is fun!" on the graphics window.
 */

"use strict";

/* Constants */

const GWINDOW_WIDTH = 500;
const GWINDOW_HEIGHT = 300;
const BALLOON_WIDTH = 140;
const BALLOON_HEIGHT = 160;
const BALLOON_LABEL = "CS is fun!";
const CORD_LENGTH = 100;

/* Main program */

function RedBalloon() {
   let gw = GWindow(GWINDOW_WIDTH, GWINDOW_HEIGHT);
   let cx = gw.getWidth() / 2;
   let cy = gw.getHeight() / 2;
   let balloonX = cx - BALLOON_WIDTH / 2;
   let balloonY = cy - (BALLOON_HEIGHT + CORD_LENGTH) / 2;
   let balloon = GOval(balloonX, balloonY, BALLOON_WIDTH, BALLOON_HEIGHT);
   balloon.setFilled(true);
   balloon.setFillColor("Red");
   let cordY = balloonY + BALLOON_HEIGHT;
   let cord = GLine(cx, cordY, cx, cordY + CORD_LENGTH);
   let label = GLabel(BALLOON_LABEL);
   label.setFont("bold 28px 'Helvetica Neue','Arial','Sans-Serif'");
   label.setColor("White");
   let labelX = cx - label.getWidth() / 2;
   let labelY = balloonY + (BALLOON_HEIGHT + label.getAscent()) / 2;
   gw.add(balloon);
   gw.add(cord);
   gw.add(label, labelX, labelY);
}
```

The objects themselves are not hard to create. What typically takes the most time when you are creating this kind of display is figuring out how to specify the sizes of each object and how to position them in the window so that everything fits together in the way you want it to appear.

The simplest strategy for specifying the sizes and other properties of graphical objects is to define them as constants, as shown in the `RedBalloon.js` example. The constants indicate that the graphics window is 500 pixels wide and 300 pixels high, that the balloon itself is 140 pixels wide and 160 pixels tall, that the message it displays is the string `"CS is fun!"`, and that the string tied to the base of the balloon is 100 pixels long.

Your primary task in writing the program is to figure out exactly how to position the graphical objects given the values of these constants. The entire figure—the balloon together with its string—is centered in the graphics window, which means that you have to figure out the coordinate locations for each of the objects relative to the center of the window. The coordinates of the center are easily computed using the following declarations, which will show up repeatedly in other examples:

```
let cx = gw.getWidth() / 2;
let cy = gw.getHeight() / 2;
```

The upper left corner of the oval representing the balloon is then shifted left from `cx` by half the width of the balloon and shifted upward from `cy` by half the total height, which is `BALLOON_HEIGHT + CORD_LENGTH`. The coordinates of the upper left corner of the oval can therefore be computed as follows:

```
let balloonX = cx - BALLOON_WIDTH / 2;
let balloonY = cy - (BALLOON_HEIGHT + CORD_LENGTH) / 2;
```

The remaining coordinates can be computed similarly. The *y*-coordinate of the top of the cord, for example, can be computed using the following expression:

```
let cordY = balloonY + BALLOON_HEIGHT;
```

Using simple decomposition

The `RedBalloon.js` program in Figure 4-10 is written as a single function. In more sophisticated graphical applications, it makes sense to decompose the program into multiple functions, each of which is responsible for part of the drawing, just as you did with the Karel programs in Chapter 1. As in Karel's world, you need to think carefully about how to decompose the problem so that each of the functions makes sense on its own.

To get a sense of how decomposition applies in a simple graphics application, suppose you have decided to draw a picture of your dream house, using a level of detail that one might find in an elementary-school art class. In the end, you want the picture on the graphics window to look like this:

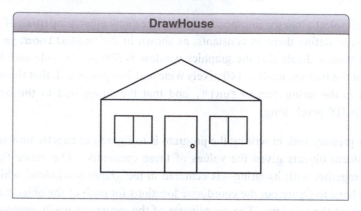

Although there are other reasonable choices, one possible strategy is to subdivide the problem into functions that draw the house frame, the door, and each of the windows. These functions would then have responsibility for drawing the parts of the picture shown in the left margin. You can then draw the entire house by making one call to **drawFrame**, one call to **drawDoor**, and two calls to **drawWindow**.

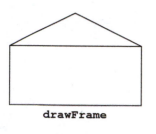

drawFrame

What you still need to do is figure out how each of these functions knows where to position its part of the picture and what the sizes of each of the components should be. As in the **RedBalloon.js** program, some of the values can be specified using constants. Some, however, have to be passed as parameters to these functions. At a minimum, the **drawWindow** function needs to know the x and y coordinates of the window so that it can draw a window in two different places.

drawDoor

Deciding which values to declare as constants and which to pass as parameters requires evaluating the tradeoffs between the two models. In general, declaring constants is simpler but limits the program's flexibility. At the same time, passing too many parameters makes functions harder to understand and use. In most applications, it makes sense to adopt a hybrid strategy in which you use constants to specify values that remain the same throughout the program and parameters to specify values that callers will want to change.

drawWindow

A complete program to draw the house appears in Figure 4-11 on the next two pages. Each of the functions takes three parameters: the graphics window **gw**, and the coordinates **x** and **y**, which specify the location on the window at which that part of the entire picture should appear. For consistency with JavaScript's graphics model, these coordinate values specify the upper left corner of that component of

> **FIGURE 4-11**   Program to draw a simple frame house

```
/*
 * File: DrawHouse.js
 * -------------------
 * This program draws a simple frame house at the center of the graphics
 * window.
 */

"use strict";

/* Constants */

const GWINDOW_WIDTH = 500;    /* The width of the graphics window      */
const GWINDOW_HEIGHT = 300;   /* The height of the graphics window     */
const HOUSE_WIDTH = 300;      /* The width of the house                */
const HOUSE_HEIGHT = 210;     /* The height of the house including the roof */
const ROOF_HEIGHT = 75;       /* The height of the roof above the frame */
const DOOR_WIDTH = 60;        /* The width of the door                 */
const DOOR_HEIGHT = 105;      /* The height of the door                */
const DOORKNOB_SIZE = 6;      /* The diameter of the doorknob          */
const DOORKNOB_INSET_X = 5;   /* The distance from the knob to the door edge */
const WINDOW_WIDTH = 70;      /* The width of each window              */
const WINDOW_HEIGHT = 50;     /* The height of each window             */
const WINDOW_INSET_X = 26;    /* The distance from outer wall to the window */
const WINDOW_INSET_Y = 30;    /* The distance from the ceiling to the window */

/* Main program */

function DrawHouse() {
   let gw = GWindow(GWINDOW_WIDTH, GWINDOW_HEIGHT);
   let houseX = (gw.getWidth() - HOUSE_WIDTH) / 2;
   let houseY = (gw.getHeight() - HOUSE_HEIGHT) / 2;
   drawFrameHouse(gw, houseX, houseY);
}

/*
 * Draws a simple frame house on the graphics window gw. The parameters
 * x and y indicate the upper left corner of the bounding box that
 * surrounds the entire house.
 */

function drawFrameHouse(gw, x, y) {
   drawFrame(gw, x, y);
   let doorX = x + (HOUSE_WIDTH - DOOR_WIDTH) / 2;
   let doorY = y + HOUSE_HEIGHT - DOOR_HEIGHT;
   drawDoor(gw, doorX, doorY);
   let leftWindowX = x + WINDOW_INSET_X;
   let rightWindowX = x + HOUSE_WIDTH - WINDOW_INSET_X - WINDOW_WIDTH;
   let windowY = y + ROOF_HEIGHT + WINDOW_INSET_Y;
   drawWindow(gw, leftWindowX, windowY);
   drawWindow(gw, rightWindowX, windowY);
}
```

FIGURE 4-11 **Program to draw a simple frame house (continued)**

```
/*
 * Draws the frame for the house on the graphics window gw.  The parameters
 * x and y indicate the upper left corner of the bounding box.
 */
function drawFrame(gw, x, y) {
   let roofY = y + ROOF_HEIGHT;
   gw.add(GRect(x, roofY, HOUSE_WIDTH, HOUSE_HEIGHT - ROOF_HEIGHT));
   gw.add(GLine(x, roofY, x + HOUSE_WIDTH / 2, y));
   gw.add(GLine(x + HOUSE_WIDTH / 2, y, x + HOUSE_WIDTH, roofY));
}

/*
 * Draws a door (with its doorknob) on the graphics window gw.  The
 * parameters x and y indicate the upper left corner of the door.
 */
function drawDoor(gw, x, y) {
   gw.add(GRect(x, y, DOOR_WIDTH, DOOR_HEIGHT));
   let doorknobX = x + DOOR_WIDTH - DOORKNOB_INSET_X - DOORKNOB_SIZE;
   let doorknobY = y + DOOR_HEIGHT / 2;
   gw.add(GOval(doorknobX, doorknobY, DOORKNOB_SIZE, DOORKNOB_SIZE));
}

/*
 * Draws a rectangular window divided vertically into two panes.  The
 * parameters x and y indicate the upper left corner of the window.
 */
function drawWindow(gw, x, y) {
   gw.add(GRect(x, y, WINDOW_WIDTH, WINDOW_HEIGHT));
   gw.add(GLine(x + WINDOW_WIDTH / 2, y,
                x + WINDOW_WIDTH / 2, y + WINDOW_HEIGHT));
}
```

the picture. For graphical objects that don't have an upper left corner, the usual strategy is to have the coordinates refer—as they do for the **GOval** class—to the upper left corner of the rectangle that encloses the object, which is called its ***bounding box.*** Thus, the coordinates for the house as a whole indicate the upper left corner of the dashed rectangle in the following diagram:

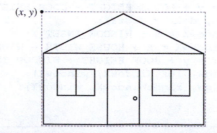

Using control structures in graphical applications

The control statements you learned about in Chapter 3 come up often in graphical programming, particularly when you need to draw many copies of the same figure in different positions on the graphics window. As an example, the program in Figure 4-12 draws five circles centered in the graphics window, like this:

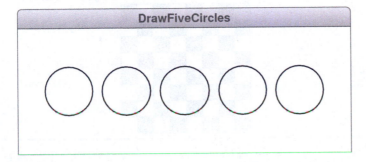

It is worth taking a look at the code for **DrawFiveCircles.js** to make sure you understand how the expressions ensure that the circles are centered.

FIGURE 4-12 **Program to draw five circles centered in the graphics window**

```
/*
 * File: DrawFiveCircles.js
 * -------------------------
 * This program draws a row of five circles centered in the graphics window.
 */

"use strict";

/* Constants */

const GWINDOW_WIDTH = 500;
const GWINDOW_HEIGHT = 200;
const CIRCLE_SIZE = 75;
const CIRCLE_SEP = 15;

/* Main program */

function DrawFiveCircles() {
   let gw = GWindow(GWINDOW_WIDTH, GWINDOW_HEIGHT);
   let cx = gw.getWidth() / 2;
   let cy = gw.getHeight() / 2;
   for (let i = 0; i < 5; i++) {
      let centerX = cx + (i - 2) * (CIRCLE_SIZE + CIRCLE_SEP);
      let circleX = centerX - CIRCLE_SIZE / 2;
      let circleY = cy - CIRCLE_SIZE / 2;
      gw.add(GOval(circleX, circleY, CIRCLE_SIZE, CIRCLE_SIZE));
   }
}
```

When you work with two-dimensional graphical designs, you often need nested loops to arrange graphical objects in both the horizontal and vertical directions. The `Checkerboard.js` program in Figure 4-13, for example, draws a checkerboard that looks like this:

FIGURE 4-13 **Program to draw a checkerboard**

```
/*
 * File: Checkerboard.js
 * -----------------------
 * This program draws a checkerboard centered in the graphics window.
 */

"use strict";

/* Constants */

const GWINDOW_WIDTH = 500;        /* Width of the graphics window  */
const GWINDOW_HEIGHT = 300;       /* Height of the graphics window */
const N_COLUMNS = 8;              /* Number of columns             */
const N_ROWS = 8;                 /* Number of rows                */
const SQUARE_SIZE = 35;           /* Size of a square in pixels    */

/* Main program */

function Checkerboard() {
   let gw = GWindow(GWINDOW_WIDTH, GWINDOW_HEIGHT);
   let x0 = (gw.getWidth() - N_COLUMNS * SQUARE_SIZE) / 2;
   let y0 = (gw.getHeight() - N_ROWS * SQUARE_SIZE) / 2;
   for (let row = 0; row < N_ROWS; row++) {
      for (let col = 0; col < N_COLUMNS; col++) {
         let x = x0 + col * SQUARE_SIZE;
         let y = y0 + row * SQUARE_SIZE;
         let sq = GRect(x, y, SQUARE_SIZE, SQUARE_SIZE);
         sq.setFilled((row + col) % 2 !== 0);
         gw.add(sq);
      }
   }
}
```

Once again, it is worth taking some time to go through the code in Figure 4-13, paying particular attention to the following details:

- The program is designed so that you can easily change the dimensions of the checkerboard by changing the values of the constants `N_ROWS` and `N_COLUMNS`.

- The checkerboard is arranged so that it is centered in the graphics window. The variables `x0` and `y0` are used to hold the coordinates of the upper left corner of the centered board.

- The decision to fill a square is made by checking whether the sum of its row number and column number is even or odd. For white squares, this sum is even; for black squares, this sum is odd. Note, however, that you don't need to include an `if` statement in the code to test this condition. All you need to do is call the `setFilled` method with the appropriate Boolean value.

Functions that return graphical objects

It is important to keep in mind that graphical objects are data values in JavaScript in precisely the same way that numbers and strings are. You can therefore assign graphical objects to variables, pass them as arguments to function calls, or have functions return them as results. Functions that return values of one of the `GObject` subclasses can be extremely useful as tools in creating graphical applications that need to display a shape with certain preset features, such as size and color.

The `Target.js` program in Figure 4-14 illustrates this feature by defining a `createFilledCircle` function that takes four arguments: the values *x* and *y* representing the coordinates of the center of the circle, a number *r* specifying the radius of the circle, and a string *color* indicating the JavaScript color name. The `Target.js` program calls `createFilledCircle` three times to create three circles that alternate in color between red and white and progressively decrease in size. The radius of the outer circle is given by the constant `OUTER_RADIUS`. The two inner circles are two-thirds and one-third that size, respectively. Running the `Target.js` program produces the following output:

FIGURE 4-14 Program to draw a red and white target on the graphics window

```
/*
 * File: Target.js
 * ----------------
 * This program draws a target at the center of the graphics window composed
 * of three concentric circles alternately colored red and white.
 */

"use strict";

/* Constants */

const GWINDOW_WIDTH = 500;
const GWINDOW_HEIGHT = 200;
const TARGET_RADIUS = 75;

/* Main program */

function Target() {
   let gw = GWindow(GWINDOW_WIDTH, GWINDOW_HEIGHT);
   let cx = gw.getWidth() / 2;
   let cy = gw.getHeight() / 2;
   gw.add(createFilledCircle(cx, cy, TARGET_RADIUS, "Red"));
   gw.add(createFilledCircle(cx, cy, 2 * TARGET_RADIUS / 3, "White"));
   gw.add(createFilledCircle(cx, cy, TARGET_RADIUS / 3, "Red"));
}

/*
 * Creates a circle of radius r centered at the point (x, y) filled
 * with the specified color and returns the initialized GOval to
 * the caller.
 */

function createFilledCircle(x, y, r, color) {
   let circle = GOval(x - r, y - r, 2 * r, 2 * r);
   circle.setColor(color);
   circle.setFilled(true);
   return circle;
}
```

■ Summary

This chapter introduced the Portable Graphics Library, which allows you to create simple pictures on the screen using lines, rectangles, ovals, and labels. Along the way, you had a chance to practice using objects in JavaScript.

Important points introduced in the chapter include:

- The graphical programs in this book use the *Portable Graphics Library,* which is a collection of graphical tools designed for use in introductory courses. That library is supplied as a single JavaScript file called **JSGraphics.js**.

- JavaScript supports a modern style of programming called the *object-oriented paradigm,* which focuses attention on data objects and their interactions.

- In the object-oriented paradigm, an *object* is a conceptually integrated entity that combines the state of that object and the operations that affect its state. Each object is a representative of a *class,* which is a template that defines the attributes and operations shared by all objects of a particular type. A single class can give rise to many different objects; each such object is an *instance* of that class.

- Objects communicate by sending *messages.* In JavaScript, those messages are implemented by calling *methods,* which are simply functions that belong to a particular class.

- Method calls in JavaScript use the receiver syntax, which looks like this:

  receiver . name (*arguments*)

  The *receiver* is the object to which the message is sent, *name* indicates the name of the method that responds to the message, and *arguments* is a list of values that convey any additional information carried by the message.

- Functions that create new objects are called *factory methods* and conventionally have names that begin with an uppercase letter.

- The first line in any JavaScript program that uses the Portable Graphics Library creates a **GWindow** object using the following declaration:

  ```
  let gw = GWindow(GWINDOW_WIDTH, GWINDOW_HEIGHT);
  ```

  The constants **GWINDOW_WIDTH** and **GWINDOW_HEIGHT** specify the dimensions of the graphics window in *pixels,* which are the tiny dots that cover the face of the display. Once you have initialized the variable **gw**, you can then create graphical objects of various kinds and add them to the window.

- This chapter introduces four classes of graphical objects—**GRect**, **GOval**, **GLine**, and **GLabel**—that represent rectangles, ovals, line segments, and text strings, respectively. Other graphical objects are introduced in later chapters.

- All graphical objects support the method **setColor**, which takes the name of the color as a string. JavaScript defines 140 standard colors whose names appear in Figure 4-5 on page 125.

- The **GRect** and **GOval** classes use **setFilled** and **setFillColor** to control whether the interior of the shape is filled and what color is used for the interior.

- The **GLabel** class uses the **setFont** method to set the font in which the label appears. The argument to **setFont** is the CSS specification of a font, which is described on page 129.

- The **GLabel** class uses a geometric model that is different from the one used by the other graphical objects. That model is illustrated in Figure 4-7 on page 131.

▆ Review questions

1. What is the name of the JavaScript library used in this chapter to implement programs that produce graphical output?

2. In your own words, define the terms *class, object,* and *method.*

3. What is a *reference?*

4. The object-oriented paradigm uses the metaphor of sending messages to model communication between objects. How does JavaScript implement this idea?

5. What is the *receiver syntax?*

6. What is a *factory method?*

7. What is the first line in every graphical program that appears in this book?

8. What are the four classes of graphical objects introduced in this chapter?

9. How do you change the color of a graphical object?

10. What is the purpose of the **setFilled** and **setFillColor** methods in the **GRect** and **GOval** classes?

11. What is the format of the argument string passed to **setFont**?

12. Define the following terms in the context of the **GLabel** class: *baseline, origin, height, ascent,* and *descent.*

13. Explain the purpose of the two following lines in the **CenteredHelloWorld** function:

    ```
    let x = (gw.getWidth() - msg.getWidth()) / 2;
    let y = (gw.getHeight() + msg.getAscent()) / 2;
    ```

    Why is there a minus sign in the calculation of the *x* coordinate and a plus sign in the calculation of the *y* coordinate?

14. When you center a **GLabel** vertically using the **getAscent** method, why does the resulting text often appear to be a few pixels too low?

15. What is the *collage model?*

16. What is meant by the term *stacking order?* What other term is often used for the same purpose?

Exercises

1. Use your program editor to create the program **GraphicsHelloWorld.js** and its associated **index.html** file exactly as they appear in Figures 4-1 and 4-2. Open the **index.html** file in your browser to show that you can get graphical programs working.

2. Write a graphical program **TicTacToeBoard.js** that draws a Tic-Tac-Toe board centered in the graphics window, as shown in the following sample run:

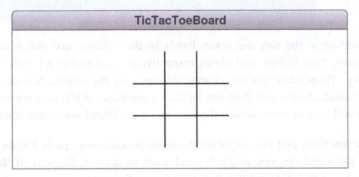

The size of the board should be specified as a constant, and the diagram should be centered in the window, both horizontally and vertically.

3. Draw a simplified version of Figure 4-7, which illustrates the geometry of the **GLabel** class. In your implementation, you should display the two strings (**"The quick brown fox"** and **"jumped over the lazy dog"**) in red using a sans-serif font that is large enough to make the guidelines easy to see. Then for each of the strings, you should draw a gray line along the baseline, the line that marks the font ascent, and the line that marks the font descent. Finally, you should draw a small filled circle indicating the baseline origin of the first string. The graphics window will then look like this:

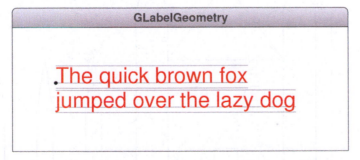

This output is a little more honest than Figure 4-7 about the font ascent, which appears slightly above the top of the uppercase characters.

4.   Use the graphics library to draw a rainbow that looks something like this:

Starting at the top, the seven bands in the rainbow are red, orange, yellow, green, blue, indigo, and violet, respectively; cyan makes a lovely color for the sky. Remember that this chapter defines only the **GRect**, **GOval**, **GLine**, and **GLabel** classes and does not include a graphical object that represents an arc. It will help to think outside the box, in a more literal sense than usual.

5.   If you think that the output produced by **DrawHouse.js** in Figure 4-11 seems a bit mundane, you might instead want to draw a diagram of the House of Usher, which Edgar Allan Poe describes as follows:

> With the first glimpse of the building, a sense of insufferable gloom
> pervaded my spirit. . . . I looked upon the scene before me—upon
> the mere house, and the simple landscape features of the domain—
> upon the bleak walls—upon the vacant eye-like windows . . . upon a
> few white trunks of decayed trees—with an utter depression of soul.

From Poe's description, you might draw a house that looks something like this:

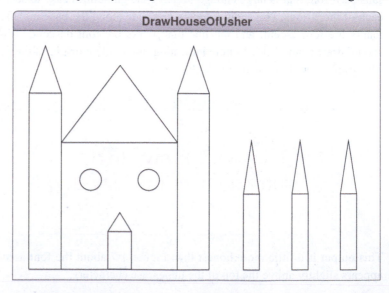

The figure on the left is the house with its "vacant eye-like windows" and the three figures on the right are a stylized rendition of the "few white trunks of decayed trees."

6. Write a program that displays a pyramid on the graphics window. The pyramid consists of bricks in horizontal rows, arranged so that the number of bricks in each row decreases by one as you move upward, as follows:

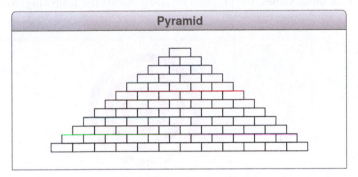

The pyramid should be centered in the window both horizontally and vertically and should use constants to define the dimensions of each brick and the height of the pyramid.

7. Rewrite (and suitably rename) the `DrawFiveCircles.js` program shown in Figure 4-12 so that the number of circles is given by the constant `N_CIRCLES`.

8. Enhance the `Checkerboard.js` program shown in Figure 4-13 so that the graphics window also displays the red and black checkers corresponding to the initial state of the game, which looks like this:

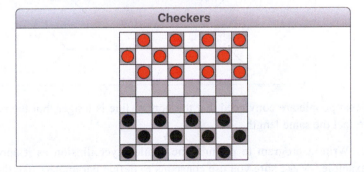

The other change in this program is that the color of the dark squares has been changed from black to gray so that the black checkers are not lost against the background.

9. Rewrite the **Target.js** program from Figure 4-14 so that the number and radii of the circles are controlled by the following constants:

```
const N_CIRCLES = 7;
const OUTER_RADIUS = 75;
const INNER_RADIUS = 10;
```

Given those values, the program should generate the following display:

10. Classical optical illusions offer a rich source of interesting graphical exercises. One of the simplest examples is the *Müller-Lyer illusion,* named after the German sociologist Franz Karl Müller-Lyer, who first described the effect in 1889. In one of its more common forms, the Müller-Lyer illusion asks the viewer which of the two horizontal lines is longer in the following figure:

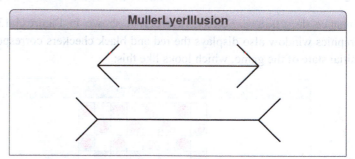

Most people are convinced that the bottom line is longer, but the two lines are in fact the same length.

Write a program to produce the Müller-Lyer illusion as it appears in this example. Make sure you use constants to define parameters like the lengths of the various lines.

11. Another illusion that shows how context affects the perception of relative size is the *Ebbinghaus illusion,* which was discovered by the German psychologist Hermann Ebbinghaus and published in a 1901 book by the British psychologist

FIGURE 4-15 The Ebbinghaus illusion: Are the inner circles the same size?

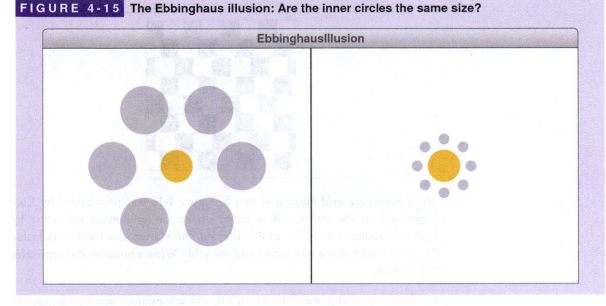

Edward Tichener. This illusion, which appears in Figure 4-15, makes it seem as if the central circle on the left is smaller than the circle on the right, even though the two are the same size. Write a program to produce this illusion.

12. Write a program to produce the **Zöllner illusion,** which was discovered by the German astrophysicist Johann Karl Friedrich Zöllner in 1860. In this illusion, the diagonal lines that run in opposite directions on every other line make it difficult to see that the horizontal lines are actually parallel:

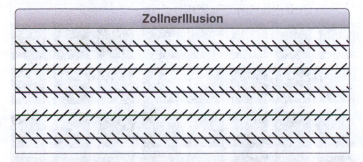

13. An even more exotic illusion is the **kindergarten illusion** (also called the **café wall illusion**), which was first described by the American psychologist Arthur Henry Pierce in 1898. In this illusion, shifting the squares slightly on each row of a checkerboard pattern makes the horizontal lines of the checkerboard appear slanted instead of straight. Starting with the `Checkerboard.js` program in Figure 4-13, make the changes necessary to produce the following image:

14. The *scintillating grid illusion* shown in Figure 4-16 was popularized by Elke Lingelbach in the 1990s and is based on an earlier illusion published by Ludimar Hermann in 1870. In this illusion, the viewer sees black dots inside the white circles at the intersections of the grid. Write a program that replicates this illusion.

15. Our visual sense is powerfully affected by our assumptions about an image. In 1911, the Italian psychologist Mario Ponzo showed that people expect objects viewed at a distance in a perspective drawing to appear smaller. If an object appears to violate the rules of perspective, our minds compensate by changing our perception of its size.

FIGURE 4-16 The scintillating grid illusion

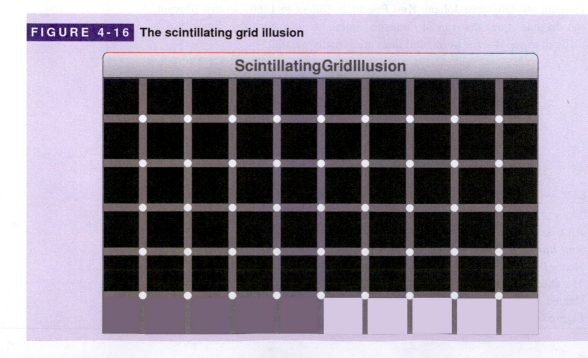

In one of its more popular forms, the ***Ponzo illusion*** illustrates this principle by superimposing two horizontal lines onto a stylized image of a railroad track receding into the distance. Because our experience assures us that the rails are equally far apart all the way down the track, a line that crosses it must be larger than one that falls entirely inside it, as illustrated in the following example:

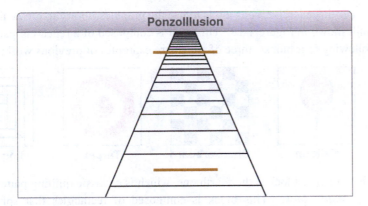

Your mission is to reproduce this image using ***one-point perspective,*** which is a technique for representing a three-dimensional scene in a two-dimensional drawing. In a drawing that uses one-point perspective, objects move toward a single ***vanishing point*** as they move farther from the viewer. This technique was developed during the early Renaissance and was used by the Florentine artist and architect Filippo Brunelleschi in a 1415 painting. Your challenge in creating the Ponzo illusion is to figure out where each of the crossties should go in the railroad track as it vanishes into the distance. The mathematical formulae you need to perform these calculations appear in Figure 4-17.

FIGURE 4-17 **Mathematics of perspective-based foreshortening**

Step 1. Define parameters	Step 2. Draw second crosstie	Step 3. Find next crosstie	Step 4. Repeat the process
V = distance to vanishing point	d = distance to next crosstie	Red line marks next crosstie.	Use the same process to find each new crosstie.
$h = \dfrac{first\ crosstie\ length}{2}$	$h' = h - \dfrac{d}{m}$	$d' = \dfrac{d - \dfrac{d^2}{mh}}{1 + \dfrac{d}{mh}}$	
Define the slope $m = \dfrac{V}{h}$			

16. Back in the early 1990s—long before JavaScript existed—Julie Zelenski and Katie Capps Parlante developed a lovely graphics assignment that we used in Stanford's introductory course for many years. The goal of the assignment was to draw a **sampler quilt,** which is composed of several different block types that illustrate a variety of quilting styles.

For this exercise, your job is to use the graphics library to create the sampler quilt shown in Figure 4-18. This quilt is composed of a repeating pattern of the following four blocks, three of which are examples of previous work:

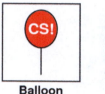

Balloon   Checkerboard   Target   Log Cabin

The only new block is the fourth one, which is a classic quilting pattern called a *log cabin block.* This block is composed of rectangles that spiral inward toward a square in the center. The width of each rectangle and the width of the central square are all the same, which means that the dimensions are determined by the block size and the number of frames in the spiral.

FIGURE 4-18 **Graphical display of a sampler quilt**

CHAPTER 5
Functions

Our module structure is based on the decomposition criteria known as information hiding. According to this principle, system details that are likely to change independently should be the secrets of separate modules.

—David Parnas, Paul Clements, and David Weiss,
"The Modular Structure of Complex Systems," 1984

(Courtesy of David Parnas)

David Parnas (1941–)

David Parnas is Professor of Software Engineering *emeritus* at the University of Limerick in Ireland, where he directed the Software Quality Research Laboratory, and has also taught at universities in Germany, Canada, and the United States. His most influential contribution to software engineering is his groundbreaking 1972 paper entitled "On the Criteria to be Used in Decomposing Systems into Modules," which provided much of the foundation for the strategy of decomposition described in this chapter. Professor Parnas also attracted considerable public attention in 1985 when he resigned from a Department of Defense panel investigating the software requirements of the proposed Strategic Defense Initiative— more commonly known as "Star Wars"—on the grounds that the requirements of the system were impossible to achieve. For his courageous stand in bringing these problems to light, Parnas received the 1987 Norbert Wiener Award from Computer Professionals for Social Responsibility.

This chapter examines in more detail the concept of a function, which was initially presented in Chapter 1 and then revisited in the context of JavaScript in Chapter 2. A function is a set of statements that have been collected together and given a name. Because functions allow the programmer to invoke the entire set of operations using a single name, programs become much shorter and much simpler. Without functions, programs would become unmanageable as they increased in size and sophistication.

In order to appreciate how functions reduce the complexity of programs, it helps to examine the role of functions from two distinct philosophical perspectives: *reductionism* and *holism*. **Reductionism** is the philosophical principle that the whole of an object can best be understood by understanding the parts that make it up. Its antithesis is **holism**, which recognizes that the whole is often more than the sum of its parts. As you try to master the discipline of dividing large programs into functions, you must learn to see the process from each of these perspectives. If you concentrate only on the big picture, you will end up not understanding the tools you need for solving problems. However, if you focus exclusively on details, you will invariably miss the forest for the trees.

When you are first learning about programming, the best approach is usually to alternate between these two perspectives. Taking the holistic view helps sharpen your intuition about the programming process and enables you to stand back from a program and say, "I understand what this function does." Taking the reductionistic view allows you to say, "I understand how this function works." Both perspectives are essential. You need to understand how functions work so that you can code them correctly. At the same time, you must be able to take a step backward and look at functions holistically, so that you also understand why they are important and how to use them effectively.

5.1 A quick review of functions

Although you have been working with functions ever since you wrote your first Karel program in Chapter 1, you have so far seen only a part of the computational power that functions provide. Before delving more deeply into the details of how functions work, it helps to review some basic terminology. First of all, a *function* consists of a set of statements that have been collected together and given a name. The act of executing the set of statements associated with a function is known as *calling* that function. To indicate a function call in JavaScript, you write the name of the function, followed by a list of expressions enclosed in parentheses. These expressions, which are called *arguments,* allow the caller to pass information to the function.

The syntax of a function definition

A typical function definition has the form shown in the syntax box on the right. The *name* component of this pattern indicates the function name, *parameters* is the list of parameter names that receive the values of the arguments, and *statements* represents the body of the function. Functions that return a value to the caller must contain at least one **return** statement that specifies the value of the function, as illustrated in the second syntax box.

These syntactic patterns are illustrated in the definition of the **max** function from Chapter 3, which looks like this:

```
function max(x, y) {
   if (x > y) {
      return x;
   } else {
      return y;
   }
}
```

```
function name (parameters) {
   statements
}
```

```
return value;
```

This function has the name **max** and takes two parameters, **x** and **y**. The statements in the body decide which of these two values is larger and then return that value.

Functions, however, are often called simply for their effect and need not return an explicit value. For example, the Karel functions in Chapter 1 and the JavaScript functions that implement complete programs don't include a **return** statement. Some languages distinguish a function that returns a value from one that doesn't by calling the latter a *procedure*. JavaScript uses the term *function* for both types. This terminology is technically accurate because JavaScript functions always return a value, which is the special value **undefined** if no **return** statement appears.

Parameter passing

The most important thing to remember about the process of calling a function is that the values of the arguments are copied to the parameter variables *in the order in which they appear*. The first argument is assigned to the first parameter variable, the second argument to the second parameter variable, and so on. The names of the parameters have nothing to do with the order in which their values are assigned. There may well be a variable named **x** in both the calling function and in the parameter list for the function being called. That reuse of the same name, however, is merely a coincidence. Local variable names and parameter names are visible only inside the function in which their declarations appear.

Unlike most modern languages, JavaScript does not check whether the number of arguments in the call matches the number of parameters specified for the function. If there are too many arguments, the extra ones are not assigned to any of the parameters and are therefore essentially ignored. If there are too few, any parameters that don't have a corresponding argument are set to **undefined**.

Optional parameters

In early versions of the language, one of the primary uses of JavaScript's rule for missing arguments was to allow a function to take optional parameters. To test whether the caller supplied an argument, the function could check the corresponding parameter variable to see if it is **undefined** and, if so, substitute a default value. Modern versions of JavaScript allow a function to specify default values by including an equal sign and the value in the parameter list. For example, the following function displays **n** consecutive integers, beginning with the value **start** if two arguments are supplied and with 1 if the second argument is missing:

```
function count(n, start = 1) {
   for (let i = 0; i < n; i++) {
      console.log(start + i);
   }
}
```

The following console session illustrates the operation of **count**, both when it is given a second argument and when it is not:

```
                         JavaScript Console
> count(3);
1
2
3
> count(2, 10);
10
11
>
```

Predicate functions

As you have seen in the earlier chapters, functions can return values of different data types. For example, the **monthName** on page 90 returns a string, the function **fact** on page 95 returns a number, and the function **createFilledCircle** on page 144 returns a **GOval**. Although functions in JavaScript can return values of any type, functions that return Boolean values deserve special attention because they play such an important role in programming. Functions that return Boolean values are called *predicate functions.*

As noted earlier in the chapter, there are only two Boolean values: **true** and **false**. Thus a predicate function—no matter how many arguments it takes or how complicated its internal processing may be—must eventually return one of these two values. The process of calling a predicate function is therefore analogous to asking a yes/no question and getting an answer. For example, the following function definition answers the question "is n an even number?" for a particular integer n supplied by the caller as an argument:

```
function isEven(n) {
   return n % 2 === 0;
}
```

A number is even if there is no remainder when you divide that number by two. If n is even, the expression n % 2 === 0 has the value true, which is returned as the value of isEven. If n is odd, the function returns false. Because isEven returns a Boolean result, you can use it directly in a conditional context. For example, the following for loop uses isEven to display all the even numbers between 1 and 100, inclusive:

```
for (let i = 1; i <= 100; i++) {
   if (isEven(i)) console.log(i);
}
```

The for loop runs through each number, and the if statement asks the simple question "is this number even?" If it is, the program calls console.log to display the number; if not, nothing happens.

If you were writing a program that works with dates, it would be useful to have a predicate function isLeapYear to determine whether a given year qualifies as a leap year. Although one tends to think of leap years as occurring once every four years, astronomical realities are not quite so tidy. Because it takes about a quarter of a day more than 365 days for the earth to complete its orbit, adding an extra day once every four years helps keep the calendar in sync with the sun, but it is still off by a slight amount. To ensure that the beginning of the year does not slowly drift through the seasons, the rule used for leap years is in fact more complicated. Leap years come every four years, except for years ending in 00, which are leap years only if they are divisible by 400. Thus, 1900 was not a leap year even though 1900 is divisible by 4. The year 2000, on the other hand, was a leap year because 2000 is divisible by 400. For any leap year, one of the following conditions must hold:

- The year is divisible by 4 but not divisible by 100, *or*
- The year is divisible by 400.

It is easy to code the correct rule in JavaScript as a predicate function, as follows:

```
function isLeapYear(year) {
   return ((year % 4 === 0) && (year % 100 !== 0)) ||
          (year % 400 === 0);
}
```

Once the function is defined, you can test for leap years like this:

```
if (isLeapYear(year)) . . .
```

 ## 5.2 Libraries

Writing a program to solve a large or difficult problem inevitably forces you to manage at least some amount of complexity. There are algorithms to design, special cases to consider, user requirements to meet, and innumerable details to get right. To make programming manageable, you must reduce the complexity of the programming process as much as possible. Functions reduce some of the complexity; libraries offer a similar reduction in programming complexity but at a higher level of detail. A function gives its caller access to a set of steps that implements a single operation. A library provides a collection of tools that share a common model. That model and its conceptual foundation constitute a *programming abstraction.*

Creating your own libraries

You can define a JavaScript library simply by combining the relevant definitions into a file whose name ends with the standard **.js** extension. For example, if you work extensively with dates in your programming, you can combine the constant definitions for the month names, the **monthName** function from page 90, and the **isLeapYear** function from page 159 into a library called **DateLib.js**, as shown in Figure 5-1 on the next page.

Once you have created the **DateLib.js** library, you can then use it in much the same way that you use any other library. All you need to do is add the line

```
<script src="DateLib.js"></script>
```

to the **index.html** file. Your JavaScript program will then have access to the constants for the month names and the functions **monthName** and **isLeapYear**. In computer science terminology, the **DateLib.js** library *exports* these constants and functions, which are collectively called *entries.*

The principle of information hiding

One of the goals of any library is to hide the complexity involved in the underlying implementation. By exporting the **isLeapYear** function, the **DateLib.js** library hides away the complexities involved in determining whether years ending in 00 are leap years. When you call the **isLeapYear** function, you don't need to have any idea how the implementation works. In fact, you don't even have to know that the special rules for century years exist. Those details are relevant only to the programmers responsible for implementing the **DateLib.js** library.

FIGURE 5-1 A simple library for working with dates

```
/*
 * File: DateLib.js
 * ------------------
 * This library exports the functions monthName and isLeapYear, along
 * with a set of constants giving names to the months of the year.
 */

/* Constants for the names of the months */

const JANUARY = 1;
const FEBRUARY = 2;
const MARCH = 3;
const APRIL = 4;
const MAY = 5;
const JUNE = 6;
const JULY = 7;
const AUGUST = 8;
const SEPTEMBER = 9;
const OCTOBER = 10;
const NOVEMBER = 11;
const DECEMBER = 12;

/*
 * Converts a numeric month in the range 1 to 12 into its name.
 */

function monthName(month) {
   switch (month) {
     case JANUARY: return "January";
     case FEBRUARY: return "February";
     case MARCH: return "March";
     case APRIL: return "April";
     case MAY: return "May";
     case JUNE: return "June";
     case JULY: return "July";
     case AUGUST: return "August";
     case SEPTEMBER: return "September";
     case OCTOBER: return "October";
     case NOVEMBER: return "November";
     case DECEMBER: return "December";
     default: return undefined;
   }
}

/*
 * Returns true if the specified year is a leap year, and false otherwise.
 */

function isLeapYear(year) {
   return year % 400 === 0 || (year % 4 === 0 && year % 100 !== 0);
}
```

Knowing how to call the `isLeapYear` function and knowing how to implement it are both important skills. It is useful to keep in mind, however, that those two skills—calling a function and implementing one—are to a large extent independent. Successful programmers often use functions that they wouldn't have a clue how to write. Conversely, programmers who implement a library function can never anticipate all the potential uses for that function.

To emphasize the difference in perspective between programmers who implement a library and those who use it, computer scientists have assigned names to programmers working in each of these roles. Naturally enough, a programmer who implements a library is called an *implementer*. Conversely, a programmer who calls functions provided by a library is called a *client* of that library.

Both functions and libraries offer a tool for hiding lower-level implementation details so that clients need not worry about them. In computer science, this technique is called *information hiding*. The fundamental idea, championed by David Parnas in the early 1970s, is that the complexity of programming systems is best managed by making sure that details are visible only at those levels of the program at which they are relevant. For example, only the programmers who implement `isLeapYear` need to know the details of its operation. Clients who merely use `isLeapYear` can remain blissfully unaware of the underlying details.

The concept of an interface

In computer science, the understanding shared between a client and an implementer is called an *interface*. Conceptually, an interface contains the information that clients need to know about a library—and no more. For clients, getting too much information can be as bad as getting too little, because additional detail is likely to make the interface more difficult to understand. Often, the real value of an interface lies not in the information it *reveals* but rather in the information it *hides*.

When you design an interface for a library, you should try to protect the client from as many of the complicating details of the implementation as possible. In doing so, it is perhaps best to think of an interface not as a communication channel between the client and the implementation, but instead as a wall that divides them.

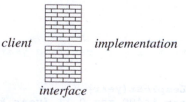

Like the wall that divided the lovers Pyramus and Thisbe in Greek mythology, the wall representing an interface contains an opening or chink that allows the two sides to communicate. In programming, that chink exposes the function definitions so that the client and implementation can share essential information. The main purpose of the wall, however, is to keep the two sides apart. Ideally, all the complexity involved in the realization of a library lies on the implementation side of the wall. An interface is successful if it supports the principle of information hiding by keeping as much complexity as possible away from the client side.

■ 5.3 A library to support randomness

To give you more insight into how libraries work, the next few sections define a library called `RandomLib.js`, which exports four functions that allow you to write programs that make seemingly random choices. Being able to simulate random behavior is necessary, for example, if you want to write a computer game that involves flipping a coin or rolling a die, but is also useful in more practical contexts. Programs that simulate random processes are said to be ***nondeterministic.***

The starting point for the `RandomLib.js` library is the `Math.random` function, which was included in Figure 2-3 in the list of functions available in the `Math` class. Calling `Math.random` returns a number in the range beginning at 0 and extending up to but not including the value 1. Every now and then, there is an application for which you need random values in precisely this range. More often than not, however, you would like to generate random values in a more general way. For example, if you are working on a game program that involves rolling a die, you would like to be able to produce a random integer between 1 and 6, inclusive. To simulate flipping a coin, it would be useful to have a function that produced a Boolean value so that `true` and `false` occurred with equal probability.

Designing the interface for the `RandomLib.js` library

The first and most important step in designing the `RandomLib.js` library consists of designing its interface, which is largely a matter of deciding what functions it should export. Those functions should be simple to use and should conceal as much of the underlying complexity as possible. They should also provide the functionality necessary to meet the needs of a wide range of clients, which means that you must have some idea of what operations clients are likely to need. Understanding those needs depends in part on your own experience, but often requires interacting with potential clients to get a better sense of their requirements.

In the context of a textbook, it is impossible to conduct a client survey. The `RandomLib.js` library developed in this chapter therefore offers those capabilities that have proven to be useful over many years of teaching Stanford's introductory programming course. The operations that students want include the following:

- *Selecting a random integer in a specified range.* If you want, for example, to simulate the process of rolling a standard six-sided die, you need to choose a random integer between 1 and 6.

- *Choosing a random real number in a specified range.* If you want to position an object at a random point in space, you need to choose random *x* and *y* coordinates within whatever limits are appropriate to the application.

- *Simulating a random event with a specific probability.* If you want to simulate flipping a coin, you need to generate the value *heads* with probability 0.5, which corresponds to 50 percent of the time.

- *Picking a random color.* In certain graphical applications, it is useful to choose a color at random to create unexpected patterns on the screen.

Translating these conceptual operations into a set of functions is a reasonably straightforward task, especially if you look at the problem from the client's perspective. The four functions exported by `RandomLib.js` are `randomInteger`, `randomReal`, `randomChance`, and `randomColor`, which correspond directly to the four operations clients are likely to use. The complete code for `RandomLib.js` appears in Figure 5-2, along with comments to help the client use these functions.

Implementing the `RandomLib.js` library

Although the client's view of these functions is relatively easy to understand, the implementations of these functions all involve some level of complexity that should be hidden from the client. This section walks through the code for each of these functions in detail.

As you can see from the comments in Figure 5-2, the `randomInteger` function takes two integers and returns an integer in the inclusive range that extends from the first argument to the second. If you wanted to simulate a die roll, you would call

```
randomInteger(1, 6)
```

The body of the `randomInteger` function fits on a single line, but it takes some thought to understand what that line does. For any values of the parameters `low` and `high`, the `randomInteger` function returns the following expression:

```
low + Math.floor((high - low + 1) * Math.random())
```

It is probably easiest to examine this expression from the inside out. The function call to `Math.random` returns a random number that can be as small as 0 but is always strictly less than 1. In mathematics, a range of real numbers that can be equal to one endpoint but not the other is called a ***half-open interval***. On a number

FIGURE 5-2 A simple random library

```
/*
 * File: RandomLib.js
 * -------------------
 * This file contains a simple library to support randomness.
 */

/*
 * Returns a random integer in the range low to high, inclusive.
 */
function randomInteger(low, high) {
   return low + Math.floor((high - low + 1) * Math.random());
}

/*
 * Returns a random real number in the half-open interval [low, high).
 */
function randomReal(low, high) {
   return low + (high - low) * Math.random();
}

/*
 * Returns true with probability p.  A missing argument defaults to 0.5.
 */
function randomChance(p = 0.5) {
   return Math.random() < p;
}

/*
 * Returns a random opaque color expressed as a string consisting of a "#"
 * followed by six random hexadecimal digits.
 */
function randomColor() {
   let str = "#";
   for (let i = 0; i < 6; i++) {
      let d = randomInteger(0, 15);
      switch (d) {
       case 0: case 1: case 2: case 3: case 4:
       case 5: case 6: case 7: case 8: case 9: str += d; break;
       case 10: str += "A"; break;
       case 11: str += "B"; break;
       case 12: str += "C"; break;
       case 13: str += "D"; break;
       case 14: str += "E"; break;
       case 15: str += "F"; break;
      }
   }
   return str;
}
```

line, a half-open interval is marked using an open circle to show that the endpoint is excluded, like this:

This text follows the standard conventions of mathematics by using square brackets to indicate closed ends of intervals and parentheses to indicate open ends. Thus, the notation [0, 1) indicates the half-open interval corresponding to this diagram.

The next step is to multiply the random value in the [0, 1) interval by the number of possible outcomes, which is given by the expression

```
(high - low + 1)
```

Having to add 1 after subtracting `low` from `high` might at first seem confusing, but this situation is analogous to the fencepost problem introduced in Chapter 1. Subtracting `low` from `high` gives the distance between these points, which therefore corresponds to the length of the fence. The number of possible outcomes is the number of integers covered by the range, keeping in mind that defining the range to be inclusive means that there is an integer—corresponding to a fencepost—at each end. In the die roll example, the length of the range is 5, but the number of possible outcomes is 6. Multiplying the result of `Math.random` by 6 produces a real number in the [0, 6) range, as follows:

The code for `randomInteger` then uses `Math.floor` to convert the real number to an integer by rounding it down to the next smallest whole number.

The last remaining step is to add the value of `low` so that the set of possible return values for `randomInteger` starts at the correct point, as illustrated on the following number line in which only the solid dots represent possible values:

The implementation of `randomReal` follows much the same strategy as the code for `randomInteger` but is simpler because it can leave out both the call to `Math.floor` and the adjustment of the range to avoid the fencepost problem, which does not apply when real numbers are involved. The code is therefore simply

```
function randomReal(low, high) {
    return low + (high - low) * Math.random();
}
```

The function `randomChance` is used to simulate random events that occur with some fixed probability. In accord with mathematical convention, a probability is represented as a number between 0 and 1, where 0 means that the event never occurs and 1 means that it always does. Calling `randomChance(p)` returns `true` with probability `p`, where the parameter `p` has a default value of 0.5. Thus, calling `randomChance(0.75)` returns `true` 75% of the time; calling `randomChance()` returns `true` 50% of the time. You can use `randomChance` to simulate flipping a coin, as illustrated by the following function, which returns `"heads"` or `"tails"` with equal probability:

```
function flipCoin() {
    return (randomChance() ? "heads" : "tails");
}
```

The only remaining function in the `RandomLib.js` library is `randomColor`, which returns a random color from the 16,777,216 opaque colors available in JavaScript. As described on page 125, JavaScript allows you to specify any of these colors using the standard web convention of writing a hashtag symbol (#) followed by six hexadecimal digits. Hexadecimal notation is discussed in detail in Chapter 7, but all you need to know to understand the implementation of `randomColor` is that hexadecimal notation augments the familiar digits 0 through 9 with the letters from **A** to **F**. The code for `randomColor` in Figure 5-2 initializes the variable `str` to the string `"#"` and then concatenates six additional characters to the end, randomly chosen from the 16 possible hexadecimal digits.

Using the `RandomLib.js` library

As an illustration of how clients might use the `RandomLib.js` library, the `Craps` function in Figure 5-3 plays the casino game called *craps*. The rules for craps appear in the comments at the beginning of the program. The code itself follows the outline imposed by the rules of the game. In particular, it rolls the dice initially and then chooses how to proceed according to the result of that first roll. Moreover, because the task of rolling two dice and determining their sum appears at different points in the program, it makes sense to make rolling two dice a separate function.

Although the `Craps` function is nondeterministic and will therefore produce different results each time, the following console log shows two possible outcomes:

```
                        JavaScript Console
> Craps();
Rolling dice:  5 + 6 = 11
That's a natural.   You win.
> Craps();
Rolling dice:  4 + 5 = 9
Your point is 9.
Rolling dice:  2 + 1 = 3
Rolling dice:  3 + 4 = 7
That's a 7.   You lose.
>
```

FIGURE 5-3 A program to play the casino game of Craps

```javascript
/*
 * File: Craps.js
 * --------------
 * This program plays the casino game of Craps.  At the beginning of
 * the game, the player rolls a pair of dice and computes the total.
 * If the total is 2, 3, or 12 (called "craps"), the player loses.
 * If the total is 7 or 11 (called a "natural"), the player wins.
 * If the total is any other number, that number becomes the "point."
 * From here, the player keeps rolling the dice until (a) the point
 * comes up again, in which case the player wins, or (b) a 7 appears,
 * in which case the player loses.  The numbers 2, 3, 11, and 12 no
 * longer have special significance after the first roll.
 */

"use strict";

function Craps() {
   let total = rollTwoDice();
   if (total === 7 || total === 11) {
      console.log("That's a natural.  You win.");
   } else if (total === 2 || total === 3 || total === 12) {
      console.log("That's craps.  You lose.");
   } else {
      let point = total;
      console.log("Your point is " + point + ".");
      let running = true;
      while (running) {
         total = rollTwoDice();
         if (total === point) {
            console.log("You made your point.  You win.");
            running = false;
         } else if (total === 7) {
            console.log("That's a 7.  You lose.");
            running = false;
         }
      }
   }
}

/*
 * Rolls two dice, displays their values, and returns their sum.
 */

function rollTwoDice() {
   let d1 = randomInteger(1, 6);
   let d2 = randomInteger(1, 6);
   let total = d1 + d2;
   console.log("Rolling dice: " + d1 + " + " + d2 + " = " + total);
   return total;
}
```

As a second example of a program that uses the `RandomLib.js` library, the `RandomCircles.js` program in Figure 5-4 displays circles of various random sizes, random colors, and random positions. The display will be different each time, but the code makes sure that the individual circles always fit inside the graphics window.

FIGURE 5-4 Program to display random circles on the screen

```
/*
 * File: RandomCircles.js
 * ----------------------
 * This program draws a set of 10 circles with different sizes, positions,
 * and colors.  Each circle has a randomly chosen color, a randomly chosen
 * radius within a specified range, and a randomly chosen position subject
 * to the condition that the circle must fit inside the graphics window.
 */

"use strict";

/* Constants */

const GWINDOW_WIDTH = 500;
const GWINDOW_HEIGHT = 300;
const N_CIRCLES = 10;
const MIN_RADIUS = 15;
const MAX_RADIUS = 50;

/* Main program */

function RandomCircles() {
   let gw = GWindow(GWINDOW_WIDTH, GWINDOW_HEIGHT);
   for (let i = 0; i < N_CIRCLES; i++) {
      gw.add(createRandomCircle());
   }
}

/*
 * Creates a randomly generated circle.  The radius is chosen randomly
 * between MIN_RADIUS and MAX_RADIUS, the location is chosen so that the
 * circle fits in the window, and the circle is given a random color.
 */

function createRandomCircle() {
   let r = randomReal(MIN_RADIUS, MAX_RADIUS);
   let x = randomReal(r, GWINDOW_WIDTH - r);
   let y = randomReal(r, GWINDOW_HEIGHT - r);
   let circle = GOval(x - r, y - r, 2 * r, 2 * r);
   circle.setFilled(true);
   circle.setColor(randomColor());
   return circle;
}
```

5.4 The mechanics of function calls

Although you can certainly get by with an intuitive understanding of how the function-calling process works, it helps to understand precisely what happens when one function calls another in JavaScript. The sections that follow describe the process in detail and then walk you through a simple example.

The steps in calling a function

Whenever a function call occurs, the JavaScript interpreter executes the following operations:

1. The calling function computes values for each argument using the bindings of local variables in its own context. Because the arguments are expressions, this computation can involve operators and other functions; the calling function evaluates these expressions before execution of the new function begins.

2. The system creates new space for all the local variables required by the new function, including any parameters. These variables are allocated together in a block, which is called a *stack frame.*

3. The value of each argument is copied into the corresponding parameter variable. For functions with more than one argument, these copies occur in order; the first argument is copied into the first parameter, and so forth. If there are more arguments than parameters, the extra argument values play no role in the initialization of the parameters. If there are more parameters than arguments, those parameters that don't have a corresponding argument are set to the value `undefined` or a default value, if one is specified.

4. The statements in the function body are executed until the program encounters a `return` statement or there are no more statements to execute.

5. The value of the `return` expression, if any, is evaluated and returned as the value of the function.

6. The stack frame created for this function call is discarded. In the process, all local variables disappear.

7. The calling program continues, with the returned value substituted in place of the call. The point to which the function returns is called the *return address.*

Although this process may seem to make at least some sense, you probably need to work through an example or two before you understand it fully. Reading through the example in the next section will give you some insight into the process, but it will be even more helpful to take one of your own programs and walk through it at the same level of detail. And while you can trace through a program on paper or a whiteboard, it may be best to get yourself a supply of 3×5 index cards and then use a card to represent each stack frame. The advantage of the index-card model is that you can create a stack of index cards that closely models the operation of the computer. Calling a function adds a card; returning from the function removes it.

The combinations function

The function-calling process is most easily illustrated in the context of a specific example. Suppose that you have a collection of six coins, which in the United States might be a penny, a nickel, a dime, a quarter, a half-dollar, and a dollar. Given those six coins, how many ways are there to choose two of them? As you can see from the full enumeration of the possibilities in Figure 5-5, the answer is 15. However, as a computer scientist, you should immediately think about the more general question: given a set containing *n* distinct elements, how many ways can you choose a subset with *k* elements? The answer to that question is computed by the ***combinations function*** $C(n, k)$, which is defined as follows:

$$C(n, k) = \frac{n!}{k! \times (n - k)!}$$

FIGURE 5-5   Illustration of the combinations function

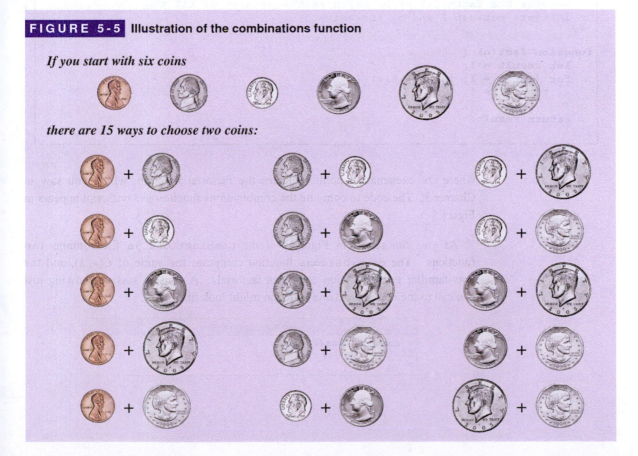

If you start with six coins

there are 15 ways to choose two coins:

FIGURE 5-6 JavaScript implementation of the mathememathical combinations function $C(n, k)$

```
/*
 * File: Combinations.js
 * -----------------------
 * This file exports an implementation of the mathematical combinations
 * function C(n, k), which is the number of ways of selecting k objects
 * from a set of n distinct objects.
 */

"use strict";

/*
 * Returns the mathematical combinations function C(n, k), which is
 * the number of ways one can choose k elements from a set of size n.
 */

function combinations(n, k) {
   return fact(n) / (fact(k) * fact(n - k));
}
/*
 * Returns the factorial of n, which is the product of all the
 * integers between 1 and n, inclusive.
 */

function fact(n) {
   let result = 1;
   for (let i = 1; i <= n; i++) {
      result *= i;
   }
   return result;
}
```

where the exclamation point indicates the factorial function, which you saw in Chapter 3. The code to compute the combinations function in JavaScript appears in Figure 5-6.

As you can see from Figure 5-6, the **Combinations.js** file contains two functions. The **combinations** function computes the value of $C(n, k)$, and the now-familiar **fact** function computes factorials. A console session showing just one call to the **combinations** function might look like this:

JavaScript Console
> combinations(6, 2)
15
>

Tracing the combinations function

While the `combinations` function is interesting in its own right, the purpose of the current example is to illustrate the steps involved in calling functions. When the user enters a function call in the console window, the JavaScript interpreter invokes the standard steps in the function-calling process.

As always, the first step is to evaluate the arguments in the current context. In this example, the arguments are the numbers 6 and 2, so the evaluation process simply keeps track of these two values.

The second step is to create a frame for the `combinations` function that contains space for the variables that are stored as part of that frame, which are the parameters and any variables that appear in declarations within the function. The `combinations` function has two parameters and no local variables, so the frame only requires enough space for the parameter variables `n` and `k`. After the JavaScript interpreter creates the frame, it copies the argument values into these variables in order. Thus, the parameter variable `n` is initialized to 6, and the parameter variable `k` is initialized to 2.

In the diagrams in this book, each stack frame appears as a rectangle surrounded by a double line. Each stack-frame diagram shows the code for the function along with a pointing-hand icon that makes it easy to keep track of the current execution point. The frame also contains labeled boxes for each of the local variables. The stack frame for the `combinations` function therefore looks like this after the parameters have been initialized but before execution of the function begins:

```
function combinations (n, k) {
☞ return fact (n) / ( fact (k) * fact (n - k) );
}
                               n        k
                              ┌────┐   ┌────┐
                              │ 6  │   │ 2  │
                              └────┘   └────┘
```

To compute the value of the `combinations` function, the program must make three calls to the function `fact`. In JavaScript, function calls are evaluated from left to right, so the first call is the one to `fact(n)`, as follows:

```
function combinations (n, k) {
    return │fact (n)│ / ( fact (k) * fact (n - k) );
}
                               n        k
                              ┌────┐   ┌────┐
                              │ 6  │   │ 2  │
                              └────┘   └────┘
```

To evaluate this function, the system must create yet another stack frame, this time for the function `fact` with an argument value of 6. The frame for `fact` has both parameters and local variables. The parameter **n** is initialized to the value of the calling argument and therefore has the value 6. The two local variables, **i** and **result**, have not yet been initialized and therefore contain the value **undefined**, which is indicated in stack diagrams as an empty box. The new frame for **fact** gets stacked on top of the old one, which allows the JavaScript interpreter to remember the values in the earlier stack frame, even though they are not currently visible. The situation after creating the new frame and initializing the parameters looks like this:

```
function combinations(n, k) {
    function fact(n) {
   ☞ let result = 1;
        for (let i = 1; i <= n; i++) {
            result *= i;
        }
        return result;
    }
}
```

n	result	i
6		

The system then executes the statements in the function **fact**. In this instance, the body of the **for** loop is executed six times. On each cycle, the value of **result** is multiplied by the loop index **i**, which means that it will eventually hold the value 720 ($1\times2\times3\times4\times5\times6$, or 6!). When the program reaches the **return** statement, the stack frame looks like this:

```
function combinations(n, k) {
    function fact(n) {
        let result = 1;
        for (let i = 1; i <= n; i++) {
            result *= i;
        }
   ☞ return result;
    }
}
```

n	result	i
6	720	7

Returning from a function involves copying the value of the **return** expression (in this case the local variable **result**), to the point at which the call occurred. The frame for **fact** is then discarded, which leads to the following configuration:

```
function combinations(n, k) {
    return fact(n) / ( fact(k) * fact(n - k) );
}
             └─720
```

n	k
6	2

The next step in the process is to make a second call to **fact**, this time with the argument **k**. In the calling frame, **k** has the value 2. That value is then used to initialize the parameter **n** in the new stack frame, as follows:

```
function combinations (n, k) {
  function fact (n) {
    ☞ let result = 1;
      for (let i = 1; i <= n; i++) {
         result *= i;
      }
      return result;              n        result    i
  }                               2
```

The computation of **fact(2)** is easier to perform in one's head than the earlier call to **fact(6)**. This time around, the value of **result** will be 2, which is then returned to the calling frame, like this:

```
function combinations (n, k) {
    return fact (n) / ( fact (k) * fact (n - k) );
}
        └─ 720        └─ 2
                                    n        k
                                    6        2
```

The code for **combinations** makes one more call to **fact**, this time with the argument **n - k**. Evaluating this call therefore creates a new stack frame with n equal to 4:

```
function combinations (n, k) {
  function fact (n) {
    ☞ let result = 1;
      for (let i = 1; i <= n; i++) {
         result *= i;
      }
      return result;              n        result    i
  }                               4
```

The value of **fact(4)** is $1 \times 2 \times 3 \times 4$, or 24. When this call returns, the system is able to fill in the last of the missing values in the calculation, as follows:

```
function combinations (n, k) {
    return fact (n) / ( fact (k) * fact (n - k) );
}
        └─ 720        └─ 2         └─ 24
                                    n        k
                                    6        2
```

The computer then divides 720 by the product of 2 and 24 to get the answer 15. This value is returned to the JavaScript interpreter running in the JavaScript console window. The interpreter prints that value on the console, like this:

```
                    JavaScript Console
> combinations(6, 2)
15
>
```

5.5 Recursive functions

The `Combinations.js` program includes a simple implementation of a function to compute factorials, which looks like this:

```
function fact(n) {
    let result = 1;
    for (let i = 1; i <= n; i++) {
        result *= i;
    }
    return result;
}
```

This implementation uses a `for` loop to cycle through the integers between 1 and `n`. Strategies based on looping are said to be *iterative.* Functions like `fact`, however, can also be implemented using a distinctly different approach that requires no loops at all. This strategy is called *recursion,* which is the process of solving a problem by breaking it down into simpler problems of the same form.

A recursive formulation of `fact`

The iterative implementation of `fact` does not take advantage of an important mathematical property of factorials. Each factorial is related to the factorial of the next smaller integer in the following way:

$$n! = n \times (n-1)!$$

Thus, 4! is 4 × 3!, 3! is 3 × 2!, and so on. To make sure that this process stops at some point, mathematicians define 0! to be 1. Thus, the conventional mathematical definition of the factorial function looks like this:

$$n! = \begin{cases} 1 & \text{if } n = 0 \\ n \times (n-1)! & \text{otherwise} \end{cases}$$

This definition is recursive, because it defines the factorial of n in terms of a simpler instance of the factorial function: finding the factorial of $n-1$. The new problem has the same form as the original, which is the fundamental characteristic of recursion. You can then use the same process to define $(n-1)!$ in terms of $(n-2)!$. Moreover, you can carry this process forward step by step until the solution is expressed in terms of 0!, which is equal to 1 by definition.

From your perspective as a programmer, the most important consequence of the definition from mathematics is that it provides a template for a recursive solution. In JavaScript, you can implement the `fact` function as follows:

```
function fact(n) {
   if (n === 0) {
      return 1;
   } else {
      return n * fact(n - 1);
   }
}
```

If `n` is 0, the result of `fact` is 1. If not, the implementation computes the result by calling `fact(n - 1)` and then multiplying the result by `n`. This implementation follows directly from the mathematical definition of the factorial function and has precisely the same recursive structure.

Tracing the recursive process

If you work from the mathematical definition, writing the recursive implementation of `fact` is straightforward. On the other hand, even though the definition is easy to write, the brevity of the solution may seem suspicious. When you are learning about recursion for the first time, the recursive implementation of `fact` seems to leave something out. Even though it clearly reflects the mathematical definition, the recursive formulation makes it hard to identify where the actual computational steps occur. When you call `fact`, for example, you want the computer to give you the answer. In the recursive implementation, all you see is a formula that transforms one call to `fact` into another one. Because the steps in that calculation are not explicit, it seems somewhat magical when the computer gets the right answer.

If you trace through the logic the computer uses to evaluate any function call, however, you discover that no magic is involved. When the computer evaluates a call to the recursive `fact` function, it goes through the same process it uses to evaluate any other function call.

To visualize the process, suppose that you have executed the statement

```
console.log("fact(4) = " + fact(4));
```

To evaluate the argument to `console.log`, JavaScript calls `fact`, which requires creating a new stack frame and copying the argument 4 into the formal parameter `n`. The frame for `fact` temporarily supersedes the frame for the original call, as shown in the following diagram:

```
console.log("fact(4) = " + fact(4));
function fact(n) {
☞ if (n === 0) {
      return 1;
   } else {
      return n * fact(n - 1);
   }
}
```
```
n
4
```

The computer now begins to evaluate the body of the function, starting with the `if` statement. Because `n` is not equal to 0, control proceeds to the `else` clause, where the program must evaluate and return the value of the expression

$$n * fact(n - 1)$$

Evaluating this expression requires computing the value of `fact(n - 1)`, which introduces a recursive call. When that call returns, all the program has to do is multiply the result by `n`. It is therefore possible to diagram the current state of the computation as follows:

```
console.log("fact(4) = " + fact(4));
function fact(n) {
   if (n === 0) {
      return 1;
   } else {
      return n * fact(n - 1);
   }
}
```
```
n
4
```
?

The next step in the computation is to evaluate the call to `fact(n - 1)`, beginning with the argument expression. Because the current value of `n` is 4, the argument expression `n - 1` has the value 3. The computer then creates a new frame for `fact` in which the formal parameter is initialized to this value. Thus, the next frame looks like this:

```
console.log("fact(4) = " + fact(4));
function fact(n) {
function fact(n) {
☞ if (n === 0) {
      return 1;
   } else {
      return n * fact(n - 1);
   }
}
```
```
n
3
```

There are now two frames labeled `fact`. In the most recent one, the computer is just starting to calculate `fact(3)`. This new frame hides the previous frame for `fact(4)`, which will not reappear until the `fact(3)` computation is complete.

Computing `fact(3)` again begins by testing the value of **n**. Since **n** is still not 0, the `else` clause instructs the computer to evaluate `fact(n - 1)`. As before, this process requires the creation of a new stack frame evaluating `fact(2)`. Following the same logic, the program must then call `fact(1)`, which in turn calls `fact(0)`, creating a total of three new stack frames, as follows:

```
console.log("fact(4) = " + fact(4));
  function fact(n) {
    function fact(n) {
      function fact(n) {
        function fact(n) {
          function fact(n) {
            ☞ if (n === 0) {
              return 1;
            } else {
              return n * fact(n - 1);     n
            }                             ┌───┐
          }                              │ 0 │
        }                                └───┘
```

At this point, however, the situation changes. Because the value of **n** is 0, the function can return its result immediately by executing the statement

```
return 1;
```

This statement returns the value 1 to the calling frame, which resumes its position on top of the stack, as shown:

```
console.log("fact(4) = " + fact(4));
  function fact(n) {
    function fact(n) {
      function fact(n) {
        function fact(n) {
          if (n === 0) {
            return 1;
          } else {
            return n * fact(n - 1);     n
          }                    ↑       ┌───┐
        }                     └─1     │ 1 │
      }                               └───┘
```

From this point, the computation proceeds back through each of the recursive calls, completing the calculation of the return value at each level. In this frame, for example, the call to `fact(n - 1)` can be replaced by the value 1, as shown in the diagram for the stack frame. In this stack frame, n has the value 1, so the result of this call is simply 1. This result gets propagated back to its caller, as shown in the following diagram:

```
console.log("fact(4) = " + fact(4));
function fact(n) {
  function fact(n) {
    function fact(n) {
      if (n === 0) {
        return 1;
      } else {
        return n * fact(n - 1);      n
      }                         1      2
    }
  }
}
```

Because n is now 2, evaluating the **return** statement causes the value 2 to be passed back to the preceding level, as follows:

```
console.log("fact(4) = " + fact(4));
function fact(n) {
  function fact(n) {
    if (n === 0) {
      return 1;
    } else {
      return n * fact(n - 1);      n
    }                         2      3
  }
}
```

At this stage, the program returns 3 × 2 to the preceding level, so that the frame for the initial call to `fact` looks like this:

```
console.log("fact(4) = " + fact(4));
function fact(n) {
  if (n === 0) {
    return 1;
  } else {
    return n * fact(n - 1);      n
  }                         6      4
}
```

The final step in the process consists of calculating 4 × 6 and returning the value 24 to the initial call.

The recursive leap of faith

The point of including the trace of the `fact(4)` computation is to convince you that JavaScript treats a recursive function just like any other function. When you are faced with a recursive function, you can—at least in theory—mimic the operation of the computer and figure out what it will do. By drawing all the frames and keeping track of all the variables, you can duplicate the entire operation and come up with the answer. If you do so, however, you will usually find that the complexity of the process ends up making the computation harder to follow.

Whenever you try to understand a recursive program, it is useful to put the underlying details aside and focus instead on a single level of the operation. At that level, you are allowed to assume that any recursive call automatically gets the right answer as long as the arguments are simpler than the original ones. This psychological strategy—assuming that any simpler recursive call will work correctly—is called the ***recursive leap of faith.*** Learning to apply this strategy is essential to using recursion in practical applications.

As an example, consider what happens if you call `fact(n)` with n equal to 4. The recursive implementation must compute the value of the expression

```
n * fact(n - 1)
```

Replacing n with its value and then evaluating n - 1 makes it clear that the result is

```
4 * fact(3)
```

Stop right there. Computing `fact(3)` is simpler than computing `fact(4)`. Because it is simpler, the recursive leap of faith allows you to assume that it works. Thus, you should assume that the call to `fact(3)` will correctly compute the value of 3!, which is 3 × 2 × 1, or 6. The value of `fact(4)` is therefore 4 × 6, or 24.

The Fibonacci function

In a mathematical treatise entitled *Liber Abbaci* published in 1202, the Italian mathematician Leonardo Fibonacci proposed a problem that has had a wide influence on many fields, including computer science. The problem was phrased as an exercise in population biology—a field that has become increasingly important in recent years. Fibonacci's problem concerns how the population of rabbits would grow from generation to generation if the rabbits reproduced according to the following, admittedly fanciful, rules:

- Each pair of fertile rabbits produces a new pair of offspring each month.
- Rabbits become fertile in their second month of life.
- Old rabbits never die.

If a pair of newborn rabbits is introduced in January, how many pairs of rabbits are there at the end of the year?

You can solve Fibonacci's problem simply by keeping a count of the rabbits at each month during the year. At the beginning of January, there are no rabbits, since the first pair is introduced sometime in that month, which leaves one pair of rabbits on February 1st. Because the initial pair of rabbits is newborn, they are not yet fertile in February, which means that the only rabbits on March 1st are the original pair of rabbits. In March, however, the original pair is now of reproductive age, which means that a new pair of rabbits is born. The new pair increases the colony's population—counting by pairs—to two on April 1st. In April, the original pair goes right on reproducing, but the rabbits born in March are as yet too young. Thus, there are three pairs of rabbits at the beginning of May. From here on, with more rabbits becoming fertile each month, the rabbit population begins to explode.

Computing terms in the Fibonacci sequence

At this point, it is useful to record the population data so far as a sequence of terms, indicated by the subscripted value t_i, each of which shows the number of rabbit pairs at the beginning of the ith month from the start of the experiment on January 1st. The sequence itself is called the *Fibonacci sequence* and begins with the following terms, which represent the results of our calculation so far:

t_0	t_1	t_2	t_3	t_4
0	1	1	2	3

You can simplify the computation of further terms in this sequence by making an important observation. Because in this problem pairs of rabbits never die, all the rabbits that were around in the previous month are still around. Moreover, every pair of fertile rabbits has produced a new pair. The number of fertile rabbit pairs capable of reproduction is simply the number of rabbits that were alive in the month before the previous one. The net effect is that each new term in the sequence must simply be the sum of the preceding two. Thus, the next several terms in the Fibonacci sequence look like this:

t_0	t_1	t_2	t_3	t_4	t_5	t_6	t_7	t_8	t_9	t_{10}	t_{11}	t_{12}
0	1	1	2	3	5	8	13	21	34	55	89	144

The number of rabbit pairs at the end of the year is therefore 144.

From a programming perspective, it helps to express the rule for generating new terms in the following more mathematical form:

$$t_n = t_{n-1} + t_{n-2}$$

An expression of this type, in which each element of a sequence is defined in terms of earlier elements, is called a ***recurrence relation.***

The recurrence relation alone is not sufficient to define the Fibonacci sequence. Although the formula makes it easy to calculate new terms in the sequence, the process has to start somewhere. In order to apply the formula, you need to have at least two terms already available, which means that the first two terms in the sequence—t_0 and t_1—must be defined explicitly. The complete specification of the terms in the Fibonacci sequence is therefore

$$t_n = \begin{cases} n & \text{if } n \text{ is 0 or 1} \\ t_{n-1} + t_{n-2} & \text{otherwise} \end{cases}$$

This mathematical formulation is an ideal model for a recursive implementation of a function `fib(n)` that computes the nth term in the Fibonacci sequence. All you need to do is plug the simple cases and the recurrence relation into the standard recursive paradigm. The recursive implementation of `fib(n)` looks like this:

```
function fib(n) {
    if (n === 0 || n === 1) {
        return n;
    } else {
        return fib(n - 1) + fib(n - 2);
    }
}
```

Gaining confidence in the recursive implementation

Now that you have a recursive implementation of the function `fib`, how can you go about convincing yourself that it works? You can always begin by tracing through the logic. Consider, for example, what happens if you call `fib(5)`. Because this is not one of the simple cases enumerated in the `if` statement, the implementation computes the result by evaluating the line

```
return fib(n - 1) + fib(n - 2);
```

which in this case is equivalent to

```
return fib(4) + fib(3);
```

At this point, the computer calculates the result of `fib(4)`, adds that to the result of calling `fib(3)`, and returns the sum as the value of `fib(5)`.

But how does the computer evaluate `fib(4)` and `fib(3)`? The answer, of course, is that it uses precisely the same strategy it did to calculate `fib(5)`. The essence of recursion is to break problems down into simpler ones that can be solved by calls to exactly the same function. Those calls get broken down into simpler ones, which in turn get broken down into even simpler ones, until at last the simple cases are reached.

On the other hand, it is best to regard this entire mechanism as irrelevant detail. Instead, just remember the recursive leap of faith. Your job at this level is to understand how the call to **fib(5)** works. In the course of walking though the execution of that function, you have managed to transform the problem into computing the sum of **fib(4)** and **fib(3)**. Because the argument values are smaller, each of these calls represents a simpler case. Applying the recursive leap of faith, you can assume that the program correctly computes each of these values, without going through all the steps yourself. For the purposes of validating the recursive strategy, you can just look the answers up in the table: **fib(4)** is 3 and **fib(3)** is 2. The result of calling **fib(5)** is therefore $3 + 2$, or 5, which is indeed the correct answer. Case closed. You don't need to see all the details, which are best left to the computer.

Efficiency of the recursive implementation

However, if you do decide to go through the details of the evaluation of the call to **fib(5)**, you will quickly discover that the calculation is extremely inefficient. The recursive decomposition makes many redundant calls, in which the computer ends up calculating the same term in the Fibonacci sequence several times. This situation is illustrated in Figure 5-7 at the top of the next page, which shows the recursive calls required in the calculation of **fib(5)**. As you can see from the diagram, the program ends up making one call to **fib(4)**, two calls to **fib(3)**, three calls to **fib(2)**, five calls to **fib(1)**, and three calls to **fib(0)**. Given that the Fibonacci function can be implemented efficiently using iteration, the explosion of steps required by the recursive implementation is more than a little disturbing.

On discovering that the simple recursive implementation of **fib(n)** is highly inefficient, many people are tempted to point their finger at recursion as the culprit. The problem in the Fibonacci example, however, has nothing to do with recursion *per se* but rather with the way in which recursion is used. By adopting a different strategy, it is possible to write a recursive implementation of the **fib** function in which the large-scale inefficiencies revealed in Figure 5-7 disappear completely.

As is often the case when using recursion, the key to finding a more efficient solution lies in adopting a more general approach. The Fibonacci sequence is not the only sequence whose terms are defined by the recurrence relation

$$t_n = t_{n-1} + t_{n-2}$$

FIGURE 5-7 Steps in the calculation of `fib(5)`

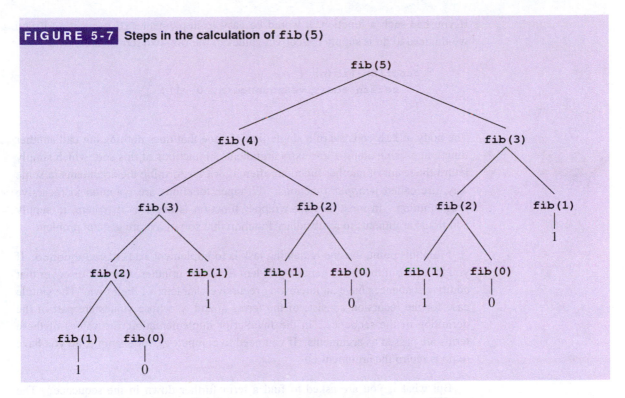

Depending on how you choose the first two terms, you can generate many different sequences. The traditional Fibonacci sequence

$$0, 1, 1, 2, 3, 5, 8, 13, 21, 34, 55, 89, 144, \ldots$$

comes from defining $t_0 = 0$ and $t_1 = 1$. If, for example, you defined $t_0 = 3$ and $t_1 = 7$, you would get this sequence instead:

$$3, 7, 10, 17, 27, 44, 71, 115, 186, 301, 487, 788, 1275, \ldots$$

Both sequences use the same recurrence relation, which specifies that each new term is the sum of the preceding two. The only way the sequences differ is in the choice of the first two terms. As a general class, sequences that follow this pattern are called *additive sequences.*

This concept of an additive sequence makes it possible to convert the problem of finding the nth term in the Fibonacci sequence into the more general problem of finding the nth term in an additive sequence whose initial terms are t_0 and t_1. Such a function requires three arguments and might be expressed in JavaScript as a function with the following header line:

```
function additiveSequence(n, t0, t1)
```

If you had such a function, it would be easy to implement `fib` using it. All you would need to do is supply the correct values of the first two terms, as follows:

```
function fib(n) {
    return additiveSequence(n, 0, 1);
}
```

The body of `fib` consists of a single line of code that does nothing but call another function, passing along a few extra arguments. Functions of this sort, which simply return the result of another function, often after transforming the arguments in some way, are called **wrapper** functions. Wrapper functions are common in recursive programming. In most cases, a wrapper function is used, as it is here, to supply additional arguments to a subsidiary function that solves a more general problem.

From this point, the one remaining task is to implement `additiveSequence`. If you think about this more general problem for a few minutes, you will discover that additive sequences have an interesting recursive character of their own. The simple case for the recursion consists of the terms t_0 and t_1, whose values are part of the definition of the sequence. In the JavaScript implementation, the values of these terms are passed as arguments. If you need to compute t_0, for example, all you have to do is return the argument `t0`.

But what if you are asked to find a term further down in the sequence? The recurisve insight you need is that the nth term in any additive sequence is simply the $n-1^{st}$ term in the additive sequence that begins one step further along. This insight makes it possible to implement the function `additiveSequence` as follows:

```
function additiveSequence(n, t0, t1) {
    if (n === 0) return t0;
    if (n === 1) return t1;
    return additiveSequence(n - 1, t1, t0 + t1);
}
```

If you trace through the steps in the calculation of `fib(5)` using this technique, you will discover that the calculation involves none of the redundant computation that made the earlier recursive formulation so inefficient. The steps lead directly to the solution, as shown in the following diagram:

```
fib(5)
  = additiveSequence(5, 0, 1)
    = additiveSequence(4, 1, 1)
      = additiveSequence(3, 1, 2)
        = additiveSequence(2, 2, 3)
          = additiveSequence(1, 3, 5)
            = 5
```

Even though the new implementation is entirely recursive, it is comparable in efficiency to the traditional iterative version of the Fibonacci function. In fact, it is possible to use more sophisticated mathematics to write a recursive implementation of `fib(n)` that is considerably more efficient than the iterative strategy. You will have a chance to code this implementation in the exercises for Chapter 10.

 Summary

In this chapter, you learned about *functions*, which enable you to refer to an entire set of operations with a single name. More importantly, by allowing the programmer to ignore the internal details and concentrate only on the effect of a function as a whole, functions provide a critical tool for reducing the conceptual complexity of programs.

The important points introduced in this chapter include:

- A *function* consists of a set of program statements that have been collected together and given a name. Other parts of the program can then *call* that function, possibly passing it information in the form of *arguments* and receiving a result *returned* by that function.

- A function that returns a value must have a `return` statement that specifies the result. Functions may return values of any type.

- Functions that return Boolean values are called *predicate functions*. Because you can use the result of such functions to specify a condition in an `if` or a `while` statement, predicate functions play an important role in programming.

- Variables declared within a function are local to that function and cannot be used outside it. Internally, all the variables declared within a function are stored together in a *stack frame*.

- *Parameters* are local variables that act as placeholders for the argument values. JavaScript initializes the parameter variables by copying the argument values in the order in which they appear. If there are more arguments than parameters, the extra ones are ignored; any extra parameters are set to `undefined` or a default value specified in the parameter list.

- When a function returns, it continues from precisely the point at which the call was made. Computer scientists refer to this point as the *return address*.

- You can create your own libraries by collecting the necessary code in a file whose name ends with the standard `.js` file type. You can then use the entries exported by this library by including the appropriate `<script>` tag in the HTML file.

- In understanding the concept of a library, it is useful to differentiate the roles of the *client,* who uses the library, and the *implementer,* who writes the necessary code. The shared understanding between the client and the implementer is called the *interface.*

- Figure 5-2 shows the code for the `RandomLib.js` library, which exports a set of functions for working with programs that simulate random behavior.

- JavaScript's implementation of function calls makes it possible for a function to call itself, because the local variables for each call are stored in different stack frames. Functions that call themselves are said to be *recursive.*

- Before you can use recursion effectively, you must learn to limit your analysis to a single level of the recursive decomposition and to rely on the correctness of all simpler recursive calls without tracing through the entire computation. Trusting these simpler calls to work correctly is often called the *recursive leap of faith.*

- Mathematical functions often express their recursive nature in the form of a *recurrence relation,* in which each new element in a sequence is defined in terms of earlier elements.

- Although some recursive functions may be less efficient than their iterative counterparts, recursion itself is not the problem. As is typical with all types of algorithms, some recursive strategies are more efficient than others.

- In order to ensure that recursive decomposition produces subproblems that are identical in form to the original, it is sometimes useful to generalize the problem. In such cases, the function exported to clients is often a *wrapper function* whose only purpose is to call a second function that implements the more general case.

Review questions

1. Define the following terms as they apply to functions: *call, argument, return.*

2. How do you specify the result of a function in JavaScript?

3. Can there be more than one `return` statement in the body of a function?

4. What is a *predicate function?*

5. Describe the differences between the roles of *client* and *implementer.*

6. What is an *interface?*

7. What four functions are exported by the `RandomLib.js` library?

8. How do you gain access to the facilities provided by the `RandomLib.js` library from some other program file?

9. What is a *half-open interval?* How is such an interval usually represented in mathematics?

10. How would you use the `randomInteger` function to generate a randomly chosen integer between 1 and 100?

11. By going through the code by hand, determine whether the `randomInteger` function works with negative arguments. What are the possible results of calling the function `randomInteger(-5, 5)`?

12. If you ran the `RandomCircle.js` program shown in Figure 5-4, you would expect to see 10 circles on the graphics window because `N_CIRCLES` has the value 10. In fact, you sometimes see fewer circles. Why might this be?

13. Describe the rules by which JavaScript assigns argument values to parameters.

14. Variables declared within a function are called *local variables.* What is the significance of the word *local* in this context?

15. What is a *stack frame?*

16. What do computer scientists mean by the term *return address?*

17. Describe the difference between the strategies of *iteration* and *recursion.*

18. What is meant by the phrase *recursive leap of faith?* Why is this concept important for you as a programmer?

19. In the section entitled "Tracing the recursive process," the text goes through a long analysis of what happens internally when `fact(4)` is called. Using this section as a model, trace the execution of `fib(3)`, sketching out each stack frame created in the process.

20. What is a *recurrence relation?*

21. How many times is `fib(1)` called if you compute `fib(10)` using the recursive implementation on page 183?

22. What is a *wrapper function?* Why are wrapper functions often useful in writing recursive functions?

Exercises

1. In contrast to most languages, JavaScript has few built-in facilities to support the creation of formatted tables, such as those in which numbers line up nicely in columns. To create this kind of formatted table, it is useful to create a library

AlignLib.js that contains the functions **alignLeft**, **alignRight** (which appears in Chapter 3) and **alignCenter**, each of which takes a value and a width and returns the value aligned appropriately within a field of that size. In each case, you need to convert the value to a string, and then add spaces on the back, front, or alternately on both ends until the string has the desired length. If the number of extra spaces needed is odd, you will have to make some decision as to how **alignCenter** operates. The comments associated with the function should document your decision.

2. Write a function **randomAverage(n)** that generates **n** random real numbers between 0 and 1 and then returns the average of those **n** values. Statistically, calling **randomAverage(n)** will produce results that become closer to 0.5 as the value of **n** increases. Write a main program that displays the result of calling **randomAverage** on 1, 10, 100, 1000, 10000, 100000, and 1000000.

3. *Heads. . . .*
    Heads. . . .
    Heads. . . .
    A weaker man might be moved to re-examine his faith, if in nothing else at least in the law of probability.

    —Tom Stoppard, *Rosencrantz and Guildenstern Are Dead,* 1967

    Write a function **consecutiveHeads(numberNeeded)** that simulates tossing a coin repeatedly until the specified number of heads appear consecutively. At that point, your program should display a line on the console that indicates how many coin tosses were needed to complete the process. The following console log shows one possible execution of the program:

    ```
    JavaScript Console
    > consecutiveHeads(3);
    Tails
    Heads
    Heads
    Tails
    Heads
    Heads
    Heads
    It took 7 tosses to get 3 consecutive heads.
    >
    ```

4. *I shall never believe that God plays dice with the world.*

    —Albert Einstein, 1947

    Despite Einstein's metaphysical objections, the current models of physics, and particularly of quantum theory, strongly suggest that nature does indeed involve random processes. A radioactive atom, for example, does not decay for any specific reason that we mortals understand. Instead, that atom has a probability of decaying randomly within a particular period of time.

Because physicists consider radioactive decay a random process, it is not surprising that random numbers can be used to simulate it. Suppose you start with a collection of atoms, each of which has a certain probability of decaying in any unit of time. You can then approximate the decay process by taking each atom in turn and deciding randomly whether it decays.

Write a function `simulateRadioactiveDecay` that models the process of radioactive decay. The first parameter is the initial population of atoms; the second is the probability that any of those atoms will decay within a year. For example, calling

```
simulateRadioactiveDecay(10000, 0.5)
```

simulates what happens over time to a sample that contains 10,000 atoms of some radioactive material, where each atom has a 50 percent chance of decaying in a year. Your function should produce a trace on the console showing how many atoms remain at the end of each year until all of the atoms have decayed. For example, the output of your function might look like this:

```
JavaScript Console
> simulateRadioactiveDecay(10000, 0.5);
There are 4916 atoms at the end of year 1.
There are 2430 atoms at the end of year 2.
There are 1228 atoms at the end of year 3.
There are 637 atoms at the end of year 4.
There are 335 atoms at the end of year 5.
There are 163 atoms at the end of year 6.
There are 93 atoms at the end of year 7.
There are 46 atoms at the end of year 8.
There are 18 atoms at the end of year 9.
There are 8 atoms at the end of year 10.
There are 2 atoms at the end of year 11.
There is 1 atom at the end of year 12.
There are 0 atoms at the end of year 13.
>
```

As the numbers indicate, roughly half the atoms in the sample decay each year. In physics, the conventional way to express this observation is to say that the sample has a *half-life* of one year.

5. Random numbers offer an interesting strategy for approximating the value of π. Imagine that you have a dartboard hanging on your wall that consists of a circle painted on a square backdrop, as in the following diagram:

What happens if you throw a sequence of darts completely randomly, ignoring any darts that miss the board altogether? Some of the darts will fall inside the colored circle, but some will be outside the circle in the white corners of the square. If the throws are random, the ratio of the number of darts landing inside the circle to the total number of darts hitting the square should be approximately equal to the ratio between the two areas. The ratio of the areas is independent of the actual size of the dartboard, as illustrated by the formula

$$\frac{darts\ falling\ inside\ the\ circle}{darts\ falling\ inside\ the\ square} \cong \frac{area\ inside\ the\ circle}{area\ inside\ the\ square} = \frac{\pi r^2}{4r^2} = \frac{\pi}{4}$$

To simulate this process in a program, imagine that the dartboard is drawn on the standard Cartesian coordinate plane with its center at the origin and a radius of 1 unit. The process of throwing a dart randomly at the square can be modeled by generating two random numbers, x and y, each of which lies between −1 and +1. This (x, y) point always lies somewhere inside the square. The point (x, y) lies inside the circle if

$$\sqrt{x^2 + y^2} < 1$$

This condition, however, can be simplified considerably by squaring each side of the inequality, which yields the following more efficient test:

$$x^2 + y^2 < 1$$

If you perform this simulation many times and compute what fraction of the darts falls inside the circle, the result will be an approximation of $\pi/4$.

Write a program that simulates throwing 10,000 darts and then uses the results to display an approximate value of π. Don't worry if your answer is correct only in the first few digits. The strategy used in this problem is not particularly accurate, even though it occasionally proves useful as an approximation technique. In mathematics, this technique is called **Monte Carlo integration,** after the capital city of Monaco, famous for its casinos.

6.   The combinations function $C(n, k)$ determines the number of ways you can choose k values from a set of n elements, ignoring the order of the elements. If the order of the value matters—so that, in the case of the coin example, choosing a penny and then a dime is seen as distinct from choosing a dime and then a penny—you need to use a different function, which computes the number of **permutations,** which are all the ways of ordering k elements taken from a collection of size n. This function is denoted as $P(n, k)$, and has the following mathematical formulation:

$$P(n, k) = \frac{n!}{(n-k)!}$$

Although this definition is mathematically correct, it is not well suited to implementation in practice because the factorials involved quickly get much too large. For example, if you use this formula to calculate the number of ways to select two cards from a standard 52-card deck (assuming that the order matters), you would end up trying to evaluate the following fraction:

$$\frac{80{,}658{,}175{,}170{,}943{,}878{,}571{,}660{,}636{,}856{,}403{,}766{,}975{,}289{,}505{,}440{,}883{,}277{,}824{,}000{,}000{,}000{,}000}{30{,}414{,}093{,}201{,}713{,}378{,}043{,}612{,}608{,}166{,}064{,}768{,}844{,}377{,}641{,}568{,}960{,}512{,}000{,}000{,}000{,}000}$$

even though the answer is the much more manageable 2652 (52 × 51).

Write a function **permutations(n, k)** that computes the $P(n, k)$ function without calling the **fact** function. Part of your job in this problem is to figure out how to compute this value efficiently. To do so, you will probably find it useful to play around with some relatively small values to get a sense of how the factorials in the numerator and denominator of the formula behave.

7. The values of the combinations function $C(n, k)$ described in this chapter are often displayed using a triangular arrangement that begins

$$C(0, 0)$$

$$C(1, 0) \quad C(1, 1)$$

$$C(2, 0) \quad C(2, 1) \quad C(2, 2)$$

$$C(3, 0) \quad C(3, 1) \quad C(3, 2) \quad C(3, 3)$$

$$C(4, 0) \quad C(4, 1) \quad C(4, 2) \quad C(4, 3) \quad C(4, 4)$$

$$C(5, 0) \quad C(5, 1) \quad C(5, 2) \quad C(5, 3) \quad C(5, 4) \quad C(5, 5)$$

and then continues for as many rows as desired. This figure is called *Pascal's Triangle* after its inventor, the seventeenth-century French mathematician Blaise Pascal. Pascal's Triangle has the interesting property that every interior entry is the sum of the two entries above it.

Write a function **displayPascalTriangle(n)** that displays Pascal's Triangle from row 0 up to row **n**, as shown in the following console log:

```
                        JavaScript Console
> displayPascalTriangle(9);
                        1
                    1       1
                1       2       1
            1       3       3       1
        1       4       6       4       1
    1       5      10      10       5       1
  1     6      15      20      15       6      1
 1    7     21     35      35      21      7     1
1   8    28    56      70      56      28     8    1
1  9   36   84    126    126      84    36    9    1
>
```

The interesting challenge in this assignment is aligning the output, for which the various functions you wrote for exercise 1 will come in handy.

8. The fact that every entry in Pascal's Triangle is the sum of the two entries above it makes it possible to calculate $C(n, k)$ recursively. Use this insight to write a recursive implementation of the `combinations` function without using any loops or calls to `fact`.

9. Spherical objects, such as cannonballs, can be stacked to form a pyramid with one cannonball at the top, sitting on top of a square composed of four cannonballs, sitting on top of a square composed of nine cannonballs, and so forth. Write a recursive function `cannonball` that takes as its argument the height of the pyramid and returns the number of cannonballs it contains. Your function must operate recursively and must not use any iterative constructs, such as `while` or `for`.

10. Rewrite the `fib` function so that it operates iteratively rather than recursively.

11. Rewrite the `digitSum` function from page 93 so that it operates recursively instead of iteratively. To do so, you need to identify both the simple cases and the necessary recursive insight.

12. Rewrite the `gcd` function that uses Euclid's algorithm shown on page 107 so that it computes the greatest common divisor recursively using the following rules:

   - If y is zero, then x is the greatest common divisor.

   - Otherwise, the greatest common divisor of x and y is always equal to the greatest common divisor of y and the remainder of x divided by y.

CHAPTER 6
Writing Interactive Programs

Quit worrying about failure. Failure's easy. Worry about
if you're successful, because then you have to deal with it.

— Adele Goldberg, interview with John Mashey, 2010

Adele Goldberg (1945–)

(Ann E. Yow-Dyson/Archive Photos/Getty Images)

Adele Goldberg received her Ph.D. in Information Science from the University of Chicago and took a research position at the Xerox Palo Alto Research Center (PARC), which introduced the graphical user interface—an idea that has since become central to modern computing. Together with others in the Learning Research Group at PARC, Goldberg designed and implemented the programming language Smalltalk, which took the ideas of object-oriented programming developed in Scandinavia and integrated them into a programming environment designed to support constructivist learning in which students build knowledge from their experiences. Drawing on the state-of-the-art technology invented at PARC, Smalltalk was among the first programming environments designed for use with graphical displays. Along with her colleagues Alan Kay and Dan Ingalls, Goldberg received the Software Systems Award from the Association for Computing Machinery, the leading professional society for computer science, in 1987.

So far, the only direct interactions you have had with JavaScript programs have taken place in the context of the JavaScript console. When you type a function call into the console window, the JavaScript interpreter then calls that function and displays the result. That style of interaction is termed *synchronous,* because user actions are synchronized with the program operation. A graphical user interface (often shortened to the acronym *GUI,* which is pronounced like *gooey*), by contrast, is *asynchronous,* in that it allows the user to intercede at any point, typically by using the mouse or the keyboard to trigger an action. Actions that occur asynchronously with respect to the program operation, such as clicking the mouse or typing on the keyboard, are generically referred to as *events.* Interactive programs that operate by responding to these events are said to be *event-driven.* The primary goal of this chapter is to teach you how to write simple event-driven programs.

Historically, the development of the graphical user interface has been closely associated with the object-oriented paradigm, which is itself commonly abbreviated as *OOP.* There are at least two reasons that the GUI and OOP have worked well together (beyond the fact that they have both become popular three-letter buzzwords in the computing industry). First, graphical displays are characterized by having many independent objects that form a hierarchical relationship that fits easily into the object-oriented paradigm. Second, it is easy to think of events as messages, which are a central foundation of the object-oriented model. Clicking the mouse, for example, sends a message to the application, which then responds in an appropriate way.

◼ 6.1 First-class functions

Before looking at the details of how event-driven programs are implemented in JavaScript, it is useful to spend a little more time considering the question of how JavaScript implements the idea of a function. In the programs you have seen so far in this book, the ideas of functions and data have remained separate. Functions provide the means for representing an algorithm; those functions then operate on data values, which act as the raw material on which computation is performed. Functions have been part of the algorithmic structure, not part of the data structure. Being able to use functions as data values, however, often makes it much easier to design effective interfaces, because this facility allows clients to specify operations as well as data.

In JavaScript, functions are values that are simultaneously part of both the algorithmic structure and the data structure of a program. Given a functional value, you can assign it to a variable, pass it as a parameter, or return it as a result. When a programming language allows functions to behave just like any other data value, computer scientists say that the language supports *first-class functions.*

Declaring functions as data values

In JavaScript, the style of function definition that you have seen is not the only way to define a function. For example, instead of writing

```
function f(x) {
    return x * x - 5;
}
```

JavaScript allows you to achieve a similar result using the following declaration:

```
let f = function(x) { return x * x - 5; };
```

This declaration introduces a new variable named **f** and initializes that variable to a function that takes an argument x and returns the value $x^2 - 5$. The syntax matches that of any other JavaScript declaration and therefore takes a semicolon at the end.

The domain of the function data type is the vast spectrum of functions that you might want to define in JavaScript. The operation that is particular to the function data type is *application,* which is the process of calling that function with a list of arguments. No matter which way you define the function **f**, you call it in the same way, so that **f(3)** produces the value 4.

In JavaScript, a function defined inside another function is called an *inner function.* The primary advantage of inner functions is that they have access to the local variables declared in the block in which the inner function is defined. The value of an inner function is therefore more than just the code that implements it. Inner functions also keep track of the variables that are defined in the current scope. This combination of code and variables is called a *closure.*

Although these two syntactic forms for function declaration are similar, there are important differences. Declaring a function as a variable separates the name of the function from its value. Although the functional value is stored in a variable named **f**, the function itself is *anonymous* in the sense that it has no name. JavaScript debuggers provide less information if you use the second form. Perhaps more importantly, JavaScript defines every inner function declared using the first style *before* it executes any of the statements of the enclosing block. This process is called *hoisting.* As a result, the definition of inner functions can come at any point within the body and need not interrupt its flow. In this book, inner functions are usually defined at the end of the function or block of statements that contains them.

Passing functions as parameters

As noted on page 196, JavaScript functions can be passed as parameters. One example of an application in which doing so makes intuitive sense is the following function:

```
function printFunctionTable(f, min, max) {
    for (let i = min; i <= max; i++) {
        console.log("f(" + i + ") = " + f(i));
    }
}
```

This first parameter is a function that takes a number and returns a result. The effect of this function is to count from **min** to **max**, generating a line of output that shows the value of the function at each of those values. For example, if **f** is defined as shown in the preceding section to be $f(x) = x^2 - 5$, calling

printFunctionTable(f, -2, 4);

produces the following output:

JavaScript Console
f(-2) = -1
f(-1) = -4
f(0) = -5
f(1) = -4
f(2) = -1
f(3) = 4
f(4) = 11

The function argument, however, can be any function, even one that comes from a library. For example, calling

printFunctionTable(Math.sqrt, 2, 9);

generates the following console log:

JavaScript Console
f(2) = 1.4142135623730951
f(3) = 1.7320508075688772
f(4) = 2
f(5) = 2.23606797749979
f(6) = 2.449489742783178
f(7) = 2.6457513110645907
f(8) = 2.8284271247461903
f(9) = 3

It is also legal to specify a function definition directly within the call, as in

printfunctionTable(function(x) { return x * x; }, 1, 4);

which displays the following table of squares:

JavaScript Console
f(1) = 1
f(2) = 4
f(3) = 9
f(4) = 16

6.2 A simple interactive example

Before becoming immersed in the details, it helps to consider a simple example that illustrates JavaScript's model for interacting with the user. The **DrawDots.js** program in Figure 6-1 draws a small dot whenever the user clicks the mouse button. For example, if you click the mouse near the upper left corner of the window, the program will draw a dot in that position, as shown in the following diagram:

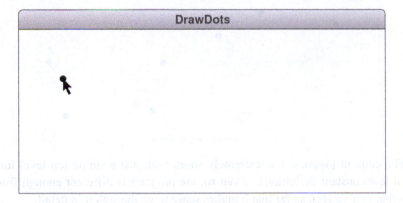

FIGURE 6-1   **Program to draw dots when the user clicks the mouse**

```
/*
 * File: DrawDots.js
 * ------------------
 * This program draws a dot every time the user clicks the mouse.
 */

"use strict";

/* Constants */

const GWINDOW_WIDTH = 500;
const GWINDOW_HEIGHT = 300;
const DOT_SIZE = 6;

/* Main program */

function DrawDots() {
    let gw = GWindow(GWINDOW_WIDTH, GWINDOW_HEIGHT);
    gw.addEventListener("click", clickAction);

    function clickAction(e) {
        let dot = GOval(e.getX() - DOT_SIZE / 2, e.getY() - DOT_SIZE / 2,
                        DOT_SIZE, DOT_SIZE);
        dot.setFilled(true);
        gw.add(dot);
    }
}
```

If you then go on to click the mouse in other positions, dots will appear there as well. You could, for example, draw a picture of the constellation Ursa Major, which is more commonly known as the Big Dipper. All you would have to do is click the mouse once in the position of each star, as follows:

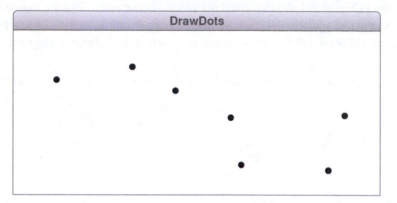

The code in Figure 6-1 is extremely short, with just a single top-level function and a few constant definitions. Even so, the program is different enough from the ones that you've seen so far that it makes sense to go through it in detail.

The first statement in the program simply creates the graphics window, precisely as you always have. The next statement establishes the link between the graphics window and the behavior specified by the **clickAction** function, which is defined at the end of the function. By executing the line

```
gw.addEventListener("click", clickAction);
```

the program tells the graphics window that it wants to respond to mouse clicks. Moreover, the response to that mouse click is specified by **clickAction**, which is called automatically whenever a click occurs.

The body of **DrawDots** ends with the definition of the **clickAction** function, which is defined everywhere inside **DrawDots** because of JavaScript's policy of hoisting functions described earlier in the chapter. The code in Figure 6-1 never calls **clickAction** explicitly. The call, when it happens, comes from the code that implements the graphics library. Functions that the program does not call directly but that instead occur in response to some event are referred to as ***callback functions.*** The name reflects the relationship between the client program and the libraries it uses. As a client, your program calls **addEventListener** to register interest in a particular event. As part of that process, you provide the library with a function that it can call when the event occurs. It is, in a way, analogous to providing a callback number. When the library implementation needs to call you back, you've given it the means to do so.

Now that you have a sense of how callback functions work in general, you are in a better position to understand the `clickAction` function, which looks like this:

```
function clickAction(e) {
    let dot = GOval(e.getX() - DOT_SIZE / 2,
                    e.getY() - DOT_SIZE / 2,
                    DOT_SIZE, DOT_SIZE);
    dot.setFilled(true);
    gw.add(dot);
}
```

The function takes a parameter `e`, which provides the function with data about the details of the event. In this case, `e` is a *mouse event,* which keeps track of the location of the mouse along with other data. Callback functions that respond to mouse events can determine the location of the mouse by invoking the methods `e.getX()` and `e.getY()`. Each of these methods returns a coordinate in pixels measured relative to the origin in the upper left corner of the window.

The body of the `clickAction` function creates a `GOval` of the size specified by `DOT_SIZE`, sets it to be filled, and then adds it to the window so that its center appears as the current mouse position. The variable `gw`, which is a local variable inside `DrawDots`, is accessible to the `clickAction` code because the definition of that function appears inside the `DrawDots` body.

6.3 Controlling properties of objects

Before moving on to look at more sophisticated examples of interactivity, it is important to have a more complete understanding of how to manipulate graphical objects that have already been placed on the screen. So far, the objects that you've added to the graphics window retain their initial location and dimensions. When you build interactive programs, you need to be able to change these properties.

The classes in the graphics library export a richer set of methods than you have had a chance to use so far. Figure 6-2 lists the complete set of methods supported by every graphical object and a few that apply only to `GRect`, `GOval`, and `GLine`. Each of the method descriptions consists of a single line that offers an overview of what the method does. For more details, you can consult the web documentation for the graphics library.

Instead of going through each of these methods in detail, this chapter presents several programming examples that introduce new methods only as they are needed. As a result, you have a chance to learn about each of the new methods in the context of an application that makes use of it.

FIGURE 6-2 Expanded list of methods available in the graphics library

Methods that control the location of the object

obj.setLocation (*x*, *y*)	Sets the location of this object to the point (*x*, *y*).
obj.move (*dx*, *dy*)	Moves the object using the displacements *dx* and *dy*.
obj.movePolar (*r*, *theta*)	Moves the object *r* pixels in direction *theta*.

Methods that control the appearance of the object

obj.setColor (*color*)	Sets the color used to display this object.
obj.setLineWidth (*width*)	Sets the width of the lines used to draw the object.
obj.setVisible (*flag*)	Sets whether this object is visible.
obj.rotate (*theta*)	Rotates the object *theta* degrees around its origin.
obj.scale (*sf*)	Scales the object by *sf* both horizontally and vertically.

Methods that control the stacking order

obj.sendBackward ()	Moves this object one step backward in the stacking order.
obj.sendForward ()	Moves this object one step forward in the stacking order.
obj.sendToBack ()	Moves this object to the back of the stacking order.
obj.sendToFront ()	Moves this object to the front of the stacking order.

Methods that return properties of the object

obj.getX ()	Returns the *x* coordinate of the object.
obj.getY ()	Returns the *y* coordinate of the object.
obj.getWidth ()	Returns the width of this object.
obj.getHeight ()	Returns the height of this object.
obj.getColor ()	Returns the color used to display this object.
obj.getLineWidth ()	Returns the width of the lines used to draw the object.
obj.isVisible ()	Checks to see whether this object is visible.
obj.contains (*x*, *y*)	Checks to see whether the point (*x*, *y*) is inside the object.

Methods available only for the GRect and GOval classes

obj.setFilled (*flag*)	Sets whether this object is filled.
obj.setFillColor (*color*)	Sets the color used to fill the interior of the object.
obj.setBounds (*x*, *y*, *width*, *height*)	Resets the boundary rectangle for the object.

Methods available only for the GLine class

obj.setStartPoint (*x*, *y*)	Changes the start point of the line without changing the end.
obj.setEndPoint (*x*, *y*)	Changes the end point of the line without changing the start.

FIGURE 6-3	**Common mouse event types**
`"click"`	The user clicks the mouse in the window.
`"dblclick"`	The user double-clicks the mouse in the window.
`"mousedown"`	The user presses the mouse button.
`"mouseup"`	The user releases the mouse button.
`"mousemove"`	The user moves the mouse with the button up.
`"drag"`	The user drags the mouse (that is, moves the mouse with the button down).

6.4 Responding to mouse events

The `"click"` event used in the `DrawDots.js` program is only one of several mouse events that JavaScript allows you to detect. The mouse events implemented by the `GWindow` class are shown in Figure 6-3. Each of these event names allows you to respond to a specific type of action with the mouse, most of which will seem familiar from using your computer. The `"mousemove"` event, for example, is generated when you move the mouse in the window without pressing the mouse button. The `"drag"` event occurs when you move the mouse while holding the button down. The name of the event comes from the fact that the interaction model of moving the mouse with the button down is often used to drag objects around on the window. You press the mouse button over an object to grab it and then drag it to the desired position.

The sections that follow offer several examples that illustrate conventional styles of using the mouse to create and reposition objects in the graphics window.

A simple line-drawing program

In all likelihood, you have already used some application that allows you to draw lines on the screen by dragging the mouse. To create a line, you press the mouse button at the point at which you'd like the line to start and then drag the mouse with the button down until you reach the point at which you want the line to end. As you drag the mouse, the application typically updates the line so that you can see what you have drawn so far. When you release the mouse button, the line stays in that position, and you can repeat the process to create as many new lines as you wish.

Suppose, for example, that you press the mouse button somewhere on the screen and then drag the mouse rightward an inch, holding the button down. What you'd like to see is the following picture:

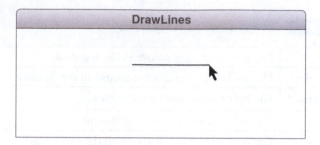

If you then move the mouse downward without releasing the button, the displayed line will track the mouse, so that you might see the following picture:

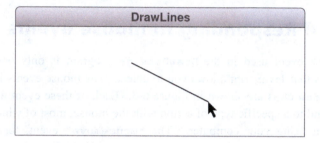

As you drag the mouse, the application repeatedly updates the line, making it appear to stretch as the mouse moves. Because the effect is precisely what you would expect if you joined the starting point and the mouse cursor with a stretchy elastic line, this technique is called *rubber-banding.*

When you release the mouse, the line stays where it is. If you then press the mouse button again on that same point, you can go ahead and draw an additional line segment by dragging the mouse to the end point of the new line, as follows:

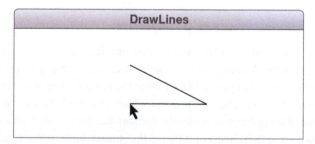

The code for this application, which appears in Figure 6-4, is remarkably short, despite the fact that the program performs what seems like a sophisticated task. As in the **DrawDots** program, the creation of the **GWindow** object at the beginning of the program follows the standard convention. The program then declares a variable called **line** that will keep track of the current line. When the program starts, there is no line, and the program records that fact by setting its initial value to the special

FIGURE 6-4 Code for the `DrawLines.js` program

```
/*
 * File: DrawLines.js
 * ------------------
 * This program lets the user draw lines on the screen by dragging the mouse.
 */

"use strict";

/* Constants */

const GWINDOW_WIDTH = 500;
const GWINDOW_HEIGHT = 300;

/* Main program */

function DrawLines() {
   let gw = GWindow(GWINDOW_WIDTH, GWINDOW_HEIGHT);
   let line = null;
   gw.addEventListener("mousedown", mousedownAction);
   gw.addEventListener("drag", dragAction);

   function mousedownAction(e) {
      line = GLine(e.getX(), e.getY(), e.getX(), e.getY());
      gw.add(line);
   }

   function dragAction(e) {
      line.setEndPoint(e.getX(), e.getY());
   }
}
```

value `null`, which is used in JavaScript to indicate an object reference that doesn't yet exist. The value of `line` is set in the code for the `"mousedown"` event and updated in the code for the `"drag"` event. The fact that one function sets this value and another function updates it means that the variable `line` must be declared in the `DrawLines` function so that both of the event-handling functions have access to it.

The function `mousedownAction` creates a new `GLine` object, assigns it to the variable `line`, and then adds the line to the window. Initially, the line starts and ends at the current position of the mouse, which means that it appears as a dot. The function `dragAction` calls the `setEndPoint` method in the `GLine` class, which, as noted in Figure 6-2, changes the point at which the line ends without changing its starting point. Doing so produces the desired rubber-banding behavior.

Dragging objects on the canvas

The `DragObjects.js` program in Figure 6-5 offers a slightly more sophisticated example of an event-driven program that uses the mouse to reposition objects on the

FIGURE 6-5 Code for the `DragObjects.js` program

```
/*
 * File: DragObjects.js
 * ---------------------
 * This program lets the user drag objects on the window.
 */

"use strict";

const GWINDOW_WIDTH = 500;
const GWINDOW_HEIGHT = 200;
const GOBJECT_WIDTH = 200;
const GOBJECT_HEIGHT = 100;

function DragObjects() {
   let gw = GWindow(GWINDOW_WIDTH, GWINDOW_HEIGHT);
   let x0 = (gw.getWidth() - GOBJECT_WIDTH) / 2;
   let y0 = (gw.getHeight() - GOBJECT_HEIGHT) / 2;
   let rect = GRect(x0, y0, GOBJECT_WIDTH, GOBJECT_HEIGHT);
   rect.setFilled(true);
   rect.setColor("Blue");
   gw.add(rect);
   let oval = GOval(x0, y0, GOBJECT_WIDTH, GOBJECT_HEIGHT);
   oval.setFilled(true);
   oval.setColor("Red");
   gw.add(oval);
   let objectBeingDragged = null;
   let lastX = 0;
   let lastY = 0;
   gw.addEventListener("mousedown", mousedownAction);
   gw.addEventListener("drag", dragAction);
   gw.addEventListener("click", clickAction);

   function mousedownAction(e) {
      lastX = e.getX();
      lastY = e.getY();
      objectBeingDragged = gw.getElementAt(lastX, lastY);
   }

   function dragAction(e) {
      if (objectBeingDragged !== null) {
         objectBeingDragged.move(e.getX() - lastX, e.getY() - lastY);
         lastX = e.getX();
         lastY = e.getY();
      }
   }

   function clickAction(e) {
      if (objectBeingDragged !== null) {
         objectBeingDragged.sendToFront();
      }
   }
}
```

display. This program begins by adding a blue rectangle and a red oval to the window, just as in the `GRectPlusGOval.js` program from Chapter 4. The rest of the main program represents the code pattern for dragging objects.

The first callback function defined in Figure 6-5 is `mousedownAction`, which responds to the user pressing the mouse button. Here, `mousedownAction` has the following definition:

```
function mousedownAction(e) {
   lastX = e.getX();
   lastY = e.getY();
   objectBeingDragged = gw.getElementAt(lastX, lastY);
}
```

The first two statements simply record the x and y coordinates of the mouse in the variables `lastX` and `lastY`. As you can see from the program, these variables are declared as local variables in the enclosing `DragObjects` function, because the program needs these values in the callback function that responds when the user drags the mouse.

The last statement in the `mousedownAction` function makes use of an important new method in the `GWindow` class. The `getElementAt` method takes an x and a y coordinate and then checks to see what object displayed on the window contains that location. Here, it is important to recognize that there are two possibilities. First, you could be pressing the mouse button on top of an object, which means that you want to start dragging it. Second, you could be pressing the mouse button somewhere else on the canvas at which there is no object to drag. If just one object exists at the specified location, `getElementAt` returns that object; if more than one object covers that space, `getElementAt` chooses the one in front of the others in the stacking order. If no objects exist at that location, `getElementAt` returns the special value `null`. In any of those cases, the `mousedownAction` function assigns that value to the variable `objectBeingDragged`, which is again declared at the level of the `DragObjects` function so that all of the callback functions can share that value.

The `dragAction` function consists of the following code:

```
function dragAction(e) {
   if (objectBeingDragged !== null) {
      objectBeingDragged.move(e.getX() - lastX,
                              e.getY() - lastY);
      lastX = e.getX();
      lastY = e.getY();
   }
}
```

The **if** statement checks to see whether there is an object to drag. If the value of **objectBeingDragged** is **null**, there is nothing to drag, so the rest of the function can just be skipped. If there is an object, you need to move it by some distance in each direction. That distance does not depend on the current coordinates of the mouse but rather on how far it has moved from where it was when you last noted its position. Thus, the arguments to the **move** method are—for both the *x* and *y* components—the location where the mouse is now minus where the mouse was at the time of the last event. Those coordinates are stored in the variables **lastX** and **lastY**. Once you have moved the object, you must then update the values of these variables to ensure that they are correct for the next call to **mouseDragged**.

The only other feature in the **DragObjects.js** program is that the application also registers its interest in **"click"** events, which trigger a call to the following function:

```
function clickAction(e) {
   if (objectBeingDragged !== null) {
      objectBeingDragged.sendToFront();
   }
}
```

The point of adding this function is to allow the user to change the stacking order, which, as noted in Chapter 2, is the order in which objects are layered on the screen. Defining this function ensures that clicking on an object sends it to the front.

In the **DragObjects.js** program, clicking on an object has the effect of moving it to the front of the stacking order. Implementing this behavior correctly, however, requires understanding JavaScript's rules for generating mouse events. A **"click"** event occurs when a **"mousedown"** event is followed within a relatively short amount of time by a **"mouseup"** event. By the time JavaScript processes the **"click"** event, the **"mousedown"** and **"mouseup"** events have already occurred. The **DragObjects.js** program does not specify any action for **"mouseup"** but does respond to the **"mousedown"** event by calling **mousedownAction**. Thus, by the time the call to **clickAction** occurs, the **mousedownAction** function will already have set the value of **objectBeingDragged**.

6.5 Timer-based animation

Interactive programs change their behavior not only in response to user events, but also over time. In a computer game, for example, objects on the screen typically move in real time. Updating the contents of the graphics window so that they change over time is called ***animation.***

The `setTimeout` and `setInterval` functions

The conventional way to implement animation in JavaScript is to use a *timer,* which is a mechanism that generates a function call after a specified delay. JavaScript timers come in two forms. The library function

> `setTimeout` (*function*, *delay*)

creates a *one-shot timer* that calls *function* after *delay* milliseconds. The function

> `setInterval` (*function*, *delay*)

creates an *interval timer* that calls *function* repeatedly every *delay* milliseconds. In each case, the function returns a numeric value that allows subsequent code to identify the timer. If you store this numeric value in a variable, you can then call `clearTimeout` or `clearInterval` (depending on the type of timer) to stop the timer process. Thus, executing

> `let timer = setInterval(step, 20);`

creates an interval timer and stores its identifying number in the variable `timer`. The interval timer then begins generating calls to the function `step` once every 20 milliseconds, or every fiftieth of a second. The name `step` is chosen here to suggest that each call represents a single step in the animation, which is called a *time step.* The `step` function receives no arguments, so any information it needs must be communicated through the local variables of the function in which `step` is defined.

Timers that initiate events every 20 milliseconds allow you to change the state of the graphics window quickly enough so that the changes seem smooth to the human eye. You can therefore move an object on the screen by creating an interval timer that executes its callback function every 20 milliseconds and then having the callback function make an incremental change to the position of that object. When the object reaches the desired final location, your program can then stop the timer by calling

> `clearInterval(timer);`

A simple example of animation

A simple example of timer-based of animation appears in Figure 6-6, which moves a square diagonally across the screen from its initial position in the upper left corner to its final position in the lower right. The program runs for `N_STEPS` time steps and computes values for the variables `dx` and `dy` so that the square moves to its final position in precisely that amount of time.

FIGURE 6-6   **Program to move a square diagonally across the screen**

```
/*
 * File: AnimatedSquare.js
 * ------------------------
 * This program animates a square so that it moves from the upper left
 * corner of the window to the lower right corner.
 */

"use strict";

/* Constants */

const GWINDOW_WIDTH = 500;
const GWINDOW_HEIGHT = 300;
const N_STEPS = 100;
const TIME_STEP = 20;
const SQUARE_SIZE = 50;

function AnimatedSquare() {
   let gw = GWindow(GWINDOW_WIDTH, GWINDOW_HEIGHT);
   let dx = (gw.getWidth() - SQUARE_SIZE) / N_STEPS;
   let dy = (gw.getHeight() - SQUARE_SIZE) / N_STEPS;
   let square = GRect(0, 0, SQUARE_SIZE, SQUARE_SIZE);
   square.setFilled(true);
   gw.add(square);
   let stepCount = 0;
   let timer = setInterval(step, TIME_STEP);

   function step() {
      square.move(dx, dy);
      stepCount++;
      if (stepCount === N_STEPS) clearInterval(timer);
   }
}
```

The operation of `AnimatedSquare.js` is shown in the following screen image, which uses an arrow to map the trajectory of the square from its initial location:

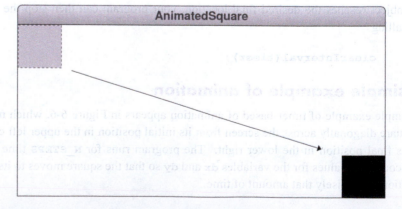

AnimatedSquare

The code for the callback function looks like this:

```
function step() {
    square.move(dx, dy);
    stepCount++;
    if (stepCount === N_STEPS) clearInterval(timer);
}
```

The first line adjusts the position of the square by the values **dx** and **dy**. The second line increments the value of **stepCount**. The third line checks to see whether **stepCount** has reached the limit and, if so, stops the timer. The **step** function has access to the variables **square**, **dx**, **dy**, **stepCount**, and **timer** because these are local variables in **AnimatedSquare**.

Tracking the state of an animation

As animations become more complex, keeping track of what objects are moving on the screen and when the next time step should occur becomes a bit tricky. Suppose, for example, that you want to add animation to the **RandomCircles.js** program in Figure 5-4 on page 169. Instead of having the circles all show up at once, what you want is for the circles to appear slowly, one at a time. Each circle begins as a single point and then grows, step by step, until it reaches its desired size. As soon as that happens, the program should create the next circle and let it grow to its full size, continuing in this fashion until all ten circles are displayed on the screen.

It is, of course, tempting to start this program by building on the earlier example. That strategy would suggest adopting the following pseudocode structure inside the main program:

```
for (let i = 0; i < N_CIRCLES; i++) {
    Create a circle.
    Animate that circle so that it grows to full size.
    Wait for that animation to complete.
}
```

Unfortunately, that strategy doesn't work in JavaScript. Unlike most languages, JavaScript does not allow programs to wait for some asynchronous task to finish and then continue with what they were doing. That restriction makes it impossible to capture the intention of the pseudocode line

> *Wait for that animation to complete.*

Interactivity in JavaScript is required to be entirely event-driven, in the sense that all actions take place in response to events that occur asynchronously with respect to the running of the program. In fact, programs in JavaScript typically run to completion before any events occur. After that, events completely determine how the application proceeds. JavaScript's event model requires a different approach, in which the **step** function that implements the animation has to keep track of the size of the current circle and determine when it has reached full size. When it has, the **step** function—and not the main program, which has stopped running by this point—must create the next circle. The **step** function therefore has the following pseudocode form:

```
function step() {
    if (the current circle is still growing) {
        Increase the size of the current circle.
    } else if (there are more circles to create) {
        Create another circle.
    } else {
        clearInterval(timer);
    }
}
```

The code for the **GrowingCircles.js** program that uses this structure appears in Figure 6-7. The code for the **createNewCircle** function is largely the same as the code for **createRandomCircle** in Figure 5-4. The only differences are that

1. The **createNewCircle** function creates circles whose initial size is 0.

2. The **createNewCircle** function records the eventual and current size of the circle in the variables **desiredSize** and **currentSize**. Setting both of these variables to 0 ensures that **createNewCircle** is called on the first time step.

The code for the **step** function follows the pseudocode outline shown earlier on this page. The only new feature is the call to the **setBounds** method, which resets the location and size of the current circle so that it grows by one pixel in each time step.

6.6 Expanding the graphics library

Ever since Chapter 4, you've been using classes from the Portable Graphics Library to create simple drawings on the screen. So far, however, you have seen only a small part of what the graphics library has to offer. Now that you know how to write programs that involve animation and interactivity, it makes sense to learn more about the graphics library and how to use it. This section introduces three new classes—**GArc**, **GPolygon**, and **GCompound**—that allow you to create much more interesting graphical displays.

FIGURE 6-7 Program to create ten circles that start as a point and then grow to full size

```javascript
/*
 * File: GrowingCircles.js
 * -----------------------
 * This program draws random circles that grow to their final size.
 */

"use strict";

/* Constants */

const GWINDOW_WIDTH = 500;
const GWINDOW_HEIGHT = 300;
const N_CIRCLES = 10;
const MIN_RADIUS = 15;
const MAX_RADIUS = 50;
const TIME_STEP = 20;
const DELTA_SIZE = 1;

function GrowingCircles() {
   let gw = GWindow(GWINDOW_WIDTH, GWINDOW_HEIGHT);
   let circlesCreated = 0;
   let desiredSize = 0;
   let currentSize = 0;
   let circle = null;
   let timer = setInterval(step, TIME_STEP);

   function createNewCircle() {
      let r = randomReal(MIN_RADIUS, MAX_RADIUS);
      let x = randomReal(r, GWINDOW_WIDTH - r);
      let y = randomReal(r, GWINDOW_HEIGHT - r);
      circle = GOval(x, y, 0, 0);
      circle.setFilled(true);
      circle.setColor(randomColor());
      desiredSize = 2 * r;
      currentSize = 0;
      return circle;
   }

   function step() {
      if (currentSize < desiredSize) {
         currentSize += DELTA_SIZE;
         let x = circle.getX() - DELTA_SIZE / 2;
         let y = circle.getY() - DELTA_SIZE / 2;
         circle.setBounds(x, y, currentSize, currentSize);
      } else if (circlesCreated < N_CIRCLES) {
         gw.add(createNewCircle());
         circlesCreated++;
      } else {
         clearInterval(timer);
      }
   }
}
```

The GArc class

The GArc class is used to display an arc formed by selecting part of the perimeter of an oval. The GArc function itself takes the following parameters:

> GArc (*x*, *y*, *width*, *height*, *start*, *sweep*)

The first four parameters specify the location and size of the rectangle that encloses the arc and therefore have precisely the same interpretation as those parameters in calls to **GRect** or **GOval**. The next two parameters specify the ***start angle,*** which is the angle at which the arc begins, and the ***sweep angle,*** which is the number of degrees through which the arc extends. In keeping with mathematical convention, angles in the graphics library are measured in degrees counterclockwise from the +*x* axis, as follows:

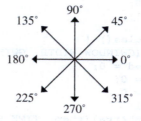

The geometric interpretation of these parameters appears in Figure 6-8. The effect of these parameters, however, is more easily demonstrated by example. The

---

FIGURE 6-8   **The geometric interpretation of the GArc parameters**

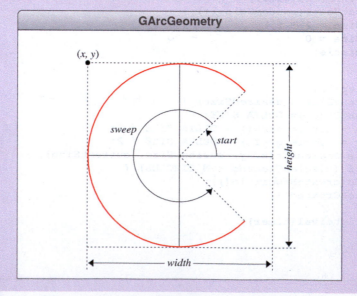

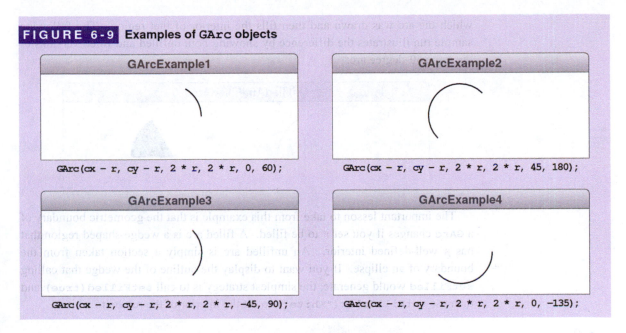

FIGURE 6-9   Examples of GArc objects

four sample runs in Figure 6-9 show the effect of the code that appears below each diagram. The code fragments create and display arcs using different values for **start** and **sweep**. Each of the arcs has a radius of **r** pixels and is centered at the point (**cx**, **cy**). The last two examples show that the values of **start** and **sweep** can be negative, in which case the angles extend in the clockwise direction.

The **GArc** class implements the methods shown in Figure 6-10. As you can see, these methods include **setFilled** and **setFillColor**, just as **GRect** and **GOval** do. It is not immediately apparent, however, exactly what filling an arc means. In the interpretation of arc-filling used in the Portable Graphics Library, the unfilled version of a **GArc** is not simply the boundary of its filled counterpart. If you display an unfilled **GArc**, only the arc itself is shown. If you call **setFilled(true)** on that arc, the graphics library connects the end points of the arc to the center from

FIGURE 6-10   Methods implemented by the GArc class

arc.**setFilled**(*flag*)	Sets whether the wedge for this arc is filled.
arc.**setFillColor**(*color*)	Sets the color used to fill the wedge for this arc.
arc.**setStartAngle**(*start*)	Sets the start angle to *start*.
arc.**getStartAngle**()	Returns the start angle.
arc.**setSweepAngle**(*sweep*)	Sets the start angle to *sweep*.
arc.**getSweepAngle**()	Returns the sweep angle.

which the arc was drawn and then fills the interior of that region. The following sample run illustrates the difference by showing both unfilled and filled versions of the same 60-degree arc:

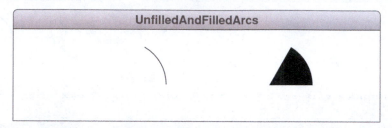

The important lesson to take from this example is that the geometric boundary of a `GArc` changes if you set it to be filled. A filled arc is a wedge-shaped region that has a well-defined interior. An unfilled arc is simply a section taken from the boundary of an ellipse. If you want to display the outline of the wedge that calling `setFilled` would generate, the simplest strategy is to call `setFilled(true)` and then use `setFillColor("White")` to set the interior of the region to white.

The `GPolygon` class

The `GPolygon` class makes it possible to display a *polygon,* which is simply the mathematical name for a closed shape whose boundary consists of straight lines. The line segments that form the outline of a polygon are called *edges.* The point at which a pair of edges meets is called a *vertex.* Many polygonal shapes are familiar from the real world. Each cell in a honeycomb is a hexagon, which is the common name for a polygon with six sides. A stop sign is an octagon with eight identical sides. Polygons, however, are not required to have equal sides and angles. The figures in the left margin, for example, illustrate four polygons that fit the general definition.

The `GPolygon` class is easy to use if you keep the following points in mind:

- Unlike the functions that create the other shapes, the `GPolygon` factory method does not create the entire figure. What happens instead is that calling `GPolygon` creates an empty polygon. Once you have created an empty polygon, you then add vertices to it by calling various other methods described later in this section.

- The origin of a `GPolygon` is not defined to be its upper left corner. Many polygons, after all, don't have an upper left corner. What happens instead is that you—as the programmer who is creating the specific polygon—choose a *reference point* that defines the location of the polygon as a whole. You then specify the coordinates for each vertex in terms of where they lie in relation to the reference point. This approach makes it easier to move the polygon as a unit.

diamond

trapezoid

T-shape

five-pointed star

The creation of a `GPolygon` is easiest to illustrate by example. Suppose that you want to create a `GPolygon` representing the diamond-shaped figure shown in the margin. Your first design decision consists of choosing where to put the reference point. For most polygons, the most convenient point is the geometric center of the figure. If you adopt that model, you then need to create an empty `GPolygon` and add four vertices to it, specifying the coordinates of each vertex relative to the coordinates of the center. Assuming that the width and height of the diamond are stored in the constants `DIAMOND_WIDTH` and `DIAMOND_HEIGHT`, you can create the diamond-shaped `GPolygon` using the following code:

```
let diamond = GPolygon();
diamond.addVertex(-DIAMOND_WIDTH / 2, 0);
diamond.addVertex(0, DIAMOND_HEIGHT / 2);
diamond.addVertex(DIAMOND_WIDTH / 2, 0);
diamond.addVertex(0, -DIAMOND_HEIGHT / 2);
```

You can then add the diamond at the center of the graphics window by executing the following statement:

```
gw.add(diamond, gw.getWidth() / 2, gw.getHeight() / 2);
```

The graphics window then looks like this:

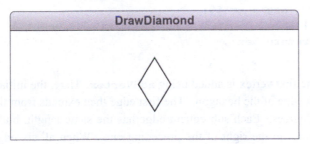

When you use the `addVertex` method to construct a polygon, the coordinates of each vertex are expressed relative to the reference point. In some cases, it is easier to specify the coordinates of each vertex in terms of the preceding one. To enable this approach, the `GPolygon` class offers an `addEdge` method, which is similar to `addVertex` except that the parameters specify the displacement from the previous vertex to the current one. You can therefore draw the same diamond by making the following sequence of calls:

```
let diamond = GPolygon();
diamond.addVertex(-DIAMOND_WIDTH / 2, 0);
diamond.addEdge(DIAMOND_WIDTH / 2, DIAMOND_HEIGHT / 2);
diamond.addEdge(DIAMOND_WIDTH / 2, -DIAMOND_HEIGHT / 2);
diamond.addEdge(-DIAMOND_WIDTH / 2, -DIAMOND_HEIGHT / 2);
diamond.addEdge(-DIAMOND_WIDTH / 2, DIAMOND_HEIGHT / 2);
```

Note that the first vertex must still be added using **addVertex**, but that subsequent ones can be defined by specifying the edge displacements.

As you work with the **GPolygon** class, you will discover that some polygons are easier to define with successive calls to **addVertex**, while others are easier to define using **addEdge**. For many polygonal figures, however, it is even more convenient to define the edges using polar coordinates. The **GPolygon** class supports this style through the method **addPolarEdge**. This method is identical to **addEdge** except that its arguments are the length of the edge and its direction, expressed in degrees counterclockwise from the $+x$ axis.

The **addPolarEdge** method makes it easy to create figures in which you know the angles of the edges but would need trigonometry to calculate the vertices. The following function, for example, uses **addPolarEdge** to create a regular hexagon in which the length of each edge is determined by the parameter **side**:

```
function createHexagon(side) {
    let hex = GPolygon();
    hex.addVertex(-side, 0);
    let angle = 60;
    for (let i = 0; i < 6; i++) {
        hex.addPolarEdge(side, angle);
        angle -= 60;
    }
    return hex;
}
```

As always, the first vertex is added using **addVertex**. Here, the initial vertex is the one at the left edge of the hexagon. The first edge then extends from that point at an angle of 60 degrees. Each subsequent edge has the same length, but sets off at an angle 60 degrees to the right of the preceding one. When all six edges have been added, the final edge ends up at the original vertex, thereby closing the polygon.

Once you have defined this method, executing the statement

```
gw.add(createHexagon(50), gw.getWidth() / 2,
                          gw.getHeight() / 2);
```

produces the following display:

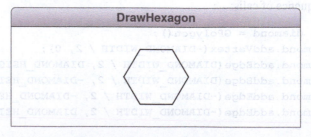

FIGURE 6-11   **Methods implemented by the `GPolygon` class**

poly.`addVertex`(*x*, *y*)	Adds a vertex at the point (*x*, *y*).
poly.`addEdge`(*dx*, *dy*)	Adds a vertex shifted by *dx* and *dy* from the preceding one.
poly.`addPolarEdge`(*r*, *theta*)	Adds a vertex shifted by *r* units in direction *theta*.
poly.`setFilled`(*flag*)	Sets whether the polygon is filled.
poly.`setFillColor`(*color*)	Sets the color used to fill the polygon.

Figure 6-11 lists the methods that apply to the `GPolygon` class. As with the other bounded figures, `GPolygon` implements `setFilled` and `setFillColor`.

As another example of using the `GPolygon` class, the `createStar` function in Figure 6-12 creates a `GPolygon` whose edges form a five-pointed star, as follows:

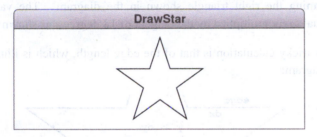

FIGURE 6-12   **Function to create a five-pointed star**

```
/*
 * Creates a GPolygon representing a five-pointed star with the reference
 * point at the center.  The size refers to the width of the star at its
 * widest point.
 */

function createStar(size) {
   let poly = GPolygon();
   let dx = size / 2;
   let dy = dx * Math.tan(18 * Math.PI / 180);
   let edge = dx - dy * Math.tan(36 * Math.PI / 180);
   poly.addVertex(-dx, -dy);
   let angle = 0;
   for (let i = 0; i < 5; i++) {
      poly.addPolarEdge(edge, angle);
      poly.addPolarEdge(edge, angle + 72);
      angle -= 72;
   }
   return poly;
}
```

Although the star is more complicated mathematically than the earlier examples, the most difficult part is determining the coordinates of the starting point at the left edge of the star. Calculating the x coordinate is easy because the starting point is simply half the width of the star to the left of its center. Calculating the distance in the y direction requires a bit of trigonometry, which can be illustrated as follows:

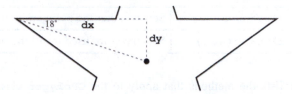

Each of the points around the periphery of a five-pointed star forms an angle that is a tenth of a complete circle, which is 36 degrees. If you draw a line that bisects that angle—leaving 18 degrees on either side—that line will hit the geometric center of the star, forming the right triangle shown in the diagram. The value of **dy** is therefore equal to **dx** multiplied by the tangent of 18 degrees, as shown in the code.

The other tricky calculation is that of the edge length, which is illustrated in the following diagram:

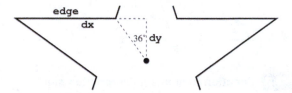

To determine the value of **edge**, you need to subtract the dotted portion of the horizontal line from its entire length, which is given by **dx**. The length of the dotted portion is easily computed using trigonometry as **dy** multiplied by the tangent of 36 degrees. Once you have computed these values, the rest of the **createStar** function follows much the same pattern as the implementation of **createHexagon**.

The GCompound class

The **GCompound** class makes it easy to assemble a collection of graphical objects into a single unit. As with **GPolygon**, calling **GCompound** creates an empty structure that you then have to fill by calling **add**, just as if you were adding those objects to the graphics window. Once you have assembled the objects, you can add the whole **GCompound** to the window, at which point it functions as a single object.

As a simple example, the function **createCrossedBox** that appears at the bottom of Figure 6-13 creates a **GCompound** consisting of a rectangle and the two diagonal lines that cross it. For example, the declaration

FIGURE 6-13 Program to rotate a crossed box around its center

```
/*
 * File: RotateCrossedBox.js
 * -------------------------
 * This program draws a crossed box and then rotates it around its center.
 */

"use strict";

/* Constants */

const GWINDOW_WIDTH = 500;
const GWINDOW_HEIGHT = 200;
const BOX_WIDTH = 200;
const BOX_HEIGHT = 100;
const TIME_STEP = 20;
const N_STEPS = 360;

/*
 * Draws a crossed box and then rotates it around its center.
 */

function RotateCrossedBox() {
   let gw = GWindow(GWINDOW_WIDTH, GWINDOW_HEIGHT);
   let box = createCrossedBox(BOX_WIDTH, BOX_HEIGHT);
   let cx = gw.getWidth() / 2;
   let cy = gw.getHeight() / 2;
   gw.add(box, cx, cy);
   let stepCount = 0;
   let timer = setInterval(step, TIME_STEP);

   function step() {
      if (stepCount < N_STEPS) {
         box.rotate(1);
         stepCount++;
      } else {
         clearInterval(timer);
      }
   }
}

/*
 * Creates a crossed box, which is a compound consisting of a GRect and
 * its two diagonals.  The reference point is at the center of the figure.
 */

function createCrossedBox(width, height) {
   let compound = GCompound();
   compound.add(GRect(-width / 2, -height / 2, width, height));
   compound.add(GLine(-width / 2, -height / 2, width / 2, height / 2));
   compound.add(GLine(-width / 2, height / 2, width / 2, -height / 2));
   return compound;
}
```

```
let box = createCrossedBox(BOX_WIDTH, BOX_HEIGHT);
```

sets the variable **box** so that it holds a new **GCompound** object that looks like this:

Like the **GPolygon** class, the **GCompound** class defines its own coordinate system in which all coordinate values are expressed relative to a reference point. This design has two advantages. First, separating the process of defining the shape and setting its coordinates means that you can define a **GCompound** without having to know exactly where it will appear. That property is particularly useful if the location of an object in the graphics window depends on its size. Second, there are often more appropriate choices to use as a reference point than the conventional upper left corner. The **createCrossedBox** function, for example, returns a **GCompound** in which the reference point is at the center, which is often a more convenient choice. The code in Figure 6-13 can then place the crossed box at the center of the window using the following code:

```
let cx = gw.getWidth() / 2;
let cy = gw.getHeight() / 2;
gw.add(box, cx, cy);
```

Executing these statements creates the following image on the graphics window:

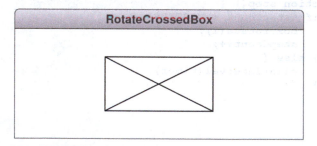

The rest of the **RotateCrossedBox** program in Figure 6-13 then uses a timer to rotate the box through a full revolution in one-degree increments. The statement

```
box.rotate(1);
```

in the callback function rotates the **GCompound** one degree counterclockwise around its reference point, which in this case is the center. After 360 steps, the callback function calls **clearInterval** to stop the timer, leaving the crossed box back in its original orientation.

Summary

In this chapter, you learned how to create interactive programs. The important points introduced in this chapter include:

- Interactive programs in JavaScript use an *event-driven* model in which the user's actions generate events that occur asynchronously with respect to the operation of the program. Each event triggers a function call that responds to that event.

- Functions in JavaScript are first-class values in the sense that they can be used in all the ways that any other value can. Functions can be assigned to variables, passed as parameters to other functions, and returned as a function result.

- The graphics library exports a large collection of methods that apply to every graphical object. A list of these methods appears in Figure 6-2 on page 202.

- Programs indicate their interest in responding to mouse events by calling the `addEventListener` method on the graphics window.

- Mouse events are associated with an event type indicated by a string. The names of the different event types appear in Figure 6-3 on page 203.

- Each call to `addEventListener` specifies the function that should respond to that type of event. These functions are generically known as *callback functions.*

- Callback functions are conventionally declared within the body of an enclosing function so that the callback function has access to the local variables of the function in which the callback function is declared.

- Callback functions used to respond to mouse events take a single parameter that includes information about the event. The only mouse-event properties used in this text are the methods `getX` and `getY`, which return the position in the window at which the mouse event occurred.

- The `GWindow` class includes a method `getElementAt(x, y)` that returns the graphical object at that location in the window. If there is no object at that location, `getElementAt` returns the special value `null`.

- The usual strategy for implementing animation in a JavaScript program is to use a *timer,* which executes a callback function after a specified delay. If the delay is 20 milliseconds or less, motion on the screen appears continuous to the eye.

- JavaScript provides two kinds of timers. The function `setTimeout` creates a *one-shot timer* that triggers an event after a delay. The function `setInterval` creates an *interval timer* that triggers an event repeatedly every time the delay time expires.

- The `GArc` class makes it possible to display elliptical arcs defined by a bounding rectangle and two angles: a *start* angle that indicates where the arc starts and a *sweep* angle that indicates how far the arc extends. Filled arcs appear as wedges in which the endpoints of the arc are connected to the center.

- The **GPolygon** class makes it possible to display an arbitrary polygon. The **GPolygon** function itself creates an empty polygon; you create the actual polygon by calling some combination of the methods **addVertex**, **addEdge**, and **addPolarEdge**.

- The **GCompound** class represents a graphical object that contains other graphical objects. Creating a **GCompound** allows the collection to be treated as a unit.

- Both the **GPolygon** and **GCompound** classes use an internal coordinate system in which the positions of the vertices or internal objects are specified with respect to a *reference point* chosen by the caller. This strategy makes it possible to create the object without knowing where it will appear in the window.

Review questions

1. In the context of JavaScript, what is an *event?*

2. Are events in JavaScript synchronous or asynchronous?

3. What reasons are offered in this chapter for the close association of graphical user interfaces and object-oriented programming?

4. Why are functions in JavaScript said to be *first-class functions?*

5. True or false: In JavaScript, you can use an explicit function definition as a parameter to some other function.

6. What are the two parameters to the **addEventListener** method?

7. What event type do you use to respond to a mouse click?

8. What are the two methods used in this chapter to get more specific information about a mouse event?

9. What is a *callback function?*

10. How does a callback function typically share information with the function that defines it?

11. What is meant by the term *rubber-banding?*

12. What value does the **getElementAt** method return if no object exists at the specified location?

13. How does the **getElementAt** method decide which object to return if more than one object covers the specified location?

14. Describe in your own words the strategy for implementing animation in JavaScript.

15. What is a *timer?*

16. What are the two library functions that create timers? How do they differ?

17. How do you stop a timer?

18. Describe the significance of the *start* and *sweep* parameters in the call to the **GArc** function.

19. What does it mean if the **sweep** argument to the **GArc** constructor is negative?

20. Describe the arcs produced by each of the following calls to **GArc**, where **cx** and **cy** are the coordinates of the center of the window and **r** has the value 100:

    a) `GArc(cx, cy, 2 * r, 2 * r, 0, 270)`

    b) `GArc(cx, cy, 2 * r, 2 * r, 135, -90)`

    c) `GArc(cx, cy, 2 * r, 2 * r, 180, -45)`

    d) `GArc(cx, cy, 3 * r, r, -90, 180)`

21. How does the **GArc** class interpret the notion of a filled arc?

22. Describe the differences between the methods **addVertex**, **addEdge**, and **addPolarEdge** in the **GPolygon** class.

23. Which of the three methods listed in the preceding question is conventionally used to add the first vertex to a **GPolygon**?

24. In your own words, describe the purpose of the **GCompound** class.

25. What advantages does the text cite for having the **GPolygon** and **GCompound** classes define their own reference point?

Exercises

1. Drawing on the **printFunctionTable** function for inspiration, implement a function

    ```
    function plot(gw, f, xMin, xMax, yMin, yMax)
    ```

    that plots the function **f** on the graphics window by creating small **GLine** segments and adding them to the graphics window. The parameters **xMin**, xMax, yMin, and yMax specify a translation between the values passed to and returned by the function and the window coordinates. The left edge of the window, for example, should correspond to the value xMin in the domain of the function.

For example, calling

```
plot(gw, Math.sin, -2 * Math.PI, 2 * Math.PI, -1, 1);
```

should generate a plot of the trigonometric sine function for values of x ranging from -2π to $+2\pi$ and displayed so that the vertical space in the window runs from -1 at the bottom to $+1$ at the top (note that this interpretation requires you to flip JavaScript's coordinate system so that it matches the traditional Cartesian model in which y values increase as you move upward). After you make this call, the graphics window should look like this:

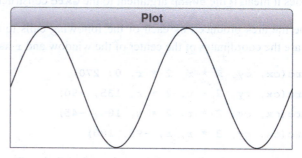

Similarly, calling

```
plot(gw, Math.sqrt, 0, 4, 0, 2);
```

should plot the Math.sqrt function on a graph that extends from 0 to 4 along the x-axis and from 0 to 2 along the y-axis, like this:

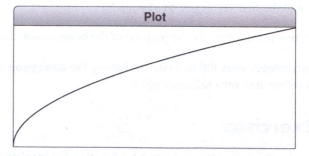

2. Modify the DrawDots program so that clicking the mouse draws a small ✗ every time you click the mouse. The ✗, which consists of two GLine objects, should be positioned so that the intersection appears at the point where the mouse was clicked.

3. In addition to line drawings of the sort generated by the **DrawLines** program, interactive drawing programs allow you to add other shapes to the canvas. In a typical drawing application, you create a rectangle by pressing the mouse at one corner and then dragging it to the opposite corner. For example, if you press the mouse at the location in the left diagram and then drag it to the position where you see the cursor in the right diagram, the program creates the rectangle shown:

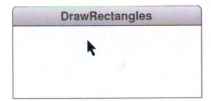 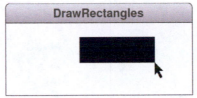

The rectangle grows as you drag the mouse. When you release the mouse button, the rectangle is complete and stays where it is. You can then go back and add more rectangles in the same way.

Although the code for this exercise is quite short, there is one important consideration that you will need to take into account. In the example above, the initial mouse click is in the upper left corner of the rectangle. Your program, however, has to work just as well if you drag the mouse in some direction other than right and down. For example, you should also be able to draw a rectangle by dragging to the left, as shown in the following illustration:

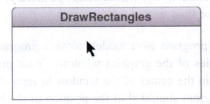 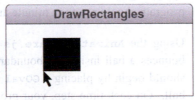

4. Use the **GOval**, **GLine**, and **GRect** classes to create a cartoon drawing of a face that looks like this:

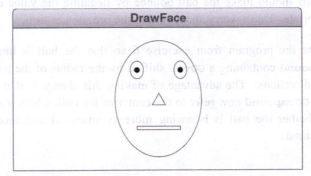

Once you have this picture, add a callback function for the **"mousemove"** event so that the pupils in the eyes follow the cursor position. For example, if you move the cursor to the lower right side of the screen, the pupils should shift so that they appear to be looking at that point, as follows:

Although it doesn't matter much when the cursor is outside the face, it is important to compute the position of the pupil independently for each eye. If you move the mouse between the eyes, for example, the pupils should point in opposite directions so that the face appears cross-eyed.

5.   Write a program that draws a filled black square in the center of the canvas. Once you have that part of the program working, animate your program so that the color of the square changes once a second to a new color chosen randomly by calling the **randomColor** function in the **RandomLib.js** library. Your program should run for a minute and then stop.

6.   Using the **AnimatedSquare.js** program as a model, write a program that bounces a ball inside the boundaries of the graphics window. Your program should begin by placing a **GOval** in the center of the window to represent the ball. On each time step, your program should shift the position of the ball by **dx** and **dy** pixels, where both **dx** and **dy** initially have the value 1. Whenever the leading edge of the ball touches one of the boundaries of the window, your program should make the ball bounce by negating the value of **dx** or **dy**, as appropriate. Don't worry about getting the program to stop.

7.   Rewrite the program from exercise 6 so that the ball is implemented as a **GCompound** containing a **GOval** shifted by the radius of the ball in both the x and y directions. The advantage of making this change is that the coordinates of the **GCompound** now refer to the center of the ball, which makes the code to see whether the ball is bouncing more symmetrical and therefore easier to understand.

8. Write a program that draws a picture of a pumpkin pie divided into equal wedge-shaped pieces where the number of pieces is indicated by the constant **N_PIECES**. Each wedge should be a separate **GArc**, filled in orange and outlined in black. The following screen image, for example, shows the diagram when **N_PIECES** is 6.

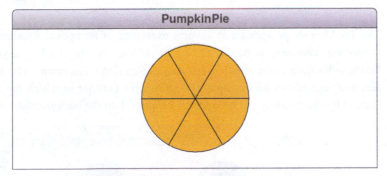

Once you have this display, add event processing to your application so that clicking on any of the wedges removes that wedge from the display. For example, if you click on the wedge in the upper right, the screen image should look like this:

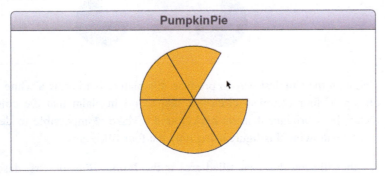

9. The title character in the PacMan series of games is easy to draw in JavaScript using a filled **GArc**. As a first step, write a program that adds a PacMan figure at the left edge of the window, as follows:

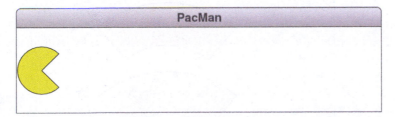

Once you have this part working, add the code to make the PacMan figure move rightward until it reaches the right edge of the graphics window. As

PacMan moves, your program should change the start and sweep angles so that the mouth appears to open and close as shown in the following image sequence:

10. The PacMan shape appears in several examples of an optical illusion called a **subjective contour,** popularized in an article by the Italian psychologist Gaetano Kanizsa in the April 1976 issue of *Scientific American.* The following screen image shows an example of a subjective contour in which the rectangle framed by the cutaway circles appears brighter than the background:

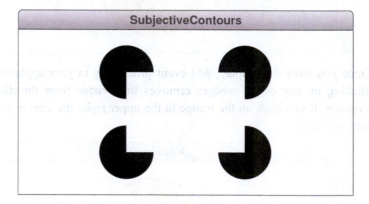

Although the simplest way to produce this picture is to draw a white rectangle on top of four complete circles, a skeptic might claim that the color of the rectangle is brighter than its background. Make it impossible to defend this claim by drawing this figure using only the four filled arcs.

11. Another illusion that uses filled arcs is the **Wundt illusion,** first described by Wilhelm Max Wundt in 1898.

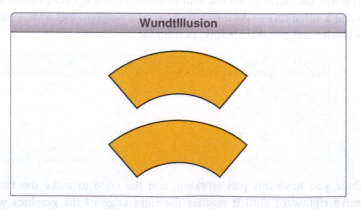

In this illusion, the lower curve looks longer than the upper curve, although the two are in fact the same size. Write a program that draws these segments using the graphics library. To do so, you need to draw a filled arc, overlay it with a smaller arc filled in white, and then complete the border with an unfilled arc.

12. Write a program that draws the following optical illusion on the graphics window:

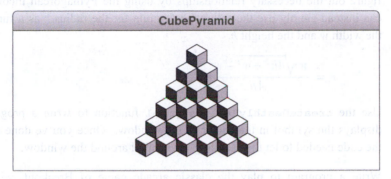

The illusion arises from the fact that it is possible to see the white surfaces as either the tops or the bottoms of cubes stacked to form a pyramid.

Each of the individual cubes is composed of three diamond-shaped polygons whose sides have different fill colors and which are rotated at different angles, as follows:

In writing this exercise, you should create a function that returns one of these cubes as a **GCompound** and then assemble the pyramid from those compounds.

13. In J. K. Rowling's *Harry Potter and the Deathly Hallows,* those who believe in the legend named in the title recognize one another through a symbol that combines three elements—a triangle representing the cloak of invisibility, a circle representing the stone of resurrection, and a line representing the elder wand—superimposed as follows:

Write a function `createDeathlyHallowsSymbol` that takes two parameters indicating the width and height of the figure and returns a `GCompound` that includes all three of these elements. The triangle should be a `GPolygon`, the circle should be a `GOval`, and the line should be a `GLine`. The geometry is straightforward for both the line and the triangle, but rather complicated for the circle, which must exactly touch the edges of the triangle. Although you could figure out the necessary relationships by using the Pythagorean theorem, you can instead simply use the following formula for the radius r as a function of the width w and the height h:

$$r = \frac{w\sqrt{4h^2 + w^2} - w^2}{4h}$$

Use the `createDeathlyHallowsSymbol` function to write a program that displays the symbol in the center of the window. Once you've done that, add the code needed to let the user drag the symbol around the window.

14. Write a program to play the classic arcade game of Breakout, which was developed in 1976 by Steve Wozniak, who would later become one of the founders of Apple. In Breakout, your goal is to clear a collection of bricks by hitting each of them with a bouncing ball.

The initial configuration of the Breakout game appears in the leftmost diagram in Figure 6-14. The colored rectangles in the top part of the screen are bricks, two rows each of red, orange, yellow, green, and blue. The slightly larger rectangle at the bottom is the paddle. The paddle is in a fixed position in the vertical dimension, but moves back and forth across the screen along with the mouse until it reaches the edge of its space.

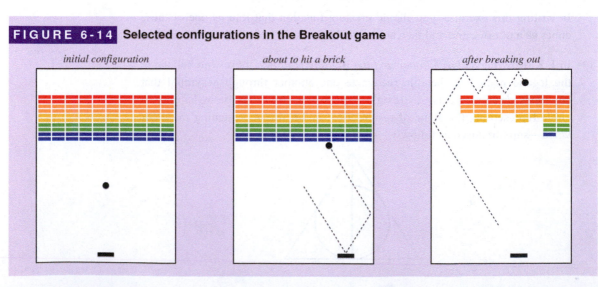

FIGURE 6-14 Selected configurations in the Breakout game

initial configuration   *about to hit a brick*   *after breaking out*

A complete Breakout game consists of three turns. On each turn, a ball is launched from the center of the window toward the bottom of the screen at a random angle. That ball bounces off the paddle and the walls of the world. Thus, after two bounces—one off the paddle and one off the right wall—the ball might have the trajectory shown in the middle diagram.

As you can see from the middle diagram, the ball is about to collide with one of the bricks on the bottom row. When that happens, the ball bounces just as it does on any other collision, but the brick disappears (which you can accomplish simply by removing it from the graphics window).

The play continues in this way until one of the following conditions occurs:

- The ball hits the lower wall, which means that you must have missed it with the paddle. In this case, the turn ends and the next ball is served, assuming that you have not already exhausted your allotment of three turns. If you have, the game ends in a loss.

- The last brick is eliminated. In this case, the game ends immediately, and you can retire victorious.

After all the bricks in a particular column have been cleared, a path will open to the top wall, as shown in the rightmost diagram in Figure 6-14. When this delightful situation occurs, the ball will often bounce back and forth several times between the top wall and the upper line of bricks without the user ever having to worry about hitting the ball with the paddle. This condition is called "breaking out." It is important to note that, even though breaking out is a very exciting part of the player's experience, you don't have to do anything special in your program to make it happen. The game operates the same as always: balls bounce off walls, collide with bricks, and obey the laws of physics.

The only part of the implementation that requires some explanation is the problem of checking to see whether the ball has collided with a brick or the paddle. The `getElementAt` method can determine whether there is an object at a particular position, but it doesn't work well to check the coordinates of the ball's center because the ball is larger than a single point. In this program, the simplest strategy is to check the four corner points on the square in which the ball is inscribed. A collision occurs if any of those points are inside a brick.

15. In New York's Times Square, you can get the news of the day by watching headlines on large display screens that show a single line of text. The headline initially begins to appear at the right edge of the screen and then moves quickly from right to left. Your job in this exercise is to write a program that simulates this type of headline display by moving a `GLabel` across the screen.

Suppose, for example, that you want to use your program to display the famous *Chicago Tribune* headline from when the paper incorrectly called the result of the 1948 presidential election:

DEWEY DEFEATS TRUMAN

Your program should create a `GLabel` containing the headline and then position it so that the entire text of the label is clipped beyond the right edge of the screen. Your program should then implement a timer-based graphical animation that moves the `GLabel` a few pixels to the left on each time step. After a few time steps, the display will show the first letter of the headline, as follows:

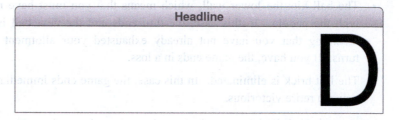

The headline continues to scroll across the screen, so that a few seconds later the entire first word is visible:

As the label continues to scroll, letters will disappear off the left edge of the screen as new letters appear on the right. Your program should continue to scroll letters toward the left until the entire `GLabel` disappears from view.

CHAPTER 7
Strings

The work [of conducting the census should] be done so far as possible by mechanical means. In order to accomplish this the records must be put in such shape that a machine could read them. This is most readily done by punching holes in cards.

— Herman Hollerith, *An Electric Tabulating System,* 1889

(Bettmann/Getty Images)

Herman Hollerith (1860–1929)

The idea of encoding text in machine-readable form dates back to the nineteenth century and the work of the American inventor Herman Hollerith. After studying engineering at City College of New York and the Columbia School of Mines, Hollerith spent a couple of years working as a statistician for the U.S. Census Bureau before accepting a teaching position at MIT. While at the Census Bureau, Hollerith had become convinced that the data produced by the census could be counted more quickly and accurately by machine. In the late 1880s, he designed and built a tabulating machine that was used to conduct the 1890 census in record time. The company he founded to commercialize his invention, originally called the Tabulating Machine Company, changed its name in 1924 to International Business Machines (IBM). Hollerith's card-based tabulating system pioneered the technique of textual encoding described in this chapter—a contribution that was reflected in the fact that early versions of the FORTRAN language used the letter H (for Hollerith) to indicate text data.

Although you have been using strings ever since Chapter 2, you have only scratched the surface of what you can do with string data. This chapter introduces the features available in the JavaScript `String` class, which provides a convenient abstraction for working with strings of characters. Understanding the various methods available in this library will make it much easier to write interesting applications. Before considering the details of the `String` class, however, it helps to take a step back and look at how computers store data in the first place.

7.1 Binary representation

Today's computers represent information in a simple but powerful form that allows information—no matter how complex—to be stored as a sequence of primitive values that can exist in only one of two possible states. Each of those primitive values is called a ***bit.***

The interpretation of the values for each bit depends on how you choose to view the underlying information. If you think of the bits that form the internal circuitry of the machine as tiny light switches, you might label those states as *off* and *on*. If you think of each bit as a logical value, you might instead use the Boolean labels *false* and *true*. However, because the word *bit* comes from a contraction of the term *binary digit,* it is more common to label those states as **0** and **1**, which are the digits of the binary number system on which computer arithmetic is based.

Binary notation

Leibniz

(GL Archive/Alamy Stock Photo)

The idea of writing numbers in binary notation predates the development of the electronic computer by more than 250 years. The German mathematician Gottfried Wilhelm von Leibniz (1646–1716) offered a detailed account of the binary system in a paper published by the French Royal Academy of Science in 1703. In that paper, Leibniz writes:

> Ordinary arithmetic calculation is performed following a progression by tens. One uses the ten characters 0, 1, 2, 3, 4, 5, 6, 7, 8, 9, which signify zero, one, and the following numbers up to nine, inclusive. On going up to ten, one starts again, and writes *ten* as 10; ten times ten, or *one hundred,* as 100; ten times one hundred, or *one thousand,* as 1000; and ten times a thousand as 10000. And so on.
>
> But instead of the progression by tens, I have used for several years the simplest progression of all, which goes by twos, which I find to be the perfection of the science of numbers. I therefore do not use any characters other than 0 and 1, and on going up to two, I start again. That is why *two* is written here as 10; and two times two or *four* as 100; and two times four or *eight* as 1000 . . .

Leibniz's second paragraph describes the binary system as "the simplest progression of all." Each digit in a binary number counts for twice as much as its neighbor on the right. That rule makes it easy to translate a number written in binary back to its decimal equivalent: all you need to do is add the place values of each digit in the number. For example, if Leibniz were to use binary notation to represent the year of his birth, he would write the number like this:

1 1 0 0 1 1 0 1 1 1 0

The following diagram shows that this value indeed corresponds to the value 1646:

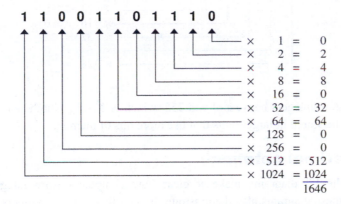

For the most part, numeric representations in this book use decimal notation for readability. If the base is not clear from the context, the text follows the usual strategy of using a subscript to denote the base. For example, the equivalence of the binary value 11001101110 and the decimal value 1646 can be made explicit by writing the numbers like this:

$$11001101110_2 = 1646_{10}$$

Storing integers as sequences of bits

The binary representation described by Leibniz makes it easy to store integers as a sequence of individual bits. In modern computer hardware, individual bits are collected together into larger units that are then treated as integral units of storage. The smallest such combined unit is called a **byte**, which consists of eight bits. Bytes are then assembled into larger structures called **words**, where a word is usually defined to be the size required to hold an integer value of the type most appropriate for the hardware. Today, machines typically organize their memory into words that are either four or eight bytes long (32 or 64 bits).

To get a sense of how computers can store integers internally, consider the byte containing the following binary digits:

0	0	1	0	1	0	1	0

That sequence of bits represents the number forty-two, which you can verify—just as Leibniz would have done—by calculating the contribution for each of the individual bits, as follows:

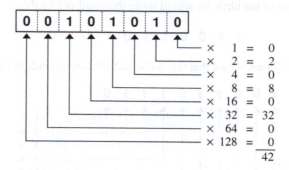

Bytes can store integers between 0 and 255, which is $2^8 - 1$. Numbers outside this range must be stored in larger units that use more bits of memory.

Hexadecimal notation

Although the bit diagrams make it clear how computers store integer values internally, these diagrams also demonstrate the fact that writing numbers in binary form is terribly inconvenient. Binary numbers are cumbersome, mostly because they tend to be so long. Decimal representations are intuitive and familiar but make it harder to understand how the number translates into bits.

For applications in which it is useful to understand how a number translates into its binary representation without having to work with binary numbers that stretch all the way across the page, computer scientists use *hexadecimal* (base 16) notation instead. In hexadecimal notation, there are sixteen digits that represent the values from 0 to 15. Although the decimal digits 0 through 9 are perfectly adequate for the first ten digits, classical arithmetic does not define the extra symbols you need to represent the remaining six. Computer science traditionally uses the letters **A** through **F** for this purpose, as follows:

$$
\begin{aligned}
\mathbf{A} &= 10 \\
\mathbf{B} &= 11 \\
\mathbf{C} &= 12 \\
\mathbf{D} &= 13 \\
\mathbf{E} &= 14 \\
\mathbf{F} &= 15
\end{aligned}
$$

What makes hexadecimal notation useful is the fact that you can easily convert between hexadecimal values and the underlying binary representation. All you need to do is combine the bits into groups of four. For example, the number forty-two can be converted from binary to hexadecimal like this:

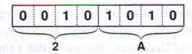

The first four bits represent the number 2, and the next four represent the number 10. Converting each of these to the corresponding hexadecimal digit gives **2A** as the hexadecimal form. You can then verify that this number still has the value 42 by adding up the digit values, as follows:

$$
\begin{array}{r}
2\ \ A \\
\times\ \ 1\ =\ 10 \\
\times\ 16\ =\ 32 \\
\hline
42
\end{array}
$$

As noted earlier, the text follows the convention of using a subscript to denote the base if it is not clear from context. Thus, the three most common representations for the number forty-two—decimal, binary, and hexadecimal—look like this:

$$42_{10} = 00101010_2 = 2A_{16}$$

The most important thing to remember, however, is that the number itself is always the same; the numeric base affects only the representation. Forty-two has an intrinsic meaning that is independent of the base, which is perhaps easiest to see in the representation an elementary school student might use:

$$\cancel{||||}\ \cancel{||||}\ \cancel{||||}\ \cancel{||||}\ \cancel{||||}\ \cancel{||||}\ \cancel{||||}\ \cancel{||||}\ ||$$

The number of tick marks in this representation is forty-two. The fact that a number is written in binary, decimal, or any other base is a property of the representation, not of the number itself. Numbers do not have bases; representations do.

Representing nonnumeric data

Although the discussion so far has focused on how computers store numbers, this chapter is about strings, which are an important example of ***nonnumeric data.*** The challenge in having computers represent nonnumeric data lies in finding a way to store that information inside the computer.

The simplest strategy for representing nonnumeric data is to assign numbers to the individual data values you need to represent. For example, the conventional way to represent the months of the year—even without a computer—is to give each month a number: January has the value 1, February has the value 2, and so on, up to December, which has the value 12. This strategy is called ***enumeration.***

Once you have enumerated a set of values, you can represent those values in memory by using the appropriate numeric code. For example, the numeric value 12 corresponds to the month of December. Internally, that value is stored as an integer expressed—as you saw in the preceding sections—as a sequence of binary digits. There is no indication in the hardware as to whether that value represents the integer 12 or the numeric representation for the month of December. The meaning of a particular value depends on how it is used. If the program uses the value arithmetically, it is interpreted as the integer 12. If it instead uses that value to select from a list of month names, that value indicates December. In either case, the number stored inside the computer is exactly the same.

The strategy of using numbers to represent nonnumeric data is one of the most important ideas in the history of computation. One of the clearest and earliest expositions of that idea comes from Ada Lovelace, daughter of the poet Lord Byron and his wife Anna Isabella Byron. In the 1840s, Lady Lovelace collaborated with the English mathematician and inventor Charles Babbage on the design of his Analytical Engine, a calculating machine that anticipated several essential features of modern computers, including the ability to solve different tasks by changing its programming. Indeed, much of what we know about the Analytical Engine—which sadly was never completed—comes from Lovelace's translation of a detailed description of Babbage's work by the Italian engineer Luigi Menabrea. Her translation, entitled *Sketch of the Analytical Engine Invented by Charles Babbage, Esq.,* was published in 1843, along with her explanatory notes that were almost three times as long as the original paper. Lovelace recognized that the algebraic patterns for which the Analytical Engine was designed could be extended to include concepts beyond simple numbers. Her notes envision a world of possibilities for the Analytical Engine that someday "might compose elaborate and scientific pieces of music of any degree of complexity or extent."

In an interview for a film about Ada Lovelace's life and work, Doron Swade, who led the effort to rebuild Babbage's earlier Difference Engine for the Science Museum in London, offers the following description of Ada's contribution:

> Ada saw something that, in some sense, Babbage failed to see. In Babbage's world, his engines were bound by number. . . . What Lovelace saw—what Ada Byron saw—was that number could represent entities other than quantity. So, once you had a machine for manipulating numbers, if those numbers represented other things—letters, musical notes—then the machine could manipulate symbols of which number was one instance."

Ada Lovelace

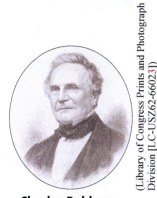

Charles Babbage

Representing characters

The primitive elements of string data are individual characters. Like the months of the year, characters can be represented inside the computer by assigning each character a numeric code. You could, for example, assign successive integers to represent each of the letters in the alphabet, using 0 for the letter **A**, 1 for letter **B**, and so on. In 1605, the English philosopher and scientist Francis Bacon did precisely that when he devised a technique for encoding messages that is now known as ***Bacon's cipher.*** What is, however, even more astonishing is that Bacon based his cipher on the binary representation of these numbers, almost a century before Leibniz published his paper on binary arithmetic. Bacon's cipher, however, was not used in practice and had little or no influence on the later development of computation.

Francis Bacon

(Georgios Kollidas/Shutterstock)

The first binary encoding scheme for characters used extensively in practice was the ***Baudot code,*** which was invented in 1870 by the French engineer Émile Baudot, one of the pioneers of the telegraph. In Baudot's scheme, each of the 26 letters was assigned a numeric code. The encoding also included a few special characters to represent the space character, the two characters that telegraph printers used to designate the end of a line, and transitions to an alternate character set used for digits and punctuation. The letters of the alphabet did not appear in order, but were instead chosen so that the most common letters, such as **E** and **T**, would require pressing just one of the five keys on the input device that Baudot designed.

Émile Baudot

(Historic Images/Alamy Stock Photo)

The fact that the letters do not appear consecutively in the Baudot code does not make the encoding scheme any less effective. The only essential characteristic of an encoding system is that the sender and receiver agree on how to convert letters to numeric codes. The need for a common encoding shared by senders and receivers increases the importance of standardization. As long as all telegraph operators used the same code, they were able to communicate with one another.

In the early years of the computing industry, standardization was complicated by the existence of incompatible character encodings. The American Standards Association (now known as the American National Standards Institute or ANSI) began work on a standardized character encoding in 1960, which was formalized in 1963 as the ***American Standard Code for Information Interchange*** or ***ASCII.*** Early IBM machines used a different character set derived from the coding system used for punched cards. That early character set evolved into a competing standard called the ***Extended Binary Coded Decimal Interchange Code*** or ***EBCDIC.*** Over time, ASCII and its successors have become the dominant standard in the industry.

In its original design, ASCII contained 128 characters, which is enough to store the uppercase and lowercase letters of the Latin alphabet, the standard decimal digits, a variety of punctuation symbols, and a set of nonprinting characters called ***control characters.*** The characters in the original ASCII set appear in Figure 7-1. The gray boxes in the table correspond to control characters that have lost their significance over time. The few remaining control characters recognized by JavaScript are indicated using a backslash (\) followed by a letter that defines that

FIGURE 7-1 The first 128 characters in ASCII

	0	1	2	3	4	5	6	7	8	9	A	B	C	D	E	F
0x	\0								\b	\t	\n	\v	\f	\r		
1x																
2x	space	!	"	#	$	%	&	'	(	)	*	+	,	-	.	/
3x	0	1	2	3	4	5	6	7	8	9	:	;	<	=	>	?
4x	@	A	B	C	D	E	F	G	H	I	J	K	L	M	N	O
5x	P	Q	R	S	T	U	V	W	X	Y	Z	[	\	]	^	_
6x	`	a	b	c	d	e	f	g	h	i	j	k	l	m	n	o
7x	p	q	r	s	t	u	v	w	x	y	z	{	|	}	~	

character's function.   For example, the character \n represents the **newline character,** which marks the end of a line. None of the other control characters are used in this book.

The characters in Figure 7-1 are arranged according to their internal values, which are expressed in hexadecimal. The character **A**, for example, appears in the row labeled **4**x and the column labeled **1**, so its internal representation is **41**$_{16}$, which is the decimal number 65. There is no need to learn these values, although certain patterns are important. This text, for example, relies on the following properties:

- The digit characters are consecutive.

- The uppercase and lowercase letters form two consecutive sequences.

The ASCII coding system quickly proved to be inadequate as computing expanded into the global environment. With the advent of the World Wide Web in the 1990s, it became necessary to expand the encoding system to embrace a broader collection of languages. The result of that expansion was a new standard called **Unicode,** which supports a much larger set of characters. The version of Unicode implemented in JavaScript allows for 65,536 (2^{16}) characters.

Unfortunately, even that expanded standard has become too small for modern computing. The current version of Unicode includes 1,114,112 characters, ranging from ancient alphabets to **emoji,** the small digital images used to express emotions or ideas in text messages. Because these symbols were added to Unicode after JavaScript was formalized, it requires extra work to include them in strings. Using those characters, moreover, requires the use of a concept called a *code point,* which was added only in version 6 of the JavaScript standard, which puts it beyond the scope of this text. Detailed information about code points is available on the web.

7.2 String operations

JavaScript supports a wide range of operations on strings beyond the simple ones you saw in Chapter 2. You already know that JavaScript uses the + operator to join strings together end to end, which is called *concatenation.* If you apply the + operator to two numbers, JavaScript adds them numerically. If the value on either side of the + operator is a string, JavaScript converts both values into strings and concatenates the two.

In addition to the + operator, JavaScript allows you to use the relational operators ===, !==, <, <=, >, and >= to compare two string values. For example, the following code checks whether the value of str is equal to "yes":

```
if (str === "yes") . . .
```

The relational operators compare strings using *lexicographic order,* which is similar to traditional alphabetical order but which uses the underlying Unicode values of each character to make the comparison. Lexicographic order means that case is significant, so "a" is not equal to "A". In lexicographic order, "a" is greater than "A" because the Unicode value for a lowercase **a** (61_{16} or 97) is greater than the Unicode value for an uppercase **A** (41_{16} or 65).

All other string operations require calling methods on a string value using the receiver syntax you learned in Chapter 4 for working with graphical objects:

receiver . name (*arguments*)

Figure 7-2 on the next page lists the most common methods that JavaScript defines as part of its String class. These methods are explored in detail in the sections that follow.

Determining the length of a string

The simplest operation that you can perform on a string value—which you already know from Chapter 2—is determining its *length,* which is the number of characters it contains. Given a JavaScript string variable str, you can determine the length by evaluating str.length. It is important to note that, in contrast to the other string operations listed in Figure 7-2, length is not defined as a method but instead as a JavaScript *property,* which is a data value associated with an object. Defining length as a property means that no parentheses appear after the property name.

As an example, if ALPHABET is defined as

```
const ALPHABET = "ABCDEFGHIJKLMNOPQRSTUVWXYZ";
```

Common operations in JavaScript's string class

String operators

str_1 **+** str_2	Concatenates str_1 and str_2 end to end and returns a new string containing the combined characters. As either operand is a string, JavaScript will convert the other to its string form.
str **+=** $suffix$	Appends $suffix$ to the end of str.
str_1 **===** str_2 str_1 **!==** str_2 str_1 **<** str_2 str_1 **<=** str_2 str_1 **>** str_2 str_1 **>=** str_2	These operators compare str_1 and str_2. The comparison is performed using lexicographic order, which is the order defined by the underlying Unicode values.

String field

str.**length**	Returns the number of characters in str.

String class method

String.fromCharCode ($code$)	Returns a one-character string with the specified Unicode value.

String methods

str.**charAt** (k)	Returns a one-character string formed from the character at index position k in str.
str.**charCodeAt** (k)	Returns the Unicode value for the character at index position k in str.
str.**substring** (p_1, p_2) str.**substring** (p_1)	Returns a new string of characters beginning at p_1 in str and extending up to but not including p_2. If p_2 is missing, the new string continues through the end of the original string.
str.**indexOf** ($pattern$) str.**indexOf** ($pattern$, k)	Searches the string str for the string $pattern$. The search starts at the beginning, or at index k, if specified. The function returns the first index at which $pattern$ appears, or −1 if it is not found.
str.**lastIndexOf** ($pattern$) str.**lastIndexOf** ($pattern$, k)	Operates like **indexOf**, but searches backward from position k. If k is missing, **lastIndexOf** starts at the end of the string.
str.**replace** ($pattern$, $replacement$)	Returns a copy of str with the first instance of $pattern$ replaced by $replacement$.
str.**split** ($pattern$)	Splits the string into an array of substrings by dividing it at instances of $pattern$. The **split** method is discussed along with arrays in Chapter 8.
str.**toLowerCase** ()	Returns a copy of str converting all characters to lowercase.
str.**toUpperCase** ()	Returns a copy of str converting all characters to uppercase.
str.**startsWith** ($prefix$)	Returns **true** if str starts with the characters in $prefix$.
str.**endsWith** ($suffix$)	Returns **true** if str ends with the characters in $suffix$.
str.**trim** ()	Returns a copy of str after removing whitespace from each end.

the expression **ALPHABET.length** has the value 26. Similarly, if you create a variable **str** using the declaration

```
let str = "";
```

the expression **str.length** has the value 0. The string containing no characters at all, which comes up frequently in programming, is called the *empty string.*

Selecting characters from a string

In JavaScript, positions within a string are numbered starting from 0. For example, the characters in **ALPHABET** are numbered as in the following diagram:

The position number written underneath each character is called its *index.*

In JavaScript, you select a character from a string by calling the **charAt** method. For example, the expression

```
ALPHABET.charAt(0)
```

selects the character **"A"** at the beginning, which is returned as a one-character string. Since character numbering in JavaScript begins at 0, the last character in a string appears at the index position that's one less than the length of the string. Thus, you can select the **"Z"** at the end of **ALPHABET** with the following expression:

```
ALPHABET.charAt(ALPHABET.length - 1)
```

JavaScript allows you to retrieve the underlying Unicode value of the character at any index position by calling **charCodeAt** with the desired index. For example,

```
ALPHABET.charCodeAt(0)
```

returns the Unicode value of the character **"A"** at index position 0, which you can determine from Figure 7-1 has the value 41_{16}, or 65. To convert from character codes to strings, you need to use the function **String.fromCharCode**, which, like the various **Math** functions, is associated with a class rather than an object. Calling **String.fromCharCode(90)**, for example, returns the one-character string **"Z"**.

Extracting parts of a string

While concatenation makes longer strings from shorter pieces, you often need to do the reverse: separate a string into the shorter pieces it contains. A string that is part of a longer string is called a *substring.* JavaScript's **String** class exports a method called **substring** that takes two parameters: the index of the first character you want to select and the index of the character that immediately follows the desired substring. For example, the method call

> `ALPHABET.substring(1, 4)`

returns the three-character substring `"BCD"`. Because indices in JavaScript begin at 0, the character at index position 1 is the character `"B"`.

The `substring` method implements the following special cases:

- If the second argument is missing, it is assumed to be the length of the string.
- If either argument is less than 0, it is assumed to be 0.
- If either argument is greater than the length of the string, it is assumed to be the length of the string.
- If the second argument is less than the first, the two arguments are swapped.

The JavaScript `String` class exports two other methods, `substr` and `slice`, that select substrings but use different conventions for defining which characters should appear. To minimize confusion, this text uses only the `substring` method.

Searching within a string

From time to time, you will find it useful to search a string to see whether it contains a particular character or substring. To support such search operations, JavaScript's `String` class exports a method called `indexOf`, which comes in two forms. The simplest form of the call is

> `str.indexOf(pattern);`

where *pattern* is the content you're looking for. When called, the `indexOf` method searches through `str` looking for the first occurrence of the pattern. If the search value is found, `indexOf` returns the index position at which the match begins. If the character does not appear before the end of the string, `indexOf` returns −1.

The `indexOf` method takes an optional second argument that indicates the index position at which to start the search. The effect of both styles of the `indexOf` method is illustrated by the following examples, which assume that the variable `str` contains the string `"hello, world"`:

> `str.indexOf("o")`   →   4
> `str.indexOf("o", 5)`   →   8
> `str.indexOf("o", 9)`   →   −1

The JavaScript `String` class also includes a `lastIndexOf` method that works like `indexOf`, except that it searches backward for a match.

Case conversion

The methods **toLowerCase** and **toUpperCase** convert any alphabetic characters in the receiver string to the specified case, leaving any other characters unchanged. For example, if **str** contains **"hello, world"**, calling **str.toUpperCase()** returns **"HELLO, WORLD"**. Similarly, calling **ALPHABET.toLowerCase()** returns **"abcdefghijklmnopqrstuvwxyz"**.

It is important to remember that the methods in JavaScript's **String** class do not change the value of the receiver but instead return an entirely new string value. Thus, calling **str.toUpperCase()** doesn't change the value of the variable **str**. If you want to change the value of **str** to its uppercase equivalent, you need to use an assignment statement to store the value back into the variable, as in

```
str = str.toUpperCase();
```

The **toUpperCase** method makes it easy to write a predicate function called **equalsIgnoreCase** that checks whether two strings are equal if the comparison ignores the distinction between uppercase and lowercase characters, as follows:

```
function equalsIgnoreCase(s1, s2) {
   return s1.toUpperCase() === s2.toUpperCase();
}
```

The startsWith, endsWith, and trim methods

Although the last three methods in Figure 7-2 don't fit easily into the other categories, they turn out to be very useful. The **startsWith** method returns **true** if the receiver string begins with the specified prefix. For example, the Boolean expression

```
answer.startsWith("y") || answer.startsWith("Y")
```

is **true** if **answer** begins with either **"y"** or **"Y"**. The **endsWith** method is symmetric and returns **true** if the string ends with the specified suffix. The **trim** method returns a copy of the string after removing all *whitespace characters* ("invisible" characters such as spaces or tabs) from both ends of the string.

Some JavaScript programmers avoid these methods because they didn't exist in early versions of JavaScript. If you need to ensure that your code runs on as many browsers as possible, you can implement these tools as predicate functions. For example, you can implement the function **startsWith** like this:

```
function startsWith(str, prefix) {
   return prefix === str.substring(0, prefix.length);
}
```

Converting between numbers and strings

Ever since Chapter 2, you have relied on the fact that the + operator, assuming that at least one of its operands is a string, automatically converts numeric values into strings before performing the concatenation. For example, the expression

```
"When I'm " + 8 * 8
```

performs the multiplication first to get 64, converts that number to a string, and then concatenates that string to the end of the characters `"When I'm "` to produce the string `"When I'm 64"`. At times, however, it is useful to exercise more control over the format of the numeric string.

One tool for formatting numbers is the `toString` method, which applies to any numeric value. With no argument, `toString` performs the same conversion as the concatenation operator and produces a string of digits. When used with numbers, `toString` allows you to specify the base as a parameter. For example, if `n` contains the value 42, calling `n.toString(16)` returns the string `"2a"`. If you prefer upper case for hexadecimal digits, you can call `toUpperCase` on the result.

To offer some control over numeric formatting, JavaScript defines the methods `toFixed`, which specifies exactly how many digits should appear after the decimal point in the converted string, and `toPrecision`, which specifies the number of significant digits. For example, calling `Math.PI.toFixed(4)` produces the string `"3.1416"`, which includes four digits following the decimal point. Calling `Math.PI.toPrecision(4)` returns `"3.142"`, which has four significant digits.

JavaScript includes two built-in functions that convert numeric strings into the numeric values signified by those strings. The `parseInt` function converts a string of digits into the corresponding numeric value. By default, `parseInt` interprets the number as a decimal value, but the function takes an optional second argument specifying the base. For example, calling `parseInt("2A", 16)` returns the value 42. The `parseFloat` function performs a similar conversion for a string representing a floating-point value, so that `parseFloat("3.14159")` returns the numeric value 3.14159.

Unfortunately, the `parseInt` and `parseFloat` functions are difficult to use if you need to ensure that the value you are scanning is a legitimate number. Each of these functions converts its argument to a number by scanning characters until it finds a character that doesn't belong in a number and then ignores any characters that come after that. Calling `parseInt("123xyz")`, for example, returns the integer 123, even though the entire argument is not a legal number.

A better strategy for converting strings to numbers is to call the built-in `Number` function, which translates its argument to a number. The `Number` function signals failure by returning **NaN**, which is short for *not a number*. In JavaScript, you check whether a value is **NaN** by calling the built-in function **isNaN**. You cannot use the **===** operator because **NaN** is traditionally defined so that it is not equal to itself. Although this definition may initially seem odd, two computations that produce **NaN** might in fact be generating different values.

7.3 Classifying characters

When you work with individual characters in a string, it is often useful to determine whether those characters fall into particular categories, such as letters or digits. To do so, you can take advantage of the fact that Unicode assigns consecutive character codes to the digits and the uppercase and lowercase letters. The fact that the digit characters are consecutive, for example, means that you can check whether a character is a digit using the following predicate function:

```
function isDigit(ch) {
    return ch.length === 1 && ch >= "0" && ch <= "9";
}
```

The Boolean expression in the **return** statement first checks that the parameter **ch** is a single-character string and, if so, checks to make sure that it appears in the inclusive range between **"0"** and **"9"** in lexicographic order. Similarly, you can check whether a character is an uppercase letter using the following function:

```
function isUpperCase(ch) {
    return ch.length === 1 && ch >= "A" && ch <= "Z";
}
```

Functions like **isDigit** and **isUpperCase** occur so frequently in applications that it is worth putting them in a library. Figure 7-3 on the next page shows the code for the **CharacterType.js** library, which exports several methods for classifying characters. If you load this library in the **index.html** that runs your application, you can check whether the variable **ch** contains a letter by calling

```
isLetter(ch)
```

If you need to implement character classifications other than those provided by **CharacterType.js**, you can use **indexOf** to see whether the character in question exists in a string constant that contains the appropriate values. The following predicate function, for example, tests whether the character **ch** is an English vowel:

```
function isEnglishVowel(ch) {
    return ch.length === 1 &&
            "AEIOUaeiou".indexOf(ch) !== -1;
}
```

FIGURE 7-3 A library to classify characters by type

```js
/*
 * File: CharacterType.js
 * -----------------------
 * This library exports a set of functions to classify a character by type.
 */

/*
 * Returns true if the character ch is a digit.
 */

function isDigit(ch) {
   return ch.length === 1 && ch >= "0" && ch <= "9";
}

/*
 * Returns true if the character ch is a letter in the Roman alphabet.
 */

function isLetter(ch) {
   return isLowerCase(ch) || isUpperCase(ch);
}

/*
 * Returns true if the character ch is a letter or a digit.
 */

function isLetterOrDigit(ch) {
   return isLetter(ch) || isDigit(ch);
}

/*
 * Returns true if the character ch is a lowercase letter.
 */

function isLowerCase(ch) {
   return ch.length === 1 && ch >= "a" && ch <= "z";
}

/*
 * Returns true if the character ch is an uppercase letter.
 */

function isUpperCase(ch) {
   return ch.length === 1 && ch >= "A" && ch <= "Z";
}

/*
 * Returns true if the character ch is a "whitespace" character.
 */

function isWhitespace(ch) {
   return ch === " " || ch === "\t" || ch === "\n" || ch === "\f" ||
          ch === "\r" || ch === "\v";
}
```

7.4 Common string patterns

Even though the methods exported by JavaScript's `String` class provide the tools you need to implement simple applications, it is usually easier to write programs by adapting code patterns that implement common operations. The two most important string patterns are iterating through the characters in a string and growing a string by concatenation. The sections that follow describe these patterns.

Iterating through the characters in a string

When you work with strings, one of the most important patterns involves iterating through the characters in a string, which requires the following code:

```
for (let i = 0; i < str.length; i++) {
    . . . body of loop that uses the character str.charAt(i) . . .
}
```

On each loop cycle, the expression `str.charAt(i)` refers to the character in the string at index position `i`. You can, for example, count the number of spaces in a string using the following function:

```
function countSpaces(str) {
    let nSpaces = 0;
    for (let i = 0; i < str.length; i++) {
        if (str.charAt(i) === " ") nSpaces++;
    }
    return nSpaces;
}
```

For some applications, it is useful to iterate through a string in the opposite direction. This style of iteration uses the following `for` loop:

```
for (let i = str.length - 1; i >= 0; i--)
```

Here, the index `i` begins at the last index position and then decreases by one on each cycle, down to and including the index position 0.

Assuming that you understand the syntax and semantics of the `for` statement, you could work out these iteration patterns from first principles each time you need them in an application. Doing so, however, would slow you down enormously. These patterns are worth memorizing so that you don't have to waste any time thinking about them. Whenever you recognize that you need to cycle through the characters in a string, some part of your nervous system between your brain and your fingers should be able to translate that idea effortlessly into the following line:

```
for (let i = 0; i < str.length; i++)
```

Growing a string through concatenation

The other string pattern that is important to memorize involves creating a new string one character at a time. The details of the loop depend on the application, but the general pattern for creating a string by concatenation looks like this:

```
let str ="";
for (whatever loop header line fits the application) {
    str += the next substring or character;
}
```

For example, the nCopies function returns a string consisting of n copies of str:

```
function nCopies(n, str) {
    let result = "";
    for (let i = 0; i < n; i++) {
        result += str;
    }
    return result;
}
```

The nCopies function is useful if, for example, you need to generate some kind of section separator in console output. One strategy for accomplishing this goal would be to use the following statement to print a line of 72 hyphens:

```
console.log(nCopies(72, "-"));
```

Combining the iteration and concatenation patterns

Many string-processing functions use the iteration and concatenation patterns together. For example, the following function reverses the argument string so that calling reverse("stressed") returns "desserts":

```
function reverse(str) {
    let result = "";
    for (let i = str.length - 1; i >= 0; i--) {
        result += str.charAt(i);
    }
    return result;
}
```

You can also implement reverse by running the loop in the forward direction and concatenating each new character to the front of the result string, as follows:

```
for (let i = 0; i < str.length; i++) {
    result = str.charAt(i) + result;
}
```

7.5 String applications

The easiest way to improve your understanding of strings is to look at several sample applications. The sections that follow walk you through four applications that use strings in different ways.

Checking for palindromes

A *palindrome* is a word that reads identically backward and forward, such as *level* or *noon*. The goal of this section is to write a predicate function `isPalindrome` that checks whether a string is a palindrome. Calling `isPalindrome("level")` should return `true`; calling `isPalindrome("xyz")` should return `false`.

As with most programming problems, there is more than one strategy for solving this problem. The following code illustrates one strategy:

```
function isPalindrome(str) {
   let n = str.length;
   for (let i = 0; i < n / 2; i++) {
      if (str.charAt(i) !== str.charAt(n - i - 1)) {
         return false;
      }
   }
   return true;
}
```

This implementation uses a `for` loop to run through each index position in the first half of the string, checking whether the character in that position matches the one in the symmetric position relative to the end of the string.

If, however, you make use of the functions you already have, you can code `isPalindrome` in a much simpler form, as follows:

```
function isPalindrome(str) {
   return str === reverse(str);
}
```

Although both implementations of `isPalindrome` return the correct result, there are various tradeoffs that may lead you to choose one over the other. The first implementation, for example, is substantially more efficient because it doesn't require creating any new strings. Despite the difference in efficiency, the second version has many advantages, particularly as an example for new programmers. For one thing, it takes advantage of existing code by making use of the **reverse** function. For another, it hides the complexity involved in calculating the index positions required by the first version. It takes at least a minute or two for most students to figure out why the code includes the selection expression `str.charAt(n - i - 1)` or why it is appropriate to use the `<` operator in the **for** loop test, as opposed to `<=`. By contrast, the line

```
return str === reverse(str);
```

reads as fluidly as English: a string is a palindrome if it is equal to the same string when you reverse it. That, after all, is precisely the definition of a palindrome.

Particularly as you are learning about programming, it is better to work toward the clarity shown in the second implementation of `isPalindrome` than to try and match the efficiency of the first. Given the speed of modern computers, it is almost always worth sacrificing some efficiency to make a program easier to understand.

Generating acronyms

An *acronym* is a new word formed by combining, in order, the initial letters of a series of words. For example, *NATO* is an acronym formed from the first letters in *North Atlantic Treaty Organization.* The goal of this section is to write a function called **acronym** that takes a string and returns its acronym. For example, calling

```
acronym("North Atlantic Treaty Organization")
```

should return the string `"NATO"`. Similarly, calling

```
acronym("port out starboard home")
```

should return the acronym `"posh"`.

When you first look at the problem, it might seem that the obvious approach is to start with the first character and then search for spaces in a **while** loop. Each time the function finds a space, it can concatenate the next character onto the end of the string variable used to hold the result. When no more spaces appear in the string, the acronym is complete. This strategy can be translated into a JavaScript implementation as follows:

```
function acronym(str) {
   let result = str.charAt(0);
   let sp = str.indexOf(" ");
   while (sp !== -1) {
      result += str.charAt(sp + 1);
      sp = str.indexOf(" ", sp + 1);
   }
   return result;
}
```

Although this implementation works for some strings, it fails for others. For example, it produces the correct algorithm only if each pair of words is separated by exactly one space. If some of the words are separated using hyphens—as in `"self-contained underwater breathing apparatus"`, which produces the acronym `"scuba"`—this implementation will fail to return the correct result. Worse still, the function will generate an error condition if the word ends with a space, because the call to `str.charAt(sp + 1)` will try to select the character after the end of the string, which doesn't exist.

Although the following implementation may at first seem harder to follow, it produces acronyms using a strategy that correctly handles the special cases in which the earlier version fails:

```
function acronym(str) {
    let result = "";
    let inWord = false;
    for (let i = 0; i < str.length; i++) {
        let ch = str.charAt(i);
        if (isLetter(ch)) {
            if (!inWord) result += ch;
            inWord = true;
        } else {
            inWord = false;
        }
    }
    return result;
}
```

This implementation uses the standard idiom to go through the string character by character, looking at each one. It determines the word boundaries by using the Boolean variable `inWord`, which is `true` if the process is scanning letters and `false` if it is scanning nonletters. New letters get added to the acronym only if the code sees a letter when `inWord` was previously `false`.

Translating English to Pig Latin

To give you more of a sense of how to implement string-processing applications, this section describes a JavaScript function that takes a line of text and translates each word in that line from English to Pig Latin, a made-up language familiar to most children in the English-speaking world. In Pig Latin, words are formed from their English counterparts by applying the following rules:

1. If the word contains no vowels, no translation is done, which means that the Pig Latin word is the same as the original.

2. If the word begins with a vowel, the Pig Latin translation consists of the original word followed by the suffix *way*.

3. If the word begins with a consonant, the Pig Latin translation is formed by extracting the string of consonants up to the first vowel, moving that collection of consonants to the end of the word, and then adding the suffix *ay*.

As an example, suppose that the English word is *scram*. Because the word begins with a consonant, you divide it into two parts: one consisting of the letters before the first vowel and one consisting of that vowel and the remaining letters:

You then interchange these two parts and add *ay* at the end, as follows:

Thus the Pig Latin word for *scram* is *amscray*. For a word that begins with a vowel, such as *apple*, you simply add *way* to the end, which leaves you with *appleway*.

The code for `PigLatin.js` appears in Figure 7-4. The file exports two functions for clients to use. The `wordToPigLatin` function converts a word to its Pig Latin equivalent. The `toPigLatin` function takes a line of text and converts the entire line to Pig Latin by divides the line into words and then converting each word. Characters that are not part of a word are copied directly to the output line so that punctuation and spacing remain unaffected. The following console log gives a few examples of the functions `toPigLatin` and `wordToPigLatin`:

```
                          JavaScript Console
> toPigLatin("this is pig latin.")
isthay isway igpay atinlay.
> wordToPigLatin("scram")
amscray
> wordToPigLatin("apple")
appleway
> wordToPigLatin("trash")
ashtray
>
```

It is worth taking a careful look at the implementations of `toPigLatin` and `wordToPigLatin` in Figure 7-4. The `toPigLatin` function finds the word boundaries in the input, which provides a useful pattern for separating a string into individual words. The `wordToPigLatin` function uses `substring` to extract pieces of the English word and then uses concatenation to put them back together in their Pig Latin form.

FIGURE 7-4 Functions to translate English to Pig Latin

```
/*
 * File: PigLatin.js
 * -----------------
 * This file defines the functions wordToPigLatin and toPigLatin.
 */

"use strict";

/*
 * Converts a multi-word string from English to Pig Latin.
 */

function toPigLatin(str) {
   let result = "";
   let start = -1;
   for (let i = 0; i < str.length; i++) {
      let ch = str.charAt(i);
      if (isLetter(ch)) {
         if (start === -1) start = i;
      } else {
         if (start >= 0) {
            result += wordToPigLatin(str.substring(start, i));
         }
         start = -1;
         result += ch;
      }
   }
   if (start >= 0) {
      result += wordToPigLatin(str.substring(start));
   }
   return result;
}

/*
 * Translates a word to Pig Latin using the following rules:
 * 1. If the word begins with a vowel, add "way" to the end of the word.
 * 2. If the word begins with a consonant, extract the leading consonants
 *    up to the first vowel, move them to the end, and then add "ay".
 * 3. If the word contains no vowels, return the word unchanged.
 */

function wordToPigLatin(word) {
   let vp = findFirstVowel(word);
   if (vp === -1) {
      return word;
   } else if (vp === 0) {
      return word + "way";
   } else {
      let head = word.substring(0, vp);
      let tail = word.substring(vp);
      return tail + head + "ay";
   }
}
```

FIGURE 7-4 Functions to translate English to Pig Latin (continued)

```
/*
 * Returns the index of the first vowel in the word, or -1 if none.
 */
function findFirstVowel(word) {
   for (let i = 0; i < word.length; i++) {
      if (isEnglishVowel(word.charAt(i))) return i;
   }
   return -1;
}

/*
 * Returns true if the character ch is an English vowel (A, E, I, O, or U).
 */
function isEnglishVowel(ch) {
   return ch.length === 1 && "AEIOUaeiou".indexOf(ch) !== -1;
}
```

Implementing simple ciphers

Codes and ciphers have been around in some form or another for most of recorded history. There is evidence to suggest that coded messages were used in ancient Egypt, China, and India, possibly as early as the third millennium BCE, although few details of the cryptographic systems have survived. In Book 6 of the *Iliad,* Homer suggests the existence of a coded message when King Proitos, seeking to have the young Bellerophontes killed,

> sent him to Lykia, and handed him murderous symbols, which
> he inscribed on a folding tablet, enough to destroy life . . .

Shakespeare's Hamlet, of course, has Rosencrantz and Guildenstern carry a similarly dangerous missive, but Hamlet's message is secured under a royal seal. In the *Iliad,* nothing in the text suggests that the message is sealed, which implies that the meaning of the "murderous symbols" must somehow be disguised.

One of the first encryption systems whose details survive is the ***Polybius square,*** developed by the Greek historian Polybius in the second century BCE. In this system, the letters of the alphabet are arranged to form a 5×5 grid in which each letter is represented by its row and column number. Suppose, for instance, that you want to transmit following English version of Pheidippides's message to Sparta:

	1	2	3	4	5
1	A	B	C	D	E
2	F	G	H	IJ	K
3	L	M	N	O	P
4	Q	R	S	T	U
5	V	W	X	Y	Z

Polybius square

THE ATHENIANS BESEECH YOU TO HASTEN TO THEIR AID

This message can be transmitted as a series of numeric pairs, as follows:

44 23 15 11 44 23 15 33 24 11 33 43 12 15 43 15 15 13 23 54
34 45 44 34 23 11 43 44 15 33 44 34 44 23 15 24 42 11 24 14

The advantage of the Polybius square is not so much that it allows for secret messages, but that it simplifies the problem of transmission. Each letter in the message can be represented by holding between one and five torches in each hand, which allows a message to be communicated visually over a great distance. By reducing the alphabet to an easily transmittable code, the Polybius square anticipates such later developments as Morse code and semaphore, not to mention modern digital encodings such as ASCII or Unicode.

In *De Vita Caesarum,* written sometime around 110 CE, the Roman historian Suetonius describes an encryption system used by Julius Caesar, as follows:

> If he had anything confidential to say, he wrote it in cipher, that is, by so changing the order of the letters of the alphabet, that not a word could be made out. If anyone wishes to decipher these, and get at their meaning, he must substitute the fourth letter of the alphabet, namely *D,* for *A,* and so with the others.

Even today, the technique of encoding a message by shifting letters a certain distance in the alphabet is called a ***Caesar cipher***. According to the passage from Suetonius, each letter is shifted three positions ahead in the alphabet. For example, if Caesar had had time to translate his final words according to his coding system, **ET TU BRUTE** would have come out as **HW WX EUXWH**, because **E** gets moved three letters ahead to **H**, **T** gets moved three to **W**, and so on. Letters that get advanced past the end of the alphabet wrap around back to the beginning, so that **X** becomes **A**, **Y** becomes **B**, and **Z** becomes **C**.

The `caesarCipher` function in Figure 7-5 translates the letters in a string according to the rules for constructing a Caesar cipher. The code uses `charCodeAt` to convert characters into their Unicode values and then uses the remainder operator to implement the cyclical shift that wraps around to the beginning of the alphabet. Once the `caesarCipher` function has computed the new character code, it uses `String.fromCharCode` to convert the Unicode value back into a string. The code makes sure that the operands to `%` are positive to guarantee correct evaluation.

The following console log demonstrates the operation of `caesarCipher`:

```
                          JavaScript Console
> caesarCipher("Et tu, Brute?", 2)
Gv vw, Dtwvg?
> caesarCipher("Gv vw, Dtwvg?", -2)
Et tu, Brute?
> caesarCipher("This is a secret message.", 13)
Guvf vf n frperg zrffntr.
> caesarCipher("Guvf vf n frperg zrffntr.", -13)
This is a secret message.
> caesarCipher("IBM 9000", -1)
HAL 9000
>
```

FIGURE 7-5 Function to encrypt a message using a Caesar cipher

```
/*
 * Encrypts a string using a Caesar cipher, in which the value of key
 * is added to each character, wrapping around to the beginning of the
 * alphabet if necessary.  The first line of the function makes sure
 * that the key value is always positive by converting negative keys
 * to the equivalent positive shift.
 */
function caesarCipher(str, key) {
   if (key < 0) key = 26 - (-key % 26);
   let result = "";
   for (let i = 0; i < str.length; i++) {
      let ch = str.charAt(i);
      if (ch >= "A" && ch <= "Z") {
         let code = ch.charCodeAt(0);
         let base = "A".charCodeAt(0);
         ch = String.fromCharCode(base + (code - base + key) % 26);
      } else if (ch >= "a" && ch <= "z") {
         let code = ch.charCodeAt(0);
         let base = "a".charCodeAt(0);
         ch = String.fromCharCode(base + (code - base + key) % 26);
      }
      result += ch;
   }
   return result;
}
```

(Private Collection/Prismatic Pictures/Bridgeman Images)

Alan Turing

Cryptography played an important role in the early history of computing. During World War II, a team of mathematicians and engineers at Bletchley Park in England used electromechanical devices to break the German Enigma code. That accomplishment, in which the pioneering computer scientist Alan Turing played a major role, proved vital to the Allied war effort. Although this work was kept secret for many years after the war, it has recently been popularized in a series of films including *Breaking the Code*, *Enigma*, and *The Imitation Game*.

7.6 Reading from the console

The graphical programs you have seen in this chapter use interactivity the way modern computers typically do. The programs create graphical displays and then let a user interact with those displays by moving a mouse. That style of interaction, however, is relatively new in the history of computing. Prior to the development of GUI technology at Xerox PARC, most interaction with the computer was accomplished through the keyboard. In 1999, the science-fiction writer Neal Stephenson wrote an essay entitled "In the beginning was the command line," in which he fondly recalls his memories of those earlier days.

Even though it may seem like ancient history, there are still situations in which reading data or commands from the console offers a useful style of human-computer interaction. If nothing else, it is often easiest to test your functions by writing simple console-based based programs that let you see the results of making particular calls. In fact, that's exactly what you've been doing when you use the JavaScript console. You type in expressions and get to see the results.

Console-based programs are also useful for illustrating programming principles. In my previous books designed to introduce the art and science of programming, one of the examples I used was a program that read a list of integers from the user and printed out their sum, as shown in the following console script:

```
JavaScript Console
> AddIntegerList();
Enter a list of integers up to a blank line.
 ? 1
 ? 2
 ? 3
 ? 4
 ?
The sum is 10.
>
```

The **AddIntegerList** function begins by giving instructions to the user and then asks the user to enter integers on the console, one per line. When the user enters a blank line after the last question mark, the program displays the sum.

Programs of this sort are somewhat tricky to write in JavaScript. JavaScript depends on an event-driven model, even for interaction with the console. It is therefore impossible for a program to print a question mark, wait for the user to enter an integer, and then continue on with the program. A JavaScript program must instead declare its interest in being notified when a line appears by supplying a callback function. That callback function is then responsible for processing the input and taking whatever actions are necessary to produce the desired result.

The code for **AddIntegerList.js** appears in Figure 7-6. The first new feature used in the program is the **requestInput** method in the **console** object. The first argument is a *prompt,* which is used to notify the user that some input is expected. The second argument is the function to be called when that input appears. The callback function takes one argument, which is the input line. If that string is empty, **processLine** displays the sum of the values entered; otherwise, **processLine** converts the string to an integer and adds it to the running total.

When you include the **JSConsole.js** library in your **index.html** file, the browser ordinarily creates a new region at the end of the **<body>** section to hold the console output and then expands that region as the program runs. For programs that accept input data, it improves the user experience if the web page creates an explicit

---

FIGURE 7-6 **Program to add a list of integers entered on the console**

```
/*
 * File: AddIntegerList.js
 * ----------------------
 * This program adds a list of integers entered on the console.
 */

"use strict";

function AddIntegerList() {
   let sum = 0;
   console.log("Enter a list of integers up to a blank line.");
   console.requestInput(" ? ", processLine);

   function processLine(line) {
      if (line === "") {
         console.log("The sum is " + sum + ".");
      } else {
         let value = Number(line);
         if (isNaN(value) || value !== Math.floor(value)) {
            console.log("Illegal integer");
         } else {
            sum += value;
         }
         console.requestInput(" ? ", processLine);
      }
   }
}
```

region for the console so that its size doesn't keep changing. You can set a fixed height for the console by including the HTML tag

inside the **<body>** section, where *h* indicates the height of the console in pixels.

Summary

In this chapter, you have learned how to use the **String** class, which makes it possible to write string-processing functions without worrying about the details of the underlying representation. The important points in this chapter include:

- The fundamental unit of information in a modern computer is a *bit,* which can be in one of two possible states. The state of a bit is usually represented in memory diagrams using the binary digits **0** and **1**, but it is equally appropriate to think of these values as *off* and *on* or *false* and *true,* depending on the application.

- Sequences of bits are combined inside the hardware to form larger structures, including *bytes,* which are eight bits long, and *words,* which are large enough to contain a standard integer.

- Computer scientists tend to record the values of bit sequences in *hexadecimal* (base 16), which allows binary values to be represented in a more compact form.

- Numbers don't have bases; representations do.

- Nonnumeric data values are represented by numbering the elements in the domain and then using those numbers as codes for the original values.

- Characters are represented internally using a coding scheme called *Unicode,* which assigns numeric values to characters from a wide range of languages.

- The `String` class represents a type that is conceptually a sequence of characters. The character positions in a string are assigned index numbers that start at 0 and extend up to one less than the length of the string.

- The most common methods exported by the `String` class appear in Figure 7-2 on page 244. Because `String` is a class, the methods use the receiver syntax instead of a more traditional functional form.

- The standard pattern for iterating through the characters in a string is

```
for (let i = 0; i < str.length; i++) {
    . . . body of loop that manipulates str.charAt(i) . . .
}
```

- The standard pattern for growing a string by concatenation is

```
let str = "";
for (whatever loop header line fits the application) {
    str += the next substring or character;
}
```

Review questions

1. Define the following terms: *bit, byte,* and *word.*

2. What is the etymology of the word *bit?*

3. Convert each of the following decimal numbers to its hexadecimal equivalent:

   a. 17
   b. 256
   c. 1729
   d. 2766

4. Convert each of the following hexadecimal numbers to decimal:

   a. 17
   b. 64
   c. **CC**
   d. **FAD**

5. What JavaScript functions allow you to convert between numbers and their corresponding string representations?

6. In your own words, state the principle of enumeration.

7. What does *ASCII* stand for?

8. What is the relationship between ASCII and Unicode?

9. By consulting Figure 7-1, determine the Unicode values of the characters `"$"`, `"@"`, `"0"`, and `"x"`.

10. True or false: In JavaScript, you can determine the length of the string stored in the variable `str` by calling `length(str)`.

11. True or false: The index positions in a string begin at 0 and extend up to the length of the string minus 1.

12. How do you extract the character at position k in a string? How would you determine the Unicode value of that character?

13. What are the arguments to the `substring` method? What happens if you omit the second argument?

14. What is *lexicographic ordering?*

15. What value does `indexOf` return if the pattern string does not appear?

16. What is the significance of the optional second argument to `indexOf`?

17. Suppose that you have declared and initialized the variable `s` as follows:

    ```
    let s = "hello, world";
    ```

    Given that declaration, what value is produced by each of the following calls:

a.	`s + "!"`	f.	`s.replace("h", "j")`
b.	`s.length`	g.	`s.substring(0, 3)`
c.	`s.charAt(5)`	h.	`s.substring(7)`
d.	`s.indexOf("l")`	i.	`s.substring(3, 5)`
e.	`s.indexOf("l", 5)`	j.	`s.substring(3, 3)`

18. What is the pattern for iterating through each character in a string?

19. How does the pattern in question 18 change if you want to iterate through the characters backward, starting with the last character and ending with the first?

20. What is the pattern for growing a string through concatenation?

Exercises

1. In exercise 18 from Chapter 3, you wrote a program to find perfect numbers. Rewrite that program so that it also displays the binary form of these numbers. As you can see if you run this program, the first few perfect numbers follow an interesting pattern when you write them out in binary. Euclid discovered this pattern more than 2000 years ago, and the 18th-century Swiss mathematician Leonhard Euler proved that all even perfect numbers follow this pattern.

2. As noted in the discussion of the built-in methods in the **String** class, the **startsWith** and **endsWith** methods are not implemented in older browsers. Using the **startsWith** function on page 247 as a model, implement the function **endsWith(str, suffix)** that checks whether **str** ends with the specified suffix.

3. Implement the function **isEnglishConsonant(ch)**, which returns **true** if **ch** is a consonant in English, that is, any alphabetic character except one of the five vowels: **"a"**, **"e"**, **"i"**, **"o"**, and **"u"**. As with the **isEnglishVowel** function presented in the text, your method should recognize both lower- and uppercase consonants.

4. Write a function **randomWord** that returns a randomly constructed "word" consisting of randomly chosen lowercase letters. The number of letters in the word should also be chosen randomly by picking a number between the values of the constants **MIN_LETTERS** and **MAX_LETTERS**.

5. Implement a function **capitalize(str)** that returns a string in which the initial character is capitalized (if it is a letter) and all other letters are converted to lower case; characters other than letters are not affected. For example, both **capitalize("BOOLEAN")** and **capitalize("boolean")** should return the string **"Boolean"**.

6. In many word games, letters are scored according to their point values, which are inversely proportional to their frequency in English words. In Scrabble™, the points are allocated as follows:

Points	Letters
1	A, E, I, L, N, O, R, S, T, U
2	D, G
3	B, C, M, P
4	F, H, V, W, Y
5	K
8	J, X
10	Q, Z

For example, the word `"FARM"` is worth 9 points in Scrabble: 4 for the *F*, 1 each for the *A* and the *R*, and 3 for the *M*. Write a function `scrabbleScore` that takes a word and returns its score in Scrabble, not counting any of the other bonuses that occur in the game. You should ignore any characters other than uppercase letters in computing the score.

7. Rewrite the `isPalindrome` function so that it operates recursively, taking advantage of the fact that a string is a palindrome if (a) its length is less than two or (b) its first and last characters match and the substring between those characters is a palindrome.

8. The concept of a palindrome is often extended to full sentences by ignoring punctuation, spacing, and differences in the case of letters. For example, the sentence

    Madam, I'm Adam.

    is a sentence palindrome, because if you look only at the letters and ignore any case distinctions, it reads identically backward and forward.

    Write a predicate function `isSentencePalindrome(str)` that returns `true` if `str` fits this definition of a sentence palindrome. For example, you should be able to use your function to reproduce the following console session:

JavaScript Console
> `isSentencePalindrome("Madam, I'm Adam.")`   true   > `isSentencePalindrome("Able was I ere I saw Elba.")`   true   > `isSentencePalindrome("Not a palindrome.")`   false   >

9. Write a function `createRegularPlural(word)` that returns the plural of `word` formed by following these standard English rules:

    a. If the word ends in *s, x, z, ch,* or *sh,* add *es* to the word.

    b. If the word ends in a *y* preceded by a consonant, change the *y* to *ies*.

    c. In all other cases, add just an *s*.

    Design a set of test cases to verify that your function works.

10. In English, the notion of an ongoing action is expressed using the present progressive tense, which involves the addition of an *ing* suffix to the verb. For example, the sentence *I think* conveys a sense that one is capable of thinking; by contrast, the sentence *I am thinking* conveys the impression that one is currently doing so. The *ing* form of the verb is called the ***present participle.***

Unfortunately, creating the present participle is not always as simple as adding the *ing* ending. One common exception is a word like *cogitate* that ends in a silent *e*. In such cases, the *e* is usually dropped, so that the participle form becomes *cogitating*. Another common exception involves words that end with a single consonant, which typically gets doubled in the participle form. For example, the verb *run* becomes *running*.

Although there are many exceptions, you can construct a large fraction of the legal participle forms in English by applying the following rules:

a. If the word ends in an *e* preceded by a consonant, take the *e* away before adding *ing*. Thus, *move* should become *moving*. If the *e* is not preceded by a consonant, it should remain in place, so that *see* becomes *seeing*.

b. If the word ends in a consonant preceded by a vowel, insert an extra copy of that consonant before adding *ing*. Thus, *jam* should become *jamming*. If, however, there is more than one consonant at the end of the word, no such doubling takes place, so that *walk* becomes *walking*.

c. In all other circumstances, simply add the *ing* suffix.

Write a function `createPresentParticiple(verb)` that takes an English verb, which you may assume is entirely lowercase and at least two characters long, and forms the participle using these rules.

11. As in most languages, English includes two types of numbers. The **cardinal numbers** (such as *one, two, three,* and *four*) are used in counting; the **ordinal numbers** (such as *first, second, third,* and *fourth*) are used to indicate a position in a sequence. In text, ordinals are usually indicated by writing the digits in the number, followed by the last two letters of the English word that names the corresponding ordinal. Thus, the ordinal numbers *first, second, third,* and *fourth* often appear in print as *1st, 2nd, 3rd,* and *4th*. The ordinals for 11, 12, and 13, however, are *11th, 12th,* and *13th*. Devise a rule that determines what suffix should be added to each number, and then use this rule to write a function `createOrdinalForm(n)` that returns the ordinal form of the number *n* as a string.

12.   *The waste of time in spelling imaginary sounds and their history*
        (or etymology as it is called) is monstrous in English . . .

                                                    —George Bernard Shaw, 1941

In the early part of the 20th century, there was considerable interest in both England and the United States in simplifying the rules used for spelling English words, which has always been a difficult proposition. One suggestion advanced as part of this movement was to eliminate all doubled letters, so that *bookkeeper* would be written as *bokeper* and *committee* would become *comite*.

Write a function `removeDoubledLetters(str)` that returns a new string in which any duplicated characters in `str` have been replaced by a single copy.

13. When large numbers are written on paper, it is traditional—at least in the United States—to use commas to separate the digits into groups of three. For example, the number one million is usually written as 1,000,000. Implement a function

    > `function addCommas(digits)`

    that takes a string of decimal digits representing a number and returns the string formed by inserting commas at every third position, starting on the right. Your implementation of the `addCommas` function should be able to reproduce the following console log:

    ```
    JavaScript Console
    > addCommas("17")
    17
    > addCommas("2001")
    2,001
    > addCommas("12345678")
    12,345,678
    > addCommas("999999999")
    999,999,999
    >
    ```

14. As written, the `PigLatin` program in Figure 7-4 behaves oddly if you enter a string that includes words beginning with an uppercase letter. For example, if you were to capitalize the first word in the sentence and the name of the Pig Latin language, you would see the following output:

    ```
    JavaScript Console
    > toPigLatin("This is Pig Latin.")
    isThay isway igPay atinLay.
    >
    ```

    Rewrite the `wordToPigLatin` function so that any word that begins with a capital letter in the English line still begins with a capital letter in Pig Latin. Thus, after you make the necessary changes in the program, the output should look like this:

    ```
    JavaScript Console
    > toPigLatin("This is Pig Latin.")
    Isthay isway Igpay Atinlay.
    >
    ```

15. Most people in English-speaking countries have played the Pig Latin game at some point in their lives. There are other invented "languages" in which words

are created using some simple transformation of English. One such language is called *Obenglobish,* in which words are created by adding the letters *ob* before the vowels (*a, e, i, o,* and *u*) in an English word. For example, under this rule, the word *english* gets the letters *ob* added before the *e* and the *i* to form *obenglobish*, which is how the language got its name.

In official Obenglobish, the `ob` characters are added only before vowels that are pronounced, which means that a word like *game* would become *gobame* rather than *gobamobe* because the final *e* is silent. While it is impossible to implement this rule perfectly, you can do a pretty good job by adopting the rule that the *ob* should be added before every vowel in the English word *except*

- Vowels that follow other vowels
- An *e* that occurs at the end of the word

Write a function `obenglobish` that takes an English word and returns its Obenglobish equivalent, using the translation rule given above. Your function should allow you to generate the following sample run:

```
                        JavaScript Console
> toObenglobish("english")
obenglobish
> toObenglobish("hobnob")
hobobnobob
> toObenglobish("gooiest")
gobooiest
> toObenglobish("amaze")
obamobaze
> toObenglobish("rot")
robot
>
```

16.
> *There is no gene for the human spirit.*
> —Tagline for the 1997 film *GATTACA*

The genetic code for all living organisms is carried in its DNA—a molecule with the remarkable capacity to replicate its own structure. The DNA molecule itself consists of a long strand of chemical bases wound together with a similar strand in a double helix. DNA's ability to replicate comes from the fact that its four constituent bases—adenosine, cytosine, guanine, and thymine—combine with each other only in the following ways:

- Cytosine on one strand links only with guanine on the other, and vice versa.
- Adenosine links only with thymine, and vice versa.

Biologists abbreviate the names of the bases by writing only the initial letter: **A**, **C**, **G**, or **T**.

Inside the cell, a DNA strand acts as a template to which other DNA strands can attach themselves. As an example, suppose that you have the following DNA strand, in which the position of each base has been numbered as it would be in a JavaScript string:

Your mission in this exercise is to determine where a shorter DNA strand can attach itself to the longer one. If, for example, you were trying to find a match for the strand

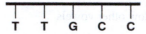

the rules for DNA dictate that this strand can bind to the longer one only at position 1:

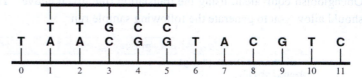

By contrast, the strand

matches at either position 2 or position 7.

Write a function

```
function findDNAMatch(s1, s2, start)
```

that returns the first position at which the DNA strand **s1** can attach to the strand **s2**. As in the **indexOf** method, the optional **start** parameter indicates the index position at which the search should start. If there is no match, **findDNAMatch** should return −1.

17. Although Caesar ciphers are simple, they are also extremely easy to break. A somewhat more secure scheme allows each letter in the message to be represented consistently by some other letter, but not one chosen by shifting the character a fixed distance in the alphabet. This kind of coding scheme is called a *letter-substitution cipher.*

The key in a letter-substitution cipher is a 26-character string that shows the enciphered counterpart of each of the 26 letters of the alphabet. For example, if the communicating parties choose **"QWERTYUIOPASDFGHJKLZXCVBNM"** as the key (which is unimaginatively generated by typing the letter keys on the keyboard in order), that key then corresponds to the following mapping:

```
A B C D E F G H I J K L M N O P Q R S T U V W X Y Z
↓ ↓ ↓ ↓ ↓ ↓ ↓ ↓ ↓ ↓ ↓ ↓ ↓ ↓ ↓ ↓ ↓ ↓ ↓ ↓ ↓ ↓ ↓ ↓ ↓ ↓
Q W E R T Y U I O P A S D F G H J K L Z X C V B N M
```

Write a function `encrypt` that takes a string and a 26-character key and returns the string after applying a letter-substitution cipher with that key. For example, your function should be able to produce the following sample run:

```
JavaScript Console
> const KEY = "QWERTYUIOPASDFGHJKLZXCVBNM";
> encrypt("Squeamish Ossifrage", KEY)
Ljxtqdoli Glloykqut
>
```

The words *squeamish ossifrage* were part of the solution to a cryptographic puzzle published in *Scientific American*. The puzzle was developed by Ron Rivest, Adi Shamir, and Leonard Adleman, who invented the widely used RSA encryption algorithm. The name of the algorithm comes from their initials.

18. Write a predicate function `isKeyLegal`, which takes a string and returns `true` if that string would be a legal key in a letter-substitution cipher. A key is legal only if it meets the following two conditions:

1. The key is exactly 26 characters long.
2. Every uppercase letter appears in the key.

These conditions automatically rule out the possibility that the key contains invalid characters or duplicated letters. After all, if all 26 uppercase letters appear and the string is exactly 26 characters long, there isn't room for anything else.

19. Letter-substitution ciphers require the sender and receiver to use different keys: one to encrypt the message and one to decrypt it when it reaches its destination. Your task in this exercise is to write a function `invertKey` that takes an encryption key and returns the corresponding decryption key. In cryptography, that operation is called *inverting* the encryption key.

The idea of inverting a key is most easily illustrated by example. Suppose, for example, that the key is `"QWERTYUIOPASDFGHJKLZXCVBNM"` as in exercise 17. That key represents the following translation rule:

```
A B C D E F G H I J K L M N O P Q R S T U V W X Y Z
↓ ↓ ↓ ↓ ↓ ↓ ↓ ↓ ↓ ↓ ↓ ↓ ↓ ↓ ↓ ↓ ↓ ↓ ↓ ↓ ↓ ↓ ↓ ↓ ↓ ↓
Q W E R T Y U I O P A S D F G H J K L Z X C V B N M
```

The translation table shows that A maps into Q, B maps into W, C maps into E, and so on. To turn the encryption process around, you have to read the translation table from bottom to top, looking to see what letter in the original text would have produced each letter in the encrypted version. For example, if you look for the letter **A** in the bottom line of the key, you discover that the corresponding letter in the original must have been **K**. Similarly, the only way to get a **B** in the encrypted message is to start with an **X** in the original one. The first two entries in the inverted translation table therefore look like this:

```
A B
↓ ↓
K X
```

If you continue this process by finding each letter of the alphabet on the bottom of the original translation table and then looking to see what letter appears on top, you will eventually complete the inverted table, as follows:

```
A B C D E F G H I J K L M N O P Q R S T U V W X Y Z
↓ ↓ ↓ ↓ ↓ ↓ ↓ ↓ ↓ ↓ ↓ ↓ ↓ ↓ ↓ ↓ ↓ ↓ ↓ ↓ ↓ ↓ ↓ ↓ ↓ ↓
K X V M C N O P H Q R S Z Y I J A D L E G W B U F T
```

The inverted key is simply the 26-character string on the bottom row, which in this case is **"KXVMCNOPHQRSZYIJADLEGWBUFT"**.

20. Write a program that reads in a list of integers on the console until the user enters a blank line. When the sentinel appears, your program should display the largest value in the list.

21. For a slightly more interesting challenge, write a program that finds both the largest and the second-largest integer in a list, prior to the entry of the blank line that ends the input. A sample run of this program might look like this:

```
JavaScript Console
> FindTwoLargest();
Enter a list of integers up to a blank line.
 ? 223
 ? 251
 ? 317
 ? 636
 ? 766
 ? 607
 ? 607
 ?
The largest value is 766.
The second-largest value is 636.
>
```

The input values in this example are the number of pages in the British hardcover editions of J. K. Rowling's *Harry Potter* series. The output therefore tells us that the longest book (*Harry Potter and the Order of the Phoenix*) has 766 pages and the second-longest book (*Harry Potter and the Goblet of Fire*) weighs in at a mere 636 pages.

CHAPTER 8
Arrays

I'm not rich because I invented VisiCalc, but I feel that I've made a change in the world. That's a satisfaction money can't buy.

— Dan Bricklin, November 1985, as quoted in Robert Slater, *Portraits in Silicon*

(Courtesy of the Computer History Museum)

Bob Frankston and Dan Bricklin

In modern computing, one of the most visible applications of the array structure described in this chapter is the electronic spreadsheet, which uses a two-dimensional array to store tabular data. The first electronic spreadsheet was VisiCalc, which was released in 1979 by Software Arts, Incorporated, a small startup company founded by MIT graduates Dan Bricklin and Bob Frankston. VisiCalc proved to be a popular application, leading many larger firms to develop competing products, including Lotus 1 2 3 and, more recently, Microsoft Excel.

Up to now, the programs in this book have worked with individual data items. The real power of computing, however, comes from the ability to work with collections of data. This chapter introduces the idea of an *array,* which is an ordered collection of values. Arrays are important in programming largely because this type of collection occur squite often in the real world. Whenever you want to represent a set of values that it makes sense to think about as forming a sequence, arrays are likely to play a role in the solution.

8.1 Introduction to arrays

An array is a collection of individual values in which the elements are identified by a sequential position. You must be able to list the individual values of an array in order: here is the first, here is the second, and so on. Conceptually, it is easiest to think of an array as a sequence of boxes, with one box for each data value in the array. Each of the values in an array is called an *element.*

Like every other data type in JavaScript, arrays can be stored in variables, passed as arguments to a function, and returned from functions as a result. And like every other data type, arrays in JavaScript support a set of operations appropriate to the type. For arrays, that set of operations allows you to manipulate both the contents and the ordering of elements. These operations are outlined in the sections that follow.

JavaScript array notation

Creating an array in JavaScript is much easier than it is in most other programming languages. All you need to do is list the elements of the array surrounded by square brackets and separated by commas. For example, the following declaration contains the numbers that correspond to coins in the United States:

```
const COINS = [ 1, 5, 10, 25, 50, 100 ];
```

After you make this definition, the value of the constant COINS is an array that corresponds to the following box diagram:

COINS

1	5	10	25	50	100
0	1	2	3	4	5

The small numbers underneath the boxes in this diagram represent the position of that value in the array, which is called its *index.* When you use JavaScript's array notation, the index numbers always begin with 0 and run up to one less than the number of elements. Thus, in an array with six elements, the index numbers are 0, 1, 2, 3, 4, and 5, as the preceding diagram shows.

Every JavaScript array has a field called `length` that contains the number of elements. The expression

    COINS.length

therefore has the value 6.

The elements of an array need not be numbers but can instead be any JavaScript value. For example, the following variable declaration defines `hogwarts` as an array containing the names of the four houses at the Hogwarts School of Witchcraft and Wizardry from J. K. Rowling's Harry Potter novels:

```
let hogwarts = [
    "Gryffindor", "Hufflepuff", "Ravenclaw", "Slytherin"
];
```

The box diagram for this array looks like this:

```
hogwarts
┌──────────────┬──────────────┬──────────────┬──────────────┐
│ "Gryffindor" │ "Hufflepuff" │ "Ravenclaw"  │ "Slytherin"  │
└──────────────┴──────────────┴──────────────┴──────────────┘
       0              1              2              3
```

The expression `hogwarts.length` has the value 4.

Array selection

To refer to a specific element within an array, you specify both the array name and the index corresponding to the position of that element within the array. The process of identifying a particular element within an array is called *selection,* and is indicated in JavaScript by writing the name of the array and following it with the index written in square brackets. For example, given the array definitions from the preceding section, the expression `COINS[2]` is 10, because that is the value at index 2 in the `COINS` array. Similarly, `hogwarts[0]` has the value `"Gryffindor"`. If you select an index position that falls outside the limits of an array, JavaScript returns the value `undefined`.

The result of a selection expression is assignable, in the sense that you can use a selection expression on the left side of an assignment statement. For example, if some future leaders of Hogwarts decided that they might need to honor a more worthy wizard, evaluating the expression

    hogwarts[3] = "Dumbledore";

would change the value of the `hogwarts` array to

```
┌──────────────┬──────────────┬──────────────┬──────────────┐
│ "Gryffindor" │ "Hufflepuff" │ "Ravenclaw"  │ "Dumbledore" │
└──────────────┴──────────────┴──────────────┴──────────────┘
       0              1              2              3
```

Arrays are often used in connection with **for** loops that step through every index position in the array. The usual pattern for doing so is analogous to the pattern for iterating through the characters in a string presented in Chapter 7:

```
for (let i = 0; i < array.length; i++) {
    . . . body of loop that uses the element array[i] . . .
}
```

The following definition of the function **listArray** offers a simple example of the use of **for** loops with arrays:

```
function listArray(array) {
    for (let i = 0; i < array.length; i++) {
        console.log(array[i]);
    }
}
```

This function simply lists the elements of **array**, one per line, on the console. For example, after defining this function, you could generate the following console session:

```
                        JavaScript Console
> let hogwarts = [
     "Gryffindor",
     "Hufflepuff",
     "Ravenclaw",
     "Slytherin"
  ];
> listArray(hogwarts);
Gryffindor
Hufflepuff
Ravenclaw
Slytherin
>
```

As a second example, the function

```
function sumArray(array) {
    let sum = 0;
    for (let i = 0; i < array.length; i++) {
        sum += array[i];
    }
    return sum;
}
```

returns the sum of the elements in the array. Calling **sumArray([1, 2, 3, 4])**, for example, returns 10 (1 + 2 + 3 + 4). Similarly, if **COINS** is defined as shown on page 274, calling **sumArray(COINS)** returns 191 (1 + 5 + 10 + 25 + 50 + 100).

FIGURE 8-1 Function to reverse an array in place

```
/*
 * File: ReverseArray.js
 * ---------------------
 * This file exports the function reverseArray, which reverses the
 * elements of an array.
 */

"use strict";

/*
 * Reverses the elements in the array.  The change is reflected in
 * the array provided by the caller because the array is passed as a
 * reference.  The parameter variable therefore refers to the same array.
 */

function reverseArray(array) {
   for (let lh = 0; lh < Math.floor(array.length / 2); lh++) {
      let rh = array.length - lh - 1;
      let tmp = array[lh];
      array[lh] = array[rh];
      array[rh] = tmp;
   }
}
```

The **reverseArray** function in Figure 8-1 offers another example of a function that takes an array parameter. The effect of this function is to reverse the order of the elements in **array**, as illustrated by the following console log:

```
                      JavaScript Console
> let hogwarts = [
      "Gryffindor",
      "Hufflepuff",
      "Ravenclaw",
      "Slytherin"
  ];
> reverseArray(hogwarts);
> listArray(hogwarts)
Slytherin
Ravenclaw
Hufflepuff
Gryffindor
>
```

It is worth spending a few minutes examining the code for **reverseArray**. The overall strategy is to use a **for** loop to go through the index positions in the first half of the array, marking that position with the variable **lh**, where the variable name is chosen to suggest the idea of a position on the left side of the array that you might point to with your left hand. The first statement in the loop body calculates the index position of the corresponding element at the right side of the array and stores that index in the variable **rh**. The last three lines of the loop body interchange these two array elements using a temporary variable to ensure that no values have been lost after the first assignment.

Passing arrays as references

The `reverseArray` function in Figure 8-1 raises a puzzling question if you think carefully about the code in light of the rules for parameter passing presented in Chapter 5. In the list of rules presented in the section entitled "The steps in calling a function," rule 3 begins like this:

3. The value of each argument is copied into the corresponding parameter variable.

It is interesting to ask whether this rule is applied when the console script calls `reverseArray`. Is the `hogwarts` array copied into the parameter variable `array`? If so, why doesn't the `reverseArray` function reverse the elements of the copy, leaving the original value of `hogwarts` unchanged?

The key to answering this question lies in understanding that the value of a JavaScript array is not the sequence of elements itself but is instead a *reference* to those elements, which indicates where the elements are stored in the computer's memory. When you pass an array as an argument to a function, JavaScript copies the reference but does not copy the actual element values. The effect of this strategy is that a function and its caller have access to the same elements.

The idea that arrays—and indeed all JavaScript objects, as you will learn in Chapter 9—are passed as references is so important that it is worth going through an example in more detail. Suppose that you have defined the following function:

```
function testReverseArray() {
   let numbers = [ 1, 2, 3, 4, 5 ];
   reverseArray(numbers);
   console.log(numbers);
}
```

Calling this function creates a new stack frame and declares the variable **numbers**. After you initialize **numbers** to an array value, the stack frame looks like this:

The important thing to note is that the elements of the array are stored *outside* the frame. The reference stored in **numbers** indicates where the array is stored.

When the program calls **reverseArray**, the new stack frame looks like this:

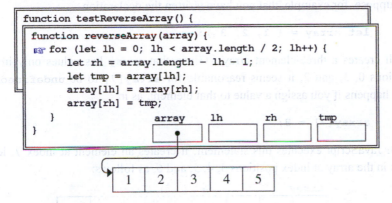

The elements of the array are still in the same place in the computer's memory as they were in the frame for **testReverseArray**. When **reverseArray** returns, the values in the **numbers** array will be reversed, as follows:

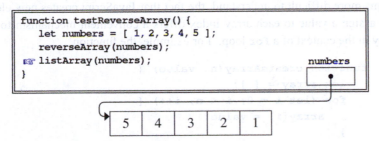

Accessing elements outside the bounds of the array

Arrays in JavaScript are implemented in a different way than arrays in most other programming languages. Internally, JavaScript arrays are implemented just like any other compound object. What makes arrays different is how programmers use them. When working with arrays, programmers conventionally use numeric indices of the sort you've already seen in this chapter. When working with objects, programmers use symbolic names to refer to individual components, as you will discover in Chapter 9. Because JavaScript uses the same internal representation for both arrays and objects, it turns out that you can violate that naming convention without generating any errors from the JavaScript interpreter.

One of the implications of the shared underlying representation between arrays and objects is that JavaScript allows you to refer to elements in an array whose indices fall outside the range of the defined elements. If you ask for the value of such an element, JavaScript returns the value **undefined**. If you assign a new value to an element outside the defined bounds, JavaScript creates that element, even if doing so leaves undefined elements interspersed among the defined ones.

Suppose, for example, that you have written the declaration

```
let array = [ 1, 2, 3 ];
```

which creates a three-element array. Given that **array** has values only in index positions 0, 1, and 2, it seems reasonable for **array[7]** to be **undefined**. But what happens if you assign a value to that element, as in

```
array[7] = 8;
```

When JavaScript executes this statement, it creates an element at index 7, leaving holes in the array at index positions 3, 4, 5, and 6, as follows:

array

1	2	3					8
0	1	2	3	4	5	6	7

Although writing code that leaves unfilled holes in the middle of an array makes programs more difficult to understand, the fact that JavaScript creates new elements as you assign a value to each array index offers a convenient mechanism to create an array in the context of a **for** loop. For example, the function

```
function createArray(n, value) {
   let array = [ ];
   for (let i = 0; i < n; i++) {
      array[i] = value;
   }
   return array;
}
```

creates an array with **n** elements, each of which is initialized to **value**.

Given this definition, calling **createArray(10, 0)** creates the following numeric array:

0	0	0	0	0	0	0	0	0	0
0	1	2	3	4	5	6	7	8	9

Similarly, calling **createArray(8, false)** creates an array of eight Boolean values, as follows:

false	false	false	false	false	false	false	false
0	1	2	3	4	5	6	7

8.2 Array operations

JavaScript offers a range of operations on arrays that are implemented as methods, as shown in Figure 8-2. Several of these methods are likely to seem familiar

---

FIGURE 8-2 Common operations in JavaScript's array class

Array field

array.**length**	Returns the number of elements in *array*.

Class method

Array.isArray(*value*)	Returns **true** if *value* is an array.

Methods that leave the original array unchanged

array.**concat**(a_1, ...)	Concatenates this array with any number of arrays and then returns a copy of the concatenated result.
array.**indexOf**(*value*) *array*.**indexOf**(*value*, *k*)	Returns the first index at which *value* appears, or −1 if no such element is found. If *k* is specified, it indicates the starting point.
array.**lastIndexOf**(*value*) *array*.**lastIndexOf**(*value*, *k*)	Operates like **indexOf**, but searches backward from position *k*. If *k* is missing, **lastIndexOf** starts at the end of the array.
array.**slice**(*start*, *finish*)	Returns a new array containing all elements beginning at *start* and ending just before *finish*.

Methods that add and remove elements from an array

array.**push**(*value*, ...)	Adds one or more values to the end of the array.
array.**pop**()	Removes and returns the last element, or **undefined** if empty.
array.**unshift**(*value*, ...)	Adds one or more values to the beginning of the array.
array.**shift**()	Removes and returns the first element, or **undefined** if empty.
array.**splice**(*index*, *count*, ...)	Removes *count* elements starting at position *index* and then inserts any additional arguments at that index position.

Methods that reorder the elements of an array

array.**reverse**()	Reverses the order of the elements in the array.
array.**sort**() *array*.**sort**(*cmp*)	Sorts the elements of the array. The **sort** method takes an optional *comparison function*, as described in the chapter.

Methods that involve both strings and arrays

str.**split**(*pattern*)	Splits *str* into an array of substrings by dividing it at instances of *pattern*. If *pattern* is the empty string, **split** returns an array of the individual characters.
array.**join**() *array*.**join**(*sep*)	Concatenates the array elements into a single string, separating the elements by a comma or the string *sep*, if specified.

because they are similar to methods in JavaScript's `String` class. For example, both arrays and strings have a `length` field that indicates the number of values, and the `indexOf` and `lastIndexOf` methods are the same for both classes. Other methods perform similar functions with slightly different names. The `concat` method for arrays corresponds to the + operator for strings, and the `slice` method is the array counterpart of `substring`.

The primary difference between the methods available for strings and those available for arrays lies in how those methods are allowed to manipulate the values to which they are applied. None of the methods in the `String` class change the contents of the original string but instead return a result by creating an entirely new string value. For example, if `str` is a string variable, calling `str.toUpperCase()` does not change the value of `str`. What happens instead is that the call returns a new string in which all characters have been converted to upper case. By contrast, most of the methods in Figure 8-2 have the effect of changing the contents of the array. These methods are detailed in the sections that follow.

Adding and removing elements of an array

The array class includes five methods that are used to add or remove elements from an array. The `push` and `pop` methods support adding and removing elements at the end of an array, the `unshift` and `shift` methods support adding and removing elements at the beginning, and the `splice` method makes it possible to add and remove elements at an arbitrary position in the array. The effect of each of these methods is illustrated in the following diagram:

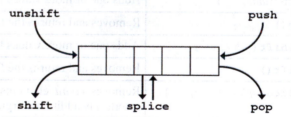

The `push` method takes any number of arguments and adds each argument to the end in turn. For example, suppose that you have used the following declaration to create an array of four strings:

```
let numbers = [ "one", "two", "three", "four" ];
```

You can then diagram the contents of `numbers` as follows:

numbers

"one"	"two"	"three"	"four"
0	1	2	3

At this point, calling `numbers.push("five")` would add the string `"five"` to the end of the array, like this:

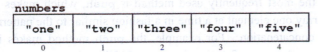

The `pop` method removes the last element in the array and returns it to the caller. Thus, if you called `numbers.pop()` in this configuration, the `pop` method would remove and return the value `"five"`, restoring the array to its previous state:

numbers

"one"	"two"	"three"	"four"
0	1	2	3

The `unshift` and `shift` methods have the same effect as `push` and `pop` except that the changes occur at the beginning of the array. For example, if you called `numbers.unshift("zero")`, the array would change as follows:

numbers

"zero"	"one"	"two"	"three"	"four"
0	1	2	3	4

Calling `numbers.shift()` in this configuration would return the string `"zero"` and restore the previous state of the array. Calling `numbers.shift()` a second time would then return the string `"one"` and leave the array in the following state:

numbers

"two"	"three"	"four"
0	1	2

Note that the `unshift` and `shift` methods change the index numbers of the remaining array elements as the initial elements are added and removed.

The `splice` method is used both to remove and add elements at an arbitrary index position in the array. The general form of the call is

array.`splice`(*index, count,* ...)

where *index* is the array index at which the deletions and insertions occur, *count* is the number of elements to delete, and any remaining arguments are inserted in its place. For example, given the most recent contents of the `numbers` array, calling `numbers.splice(1, 1, "by")` would change the array as follows:

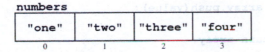

Although **splice** is by far the most flexible method available for adding and removing array elements, it is by no means the most important to learn. In my experience, the most frequently used method is **push**, which makes it possible to expand an array one element at a time in a fashion similar to the pattern for growing a string by concatenation. For example, the **push** method makes it possible to rewrite the **createArray** function from page 280 like this:

```
function createArray(n, value) {
   let array = [ ];
   for (let i = 0; i < n; i++) {
      array.push(value);
   }
   return array;
}
```

The **push** and **pop** methods allow the JavaScript array class to implement a remarkably useful data structure called a *stack,* which is a list in which values are added and removed only at the end. This restriction implies that the last item added to a stack is always the first item that gets removed. Stacks are important in computer science partly because nested function calls behave in a stack-oriented fashion. Thus, the function called most recently is the first function that returns.

A common (but possibly apocryphal) explanation for the words *stack, push,* and *pop* is that the stack model derives from the way plates are stored in a cafeteria. Suppose, for example, that you are in a cafeteria where customers pick up their own plates from a spring-loaded column that makes it possible to take only the top plate, as illustrated in the following diagram:

When a dishwasher adds a new plate, it goes on the top of the stack, pushing the others down slightly as the spring is compressed, as follows:

Customers can take plates only from the top of the stack. When they do, the remaining plates pop back up. The last plate added to the stack is the first one a customer takes.

Similarly, the **push** and **shift** methods work together to implement a useful data structure that computer scientists call a *queue,* which is analogous to a waiting line. The **push** method adds new elements to the end of the line; the **shift** method removes them from the front. You will learn more about stacks and queues if you continue your study of computer science beyond what is covered in this book.

Methods that reorder the elements of an array

The array class includes two methods—**reverse** and **sort**—that reorder the elements of an existing array. Each of these functions changes the original contents of the array and returns the updated array as its value, making it possible to embed calls to these functions inside larger expressions.

The **reverse** method is a more efficient, built-in version of the **reverseArray** function presented earlier in this chapter. Because **reverse** is a method and **reverseArray** is a function, you apply these operations differently. To reverse an array using the **reverseArray** function, clients would call

```
reverseArray(array);
```

To achieve the same result using the **reverse** method, clients would instead write

```
array.reverse();
```

The **sort** method rearranges the elements of an array so that they appear in ascending order. If you call **sort** with no argument, JavaScript sorts the array according to the how the elements would appear when printed. This interpretation makes sense for arrays of strings but produces counterintuitive results if the array contains numeric values. For example, if you define **array** as

```
let array = [ 222, 33, 4, 1111 ];
```

you might hope that calling

```
array.sort();
```

would sort the array numerically. It doesn't. What JavaScript does is sort the array lexicographically using the string representation of the numbers, as follows:

array

1111	222	33	4

Fortunately, JavaScript allows you to control how **sort** reorders the elements by passing it a ***comparison function.*** A comparison function takes two arguments and returns a number whose sign indicates the ordering relationship between those values. That return value must be negative if the first value should precede the second, positive if the first value should follow the second, and zero if the values should be sorted to the same position. For example, you can sort **array** numerically by calling **array.sort(sortNumerically)**, where **sortNumerically** is

```
function sortNumerically(n1, n2) {
   return n1 - n2;
}
```

Similarly, if **lines** is an array of strings, you can sort the array alphabetically without regard to case by supplying the following comparison function:

```
function sortIgnoringCase(s1, s2) {
   s1 = s1.toUpperCase();
   s2 = s2.toUpperCase();
   if (s1 < s2) return -1;
   if (s1 > s2) return 1;
   return 0;
}
```

Although the **sort** method always rearranges the elements of the array so that they appear in ascending order, it is easy to sort an array in descending order by using a different comparison function. The most general solution is to define the following function, which takes one comparison function and returns a new one that calls the original function with the arguments reversed:

```
function reverseComparison(cmp) {
   return function(v1, v2) { return cmp(v2, v1); };
}
```

You can use **reverseComparison** to invert the sense of any comparison function. For example, you can sort **list** in reverse without regard to case like this:

```
lines.sort(reverseComparison(sortIgnoringCase));
```

Converting between strings and arrays

The list of array operations in Figure 8-2 includes two methods that make it easy to convert back and forth between strings and arrays. The **split** method in the **String** class separates a string into individual substrings by dividing it at each instance of a pattern and then returns an array of the strings marked by those divisions. For example, if **str** contains the string **"16-Jul-1969"** (the date of the Apollo 11 moon landing), calling **str.split("-")** returns the following array:

"16"	"Jul"	"1969"

The `join` method in the array class reverses the process. If, for example, you were to call `join("-")` on an array containing these three elements, you would get the string `"16-Jul-1969"`.

You do have to take some care in using `split` if the separator pattern can appear at the beginning or end of the string. In such cases, the array that `split` returns will contain empty strings because its argument represents a separator, which always stands between two substrings. For example, if the variable `dir` contains `"/usr/bin/"` (a directory that several popular operating systems use to store command-line applications), calling `str.split("/")` returns the following four-element array:

""	"usr"	"bin"	""

This situation is analogous to the fencepost problem introduced in Chapter 1. If there are three instances of a separator character in a string, those separators divide the string into four pieces.

The possibility of an extraneous separator at the end of a string is particularly important when a string consists of a sequence of lines ending with the newline character, which is represented in a JavaScript as `\n`. As an example, the first page of Dr. Seuss's *One Fish, Two Fish, Red Fish, Blue Fish* contains the words of the title divided into lines, which are stored internally like this:

`title`

Calling `title.split("\n")` would return an array with five elements, the last of which is the empty string corresponding to the characters after the final newline. What you almost certainly want instead is to divide the title into its four component lines using the following function:

```
function splitLines(text) {
    let lines = text.split("\n");
    if (lines.length > 0 &&
        lines[lines.length - 1] === "") {
        lines.pop();
    }
    return lines;
}
```

FIGURE 8-3 Functions exported by the `ArrayLib.js` library

`createArray`(*n, value*)	Creates an array of *n* elements, each initialized to *value*.
`listArray`(*array*)	Prints the elements of *array* on the console, one per line.
`reverseComparison`(*cmp*)	Takes a comparison function and returns a new one that compares its values in the opposite order.
`splitLines`(*text*)	Splits a string containing newline characters into an array of lines in which the newlines have been removed.
`readLineArray`(*prompt, fn*) `readIntArray`(*prompt, fn*) `readNumberArray`(*prompt, fn*)	Each of these functions reads input lines from the console, printing *prompt* before each input line. When the user enters a blank line, JavaScript invokes the callback function, passing in an array of the appropriate type. If an illegal value is entered for either `readIntArray` or `readNumberArray`, the user is given a chance to retry.

The `ArrayLib.js` library

Several of the functions in this chapter are sufficiently useful that it makes sense to put them in a library. The `ArrayLib.js` library outlined in Figure 8-3 includes the functions `createArray`, `listArray`, `reverseComparison`, and `splitLines` you have already seen, along with three additional functions—`readLineArray`, `readIntArray`, and `readNumberArray`—which simplify the process of writing test programs that involve arrays. Each of these functions reads input from the console up to a blank line and then passes an array of the input values to the specified callback function. For example, the following function serves as a test of the `sumArray` function from page 276:

```
function TestSumArray() {
   console.log("Enter a list of numbers.");
   readNumberArray(" ? ", processArray);
   function processArray(array) {
      console.log("The sum is " + sumArray(array));
   }
}
```

8.3 Using arrays for tabulation

The data structure of a program is typically designed to reflect the organization of data in the real-world domain of the application. In general, whenever an application involves data that can be represented in the form of a list with elements a_0, a_1, a_2, and so on, an array is the natural choice for the underlying representation.

It is also quite common for programmers to refer to the index of an array element as a ***subscript,*** reflecting the fact that arrays are used to hold data that would typically be written with subscripts in mathematics.

There are, however, important uses of arrays in which a different relationship exists between the data in the application domain and the data in the program. Instead of storing the data values in successive elements of an array, it makes more sense for some applications to use the data to generate array indices. Those indices are then used to select elements in an array that record some statistical property of the data as a whole. Understanding how this approach works and appreciating how it differs from more traditional uses of arrays requires looking at a concrete example.

The exercises for Chapter 7 ask you to write a program that implements a letter-substitution cipher, which encrypts a message by replacing each letter in the input text with an encoded version of that letter determined through the use of a secret key. Although the task of implementing a letter-substitution cipher is an interesting problem in its own right, an even more interesting computational problem is figuring out how you might break a letter-substitution cipher if you did not have access to the key.

The problem of breaking a letter-substitution cipher is so straightforward that it often appears in recreational puzzles called ***cryptograms.*** Edgar Allan Poe was a great fan of cryptograms and described a technique for solving them in his 1843 novel *The Gold Bug:*

> My first step was to ascertain the predominant letters, as well as the least frequent. Counting all, I constructed a table thus:
>
> . . .
>
> Now, in English, the letter which most frequently occurs is *e*. Afterwards, the succession runs thus: *a o i d h n r s t u y c f g l m w b k p q x z.* *E* however predominates so remarkably that an individual sentence of any length is rarely seen, in which it is not the prevailing character.

Edgar Allan Poe

As it happens, Poe's list of the most common letters is by no means accurate. Computerized analysis reveals that the 12 most common letters in English are

$$E \quad T \quad A \quad O \quad I \quad N \quad S \quad H \quad R \quad D \quad L \quad U$$

Given that computerized analyses of English text were not available in his day, Poe can perhaps be excused for making a few mistakes. Poe was, however, entirely correct in his claim that the first step in discovering the hidden meaning of a cryptogram is to construct a table showing how often each letter appears. A program that does just that appears in Figure 8-4 on the next page.

FIGURE 8-4 Program to count letter frequencies

```
/*
 * File: CountLetterFrequencies.js
 * -----------------------------------
 * This function displays a table of letter frequencies.
 */

"use strict";

/*
 * Displays a letter-frequency table for input, which is either a string
 * or an array of strings.  Letters that never appear are not included
 * in the table.
 */

function countLetterFrequencies(input) {
   const LETTER_BASE = "A".charCodeAt(0);
   displayFrequencyTable(createFrequencyTable(input));

   function createFrequencyTable(input) {
      if (!Array.isArray(input)) input = [ input ];
      let letterCounts = createArray(26, 0);
      for (let i = 0; i < input.length; i++) {
         let line = input[i];
         for (let j = 0; j < line.length; j++) {
            let ch = line.charAt(j).toUpperCase();
            if (isLetter(ch)) {
               letterCounts[ch.charCodeAt(0) - LETTER_BASE]++;
            }
         }
      }
      return letterCounts;
   }

   function displayFrequencyTable(letterCounts) {
      for (let i = 0; i < 26; i++) {
         let count = letterCounts[i];
         if (count > 0) {
            let ch = String.fromCharCode(LETTER_BASE + i);
            console.log(ch + ": " + count);
         }
      }
   }
}

/* Test program */

function TestCountLetterFrequencies() {
   console.log("Enter lines of text, ending with a blank line.");
   readLineArray("", countLetterFrequencies);
}
```

The test program in the `CountLetterFrequencies.js` file uses the function `readLineArray` from `ArrayLib.js` to read an array of lines from the user. The callback function is `countLetterFrequencies`, which divides its work between the helper functions `createFrequencyTable` and `displayFrequencyTable`. The `createFrequencyTable` function returns an array of 26 integers, each of which stores how many times that letter appears. The `displayFrequencyTable` then uses that array to display the letter frequencies on the console.

As noted in the comments describing the `countLetterFrequencies` function, the `input` parameter can be either a single string or an array of strings. The easiest way to support such flexibility in the parameter types is to have the code convert one case to the other. In this example, `createFrequencyTable` begins by checking to see whether the parameter is an array. If it isn't, the code takes the single string parameter and creates an array containing only that element.

The following sample run illustrates the operation of the test program using the first page of Dr. Seuss's *One Fish, Two Fish, Red Fish, Blue Fish* as its input:

```
                    CountLetterFrequencies
Enter lines of text, ending with a blank line.
One fish
Two fish
Red fish
Blue fish

B: 1
D: 1
E: 3
F: 4
H: 4
I: 4
L: 1
N: 1
O: 2
R: 1
S: 4
T: 1
U: 1
W: 1
```

The output shows that the file contains four copies of the letters *F, I, S,* and *H* (one for each of the four appearances of *fish*), three *E*'s, two *O*'s, and a smattering of letters that each appear exactly once. Note that letters that never appear in the input are not shown in the output.

The implementation strategy used in `countLetterFrequencies` is to create an array of 26 integers and then to use the character code for the input characters to select the appropriate element within the array. Each element in the array contains an integer representing the current count of the letter that corresponds to that index. Thus, the element at the beginning of the array corresponds to the number of *A*'s, and the element at the end of the array corresponds to the number of *Z*'s. If you call the array `letterCounts`, you can initialize it by writing

```
let letterCounts = createArray(26, 0)
```

This declaration uses the `createArray` function defined on page 280 to allocate space for an array with 26 elements, as shown in this diagram:

`letterCounts`

0	0	0	0	0	0	0	0	0	0	0	0	0	0	0	0	0	0	0	0	0	0	0	0	0	0
0	1	2	3	4	5	6	7	8	9	10	11	12	13	14	15	16	17	18	19	20	21	22	23	24	25

Each time a letter appears in the input, you need to increment the corresponding element in `letterCounts`. Finding the element to increment is simply a matter of converting the character into an integer in the range 0 to 25 by converting the character to uppercase and then subtracting the Unicode value of `"A"`, which is stored in `LETTER_BASE`. If the input character is stored in the variable `ch`, the code necessary to increment the appropriate element in `letterCounts` looks like this:

```
letterCounts[ch.charCodeAt(0) - LETTER_BASE]++;
```

The code for `displayFrequencyTable` has to perform the same conversion in the opposite direction. The values of `i` in the `for` loop run from 0 to 25. To convert that integer to a character requires the following code:

```
let ch = String.fromCharCode(LETTER_BASE + i);
```

8.4 Reading text from files

In a practical application to count letter frequencies, you would not want the user to have to enter the text of each line but would instead like to read the data from a file containing the input text. Unfortunately, files and JavaScript do not play well together. JavaScript's primary use is to implement interactive content that runs in a browser. For security reasons, JavaScript programs running in a browser are not allowed to read arbitrary files on the user's computer. If that were possible, malicious websites could collect sensitive data from the user's file system. The one exception to this rule is that JavaScript code running in a browser can read files if the user chooses a file in a dialog initiated in response to an explicit user command.

The use of files in JavaScript is further complicated by the fact that reading the contents of a file might take some time, depending on the size of the file. Most languages therefore include library functions that read data from a file and wait for that process to complete before proceeding. That model, however, is not appropriate for JavaScript, which doesn't support the concept of suspending execution until an operation is complete. If you need to read a file in JavaScript, you call a library function to start the operation, passing in a callback function that is invoked when the read operation is complete.

To make it possible to work with files, the code supplied with this book includes a library called `JSFileChooser.js` that supports reading a text file within the security constraints that JavaScript imposes. To use the library, you simply call `JSFileChooser.chooseTextFile`, passing in a function that is called with the complete text of the file once the read operation is complete. For example, you can use the following function to count letter frequencies in a file chosen by the user:

```
function CountLetterFrequenciesInFile() {
     JSFileChooser.chooseTextFile(countLetterFrequencies);
}
```

This function displays a button inviting the user to choose a file. Pressing that button brings up a dialog that allows the user to browse the directory hierarchy to find the desired file. When the user selects a file, the browser reads the contents of the file as a string and then passes that string to `countLetterFrequencies`. As noted in the preceding section, the parameter to `countLetterFrequencies` can be either a string or an array of strings, so it works perfectly well to pass the entire contents of the file to `countLetterFrequencies`.

The `CountLetterFrequenciesInFile` program can work with arbitrarily large files. If the user, for example, chooses a file containing the full text of George Eliot's *Middlemarch,* the program produces the following output:

```
                    CountLetterFrequenciesInFile
A: 114157
B: 23269
C: 34031
D: 61046
E: 166989
F: 30826
G: 30055
H: 89636
I: 99651
J: 1695
K: 11010
L: 56865
M: 37816
N: 96887
O: 108561
P: 21922
Q: 1441
R: 79808
S: 88555
T: 123433
U: 40647
V: 12792
W: 34508
X: 2069
Y: 28700
Z: 249
```

If you sort this output by letter frequency in descending order, you discover that the 12 most common letters in *Middlemarch* are

$$E \quad T \quad A \quad O \quad I \quad N \quad H \quad S \quad R \quad D \quad L \quad U$$

The only difference between this frequency table and the statistical results for modern English presented on page 289 is that the *H* and the *S* are reversed. In general, the more text you analyze, the closer the frequencies will come to those calculated for modern English.

8.5 Multidimensional arrays

In JavaScript, the elements of an array can be of any type. In particular, the elements of an array can themselves be arrays. Arrays of arrays are called *multidimensional arrays.* The most common form of multidimensional array is the two-dimensional array, which is most often used to represent data in which the individual entries form a rectangular structure marked off into rows and columns. This type of two-dimensional structure is called a *matrix.* Arrays of three or more dimensions are also legal in JavaScript but occur less frequently.

As an example of a two-dimensional array, suppose you wanted to represent a game of Tic-Tac-Toe as part of a program. As you probably know, Tic-Tac-Toe is played on a board consisting of three rows and three columns, as follows:

Players take turns placing the letters *X* and *O* in the empty squares, trying to line up three identical symbols horizontally, vertically, or diagonally.

To represent the Tic-Tac-Toe board, the most natural strategy is to use a two-dimensional array with three rows and three columns. Each of the elements is a string, which must be one of the following: `""` (representing an empty square), `"X"`, and `"O"`. Because the board is initially empty, the declaration looks like this:

```
let board = [ [ "", "", "" ],
              [ "", "", "" ],
              [ "", "", "" ] ];
```

Given this declaration, you can refer to the characters in the individual squares by supplying two indices, one specifying the row number and another specifying the column number. In this representation, each number varies over the range 0 to 2, and the individual positions on the board have the following designations:

board[0][0]	board[0][1]	board[0][2]
board[1][0]	board[1][1]	board[1][2]
board[2][0]	board[2][1]	board[2][2]

8.6 Image processing

In modern computing, one of the most important applications of two-dimensional arrays occurs in the field of computer graphics. As you learned in Chapter 4, graphical images are composed of individual pixels. Figure 4-4 on page 124 offers a magnified view of the screen that shows how the pixels create the image as a whole. Those images are most easily represented using two-dimensional arrays.

The GImage class

The Portable Graphics Library defines the **GImage** class as a graphical object that contains image data encoded using one of the standard formats. The three most common are the Portable Network Graphics (PNG) format, the Joint Photographic Experts Group (JPEG) format, and the Graphics Interchange Format (GIF). Although most browsers are capable of displaying images encoded in other formats as well, you can maximize the portability of your program by sticking to the most common formats. The image files distributed with this book appear in PNG format.

Displaying an image requires two steps. The first step is to create or download an image file in one of the standard formats. The name of the image file should end with an extension that identifies the encoding format, which is typically **.png**. That file, moreover, must be stored in the same directory as the **index.html** file. The second step is to create a **GImage** object and add it to the graphics window, just as you would with any other graphical object. For example, if you have an image file called **MyImage.png**, you can display that image in the upper left corner of the graphics window using the following line:

```
gw.add(GImage("MyImage.png"));
```

Determining the properties of an image

Unfortunately, the situation is not quite so simple if you need to use properties of an image to determine where the image should be placed. Suppose, for example, you wanted to center the image in the graphics window. Like the other classes that represent graphical objects, **GImage** implements **getWidth** and **getHeight**, which suggests that you could center the image using the following code:

```
let image = GImage("MyImage.png");
let x = (gw.getWidth() - image.getWidth()) / 2;
let y = (gw.getHeight() - image.getHeight()) / 2;
gw.add(image, x, y);
```

The problem with this code segment is that JavaScript implements reading an image as an asynchronous operation. Calling the **GImage** function starts the process of reading the image but does not wait for that process to complete. The implementation of the **GImage** class knows how to update the image on the graphics window when the image is fully loaded, but it is impossible to get any information about the image until that process is complete. In particular, you can't determine the size of the image by calling **getWidth** and **getHeight**. Since you need this information to center the image, you have to make sure that the image is fully loaded before you can determine where to place it in the window.

Like the **GWindow** class, the **GImage** class implements the **addEventListener** method, which takes the name of an event and a callback function that is called when the event occurs. For **GImage**, the relevant event is the **"load"** event, which is triggered when the image is fully loaded. The **addEventListener** method makes it possible to center an image using the following code:

```
let image = GImage("MyImage.png");
image.addEventListener("load", displayImage);

function displayImage() {
   let x = (gw.getWidth() - image.getWidth()) / 2;
   let y = (gw.getHeight() - image.getHeight()) / 2;
   gw.add(image, x, y);
}
```

You also need to use a callback function if you need to scale an image so that it has the desired size. The code for the **EarthImage.js** program in Figure 8-5 illustrates the use of scaling to display an image so that it fills the available space in the window. The image, which shows the earth as seen by the Apollo 17 astronauts on their way to the moon in December 1972, is stored in an image file named **EarthImage.png**. The **EarthImage.js** program reads that image file into a **GImage** object and the callback function then adds that object to the window.

The **EarthImage.js** program introduces one new method from the graphics library that is particularly useful for images. The **scale** method changes the image

FIGURE 8-5   Program to draw an image of the earth taken from Apollo 17

```
/*
 * File: EarthImage.js
 * --------------------
 * This program draws a picture of the earth taken by Apollo 17 along with
 * a photo credit.
 */

"use strict";

/* Constants */

const GWINDOW_WIDTH = 400;
const GWINDOW_HEIGHT = 415;
const CITATION_FONT = "12px 'Helvetica Neue'";
const CITATION_Y = 3;

function EarthImage() {
   let gw = GWindow(GWINDOW_WIDTH, GWINDOW_HEIGHT);
   let image = GImage("EarthImage.png");
   image.addEventListener("load", displayImage);
   let citation = GLabel("Courtesy NASA/JPL-Caltech ");
   citation.setFont(CITATION_FONT);
   let x = gw.getWidth() - citation.getWidth();
   let y = gw.getHeight() - CITATION_Y;
   gw.add(citation, x, y);

   function displayImage() {
      image.scale(gw.getWidth() / image.getWidth());
      gw.add(image, 0, 0);
   }
}
```

size by the specified scale factor. If the variable **image** contains a **GImage** object, calling

```
        image.scale(0.5);
```

resizes the object to make it half as big in each dimension. Similarly, calling

```
        image.scale(2);
```

doubles its size.

In the **EarthImage.js** program in Figure 8-5, calling

```
        image.scale(gw.getWidth() / image.getWidth());
```

scales the image so that it fills the entire width of the window. The program, however, cannot perform this calculation without knowing the width of the image, which is available only in the callback function. Loading the `index.html` file for the `EarthImage.js` program produces the following display:

The `EarthImage.js` program also illustrates the inclusion of a citation along with an image. When you use existing images, you need to be aware of possible restrictions on the use of intellectual property. Most of the images you find on the web are protected by copyright. Under copyright law, you must obtain permission from the copyright holder in order to use the image, unless your use of the image satisfies the guidelines for "fair use"—a doctrine that has unfortunately become much more murky in the digital age. Under "fair use" guidelines, you could almost certainly use a copyrighted image in a paper that you write for a class. On the other hand, you could not put that same image into a commercially published work without first securing—and probably paying for—the right to do so.

Even in cases in which your use of an image falls within the "fair use" guidelines, it is important to give proper credit to the source. As a general rule, whenever you find an image on the web that you would like to use, you should first check to see whether that website explains its usage policy. Many of the best sources for images on the web have explicit guidelines for using their images. Some images are absolutely free, some are free for use with citation, some can be used in certain contexts but not others, and some are completely restricted. For example, the website for the National Aeronautics and Space Administration (`http://www.nasa.gov`) has an extensive library of images about the exploration of space. As the website explains, you can use these images freely as long as you include the citation "Courtesy NASA/JPL-Caltech" along with the image. The **EarthImage.js** program follows these guidelines and includes the requested citation on the page with the image.

Representation of images

In JavaScript, an image is a rectangular array in which the image as a whole is a sequence of rows, and each row is a sequence of individual pixel values. The value of each element in the array indicates the color that should appear in the corresponding pixel position on the screen. From Chapter 4, you know that you can specify a color in JavaScript by indicating the intensity of each of the primary colors. Each of those intensities ranges from 0 to 255 and therefore fits in an eight-bit byte. The color as a whole is stored in a 32-bit integer that contains the red, green, and blue intensity values along with a measure of the transparency of the color, represented by the Greek letter alpha (α). For the opaque colors used in most images, the value of α is always 255 in decimal, which is **11111111** in binary or **FF** in hexadecimal.

As an example, the following diagram shows the four bytes that form the color **PINK**, which JavaScript defines using the hexadecimal values **FF**, **C0**, and **CB** as the red, green, and blue components. Translating those values to their binary form gives you the following:

α	red	green	blue
1 1 1 1 1 1 1 1	1 1 1 1 1 1 1 1	1 1 0 0 0 0 0 0	1 1 0 0 1 0 1 1

The fact that JavaScript packs all the information about a color into a 32-bit integer means that you can store an image as a two-dimensional array of integers. Each element of the entire array contains one row of the image. In keeping with JavaScript's coordinate system, the rows of an image are numbered from 0 starting at the top. Each row is an array of integers representing the value of each pixel as you move from left to right.

Using the GImage class to manipulate images

The **GImage** class in the graphics library exports several methods that make it possible to perform basic image processing. As long as certain conditions are met concerning the source of the image, you can obtain the two-dimensional array of pixel values by calling **getPixelArray**. Thus, if the variable **image** contains a **GImage**, you can retrieve its pixel array by calling

```
let pixelArray = image.getPixelArray();
```

The height of the image is equal to the number of rows in the pixel array. The width is the number of elements in any of the rows, each of which has the same length in a rectangular image. Thus, you can initialize variables to hold the height and width of the pixel array like this:

```
let height = pixelArray.length;
let width = pixelArray[0].length;
```

Unfortunately, many browsers do not allow JavaScript programs to obtain the pixel array from an arbitrary image. As was true for reading text files, the security features implemented as part of the browser prohibit JavaScript code from reading the contents of an image unless the user explicitly selects that image. To make it possible to write programs that manipulate images, **GImage** includes the class method **GImage.chooseImage**, which allows the user to choose an image from a file in a way that makes the image data available. The **GImage.chooseImage** function requires a callback function, which is passed the fully loaded **GImage** when JavaScript finishes reading the data.

The **ChooseImage.js** program in Figure 8-6 illustrates the use of the **GImage.chooseImage** method to choose an image file. In this program, the **displayImage** function callback function takes the fully loaded image as an

---

FIGURE 8-6 Program that allows the user to choose an image

```javascript
/*
 * File: ChooseImage.js
 * --------------------
 * This program illustrates the process of choosing an image file.
 */

"use strict";

/* Constants */

const GWINDOW_WIDTH = 500;
const GWINDOW_HEIGHT = 400;

/* Main program */

function ChooseImage() {
   let gw = GWindow(GWINDOW_WIDTH, GWINDOW_HEIGHT);
   GImage.chooseImage(displayImage);

   function displayImage(image) {
      let x = (gw.getWidth() - image.getWidth()) / 2;
      let y = (gw.getHeight() - image.getHeight()) / 2;
      gw.add(image, x, y);
   }
}
```

argument and then uses the **getWidth** and **getHeight** methods to center the image in the window.

The **GImage** class includes several methods to simplify the task of manipulating image data. These methods appear in Figure 8-7. As you can see from the first section of the figure, the **GImage** class supports two factory methods, one for reading data from a file and one to construct a **GImage** from a two-dimensional array. Given an initialized image, the **getPixelArray** method returns the array of pixels stored within the image. The **GImage** class also exports class methods for retrieving the red, green, and blue components of a pixel from an integer and for assembling red, green, and blue values into the corresponding integer form.

These new capabilities in the **GImage** class make it possible for you to write programs to manipulate images, in much the same way that a commercial system

---

FIGURE 8-7   Useful methods in the GImage class

Factory methods to create a GImage

GImage (*filename*)	Creates a new **GImage** by reading the image data from the specified file.
GImage (*array*)	Creates a new **GImage** from the pixel array.

Method to specify a callback function

image.**addEventListener** ("load", *fn*)	Adds a callback function to the image that is called when the image is fully loaded.

Method to read the individual pixels in an image

image.**getPixelArray** ()	Returns the pixel array for this image.

Class methods

GImage.chooseImage (*fn*)	Allows the user to open a file chooser and select an image file. Once the image is selected, JavaScript waits for the image to be loaded and then calls the callback function *fn*, passing in the **GImage** object.
GImage.getRed (*pixel*)	Returns the red component of the pixel as an integer between 0 and 255.
GImage.getGreen (*pixel*)	Returns the green component of the pixel as an integer between 0 and 255.
GImage.getBlue (*pixel*)	Returns the blue component of the pixel as an integer between 0 and 255.
GImage.createRGBPixel (*r*, *g*, *b*)	Creates a pixel value from the specified *r*, *g*, and *b* components, each of which is between 0 and 255.
GImage.createPixelArray (*width*, *height*)	Creates a pixel array of the specified size.

like Adobe Photoshop™ does. The general strategy consists of the following three steps, all of which must be performed after the image is fully loaded:

1. Use `getPixelArray` to obtain the array of pixel values.
2. Perform the desired transformation by manipulating the values in the array.
3. Call the `GImage` function to create a new object from the modified array.

The following function definition uses this pattern to flip an image vertically:

```
function flipVertical(image) {
   let array = image.getPixelArray();
   array.reverse();
   return new GImage(array);
}
```

A more substantive problem is that of converting a color image to *grayscale,* a format in which all the pixels are either black, white, or some intermediate shade of gray. To do so, you need to go through each element in the pixel array and replace each pixel with a shade of gray that approximates the apparent brightness of that color. In computer graphics, that apparent brightness is called *luminance.*

The goal of a grayscale conversion is to produce a shade of gray that approximates the brightness of each pixel to the eye. As it turns out, luminance does not depend on the color components equally and is controlled much more strongly by how much green appears in the pixel than by the amount of red or blue. Red and blue tend to make an image appear darker, while green tends to lighten it up. The formula for luminance adopted by the standards committee responsible for television signals in the United States looks like this:

$$luminance = 0.299 \times red + 0.587 \times green + 0.114 \times blue$$

A complete program to produce a grayscale image appears in Figure 8-8. The main program begins by allowing the user to choose an image and then waits until the image is loaded. The `displayImages` callback function then displays the original and grayscale images side by side, like this:

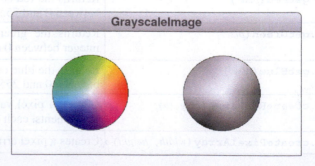

FIGURE 8-8 Program to convert an image to grayscale

```
/*
 * File: GrayscaleImage.js
 * -----------------------
 * This program displays an image together with its grayscale equivalent.
 */

"use strict";

/* Constants */

const GWINDOW_WIDTH = 500;
const GWINDOW_HEIGHT = 400;
const IMAGE_SEP = 50;

/* Main program */

function GrayscaleImage() {
   let gw = GWindow(GWINDOW_WIDTH, GWINDOW_HEIGHT);
   GImage.chooseImage(displayImages);

   function displayImages(image) {
      gw.add(image, (gw.getWidth() - IMAGE_SEP) / 2 - image.getWidth(),
                    (gw.getHeight() - image.getHeight()) / 2);
      let grayscale = createGrayscaleImage(image);
      gw.add(grayscale, (gw.getWidth() + IMAGE_SEP) / 2,
                        (gw.getHeight() - image.getHeight()) / 2);
   }
}

/* Creates a grayscale image based on the luminance of each pixel */

function createGrayscaleImage(image) {
   let array = image.getPixelArray();
   let height = array.length;
   let width = array[0].length;
   for (let i = 0; i < height; i++) {
      for (let j = 0; j < width; j++) {
         let gray = luminance(array[i][j]);
         array[i][j] = GImage.createRGBPixel(gray, gray, gray);
      }
   }
   return GImage(array);
}

/* Returns the luminance of a pixel using the NTSC formula */

function luminance(pixel) {
   let r = GImage.getRed(pixel);
   let g = GImage.getGreen(pixel);
   let b = GImage.getBlue(pixel);
   return Math.round(0.299 * r + 0.587 * g + 0.114 * b);
}
```

▮ Summary

In this chapter, you have learned how to use *arrays,* which are the primary data structure that JavaScript uses to represent ordered lists of data. The important points introduced in this chapter include:

- Like most languages, JavaScript includes a built-in *array* type for storing an ordered collection of elements. Each element in an array has an integer index that indicates its position in the array. In JavaScript, index numbers for arrays begin with 0, just as character positions do for strings.

- JavaScript arrays are most often created by enclosing a list of the elements in square brackets, separated by commas.

- The number of elements in a JavaScript array is stored in a field called **length**.

- You can select a particular element of an array by indicating the index of the desired element in square brackets after the array name. This operation is called *selection.*

- Arrays are often used together with **for** loops that allow you to cycle through the elements of the array.

- Arrays in JavaScript are stored as *references* to the memory containing the values of the array. An important implication of this design is that passing an array as a parameter does not copy the elements. Instead, JavaScript copies the reference value, which specifies the internal location of the array data. As a result, if a function changes the values of any elements of an array passed as a parameter, those changes will be visible to the caller.

- Arrays support a variety of operations implemented as methods. The most important array methods are listed in Figure 8-2 on page 281.

- Although JavaScript offers little support for data files, the code supplied with this book includes a **JSFileChooser.js** library that exports methods that allow the user to select a file.

- JavaScript supports arrays with any number of dimensions, which are represented as arrays of arrays.

- Images are represented as two-dimensional arrays of integers, each of which specifies the color of a pixel as a combination of its red, green, and blue color components.

- The graphics library includes a class called **GImage** that supports images in a way that gives clients access to the underlying pixel array.

Review questions

1. Define the following terms as they apply to arrays: *element, index, length,* and *selection.*

2. How would you create an array called **dwarves** containing the names of the 13 dwarves who arrived at Bilbo's doorstep in J. R. R. Tolkien's fantasy *The Hobbit?* Their names, in the order in which they appeared, are Dwalin, Balin, Kili, Fili, Dori, Nori, Ori, Oin, Gloin, Bifur, Bofur, Bombur, and Thorin.

3. How do you determine the length of an array?

4. True or false: Arrays violate the following rule for parameter passing as expressed in the following sentence from Chapter 5: The value of each argument is copied into the corresponding parameter variable.

5. The following diagram appears in the chapter to illustrate the effect of the five array methods that add and remove elements from an array, but the method names are missing from this version:

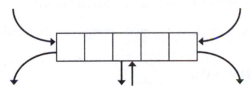

    Supply the missing method names, ideally without looking back at the chapter.

6. Trace the execution of the following program and show the output for each call to **console.log**:

```
function ArrayMethodsReview() {
   let array = [ 0, 1 ];
   array.push(2);
   console.log("array = [" + array + "]");
   array.unshift(array.pop());
   console.log("array = [" + array + "]");
   array.splice(1, 0, 0);
   console.log("array = [" + array + "]");
}
```

7. How does a comparison function used in conjunction with the **sort** method indicate the result of the comparison?

8. Why does JavaScript place significant restrictions on the use of files?

9. In your own words, explain how to use `JSFileChooser.chooseTextFile` to read a text file.

10. What is a multidimensional array?

11. The text uses the following declaration to initialize an empty Tic-Tac-Toe board:

```
let board = [ [ "", "", "" ],
              [ "", "", "" ],
              [ "", "", "" ] ];
```

Would this declaration accomplish the same task?

```
let board = createArray(3, createArray(3, ""));
```

Think carefully about how arrays are represented before offering your answer.

12. What class from the graphics library makes it possible to display images on the graphics window?

13. Describe how images are represented internally.

14. How do you extract the pixel array from an image?

15. Given a pixel array, how do you determine the width and height of the image?

■ Exercises

1. In statistics, a collection of data values is usually referred to as a ***distribution.*** A primary purpose of statistical analysis is to find ways to compress the complete set of data into summary statistics that express properties of the distribution as a whole. The most common statistical measure is the ***mean*** (traditionally denoted by the Greek letter μ), which is simply the traditional average. Another common statistical measure is the ***standard deviation*** (traditionally denoted as σ), which provides an indication of how much the values in a distribution $x_1, x_2, \ldots, x_n$ differ from the mean. If you are computing the standard deviation of a complete distribution as opposed to a sample, the standard deviation can be expressed as follows:

$$\sigma = \sqrt{\frac{\sum_{i=1}^{n}(\mu - x_i)^2}{n}}$$

The uppercase sigma (Σ) indicates a summation of the quantity that follows, which in this case is the square of the difference between the mean and each individual data point.

Create a library called `StatsLib.js` that exports the functions **mean** and **stdev**, each of which takes an array of numbers representing a distribution and returns the corresponding statistical measure. Make sure that the comments are sufficient for clients to understand how to use these functions.

2. Implement a function `createIndexArray(n)` that returns an array of n integers, each of which is set to its index in the array. For example, calling `createIndexArray(10)` should return the array

0	1	2	3	4	5	6	7	8	9
0	1	2	3	4	5	6	7	8	9

3. Both the **reverseArray** function defined in this chapter and the **reverse** method that is defined for all array objects change the values in the calling array. An alternative approach, which was adopted for the **reverse** function for strings in Chapter 7, is to return a new array leaving the original unchanged. Use this strategy to implement a function `createReversedArray(array)` that returns an array whose elements are the reverse of the original values without changing the contents of **array**. Your function should allow you to generate the following console log:

```
JavaScript Console
> let hogwarts = [
    "Gryffindor",
    "Hufflepuff",
    "Ravenclaw",
    "Slytherin"
  ];
> hogwarts
Gryffindor,Hufflepuff,Ravenclaw,Slytherin
> createReversedArray(hogwarts)
Slytherin,Ravenclaw,Hufflepuff,Gryffindor
> hogwarts
Gryffindor,Hufflepuff,Ravenclaw,Slytherin
>
```

4. Write a program that checks whether the parentheses, brackets, and curly braces in a string are properly matched. If, for example, you look at the string

```
{ s = 2 * (a[2] + 3); x = (1 + (2)); }
```

you will discover that all the bracketing operators are correctly nested, with each open parenthesis matched by a close parenthesis, each open bracket matched by a close bracket, and so on. On the other hand, the following strings are all unbalanced for the reasons indicated:

`(([])`	*The line is missing a close parenthesis.*
`)(`	*The close parenthesis comes before the open parenthesis.*
`{(})`	*The bracketing operators are improperly nested.*

The easiest way to solve this problem is to go through the string character by character ignoring all characters except for the bracketing operators. If you see one of the opening operators (a left parenthesis, left bracket, or left brace), push that operator on a stack that keeps track of the unmatched operators. When you see a closing operator (a right parenthesis, right bracket, or a right brace), pop the stack and make sure that the operators match.

5. Write a comparison function `sortAsTitles` that takes two strings and compares them, subject to the following rules:

   - The comparison should ignore differences in case.
   - All punctuation marks except spaces should be ignored.
   - The words *a, an,* and *the* at the beginning of a title should be ignored.

6. Use the `split`, `join`, and `sort` methods to write a function `sortLetters` that rearranges the characters in a string so that they appear in lexicographic order. For example, calling `sortLetters("cabbage")` should return the string `"aabbceg"`.

7. A *histogram* is a graph that displays a set of values by dividing the data into separate ranges and then indicating how many data values fall into each range. For example, given the set of exam scores

   $$100, 95, 47, 88, 86, 92, 75, 89, 81, 70, 55, 80$$

   a traditional histogram would have the following form:

   ```
                                        *
                                        *
                                        *
                               *        *    *
                          *    *        *    *    *    *
        _____
        00s  10s  20s  30s  40s  50s  60s  70s  80s  90s  100
   ```

The asterisks in the histogram indicate one score in the 40s, one in the 50s, five in the 80s, and so forth. When you generate histograms on the console, however, it is easier to display them sideways on the page, like this:

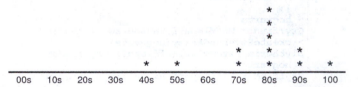

```
                            Histogram
        00s:
        10s:
        20s:
        30s:
        40s:  *
        50s:  *
        60s:
        70s:  **
        80s:  *****
        90s:  **
        100:  *
```

Write a program called **Histogram** that allows the user to select a file containing exam scores ranging from 0 to 100 and then displays a histogram of those scores, divided into the ranges 0–9, 10–19, 20–29, and so forth, up to the range containing only the value 100. Your function should match the format shown in the sample run as closely as possible.

8. A *magic square* is a two-dimensional array of integers in which the rows, columns, and diagonals all add up to the same value. One of the most famous magic squares appears in the 1514 engraving *Melencolia I* by Albrecht Dürer shown in Figure 8-9, in which a 4×4 magic square appears at the upper right, just under the bell. In Dürer's square, which can be read more easily in the magnified inset shown at the right of the figure, all four rows, all four columns, and both diagonals add up to 34. A more familiar example is the following 3×3 magic square in which each of the rows, columns, and diagonals add up to 15, as shown:

FIGURE 8-9   Magic square in Albrecht Dürer's *Melencolia I* (1514)

(Artokoloro Quint Lox Ltd./Alamy Stock Photo)

16	3	2	13
5	10	11	8
9	6	7	12
4	15	14	1

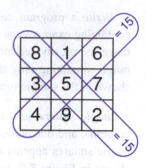

Implement a predicate function

```
function isMagicSquare(square)
```

that tests to see whether **square** is a magic square. Your function should work for matrices of any size. If you call **isMagicSquare** with an array with a different number of rows and columns, your function should return **false**.

9.   In the game of Minesweeper, a player searches for hidden mines on a rectangular grid that might—for a very small board—look like this:

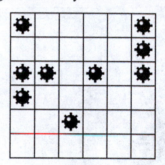

One way to represent that grid in JavaScript is to use an array of Boolean values marking mine locations, where **true** indicates the location of a mine. You could, for example, initialize the variable **mineLocations** to this array by writing the following declaration:

```
let mineLocations = [
    [  true,  false,  false,  false,  false,   true ],
    [ false,  false,  false,  false,  false,   true ],
    [  true,   true,  false,   true,  false,   true ],
    [  true,  false,  false,  false,  false,  false ],
    [ false,  false,   true,  false,  false,  false ],
    [ false,  false,  false,  false,  false,  false ]
];
```

Write a function

```
function countMines(mines)
```

that goes through the array of mines and returns a new array with the same dimensions that indicates how many mines are in the neighborhood of each location. If a location contains a mine, the corresponding entry in the matrix returned by `countMines` should be −1. In Minesweeper, the neighborhood consists of the eight adjacent locations as long as those locations are inside the array. For example, the declaration

```
let mineCounts = countMines(mineLocations)
```

should initialize `mineCounts` as follows:

−1	1	0	0	2	−1
3	3	2	1	4	−1
−1	−1	2	−1	3	−1
−1	4	3	2	2	1
1	2	−1	1	0	0
0	1	1	1	0	0

10. Over the last couple of decades, a logic puzzle called *Sudoku* has become popular throughout the world. In Sudoku, you start with a 9×9 array of integers in which some of the cells have been filled with a digit between 1 and 9 as shown on the left side of Figure 8-10. Your job in the puzzle is to fill each of the empty spaces with a digit between 1 and 9 so that each digit

FIGURE 8-10 Typical Sudoku puzzle and its solution

		2	4		5	8		
	4	1	8				2	
6				7			3	9
2				3			9	6
		9	6		7	1		
1	7			5				3
9	6			8				1
	2			9	5	6		
		8	3		6	9		

3	9	2	4	6	5	8	1	7
7	4	1	8	9	3	6	2	5
6	8	5	2	7	1	4	3	9
2	5	4	1	3	8	7	9	6
8	3	9	6	2	7	1	5	4
1	7	6	9	5	4	2	8	3
9	6	7	5	8	2	3	4	1
4	2	3	7	1	9	5	6	8
5	1	8	3	4	6	9	7	2

appears exactly once in each row, each column, and each of the smaller 3×3 squares. The solution appears at the right side of Figure 8-10. Each Sudoku puzzle is carefully constructed so that there is only one solution.

Although the algorithmic strategies you need to solve Sudoku puzzles lie beyond the scope of this book, you can easily write a function that checks to see whether a proposed solution follows the Sudoku rules against duplicating values in a row, column, or outlined 3×3 square. Write a function

```
function checkSudokuSolution(puzzle)
```

that performs this check and returns **true** if the **puzzle** is a valid solution.

11. Write a method **flipHorizontal** that works similarly to the **flipVertical** method presented in the chapter except that it reverses the picture in the horizontal dimension. Thus, if you had a **GImage** containing the image on the left (of Jan Vermeer's *The Milkmaid,* c. 1659), calling **flipHorizontal** on that image would return a new **GImage** as shown on the right:

(World History Archive/Alamy Stock Photo)

12. Write a method **rotateLeft** that takes a **GImage** and produces a new **GImage** in which the original has been rotated 90 degrees to the left.

CHAPTER 9
Objects

I have always tried to identify and focus in on what is essential
and yields unquestionable benefits. For example, the inclusion
of a coherent and consistent scheme of data type declarations
in a programming language I consider essential.

—Niklaus Wirth, Turing Award Lecture, 1984

(Courtesy of Niklaus Wirth)

Niklaus Wirth (1934–)

Swiss computer scientist Niklaus Wirth designed and engineered several early programming languages
including Euler, PL360, Algol-W, and Pascal, which became the standard language for introductory
computer science throughout the 1970s and 1980s. Although Grace Hopper's COBOL language described
on page 79 included support for data records, Pascal was the first programming language to integrate the
record concept into the type system in a consistent way. In 1975, Wirth published an influential book
entitled *Algorithms + Data Structures = Programs,* which offers an eloquent defense of the idea that data
structures are as fundamental to programming as algorithms. Niklaus Wirth received the ACM Turing
Award in 1984.

When you learned about arrays in Chapter 8, you took your first steps toward understanding an extremely important idea in computer programming: the use of compound data structures to represent complex collections of information. When you declare an array in the context of a program, you are able to combine an arbitrarily large number of data values into a single structure that has integrity as a whole. Then, if you need to do so, you can select particular elements of that array and manipulate them individually. But you can also treat the array as a unit and manipulate it all at once.

The ability to take individual values and organize them into coherent units is one of the fundamental features of modern programming languages. Functions allow you to unify many independent operations under a single name. Compound data structures—of which arrays are only one example—offer the same facility in the data domain. In each case, being able to combine the tiny pieces of a program into a single, higher-level structure provides both conceptual simplification and a significant increase in your power to express ideas in programming. The power of unification is hardly a recent discovery; it has given rise to social movements and to nations, as reflected in the labor anthem that proclaims "the union makes us strong" and the motto *"E Pluribus Unum"*—"out of many, one"—on the Great Seal of the United States.

Although arrays are a powerful tool when you need to model real-world data that can be represented as a list of ordered elements, it is also important to be able to combine unordered data values into a single unit. This chapter describes how JavaScript supports such assembled collections of data values and how to use those values effectively in programs.

■ 9.1 Objects in JavaScript

One of the challenges in explaining JavaScript's approach to structured data is that JavaScript uses the word *object* to refer to two different ideas. In languages like Java and C++ that support the object-oriented paradigm, the term *object* refers to a structure that combines data and behavior. As you will see later in this chapter, JavaScript allows objects to assume that role. JavaScript also uses the word *object* to refer to an older data model that is traditionally called a *record,* which is simply a collection of values that has integrity as a unit. The chapter begins by exploring this more primitive model and then builds the more modern concept of an object on top of that foundation, just as JavaScript itself does. The chapter then introduces the notion of *encapsulation,* which is the idea that an object should serve as a barrier between the client and the implementation.

Encapsulation has advantages for both the client and the implementer. On the one hand, encapsulation benefits the client by hiding the complexity associated with the implementation details. On the other, encapsulation protects the implementation from careless or malicious clients by restricting the set of operations that clients can perform. Encapsulation is one of two fundamental properties of object-oriented programming. The second is inheritance, which is covered in Chapter 11.

Objects as records

Objects in JavaScript are similar to arrays in that they allow multiple data values to be considered as a unit. The fundamental difference lies in how the individual data values are identified. In an array, each of the elements is identified by an index number. In an object, each of the internal components, which are generally called *properties* in JavaScript, is identified by a name.

Objects are useful whenever you have to model a collection of data that has individual components but nonetheless represents an integrated whole. If, for example, you are designing a payroll system for a company, each individual employee has a variety of attributes such as name, job title, and salary, but it still makes sense to think of all those components as a single entity that describes a particular employee. At the rather small firm of Scrooge and Marley that appears in *A Christmas Carol* by Charles Dickens, the data for the two employees might look something like this:

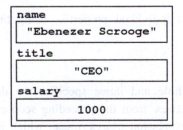
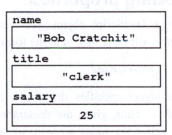

Each of the two objects in this diagram is a combination of three distinct parts: a **name** property indicating the name of the employee, a **title** property indicating the job title, and a **salary** property indicating the annual compensation. Programs can treat these employee objects at either of two levels. At the holistic level, an employee acts as a single data value. You can assign it to a variable, pass it as a parameter, or return it as a result. When you need to take a more reductionistic view, you can select and manipulate the individual properties.

Creating objects

JavaScript makes it easier to create compound objects than most other modern languages do. To create a compound object, you simply enclose a set of property specifications inside curly braces. Each property specification consists of the property name and its value separated by a colon, with the property specifications themselves separated by commas. The following line, for example, declares the variable `clerk` containing the information for Bob Cratchit:

```
let clerk =
    { name: "Bob Cratchit", title: "clerk", salary: 25 };
```

If the name of a property is a legal JavaScript identifier, it typically appears without quotation marks in JavaScript code. You can, however, use any sequence of characters as a property name by enclosing the name in quotation marks.

Like arrays, objects in JavaScript are treated as references to the actual value. The value of `clerk` is therefore diagrammed most accurately like this:

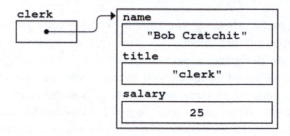

Selecting properties

Given a JavaScript object, you can select individual properties using the ***dot operator,*** which is written in the form

> *object*.*name*

where *object* specifies the object as a whole and *name* specifies the desired property. Thus, given the declaration of `clerk` from the preceding section, you could select the `name` property using the expression `clerk.name`, which in this case has the string value `"Bob Cratchit"`.

Fields are also assignable. For example, when the reformed Mr. Scrooge tells Bob Cratchit, "I am about to raise your salary," he could do so by writing

```
clerk.salary += 5;
```

which gives the underpaid clerk an extra five pounds a year. Moreover, because objects are stored as references, any changes made to the properties of an object passed as a parameter to a function will persist after that function returns. For example, if Ebenezer Scrooge decided to be even more generous, he could define the following function and then use it to double the salary of any employee:

```
function doubleSalary(employee) {
    employee.salary *= 2;
}
```

JavaScript Object Notation (JSON)

JavaScript's compact syntax for declaring objects is so convenient that it has given rise to a new standard for representing compound objects that makes it easier to share data between applications, even if they are coded in different languages. This model is called *JavaScript Object Notation,* which is typically shortened to *JSON.* JSON is a subset of JavaScript's standard notation for objects in which two additional conditions apply. First, the names of each property must be enclosed in double quotation marks. Second, the values associated with each property name must be in one of the following forms:

- A legal JavaScript number
- A Boolean constant, which must be either `true` or `false`
- A string value enclosed in double quotation marks
- The constant value `null`
- An array written using square brackets, as described in Chapter 8
- An embedded JSON object

The rest of this book contains several examples of objects that use the JSON rules.

9.2 Using objects as maps

The examples you have seen so far in this chapter use the dot operator to select properties of an object, which is by far the most common approach. The dot operator, however, requires you to know the name of the property at the time you write the program. For certain applications, it is useful to select a property whose name is either entered by the user or calculated from other data as the program runs. JavaScript allows that form of selection as well, which has the form

> *object* [*name*]

where *object* is the object from which the selection is made and *name* is a string expression indicating the property name. For example, if the variable `clerk` is defined as shown on the previous page, you can select the component containing the clerk's salary either by writing `clerk.salary` or by writing `clerk["salary"]`. Both forms select the property named `"salary"` from the object stored in `clerk`.

The bracketed form of object selection is typically used to implement a data structure that computer scientists call a *map,* which is conceptually similar to a dictionary. A dictionary allows you to look up a word to find its meaning. A map is a generalization of the dictionary concept that provides an association between an identifying tag called a *key* and an associated *value,* which is often a much larger and more complicated structure. In the dictionary example, the key is the word you're looking up, and the value is its definition.

Maps have many applications in programming. For example, an interpreter for a programming language needs to be able to assign values to variables, which can then be referenced by name. A map makes it easy to maintain the association between the name of a variable and its corresponding value.

Translating airport codes to cities using a map

If you fly at all frequently, you quickly learn that every airport in the world has a three-letter code assigned by the International Air Transport Association (IATA). For example, the John F. Kennedy airport in New York City is assigned the three-letter code JFK. Other codes, however, are considerably harder to recognize. Most web-based travel systems offer some means of looking up these codes as a service to their customers.

A simple way to implement this facility is to create a map whose keys are the airport codes and whose values are the city names. If you store the map in a constant called **AIRPORT_CODES**, all you need to do to find the city corresponding to the three-letter airport code is evaluate the expression **AIRPORT_CODES[code]**. If **AIRPORT_CODES** contains a property matching the three-letter code for the airport, the expression will return the corresponding city name from the map. If there is no property matching the code, the value of the expression is **undefined**.

Initializing a map

The interesting question is how to initialize **AIRPORT_CODES**. In most languages, the traditional approach would be to read the data from a file containing the three-letter code for each airport along with the name of the city served by that airport. As noted in Chapter 8, however, the security restrictions imposed by JavaScript make it difficult to work with data files. Given those restrictions, the most straightforward approach to initializing a map like **AIRPORT_CODES** is to include the JSON representation of the complete map in a JavaScript file and then load it using a **<script>** tag, just as you would load a JavaScript library. For the application that translates three-letter airport codes to city names, you could store the data in the file **AirportCodes.js** shown in Figure 9-1 at the top of the next page. The complete list of three-letter codes is long but still fits easily in a JavaScript file.

The **AirportCodes.js** data file need not reside on the same server that runs the application. Because web pages often use libraries from standard repositories on the web, browsers allow the **index.html** file to load scripts from any URL. This file, for example, might be stored on the IATA website, which would then be able to update the map whenever a new airport code was assigned. Web applications that need this information could then load the **AirportCodes.js** file directly from that website.

FIGURE 9-1 JavaScript data file exporting the map from airport codes to city names

```
/*
 * File: AirportCodes.js
 * ---------------------
 * This file exports the complete list of three-letter airport codes as
 * a constant map in JSON format.
 */

const AIRPORT_CODES = {
   "ATL": "Atlanta, GA, USA",
   "ORD": "Chicago, IL, USA",
   "LHR": "London, England, United Kingdom",
   "HND": "Tokyo, Japan",
   "LAX": "Los Angeles, CA, USA",
   "CDG": "Paris, France",
   "DFW": "Dallas/Ft Worth, TX, USA",
   "FRA": "Frankfurt, Germany",
   "PEK": "Beijing, China",
   . . . over 2500 more airport codes . . .
};
```

The `FindAirportCodes.js` program in Figure 9-2 illustrates how to use the `AIRPORT_CODES` map in an application. The program reads three-letter codes from the user and displays the corresponding city name, as shown in the following sample run:

```
                      FindAirportCodes
Airport code: LHR
London, England, United Kingdom
Airport code: LAX
Los Angeles, CA, USA
Airport code: XXX
There is no airport code XXX
Airport code:
```

Iterating through keys in a map

In some applications, it is useful to be able to iterate through all the keys in a map. For example, if you wanted to list all the airports serving a particular country or city, one approach would be to go through all the keys in the map and list every key for which the location value contained the desired country or city name. To make such applications possible, JavaScript includes the following special form of the `for` statement, which executes the body of the loop once for each key in a map:

```
for (let key in map) {
   . . . body of the loop . . .
}
```

FIGURE 9-2 Program to translate airport codes to city names

```
/*
 * File: FindAirportCodes.js
 * -------------------------
 * This program looks up three-letter airport codes in a constant map
 * called AIRPORT_CODES, which is loaded independently.
 */

"use strict";

function FindAirportCodes() {
   console.requestInput("Airport code: ", processLine);

   function processLine(line) {
      if (line !== "") {
         let city = AIRPORT_CODES[line];
         if (city === undefined) {
            console.log("There is no airport code " + line);
         } else {
            console.log(city);
         }
         console.requestInput("Airport code: ", processLine);
      }
   }
}
```

In this pattern, *key* is the name of a variable that holds the values of the keys and *map* is the variable containing the map.

The `FindAirportsByLocation.js` program in Figure 9-3 uses this form of the `for` loop to implement a console-based application to find the airports serving a particular location. A sample run of this application might look like this:

```
                    FindAirportsByLocation
Location: San Francisco
SFO: San Francisco, CA, USA
Location: London
LHR: London, England, United Kingdom
ELS: East London, South Africa
GON: Groton / New London, CT, USA
LCY: London, England, United Kingdom
LDY: Londonderry, Northern Ireland, United Kingdom
LGW: London, England, United Kingdom
LTN: London, England, United Kingdom
STN: London, England, United Kingdom
YXU: London, Ontario, Canada
Location:
```

When you use a `for` loop to iterate through the elements of a map, it is important to make no assumptions about the order in which those keys appear. You

---

FIGURE 9-3   **Program to list the airport codes serving a particular location**

```
/*
 * File: FindAirportsByLocation.js
 * ---------------------------------
 * This program lists all the airports in a specified location.
 */

"use strict";

function FindAirportsByLocation() {
   console.requestInput("Location: ", processLine);

   function processLine(line) {
      if (line !== "") {
         for (let code in AIRPORT_CODES) {
            let location = AIRPORT_CODES[code];
            if (location.indexOf(line) !== -1) {
               console.log(code + ": " + location);
            }
         }
         console.requestInput("Location: ", processLine);
      }
   }
}
```

---

cannot assume, for example, that the keys will be delivered in alphabetical order. If you need to ensure that the keys appear alphabetically, you need to store the keys in an array and then call **sort** to put the elements into the desired order.

9.3 Representing points

As noted in section 9.1, one of the advantages of using objects is that doing so makes it possible to combine several related pieces of information into a composite value that can be manipulated as a unit. An important practical application of this principle arises when you need to represent a point in two-dimensional space, such as the drawing surface of the graphics window. So far, the graphical programs in this text have kept track of independent x and y coordinates, which is sufficient for many applications. As you move on to more complex graphical programs, however, it is useful to store the x and y values in an integrated unit called a ***point***.

Combining the x and y coordinates into a single object makes it possible to work with points as composite values, which means that you can manipulate them like any other data value. You can assign a point to a variable, create an array of points, pass a point as an argument to a function, and return a point as a result. This last example—returning a point as the result of a function call—adds a new capability that would otherwise be difficult to achieve. A JavaScript function is allowed to return only a single value, so there is no way for a function to return the *x* and *y* coordinates independently. A function can, however, return a point, which acts as a single value. The caller can then extract its *x* and *y* coordinates.

Strategies for creating points

The expressiveness of JavaScript's syntax for creating objects makes it possible to use points in an application without defining a new type. For example, the following declarations define two point-valued variables:

```
let origin = { x: 0, y: 0 };
let lowerRight = { x: GWINDOW_WIDTH, y: GWINDOW_HEIGHT };
```

The first declaration defines the variable `origin` to be the point (0, 0) at the upper left corner of the window; the second defines the variable `lowerRight` to be the point in the lower right corner, assuming that the constants `GWINDOW_WIDTH` and `GWINDOW_HEIGHT` are set up as in the earlier graphical examples. Once you have these variables, you can use the following statement to create a `GLine` that runs diagonally across the window:

```
GLine(origin.x, origin.y, lowerRight.x, lowerRight.y)
```

Although many JavaScript applications create new objects using JavaScript's curly-brace notation, it often improves the structure of your code to provide a function that creates the new object. Doing so has a couple of advantages. Most importantly, the name of the function that creates the new object also serves as a name for the type of value the function creates. For example, the factory method

```
function Point(x, y) {
    return { x: x, y: y };
}
```

creates and returns an object whose conceptual type is `Point`, even though there is no difference internally between objects created using the `Point` function and those created using JavaScript's standard format for objects. In keeping with the convention for defining factory methods that serve as types, the name `Point` begins with an uppercase letter, just as `GRect` and `GOval` do.

Many students find it confusing at first to see property definitions like **x: x** in the **return** statement. The **x** that comes before the colon specifies the name of the property; the **x** that comes after the colon is an expression indicating the value, which in this case is the argument **x**. Factory methods often contain expressions in which the property names and the property values match. In fact, the pattern of creating an object using a variable whose name matches its value has become so common that the ECMA 5.0 standard allows you to leave out the property names in this case. Thus, it is now legal in JavaScript to write the `Point` method like this:

```
function Point(x, y) {
   return { x, y };
}
```

Given this definition of `Point`, the declarations for the variables `origin` and `lowerRight` can be rewritten like this:

```
let origin = Point(0, 0);
let lowerRight = Point(GWINDOW_WIDTH, GWINDOW_HEIGHT);
```

Adding methods to the `Point` object

Although the `Point` method in the preceding section is useful in creating graphical applications, it doesn't follow the principles of modern object-oriented design. As noted at the beginning of section 9-1, one of the core principles of object-oriented programming is encapsulation, which is the idea that objects should serve as a barrier between the client and the underlying implementation. That separation reduces complexity by hiding the internal structure of the code from clients who have no need to understand the details. At the same time, encapsulation increases the security of the implementation by preventing clients from making changes to the internal state of an object, because doing so might compromise its integrity.

To see how the notion of encapsulation might apply to the design of a `Point` type, it may help to think about how the current implementation of `Point` differs from that of the classes in the graphics library. In some ways, the strategy for representing a `Point` is similar to that of representing a `GRect`. In much the same way that the `Point` factory method creates a new object whose conceptual type is `Point`, the `GRect` factory creates a new object whose conceptual type is `GRect`. The most obvious difference lies in the way clients refer to component values within the object. Given a `Point` object as it is currently defined, clients select the `x` and `y` properties using the dot operator. Given a `GRect` object, clients obtain its coordinates by calling the methods `getX` and `getY`. Although a `GRect` logically has an x and a y position, it is not possible for the client to make direct references to those internal properties.

Modern programming practice strongly favors the method-based model over using the dot operator to select internal properties. Using methods mediates the interaction between the client and the implementation and therefore provides a reasonable level of encapsulation.

To apply this strategy of encapsulation to the `Point` type, you need to learn how to add methods to a JavaScript object. At a minimum, the `Point` type needs to define the methods `getX` and `getY` so that clients can obtain the coordinates of the point without referring directly to the `x` and `y` properties. Thus, instead of having clients write

```
pt.x
```

you would like to make it possible for them to write

```
pt.getX()
```

Methods that return the value of a property are called **getters.** Methods that change the value of a property—which are far less common—are called **setters.**

Adding methods to the `Point` type is not as hard as you might at first imagine. The receiver syntax used for method calls looks very much like the operation of selecting a property from an object and is in fact implemented in precisely that way. The name `getX` is simply a property in a `Point` object, just as `x` is. The difference is that the value of the `getX` property is a function that returns the value of the internal `x` component. JavaScript functions are, after all, first-class objects, and it is perfectly appropriate to store a function value in a property of an object. The only complication in writing the `getX` function is that its implementation must have some way of gaining access to the value of the *x* component of the point.

One very common—but by no means the best—approach in JavaScript is to store the *x* and *y* coordinates as properties in the object. The `getX` and `getY` methods can then use the keyword `this` to refer to the current object. In JavaScript, any method call that uses the syntax *receiver*.*name*(*arguments*) stores a reference to *receiver* in the keyword `this` so that the object is available inside the implementation of the method. For example, if you call

```
pt.getX()
```

the implementation of `getX` can refer to the `x` property of the receiver as `this.x`. This strategy allows you to define the following implementation of the factory method `Point`, which creates an object containing properties named `x` and `y` along with methods for obtaining the corresponding values using the receiver syntax:

```
function Point(x, y) {
   return {
      x: x,
      y: y,
      getX: function() { return this.x; },
      getY: function() { return this.y; }
   };
}
```

Although this implementation is technically correct, it represents such a violation of the principles of object-oriented design as to merit the bug symbol. The problem is that this version of **Point** leaves the properties **x** and **y** exposed to the client. Given a point **pt**, the client need not call **pt.getX()** to obtain the *x* coordinate, but can instead simply write **pt.x**, bypassing the **getX** method altogether. Worse still, the client can reach in and change the values of the **x** and **y** properties without going through methods in the class. Allowing this kind of access undermines the principle of encapsulation.

The key to a better strategy lies in recognizing that any function defined inside the factory method for **Point** already has access to the values of **x** and **y** because they are part of the closure that contains the local variables of the factory method. Thus, **getX** and **getY** can simply return these values without using the keyword **this** at all, as illustrated in the following version of the factory method:

```
function Point(x, y) {
    function getX() { return x; }
    function getY() { return y; }
    return { getX, getY };
}
```

The **return** statement at the end of the factory method returns an object with only two public properties, which are the methods **getX** and **getY**. The object does not include the definitions of the **x** and **y** properties, which are private to the closure.

All classes in this book use this closure-based approach, which is adapted from a model recommended by Doug Crockford, who was introduced on page 39. This strategy has two primary advantages. First, it hides the underlying representation from the client. Second, this strategy eliminates the need for the keyword **this**, which is a common source of confusion in JavaScript.

The **toString** method

The one remaining feature that is useful to add to the definition of the **Point** class is a method that defines how the object should be converted to a string. When JavaScript needs to determine how an object should be represented as a string, it checks to see whether that object includes a method called **toString**. If it does, JavaScript calls that method and then uses the result as the string representation for the object. For example, if you call

```
console.log(Point(2, 3))
```

JavaScript will automatically invoke the **toString** method of the **Point** object to produce the string " **(2, 3)** ", which is then displayed on the console.

Adding `toString` to the `Point` class gives rise to the final version of the `Point` class, which appears in Figure 9-4 along with a simple test program. The only statement other than function definitions inside the `Point` factory method is

```
return { getX, getY, toString };
```

which returns an object whose only accessible properties are the three exported methods. The values of the variables remain safely encapsulated inside the closure.

FIGURE 9-4 Implementation of the `Point` class

```
/*
 * File: Point.js
 * --------------
 * This file defines a simple class for representing encapsulated points.
 * In this implementation, the values of the variables x and y are stored
 * in the closure of the factory method and are therefore private to the
 * implementation.  The client can obtain these values using the getter
 * methods getX and getY but cannot change these values.
 */

/*
 * Creates a new Point object using the specified x and y coordinates.
 */
function Point(x, y) {
   return { getX, getY, toString };
/*
 * Returns the x component of the point.
 */
   function getX() {
      return x;
   }

/*
 * Returns the y component of the point.
 */
   function getY() {
      return y;
   }

/*
 * Converts the point to a string in the form (x, y).
 */
   function toString() {
      return "(" + x + ", " + y + ")";
   }
}
```

In the code shown in Figure 9-4, the definitions of the methods `getX`, `getY`, and `toString` appear after the `return` statement. This ordering is possible because JavaScript applies a process called *hoisting* to the inner functions as described in Chapter 5. As a result, the definitions of these methods are available at every point inside the factory method. The advantage of relying on hoisting is that doing so ensures that the code that implements the factory method is not separated from the method header by the definitions of the inner functions, which can easily run for more than a page in a class that exports several public methods. Constants and variables declared using the `let` keyword, however, are not hoisted in JavaScript and must therefore be defined before they are used.

Using points in an application

Point-valued objects are often useful in graphical programs. As an example, the `YarnPattern.js` program in Figure 9-5 creates beautiful patterns using only `GLine` objects. Each of the `GLine` objects connects two points stored in an array using a process that you can easily carry out in the real world. Conceptually, the process begins by arranging pegs around the perimeter of the window so that they are evenly spaced along all four edges. To get a sense of how this program operates, imagine that you start with a smaller graphics window in which the pegs are numbered clockwise from the upper left:

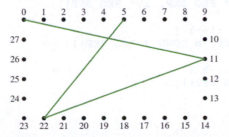

From here, you create a figure by winding a single piece of yarn through the pegs, starting at peg 0 and then moving ahead **DELTA** spaces on each cycle. For example, if **DELTA** is 11, the yarn goes from peg 0 to peg 11, then from peg 11 to peg 22, and then (counting past the beginning) from peg 22 to peg 5, as follows:

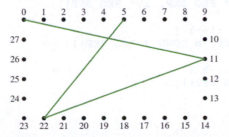

FIGURE 9-5 Program to simulate threading yarn around a series of pegs

```javascript
/*
 * File: YarnPattern.js
 * --------------------
 * This program uses the GLine class to simulate winding a piece of
 * yarn around an array of pegs along the edges of the graphics window.
 */

"use strict";

const PEG_SEP = 12;        /* The separation between pegs in pixels  */
const N_ACROSS = 80;       /* Number of PEG_SEP units horizontally   */
const N_DOWN = 50;         /* Number of PEG_SEP units vertically     */
const DELTA = 113;         /* Number of pegs to skip on each cycle   */

/* Main program */

function YarnPattern() {
   let gw = GWindow(N_ACROSS * PEG_SEP, N_DOWN * PEG_SEP);
   let pegs = createPegArray();
   let thisPeg = 0;
   let nextPeg = -1;
   while (thisPeg !== 0 || nextPeg === -1) {
      nextPeg = (thisPeg + DELTA) % pegs.length;
      let p0 = pegs[thisPeg];
      let p1 = pegs[nextPeg];
      let line = GLine(p0.getX(), p0.getY(), p1.getX(), p1.getY());
      line.setColor("Green");
      gw.add(line);
      thisPeg = nextPeg;
   }
}

/*
 * Creates an array of pegs around the perimeter of the graphics window.
 */

function createPegArray() {
   let pegs = [ ];
   for (let i = 0; i < N_ACROSS; i++) {
      pegs.push(Point(i * PEG_SEP, 0));
   }
   for (let i = 0; i < N_DOWN; i++) {
      pegs.push(Point(N_ACROSS * PEG_SEP, i * PEG_SEP));
   }
   for (let i = N_ACROSS; i > 0; i--) {
      pegs.push(Point(i * PEG_SEP, N_DOWN * PEG_SEP));
   }
   for (let i = N_DOWN; i > 0; i--) {
      pegs.push(Point(0, i * PEG_SEP));
   }
   return pegs;
}
```

The process continues until the yarn returns to peg 0, creating the following pattern:

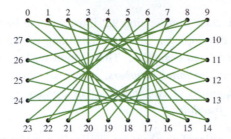

The program in Figure 9-5 begins by calling **createPegArray** to create the array of points around the perimeter. The code creates pegs from left to right across the top, from top to bottom along the right side, from right to left across the bottom, and finally from bottom to top along the left side. When **createPegArray** returns, the **YarnPattern** program starts at peg 0 and then advances **DELTA** steps on each cycle until the index loops back to 0. On each cycle, **YarnPattern** creates a **GLine** object to connect the current point in the array with the previous one.

Figure 9-6 shows a larger example of the output produced by **YarnPattern.js** that uses the values of **N_ACROSS** and **N_DOWN** shown in the program listing.

FIGURE 9-6 Sample run of the yarn-pattern program

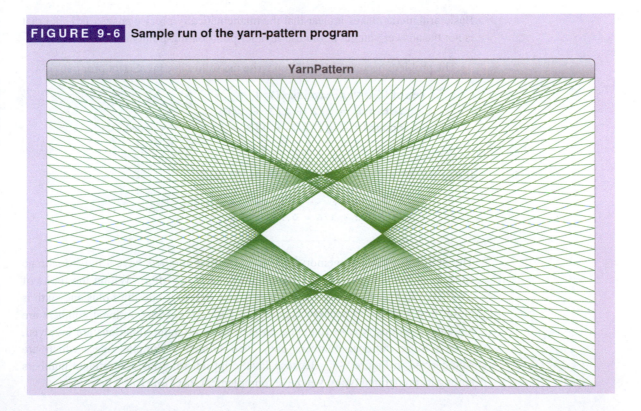

9.4 Rational numbers

Although the `Point` class from section 9.2 illustrates the basic mechanics used to define a new class, developing a solid understanding of the topic requires you to consider more sophisticated examples. This section walks you through the design of a class to represent *rational numbers,* which are those numbers that can be represented as the quotient of two integers. In elementary school, you probably called these numbers *fractions.*

In some respects, rational numbers are similar in concept to JavaScript numbers containing a decimal point, which as noted in Chapter 2 are represented internally as floating-point numbers. Both rational numbers and floating-point numbers can represent fractional values, such as 1.5, which is the rational number 3/2. The difference is that rational numbers are exact, while the built-in implementation of floating-point numbers relies on approximations limited by the hardware precision.

To get a sense of why this distinction might be important, consider the arithmetic problem of adding together the following fractions:

$$\frac{1}{2} + \frac{1}{3} + \frac{1}{6}$$

Basic arithmetic makes it clear that the mathematically precise answer is 1, but that is not the answer you get if you use JavaScript's floating-point arithmetic.

The problem becomes clear if you write the following JavaScript program:

```
function FractionSum() {
   let sum = 1/2 + 1/3 + 1/6;
   console.log("1/2 + 1/3 + 1/6 = " + sum);
}
```

If you run this program, you get the following result:

FractionSum
1/2 + 1/3 + 1/6 = 0.9999999999999999

The problem is that the memory cells used to store numbers have a limited storage capacity, which in turn restricts the precision they can offer. Within the limits of JavaScript's standard arithmetic, the sum of one-half plus one-third plus one-sixth is closer to 0.9999999999999999 than it is to 1.0. By contrast, rational numbers are not subject to this type of rounding error because no approximations are involved. What's more, rational numbers obey well-defined arithmetic rules, which are summarized in Figure 9-7. Because JavaScript does not include rational numbers among its predefined types, you have to implement `Rational` as a new class.

FIGURE 9-7 Rules for rational arithmetic

Addition

$$\frac{a}{b} + \frac{c}{d} = \frac{ad + bc}{bd}$$

Multiplication

$$\frac{a}{b} \times \frac{c}{d} = \frac{ac}{bd}$$

Subtraction

$$\frac{a}{b} - \frac{c}{d} = \frac{ad - bc}{bd}$$

Division

$$\frac{a}{b} \div \frac{c}{d} = \frac{ad}{bc}$$

A general strategy for defining new classes

When you work in object-oriented languages, designing new classes is the most important skill you need to master. As with much of programming, designing a new class is as much an art as it is a science. Designing a class requires a strong sense of aesthetics and sensitivity to the needs of any clients who will use that class as a tool. Experience and practice are the best teachers, but following a general design framework can help get you started along this path.

From my own experience, I've often found the following approach helpful:

1. *Think generally about how clients are likely to use the class.* From the very beginning of the process, it is essential to remember that library classes are designed to meet the needs of clients and not for the convenience of the implementer. In a professional context, the most effective way to ensure that a new class meets those needs is to involve clients in the design process. At a minimum, however, you need to put yourself in the client role as you sketch the outlines of the class design.

2. *Determine what information belongs in the private state of each object.* Although the private data contained in the closure of the factory method is conceptually part of the implementation, it simplifies the later design phases if you have an intuitive sense of what information objects of this class contain.

3. *Determine the parameters needed for the factory method.* Whenever a client creates a new instance of your class, the first step in the process is making a call to the factory method. As part of the design phase, you need to decide what information the client will want to supply at the time the object is created, which in turn determines what parameters the factory method will need. In the case of the **Point** class, the client must supply the x and y coordinates.

4. *Enumerate the operations that will become the public methods of the class.* In this phase, the goal is to define the names and parameters for the methods exported by the class, thereby adding specificity to the general outline you developed at the beginning of the process.

5. *Code and test the implementation.*   Once you have completed the overall design, you need to implement it. Writing the actual code is not only essential to having a working program but also offers validation for the design. As you write the implementation, it is sometimes necessary to revisit the interface design if, for example, you discover that a particular feature is difficult to implement at an acceptable level of efficiency. As the implementer, you also have a responsibility to test your implementation to ensure that the class delivers the functionality it advertises in the interface.

The sections that follow carry out these steps for the `Rational` class.

Adopting the client perspective

As a first step toward the design of the `Rational` class, you need to think about what features your clients are likely to need. In a large company, you might have various implementation teams that need to use rational numbers and could give you a good sense of what operations should be part of that class. In that setting, it would be useful to work together with those clients to agree on a set of design goals.

Since this example is a textbook scenario, however, it isn't possible for you to schedule meetings with prospective clients. The primary purpose of the example is to illustrate the structure of class definitions in JavaScript. Given these limitations and the need to manage the complexity of the example, it makes sense to limit the design goals so that the `Rational` class implements only the arithmetic operations defined in Figure 9-7.

Specifying the private state of the `Rational` class

For the `Rational` class, the private state is easy to specify. A rational number is defined as the quotient of two integers. Each rational object must therefore keep track of these two values. The variables will be declared as local to the factory method, which makes them available to any methods defined inside the closure, but hides them completely from the client. In the implementation, these variables are called `num` and `den`, which are abbreviations of the mathematical terms *numerator* and *denominator* used to refer to the upper and lower parts of a fraction.

Defining the factory method for the `Rational` class

Given that a rational number represents the quotient of two integers, the factory method will presumably take two numbers representing the components of the fraction. Defining the factory method in this way makes it possible, for example, to define the rational number one-third by calling `Rational(1, 3)`. That decision suggests that the header line for the factory method should look like this:

```
function Rational(num, den)
```

Although the similar definition in the `Point` class did not require any further manipulation of the parameters, it makes sense to think at this point whether there are any additional options you would like to offer to the client or any constraints that need to be imposed on the arguments. For example, it might be useful to allow clients to create `Rational` objects from integers by passing a single argument to the factory method, so that the call `Rational(2)` is treated automatically as if it were a call to `Rational(2, 1)` signifying the integer 2. That feature is easy to implement by specifying a default value of 1 for the second argument, as follows:

```
function Rational(num, den = 1)
```

Similarly, it might be useful to ensure that the value passed for `den` is not 0, because division by zero is not legal in a rational number. Although Chapter 11 describes other strategies for reporting errors, it is consistent with JavaScript's conventions for arithmetic to return the constant `NaN`, signifying that the result is not a number. The beginning of the `Rational` factory method might therefore look like this:

```
function Rational(num, den = 1) {
    if (den === 0) return NaN;
```

There are, however, additional constraints that you might want to impose on the values of `num` and `den` stored within the closure. If the client is given unconstrained choice for the numerator and denominator, there will be many different ways to represent the same rational number. For example, the rational number one-third can be written as a fraction in any of the following ways:

$$\frac{1}{3} \qquad \frac{2}{6} \qquad \frac{100}{300} \qquad \frac{-1}{-3}$$

Because these fractions all represent the same rational number, it is inelegant to allow arbitrary combinations of numerator and denominator values in a `Rational` object. It simplifies the implementation if every rational number has a consistent, unique representation.

Mathematicians achieve this goal by insisting on the following rules:

- The denominator is always positive, which means that the sign of the value is stored with the numerator. Thus, if the denominator supplied by the client is negative, it is necessary to invert the sign of both the numerator and the denominator.

- The rational number 0 is always represented as the fraction 0/1. Without this rule, there would be many distinct representations for the rational number 0.

- The fraction is always expressed in lowest terms, which means that any common factors are eliminated from the numerator and the denominator. In practice, the easiest way to reduce a fraction to lowest terms is to divide both the numerator and the denominator by their greatest common divisor. Fortunately, you already know how to compute the greatest common divisor using Euclid's algorithm, which appears as the function `gcd` on page 107.

Implementing these rules requires the following code in the factory method, which still needs the definitions of the exported methods and the `return` statement:

```
function Rational(num, den = 1) {
   if (den === 0) return NaN;
   if (num === 0) {
      den = 1;
   } else {
      if (den < 0) {
         den = -den;
         num = -num;
      }
      let g = gcd(Math.abs(num), den);
      num = num / g;
      den = den / g;
   }
```

Defining methods for the `Rational` class

In light of the earlier decision to limit the functionality of the `Rational` class to the arithmetic operators, figuring out what methods to export is a relatively easy task. If nothing else, it is necessary to export methods for the four arithmetic operators, which are abbreviated to the following three-letter forms: `add`, `sub`, `mul`, and `div`. Because these are methods, JavaScript requires you to call them using the receiver syntax, which means that you need to use the following line to add the rational values stored in the variables `a`, `b`, and `c`:

```
let sum = a.add(b).add(c);
```

Although there are other methods that would make sense in a professionally designed version of the `Rational` class, the only additional facilities defined in this implementation are a `toString` method and the methods `getNum` and `getDen`, which return the numerator and denominator components of the `Rational` object. The reason for including these getter methods as part of the object will become clear in the discussion of the implementation.

Implementing the `Rational` class

The final step in the process is writing the code for the `Rational` class, which appears in full in Figure 9-8 on the next two pages. Particularly given the fact that

FIGURE 9-8 Implementation of the Rational class

```
/*
 * File: Rational.js
 * ------------------
 * This file defines a simple class for representing rational numbers,
 * which are the quotients of two integers.
 */

"use strict";

/*
 * Creates a new Rational object with num as its numerator and den as its
 * denominator.  If den is not supplied, the Rational number creates an
 * integer by assigning a default value of 1.  The implementation ensures
 * that the following conditions hold for each rational number:
 *
 *    1. The denominator must be greater than 0.
 *    2. The number 0 is always represented as 0/1.
 *    3. The fraction is always reduced to lowest terms.
 */

function Rational(num, den = 1) {
   if (den === 0) return NaN;
   if (num === 0) {
      den = 1;
   } else {
      if (den < 0) {
         den = -den;
         num = -num;
      }
      let g = Rational.gcd(Math.abs(num), den);
      num = num / g;
      den = den / g;
   }
   return { add, sub, mul, div, getNum, getDen, toString };

/*
 * Creates a new Rational by adding r to this Rational object.
 */

   function add(r) {
      return Rational(num * r.getDen() + r.getNum() * den,
                      den * r.getDen());
   }

/*
 * Creates a new Rational by subtracting r from this Rational object.
 */

   function sub(r) {
      return Rational(num * r.getDen() - r.getNum() * den,
                      den * r.getDen());
   }
```

FIGURE 9-8 Implementation of the `Rational` class (continued)

```
/*
 * Creates a new Rational by multiplying this Rational object by r.
 */

   function mul(r) {
      return Rational(num * r.getNum(), den * r.getDen());
   }

/*
 * Creates a new Rational by dividing this Rational object by r.
 */

   function div(r) {
      return Rational(num * r.getDen(), den * r.getNum());
   }

/*
 * Returns the numerator of this Rational object.
 */

   function getNum() {
      return num;
   }

/*
 * Returns the denominator of this Rational object.
 */

   function getDen() {
      return den;
   }

/*
 * Converts this Rational object to a string.
 */

   function toString() {
      if (den === 1) return "" + num;
      return num + "/" + den;
   }

}
/*
 * Calculates the greatest common divisor using Euclid's algorithm.
 */

Rational.gcd = function(x, y) {
   let r = x % y;
   while (r !== 0) {
      x = y;
      y = r;
      r = x % y;
   }
   return y;
}
```

the most complex part of the implementation is the factory method for which you have already seen the necessary code, the contents of `Rational.js` are reasonably straightforward.

As is true for any JavaScript class that maintains its local state as part of a closure, all the code in Figure 9-8 appears inside the factory method. Because the definitions of the exported methods appear within the body of the factory method for the `Rational` class, they have access to the parameter variables `num` and `den` as well as to the other functions. The factory method looks like this in pseudocode:

```
function Rational(num, den = 1) {
        Code to ensure that the parameter variables conform to the necessary rules.
        A statement that creates and returns the encapsulated object.
        Function definitions for the exported methods.
}
```

The code for the arithmetic operators follows directly from their mathematical definitions. The implementation of the `add` method, for example, looks like this:

```
function add(r) {
    return Rational(num * r.getDen() + r.getNum() * den,
                    den * r.getDen());
}
```

The arguments to `Rational` are simply the values required by the addition formula:

$$\frac{a}{b} + \frac{c}{d} = \frac{ad + bc}{bd}$$

In the `add` method, the values a and b refer to the numerator and denominator of the current `Rational` object, which are available in the variables `num` and `den`. The values c and d refer to the corresponding components of the `Rational` object passed as the variable `r`. Because these values are not part of the current closure, the code needs to call the `getNum` and `getDen` methods to retrieve these values. Those methods must therefore be exported as part of the class.

The `return` statement in the `add` method calls the `Rational` factory method with the computed values of the numerator and denominator for the result. The code in the factory method ensures that the result is properly reduced to lowest terms and meets the other requirements imposed on the properties maintained inside each `Rational` object.

Defining the `Rational` class makes it possible to demonstrate that rational arithmetic is exact. Running the program

```
function RationalSum() {
    let a = Rational(1, 2);
    let b = Rational(1, 3);
    let c = Rational(1, 6);
    let sum = a.add(b).add(c);
    console.log("1/2 + 1/3 + 1/6 = " + sum);
}
```

produces the following console log:

RationalSum
1/2 + 1/3 + 1/6 = 1

Defining class methods

The final notable feature of the `Rational.js` implementation in Figure 9-8 is the definition of the `gcd` function. Although the `gcd` function is not conceptually a part of the `Rational` class, it is useful enough to export it to clients. At the same time, it doesn't make sense to export `gcd` as a method like `add` or `sub` because it doesn't apply to a `Rational` object but is instead a class method very much like the functions in the `Math` library. The code at the end of Figure 9-8 illustrates how to define `gcd` as a method that belongs to the `Rational` class rather than to an object.

9.5 Linking objects together

In JavaScript, all objects are stored as references. This fact makes it possible to record connections among different values in a larger data structure. When one object contains a reference to another, those objects are said to be **linked.** If you go on to take more advanced computer science courses, you will see many examples of linked objects. As a preview of those coming attractions, the rest of this section introduces a fundamental data structure called a **linked list** in which the references connect individual data values in a single linear chain.

My favorite example of a linked list takes its inspiration from the following passage in *The Return of the King* by J. R. R. Tolkien:

> For answer Gandalf cried aloud to his horse. "On, Shadowfax! We must hasten. Time is short. See! The beacons of Gondor are alight, calling for aid. War is kindled. See, there is the fire on Amon Dîn, and flame on Eilenach; and there they go speeding west: Nardol, Erelas, Min-Rimmon, Calenhad, and the Halifirien on the borders of Rohan."

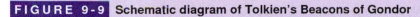

FIGURE 9-9   Schematic diagram of Tolkien's Beacons of Gondor

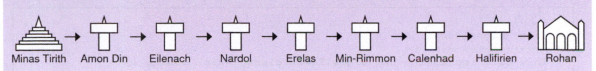

In adapting this scene for the concluding episode in his *Lord of the Rings* film trilogy, Peter Jackson produced an evocative interpretation of this scene. After the first beacon is lit in the towers of Minas Tirith, we see the signal pass from mountaintop to mountaintop as the keepers of each signal tower, ever vigilant, light their own fires when they see the triggering fire at the preceding station. The message of Gondor's danger thus passes quickly over the many leagues that separate it from Rohan, as illustrated in Figure 9-9.

To simulate the Beacons of Gondor in JavaScript, you need to use an object to represent each of the towers in the chain. Those objects are instances of a `SignalTower` class that contains the name of the tower along with a reference to the next tower in the chain. Thus, the structure representing Minas Tirith contains a reference to the one used for Amon Din, which in turn contains a reference to the structure for Eilenach, and so on, up to a `null` value that marks the end of the chain. If you adopt this approach, the internal structure of the linked list appears as shown in Figure 9-10. Each of the individual `SignalTower` structures represents a *cell* in the linked list, and the internal pointers are called *links.*

The code in Figure 9-11 on the next page implements the `SignalTower` class, which exports two methods—`getName` and `signal`—each of which is described in the comments that precede the method. The `SignalTower` implementation also exports a class method called `createChain` that creates a list of `SignalTower` objects from an array of names. The program in Figure 9-12 on page 341 simulates the process of lighting the Beacons of Gondor by creating the linked list of towers and then calling `signal` on the first tower in the list.

FIGURE 9-10   Linked list representing the Beacons of Gondor

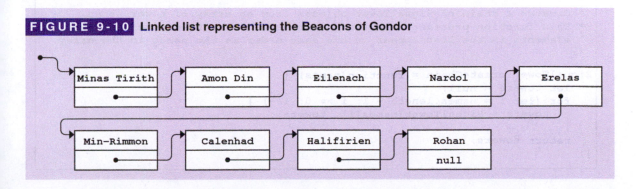

FIGURE 9-11 Class definition to represent a signal tower

```
/*
 * File: SignalTower.js
 * --------------------
 * This file implements the SignalTower class, which models a
 * communications outpost of the sort used to convey the call for
 * assistance from Minas Tirith to Rohan in J. R. R. Tolkien's
 * Return of the King.  Clients can call the  SignalTower factory
 * method directly, although it is usually more convenient to call the
 * class method SignalTower.createChain with an array of tower names.
 */

"use strict";

/*
 * Creates a new SignalTower object from the tower's name and an
 * optional link to the next SignalTower in the chain.
 */

function SignalTower(name, link = null) {
   return { getName, signal };

/*
 * Returns the name of the tower.
 */

   function getName() {
      return name;
   }

/*
 * Simulates the lighting of this signal tower and then propagates that
 * signal forward to the tower to which this tower is linked, if any.
 */

   function signal() {
      console.log("Lighting " + name);
      if (link !== null) link.signal();
   }

}

/*
 * Creates a chain of SignalTower objects from an array of tower names.
 * This function processes the array in reverse order to ensure that the
 * elements in the list appear in the same order as the names in the array.
 */

SignalTower.createChain = function(names) {
   let towers = null;
   for (let i = names.length - 1; i >= 0; i--) {
      towers = SignalTower(names[i], towers);
   }
   return towers;
};
```

FIGURE 9-12 Program to simulate the Beacons of Gondor

```
/*
 * File: BeaconsOfGondor.js
 * ----------------------
 * This program illustrates the concept of a linked list by simulating the
 * Beacons of Gondor story from J. R. R. Tolkien's Return of the King.
 */

"use strict";

/* Constants */

const TOWER_NAMES = [
    "Minas Tirith",
    "Amon Din",
    "Eilenach",
    "Nardol",
    "Erelas",
    "Min-Rimmon",
    "Calenhad",
    "Halifirien",
    "Rohan"
];

/* Main program */

function BeaconsOfGondor() {
    let beacons = SignalTower.createChain(TOWER_NAMES);
    beacons.signal();
}
```

The most interesting method in the implementation of the `SignalTower` class is `signal`, which looks like this:

```
function signal() {
    console.log("Lighting " + name);
    if (link !== null) link.signal();
}
```

The implementation uses `console.log` to report the lighting of the current tower. If this tower is linked to another one, it invokes the `signal` method on that tower. Although this pattern represents a recursive invocation of `signal`, it is far easier to think of the operation in terms of the object-oriented metaphor of sending messages. When one tower receives a signal, it lights its signal fire, which sends a signal to the next tower in the chain.

Summary

This chapter introduces the concept of an *object,* which is a data structure used to represent a collection of values. Like arrays, objects combine multiple values into a single unit. In an array, individual elements are selected using a numeric index; in an object, individual properties are selected by name. JavaScript also uses objects to implement *encapsulation,* which provides a barrier between data and behavior.

The important points introduced in this chapter include:

- You can create an object in JavaScript by enclosing a series of name-value pairs inside curly braces. For example, the expression `{ name: "two", value: 2 }` defines an object whose `name` property is the string `"two"` and whose `value` property is the number 2.

- Given a JavaScript object, you can select individual properties using the dot operator, which is followed by the name of the property without quotation marks. You can also select an individual property using square brackets to surround a string-valued expression that specifies the name of the property.

- Like arrays, objects are treated as *references*, which means that they are not copied when the object is assigned or passed as a parameter.

- Objects in JavaScript implement an important data abstraction called a *map,* which is a structure that provides an association between keys and values.

- Modern programming style discourages clients from manipulating the values of individual properties directly. Programs that use the object-oriented model provide access to the data only through the use of *methods.* The values of the internal data appear only in the factory method closure, which means that clients have no direct access to these values. This strategy for implementing classes supports the principle of *encapsulation,* which is the idea that an object should serve as a barrier that separates the client from the underlying implementation.

- You can indicate the order of elements in a sequence by storing a pointer with each value linking it to the one that follows it. In programming, structures designed in this way are called *linked lists.* The pointers that connect one value to the next are called *links.*

- The conventional way to mark the end of a linked list is to store the pointer constant `null` in the link property of the last object.

Review questions

1. What word does JavaScript use for the individual components of an object?

2. What does *JSON* stand for?

3. What is the *dot operator* and how is it used?

4. True or false: If you pass a JavaScript object as a parameter to a function, the function receives a copy of the object and therefore cannot change the properties of the original.

5. What is a *map*? How do you implement the map concept in JavaScript?

6. How do you iterate through the keys in a map?

7. True or false: Iterating through the keys in a map always processes the keys in alphabetical order.

8. True or false: Modern programming practice discourages direct access to the data properties in an object.

9. In your own words, describe the concept of *encapsulation*.

10. What would happen if you changed the value of **DELTA** in **YarnProgram.js** from 113 to 104? Would the picture be as striking? Why or why not?

11. How do you add a method to an object?

12. How does JavaScript make it possible to hide the internal representation of a class from its clients?

13. What are *getters* and *setters?*

14. What is the special role of the **toString** method in an object?

15. What is a *rational number?*

16. What restrictions does the factory method for the **Rational** class place on the values of the **num** and **den** variables?

17. How do you define a class method in JavaScript?

18. What is a *linked list?*

19. What is the conventional strategy for indicating the end of a linked list?

Exercises

1. Write a function **printPayroll** that takes an array of employees, each of which is defined as a simple JavaScript object, and prints on the console a list for each employee showing the name, title, and salary. For example, if **SCROOGE_AND_MARLEY** has been initialized as a two-element array containing

the entries for Ebenezer Scrooge and Bob Cratchit shown in the chapter, your function should be able to generate the following sample run:

```
JavaScript Console
> printPayroll(SCROOGE_AND_MARLEY);
Ebenezer Scrooge (CEO)       1000
Bob Cratchit (clerk)           25
>
```

This implementation of `printPayroll` uses the `alignLeft` and `alignRight` functions from exercise 1 in Chapter 5 to align the name and title at the left of a 25-character field and the salary at the right of a six-character field.

2. The game of **dominos** is played using pieces that are usually black rectangles with some number of white dots on each side. For example, the domino

is called the 4-1 domino, with four dots on its left side and one on its right.

Define a simple `Domino` class that represents a traditional domino. Your class should export the following entries:

- A factory method that takes the number of dots on each side

- A `toString` method that creates a string representation of the domino

- Two getter methods named `getLeftDots` and `getRightDots`

As with the examples in the text, the data structures that maintain the number of dots should be private to the class.

Test your implementation of the `Domino` class by writing a program that creates a full set of dominos from 0-0 to 6-6 and then displays those dominos on the console. A full set of dominos contains one copy of each possible domino in that range, disallowing duplicates that result from flipping a domino over. Thus, a domino set has a 4-1 domino but not a separate 1-4 domino.

3. Define a `Card` class suitable for representing a standard playing card, which is identified by two components: a **rank** and a **suit.** The rank is stored as an integer between 1 and 13 in which an ace is a 1, a jack is an 11, a queen is a 12, and a king is a 13. The suit is also represented internally as an integer, which has will always be equal to one of the following four constants:

```
const CLUBS = 0;
const DIAMONDS = 1;
const HEARTS = 2;
const SPADES = 3;
```

The `Card` class should export the following methods:

- A factory method that takes either of two forms. If `Card` is called with two arguments, as in `Card(10, DIAMONDS)`, it should create a card from those components. If `Card` is called with one argument, it should interpret the argument as a string composed of a rank (either a number or the first letter of a symbolic name) and the first letter of the suit, as in `"10D"` or `"QS"`.

- A `toString` method that converts the card to a string as described in the outline of the factory method. The card `Card(QUEEN, SPADES)`, for example, should have the string representation `"QS"`.

- The getter methods `getRank` and `getSuit`.

In addition to the `Card` class itself, the `Card.js` file should export the constants that define the suits along with the names of the four ranks that are usually named rather than numbered (`ACE`, `JACK`, `QUEEN`, `KING`). Your implementation should make it possible to run the following test program:

```
function TestCardClass() {
   for (let suit = CLUBS; suit <= SPADES; suit++) {
      let str = "";
      for (let rank = ACE; rank <= KING; rank++) {
         if (rank > ACE) str += ", ";
         str += Card(rank, suit);
      }
      console.log(str);
   }
}
```

The output of the `TestCardClass` program should look like this:

TestCardClass
AC, 2C, 3C, 4C, 5C, 6C, 7C, 8C, 9C, 10C, JC, QC, KC
AD, 2D, 3D, 4D, 5D, 6D, 7D, 8D, 9D, 10D, JD, QD, KD
AH, 2H, 3H, 4H, 5H, 6H, 7H, 8H, 9H, 10H, JH, QH, KH
AS, 2S, 3S, 4S, 5S, 6S, 7S, 8S, 9S, 10S, JS, QS, KS

4. In Roman numerals, characters of the alphabet are used to represent integers as shown in this table:

symbol	value
I	1
V	5
X	10
L	50
C	100
D	500
M	1000

Each character in a Roman numeral stands for the corresponding value. Ordinarily, the value of the Roman numeral as a whole is the sum of the individual character values in the table. Thus, the string `"LXXVI"` denotes $50 + 10 + 10 + 5 + 1$, or 76. The only exception occurs when a character corresponding to a smaller value precedes a character representing a larger one, in which case the value of the first letter is subtracted from the total, so that the string `"IX"` corresponds to $10 - 1$, or 9.

Write a function `romanToDecimal` that takes a string representing a Roman numeral and returns the corresponding decimal number. To find the values of each Roman numeral character, your function should look that character up in a map that implements the Roman numeral conversion. If the string contains characters that are not in the table, `romanToDecimal` should return –1.

5. In May of 1844, Samuel F. B. Morse sent the message "What hath God wrought!" by telegraph from Washington to Baltimore, heralding the beginning of the age of electronic communication. In his 1998 book, *The Victorian Internet,* British journalist Tom Standage goes so far as to argue quite plausibly that the impact of the telegraph on the 19th-century world was in many ways more profound than the impact of the Internet on the 20th.

To make it possible to communicate information using only the presence or absence of a single tone, Morse designed a coding system in which letters and other symbols are represented as coded sequences of short and long tones, traditionally called *dots* and *dashes*. In Morse code, the 26 letters are represented by the codes in Figure 9-13.

Write a program that reads in lines from the user and translates each line either to or from Morse code, depending on the first character of the line:

- If the line starts with a letter, you need to translate it to Morse code. Any characters other than the 26 letters should simply be ignored.

Samuel F. B. Morse

(Everett Historical/Shutterstock)

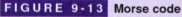

FIGURE 9-13 Morse code

A	·▬	H	····	O	▬▬▬	V	···▬
B	▬···	I	··	P	·▬▬·	W	·▬▬
C	▬·▬·	J	·▬▬▬	Q	▬▬·▬	X	▬··▬
D	▬··	K	▬·▬	R	·▬·	Y	▬·▬▬
E	·	L	·▬··	S	···	Z	▬▬··
F	··▬·	M	▬▬	T	▬		
G	▬▬·	N	▬·	U	··▬		

- If the line starts with a period (dot) or a hyphen (dash), it should be read as a series of Morse code characters that you need to translate back to letters. You may assume that each sequence of dots and dashes in the input string will be separated by spaces, and you are free to ignore any other characters that appear. Because there is no encoding for the space between words, the characters of the translated message will be run together when your program translates in this direction.

The program should end when the user enters a blank line. A sample run of this program (taken from the messages between the Titanic and the Carpathia in 1912) might look like this:

```
                         MorseCode
Morse code translator
> SOS TITANIC
... --- ...  - .. - .- -. .. -.-.
> WE ARE SINKING FAST
.-- .  .- .-. .  ... .. -. -.- .. -. --.  ..-. .- ... -
> .... . .- -.. .. -. --. ..-. --- .-. -.-- --- ..-
HEADINGFORYOU
>
```

6. Even though the **CountLetterFrequencies** program appeared in Chapter 8 as an illustration of how arrays can be used for tabulation, its operation is conceptually more closely related to the idea of a map in which each individual letter serves as a key whose corresponding value is the letter count. Rewrite the **CountLetterFrequencies.js** program so that it uses a map rather than an array in its implementation. As before, the table of letter frequencies should appear in alphabetical order.

7. Objects make it possible to circumvent JavaScript's restriction that functions can return only a single value. Rewrite the **centimetersToFeetAndInches** function from page 56 so that it returns an object with properties named **feet** and **inches** instead of a string.

8. Write a function **midpoint** that takes two values of type **Point** and returns a new **Point** object whose coordinates define the midpoint of the line segment specified by the two parameters. For example, if the variables **upperLeft** and **lowerRight** are defined as

```
let upperLeft = Point(0, 0);
let lowerRight = Point(GWINDOW_WIDTH, GWINDOW_HEIGHT);
```

calling **midpoint(upperLeft, lowerRight)** should return a point whose coordinates mark the center of the window.

9. The **Rational** class presented in the text defines the methods **add**, **sub**, **mul**, and **div** but offers no way to compare two rational values other than

subtracting one `Rational` value from another and looking at the sign of the numerator. Add the methods `equalTo`, `lessThan`, and `greaterThan` to the `Rational.js` file. Each of these methods should compare the current `Rational` object to a second one passed as an argument and return a Boolean value indicating whether the specified relation holds between the two values.

10. There is no reason to restrict the process of passing a visual signal to a single chain of towers as the `SignalTower.js` implementation in Figure 9-11 does. There could, after all, be several towers watching for the signal from Minas Tirith, each of which would respond by lighting its own signal fire and then propagating that signal to its links. The process of forwarding a signal to subsequent towers can split into multiple paths at each tower, leading to a branching structure that computer scientists call a *tree*.

   Rewrite the `SignalTower` class so that it stores an array of linked towers rather than a single linked tower. The `signal` method must then signal each tower in the array. An important part of this exercise is to design an interface that supports creating the tree of towers in a way that is convenient for clients.

   Validate your design and implementation by writing a test program that creates a tree-structured set of towers and shows that the signal is correctly propagated through the towers in the tree.

CHAPTER 10
Designing Data Structures

> Modularity based on abstraction is the way things are done.
> —Barbara Liskov, Turing Award Lecture, 2009

(Courtesy of Barbara Liskov)

Barbara Liskov (1939–)

Barbara Liskov earned her bachelor's degree in mathematics from the University of California at Berkeley in 1961. After being introduced to computers and programming through jobs at the MITRE Corporation and Harvard University, Liskov returned to California, where she received her Ph.D. in Computer Science from Stanford University in 1968. For most of her career, Liskov was Professor of Electrical Engineering and Computer Science at the Massachusetts Institute of Technology, where she conducted pioneering work on data abstraction in programming languages. The ideas that she championed about the importance of encapsulation have since become commonplace. For her many contributions, Liskov received the ACM Turing Award in 2009. On that occasion, MIT Provost L. Rafael Rife observed "every time you exchange e-mail with a friend, check your bank statement online or run a Google search, you are riding the momentum of her research."

Chapters 8 and 9 introduced you to the concepts of arrays and objects, both of which make it possible to represent collections of data values. Those chapters, however, concentrate on the low-level details of how arrays and objects are implemented in JavaScript. This chapter focuses instead on how you can use arrays and objects to implement data structures that are useful in applications, which requires thinking about data structures in a more holistic way.

◼ 10.1 Abstract data types

In Chapter 9, you learned about encapsulation and how to use it to define classes in which the variables that maintain the internal data are stored in the closure of a factory method and therefore are inaccessible to clients. Those classes are examples of a more general concept in computer science called an *abstract data type* or *ADT,* which corresponds in JavaScript to a class that uses encapsulation to separate its behavior from the details of its representation. As a client of an ADT, you know what the methods of that class do but not how those methods are implemented.

As a programming model, ADTs offer the following advantages:

- *Simplicity.* Hiding the internal representation from the client means that there are fewer details for the client to understand.

- *Flexibility.* Because a class is defined in terms of its public behavior, the programmer who implements a class is free to change the internal representation. As with any abstraction, it is appropriate to change the implementation as long as the interface remains the same.

- *Security.* The interface boundary acts as a wall that protects the implementation and the client from each other. If a client program has access to the representation, it can change the values in the underlying data structure in unexpected ways. Keeping the representation private prevents the client from making such changes.

The two examples of ADTs from Chapter 9—the `Point` class from section 9.3 and the `Rational` class from section 9.4—are unusually simple in that the internal state consists only of the parameters to the factory method. Moreover, once you have created a `Point` or a `Rational` object, the internal state never changes. Such classes are said to be *immutable.* Immutable classes have many advantages, particularly in applications that use more than one processor.

In practice, many classes need to maintain internal state information that changes over time. The variables that keep track of that state information must be declared as local variables in the factory method so that they become part of its closure. Several of the ADT examples introduced in this chapter illustrate this strategy.

10.2 Implementing a token scanner

In Chapter 7, the most sophisticated example of string processing is the Pig Latin translator. As it appears in Figure 7-4, the `PigLatin` program decomposes the problem into two phases: the `toPigLatin` function divides the input line into words and then calls `wordToPigLatin` to convert each word to its Pig Latin form. The first phase of this decomposition is not at all specific to the Pig Latin domain. Many applications need to divide a string into words, or more generally, into logical units that are typically longer than a single character. In computer science, such units are typically called *tokens*.

Because the problem of dividing a string into individual tokens comes up frequently in applications, it is useful to build a library package that takes care of that task. The next few sections walk through the design of a `TokenScanner` ADT that is both simple to use and flexible enough to meet the needs of clients.

What clients want from a token scanner

As always, the best way to begin the design of the `TokenScanner` class is to look at the problem from the client's perspective. Every client that wants to use a scanner starts with a source of tokens, which is presumably a string, although it may be one read from the contents of a data file. What the client needs is some way to retrieve individual tokens from that input source.

There are several strategies for designing a `TokenScanner` class that offers the necessary functionality. You could, for example, have the token scanner return an array containing the entire list of tokens. That strategy, however, isn't appropriate for applications that work with very long strings, because the scanner has to create a single array containing the entire list of tokens. A more space-efficient approach is to have the scanner deliver its tokens one at a time. When you use this design, the process of reading tokens from a scanner has the following pseudocode form:

> *Create the token scanner and initialize it to read from some string.*
> **while** (*more tokens are available*) {
>   *Read the next token.*
> }

This pseudocode structure immediately suggests the sort of methods that the `TokenScanner` class will need to provide for its clients. From this example, you would expect `TokenScanner` to export the following methods:

- A `TokenScanner` factory method that allows clients to specify the input string
- A `hasMoreTokens` method that tests whether there are tokens left to process
- A `nextToken` method that scans and returns the next token

These methods define the operational structure of a token scanner and do not depend on the characteristics of the client application. Different applications, however, define tokens in different ways, which means that the **TokenScanner** class must give the client some control over what types of tokens are recognized.

The need to recognize different types of tokens is easiest to illustrate by offering a few examples. As a starting point, it is useful to revisit the problem of translating English into Pig Latin. If you rewrite the **PigLatin** program to use the token scanner, you can't ignore the spaces and punctuation marks, because those characters need to be part of the output. In the context of the Pig Latin problem, tokens fall into one of two categories:

1. A string of consecutive letters and digits representing a word

2. A single-character string consisting of a space or punctuation mark

If you give the token scanner the input

        This is Pig Latin.

calling **nextToken** repeatedly must return the following sequence of eight tokens:

    This □ is □ Pig □ Latin .

Other applications, by contrast, are likely to define tokens in different ways. The JavaScript interpreter inside your web browser, for example, uses a token scanner to divide a program into tokens that make sense in the programming context, including identifiers, constants, operators, and other symbols that define the syntactic structure of the language. For example, if you give the token scanner the line

        let area = 3.14159265 * r * r;

you would like it to deliver the following sequence of tokens:

    let area = 3.14159265 * r * r ;

These two applications differ somewhat in the definition of a token. In the Pig Latin translator, anything that's not a sequence of letters and digits is returned as a single-character token, including the spaces. By contrast, token scanners for programming languages often ignore whitespace characters and treat floating-point numbers as a single token.

As you will learn if you go on to take a course on compilers, it is possible to build a token scanner that allows the client to specify what constitutes a legal token, typically by supplying a precise set of rules. That design offers the greatest possible generality. Generality, however, sometimes comes at the expense of simplicity. If you force clients to specify the rules for token formation, they need to learn how to write those rules, which is similar in many respects to learning a new language. Worse still, the rules for token formation are often difficult for clients to get right, particularly if they need to recognize a complex pattern, such as the one that compilers use to recognize numbers.

If your goal in the interface is to maximize simplicity, it is probably best to design the **TokenScanner** class so that clients can enable specific options that allow the token scanner to recognize token types in particular application contexts. If all you want is a token scanner that collects consecutive alphanumeric characters into words, you use the **TokenScanner** class in its simplest possible configuration. If you instead want the **TokenScanner** class to identify the units in a JavaScript program, you can, for example, enable an option that tells the scanner to ignore whitespace characters, which means that the **TokenScanner** class must export a method to control that option. The simplest strategy is to have the **TokenScanner** class create a token scanner that returns whitespace characters by default and to export an **ignoreWhitespace** method that changes that behavior. The set of methods exported by this implementation of a token scanner appear in Figure 10-1. The implementation of the **TokenScanner** class is not particularly difficult and appears in Figure 10-2 on the next two pages.

As always, one of the first decisions you have to make in writing the code is what information needs to be maintained in the private state of the class. In this implementation, the private state consists of the following:

- The parameter **str**, which contains the input string for the token scanner

- The variable **cp**, which keeps track of the current position in the string

- The variable **ignoreWhitespaceFlag**, which indicates if this option is enabled

The code in the factory method sets these variables to their initial values and then returns an object containing the public methods exported by the class, as follows:

```
return { nextToken, hasMoreTokens, ignoreWhitespace };
```

FIGURE 10-1 Methods exported by the simplified TokenScanner class

TokenScanner (*str*)	Initializes a scanner object that reads tokens from the specified string.
nextToken()	Returns the next token from this scanner. If **nextToken** is called when no tokens are available, it returns the empty string.
hasMoreTokens()	Returns **true** if there are more tokens to read.
ignoreWhitespace()	Tells the scanner to ignore whitespace characters.

FIGURE 10-2 Implementation of the simplified `TokenScanner` class

```
/*
 * File: TokenScanner.js
 * ----------------------
 * This file implements a simple version of a token scanner class.  A token
 * scanner is an abstract data type that divides a string into individual
 * tokens, which are strings of consecutive characters that form logical
 * units.  This simplified version recognizes two token types:
 *
 *    1. A string of consecutive letters and digits
 *    2. A single character string
 *
 * To use this class, you must first create a TokenScanner instance using
 * the declaration
 *
 *    let scanner = TokenScanner(str);
 *
 * Once you have initialized the scanner, you can retrieve the next token
 * from the token stream by calling
 *
 *    let token = scanner.nextToken();
 *
 * To determine whether any tokens remain to be read, you can either
 * call the predicate method scanner.hasMoreTokens() or check to see
 * whether nextToken returns the empty string.
 *
 * The following code fragment serves as a pattern for processing each
 * token in the string str:
 *
 *    let scanner = TokenScanner(str);
 *    while (scanner.hasMoreTokens()) {
 *       let token = scanner.nextToken();
 *       . . . code to process the token . . .
 *    }
 *
 * By default, TokenScanner treats whitespace characters as operators
 * and returns them as single-character tokens.  You can ignore these
 * characters by making the following call:
 *
 *    scanner.ignoreWhitespace();
 */

"use strict";

/*
 * Creates a new TokenScanner object that scans the specified string.
 */

function TokenScanner(str) {
   let cp = 0;
   let ignoreWhitespaceFlag = false;
   return { nextToken, hasMoreTokens, ignoreWhitespace };
```

FIGURE 10-2 Implementation of the simplified TokenScanner class (continued)

```
/*
 * Returns the next token from this scanner.  If nextToken is called
 * when no tokens are available, it returns the empty string.
 */

   function nextToken() {
      if (ignoreWhitespaceFlag) skipWhitespace();
      if (cp === str.length) return "";
      let token = str.charAt(cp++);
      if (isLetterOrDigit(token)) {
         while (cp < str.length && isLetterOrDigit(str.charAt(cp))) {
            token += str.charAt(cp++);
         }
      }
      return token;
   }

/*
 * Returns true if there are more tokens for this scanner to read.
 */

   function hasMoreTokens() {
      if (ignoreWhitespaceFlag) skipWhitespace();
      return cp < str.length;
   }
/*
 * Tells the scanner to ignore whitespace characters.
 */

   function ignoreWhitespace() {
      ignoreWhitespaceFlag = true;
/*
 * Skips over any whitespace characters before the next token.
 */

   function skipWhitespace() {
      while (cp < str.length && isWhitespace(str.charAt(cp))) {
         cp++;
      }
   }
}
```

It is worth going through the code in Figure 10-2 to make sure that you understand it. In particular, it is worth spending a minute or two looking at the implementation of **nextToken**. Two statements in this method use the expression **str.charAt(cp++)** to retrieve the next character. This is first example you've seen of an expression that uses the result of the increment operator in the context of an enclosing expression. As described in Chapter 2, the expression **cp++** adds one to the value of `cp` but then returns its previous value to the enclosing expression. The character selected from `str` is therefore the one marked by the index `cp` *before* that variable is incremented.

The `TokenScanner` class makes it easier to write many applications. You can, for example, simplify `PigLatin.js` by rewriting `lineToPigLatin` like this:

```
function toPigLatin(str) {
   let result = "";
   let scanner = TokenScanner(str);
   while (scanner.hasMoreTokens()) {
      let token = scanner.nextToken();
      if (isLetter(token.charAt(0))) {
         token = wordToPigLatin(token);
      }
      result += token;
   }
   return result;
}
```

Although the new implementation of `toPigLatin` is not much shorter than the original, the code is conceptually simpler. The original code had to operate at the level of individual characters; the new version gets to work with complete words, because the `TokenScanner` class takes care of the low-level details.

The `JSTokenScanner` class

The libraries supplied with this book include a library called `JSTokenScanner.js`, which exports a class that offers considerably more flexibility that the simplified `TokenScanner` class implemented in the preceding section. The methods exported by the `JSTokenScanner` appear in Figure 10-3 on the next page. The additional features available in the `JSTokenScanner` class include the following:

- The `setInput` method makes it possible to set a new input string without changing the scanner parameters.

- The `saveToken` method makes it possible to put a token back into the token stream where it can then be read again by a subsequent call to `nextToken`.

- The token scanner supports options for reading numbers, quoted strings, and multicharacter operators and for ignoring JavaScript-style comments.

- The `getTokenType` method makes it possible to identify different types of tokens, such as numbers, strings, operators, and identifiers.

FIGURE 10-3 Methods exported by the library implementation of the `JSTokenScanner` class

Factory method

`JSTokenScanner` (*str*)	Initializes a scanner object. The source for the tokens is initialized from the specified string. If no string is provided, the client must call `setInput` before reading tokens from the scanner.

Methods for reading tokens

`hasMoreTokens ()`	Returns `true` if there are more tokens to read from the input source.
`nextToken ()`	Returns the next token from this scanner. If `nextToken` is called when no tokens are available, it returns the empty string.
`saveToken (token)`	Saves the specified token so that it will be returned on the next call to `nextToken`.

Methods for controlling scanner options

`ignoreWhitespace ()`	Tells the scanner to ignore whitespace characters.
`ignoreComments ()`	Tells the scanner to ignore comments, which can be in either the slash-star or slash-slash form.
`scanNumbers ()`	Tells the scanner to recognize any legal number as a single token. The syntax for numbers is the same as that used in JavaScript.
`scanStrings ()`	Tells the scanner to return a string enclosed in quotation marks as a single token. The quotation marks (which may be either single or double quotes) are included in the scanned token.
`addWordCharacters` (*str*)	Adds the characters in `str` to the set of characters legal in a word.
`addOperator` (*op*)	Defines a new multicharacter operator. The scanner will return the longest defined operator, but will always return at least one character.

Miscellaneous methods

`setInput` (*str*)	Sets the input source for this scanner to the specified string. Any tokens remaining in the previous source are lost.
`getTokenType` (*token*)	Returns the type of the token, which must be one of the following constants: `EOF`, `SEPARATOR`, `WORD`, `NUMBER`, `STRING`, `OPERATOR`.
`getPosition ()`	Returns the current position of the scanner in the input stream.
`getStringValue` (*token*)	Removes the quotation marks from a string token and interprets any escape characters.
`getNumberValue` (*token*)	Returns the numeric value of a token.
`verifyToken` (*expected*)	Reads the next token and makes sure it matches the string *expected*.
`isWordCharacter` (*ch*)	Returns `true` if the character *ch* is valid in a word.
`isValidIdentifier` (*token*)	Returns `true` if `token` is a valid word token.

10.3 Efficiency and representation

One of the great advantages of separating the behavior of an abstract data type from its underlying representation is that doing so makes it possible to change that representation without forcing clients to change their programs. As long as the exported methods retain the same parameter structure and continue to have the same effect, the client has no reason to be concerned about how the information is stored on the implementation side of the interface. If, for example, the programmer maintaining the abstract data type comes up with a more efficient representation or a better algorithm, implementing that improvement will have no negative impact on the client.

The next several sections illustrate this idea by looking at several different strategies for implementing a library package that maintains a list of the legal words in English. Although such a package has conceptual similarities to a dictionary, computer scientists commonly refer to a word list that lacks associated definitions as a *lexicon*. A lexicon of English words has many useful applications, ranging from checking the spelling in a document to playing word games. At a minimum, an abstract data type implementing an English lexicon must support the following operations:

- Testing whether a string of characters is in the lexicon
- Processing every word in the lexicon in alphabetical order

Making these operations *possible* is only part of implementer's challenge. Clients also want the operations to be *efficient* so the programs they write don't take an unreasonable amount of time. As you will soon discover, the design choices you make for the lexicon can have a dramatic effect on how quickly these operations run.

Implementing the lexicon without encapsulation

Before looking at how different implementations might affect the performance of an English lexicon, it helps to consider how one might implement the necessary operations without defining an abstract data type. Although the number of words in English is large, it works perfectly well in JavaScript to define a constant array containing the entire list, as follows:

```
const ENGLISH_WORDS = [
   "a", "aa", "aah", "aahed", "aahing", "aahs",
   . . . approximately 25,000 more lines . . .
   "zymurgies", "zymurgy", "zyzzyva", "zyzzyvas"
];
```

A file containing this array loads surprisingly quickly, even over a web connection. Moreover, it is easy—although not necessarily efficient—to implement each of the required operations. Clients can iterate through every English word as follows:

```
let nWords = ENGLISH_WORDS.length;
for (let i = 0; i < nWords; i++) {
   let word = ENGLISH_WORDS[i];
   . . . perform whatever operations are required using that word . . .
}
```

Similarly, you can use the built-in `indexOf` method to check whether the variable `str` contains a valid English word like this:

```
if (ENGLISH_WORDS.indexOf(str.toLowerCase()) !== -1) . . .
```

Implementing the lexicon in this form, however, has two serious flaws. First, using `indexOf` to check whether a word is in the lexicon is highly inefficient, as you will see in the next few pages. Perhaps more importantly, giving clients direct access to the **ENGLISH_WORDS** array and telling them what array operations to use makes it impossible to eliminate the inefficiency. Exposing the underlying representation limits the scope of possible changes because clients come to depend on a particular design.

Abstract data types eliminate the problem by separating behavior and representation. As long as the methods supported by the abstract type remain the same, the implementer is free to change the internal data structures.

In order to implement **EnglishLexicon** as an abstract type, you must define a factory method that exports methods to support the required operations. Clients declare a lexicon object by calling its factory method and assigning the result to a variable, as follows:

```
let english = EnglishLexicon();
```

The **EnglishLexicon** class then exports the necessary operations as methods. Checking to see whether a word is contained in the lexicon is easily implemented as a predicate method called **contains** that returns **true** if the argument is a word in the lexicon. Thus, given the variable **english**, you could check whether the variable **str** contains a legal word by calling

```
english.contains(str)
```

Designing the method that supports processing each word in alphabetical order requires a little more thought. The code pattern for cycling through each word shown at the top of this page makes an unjustified assumption about the operations that the `EnglishLexicon` class must support. The list of required operations includes "processing every word in the lexicon in alphabetical order." There is, however, no requirement that the client be able to select the word at a particular index. Some implementation strategies make it possible to process every word in order but offer no efficient way to select, for example, the word at index `k`.

A useful strategy for allowing clients to process the words in order is to export a method that calls a client-supplied callback function on each of the words. In computer science, a method that applies an operation to every element of a data structure is called a ***mapping function.*** The `EnglishLexicon` class implements that strategy by exporting a method called **map**, which takes a function and then calls that function on every word in alphabetical order. You can, for example, display every word in the lexicon by calling

```
english.map(displayWord);
```

where `displayWord` has the following definition:

```
function displayWord(word) {
   console.log(word);
}
```

Encapsulating the array-based implementation

To create an abstract data type that fulfills the requirements of a lexicon, it is easiest to start with the earlier array-based implementation, even though it is unworkably inefficient. The code in Figure 10-4 on the next page implements the `contains` and `map` methods using an array-based model.

Although the implementation in Figure 10-4 works, the strategy for looking up a word in the lexicon is so inefficient that it would be impossible to use in most applications. This claim, however, raises important questions. What does it mean for an implementation to be inefficient? How can one measure the efficiency of an implementation and its underlying algorithms?

Empirical measurements of efficiency

One approach to measuring efficiency is to conduct empirical measurements. In JavaScript, the class method `Date.now` returns the number of milliseconds that have elapsed since midnight on January 1, 1970, as measured at the prime meridian at Greenwich in the United Kingdom. Although this time zone is still commonly referred to as ***Greenwich Mean Time*** or ***GMT,*** its official name is now ***UTC,*** an abbreviation chosen as a compromise between the English and French renderings of ***coordinated universal time.*** The UTC standard, which originated with the Unix operating system in 1970, is now common across a wide range of operating systems

FIGURE 10-4 Array-based implementation of the English lexicon

```
/*
 * File: ArrayBasedLexicon.js
 * ----------------------------
 * This file implements the EnglishLexicon class using a sorted array to
 * store the words.  This strategy makes it easy to cycle through the
 * words in alphabetical order.  Testing whether a word is in the lexicon,
 * however, runs very slowly because the implementation uses indexOf.
 */

"use strict";

/*
 * This class implements a lexicon containing all English words.
 */

function EnglishLexicon() {
   const ENGLISH_WORDS = [
      "a", "aa", "aah", "aahed", "aahing", "aahs", "aal", "aalii",
      ... entries for the other English words ...
      "zymosis", "zymotic", "zymurgies", "zymurgy", "zyzzyva", "zyzzyvas"
   ];
   return { contains, map };

/*
 * Returns true if the word appears in the lexicon.
 */

   function contains(word) {
      return ENGLISH_WORDS.indexOf(word.toLowerCase()) !== -1;
   }

/*
 * Goes through the lexicon in alphabetical order, calling fn on each word.
 */

   function map(fn) {
      for (let i = 0; i < ENGLISH_WORDS.length; i++) {
         fn(ENGLISH_WORDS[i]);
      }
   }
}
```

and programming languages. The existence of a time standard makes it possible to compute elapsed time while running a program using the following code pattern:

```
let start = Date.now();
... code for some operation whose running time you want to measure ...
let elapsed = Date.now() - start;
```

This technique cannot be used to measure the elapsed time of an operation that runs in less than a millisecond because the lack of precision in the `Date.now` function makes it impossible to measure such small time intervals accurately. For example, a single call to `contains` would almost certainly finish in less than a millisecond, which means that `elapsed` would very likely have the value 0. To get an accurate measurement, it is necessary to see how long it takes to complete many calls to `contains`. For example, the following function goes through every word in the lexicon and determines how long it takes to check them all:

```
function TestLexiconTiming() {
   let english = EnglishLexicon();
   let start = Date.now();
   english.map(checkWord);
   let elapsed = Date.now() - start;
   console.log("Time: " + elapsed + " milliseconds");

   function checkWord(word) {
      if (!english.contains(word)) {
         console.log("contains failed for " + word);
      }
   }
}
```

Running `TestLexiconTiming` produces output that looks something like this, although the exact timings will vary from machine to machine:

TestLexiconTiming
Time: 35772 milliseconds

It is important to look carefully at this number. Checking every word in the lexicon takes almost 36 seconds—more than half a minute! Computers are supposed to be fast. Why does looking up a few hundred thousand words take so long?

One possible answer to this question is that looking up words in a lexicon is somehow fundamentally a slow operation. The problem, however, might instead lie in the array-based implementation of `EnglishLexicon`. It is definitely worth exploring other possibilities.

Using a map to implement the lexicon

Another strategy for implementing a lexicon is to store the words as the keys in a map. The code for a map-based implementation of `EnglishLexicon` appears in Figure 10-5. The keys in `ENGLISH_WORD_MAP` are the English words, and the

FIGURE 10-5 Map-based implementation of the English lexicon

```javascript
/*
 * File: MapBasedLexicon.js
 * ----------------------------
 * This file implements the EnglishLexicon class using a map to store
 * the words.  This strategy offers fast lookup times but requires time
 * to prepare the sorted word list on the first call to map.
 */

"use strict";

/*
 * This class implements a lexicon containing all English words.
 */

function EnglishLexicon() {
   const ENGLISH_WORD_MAP = {
      a:true, aa:true, aah:true, aahed:true, aahing:true, aahs:true,
      ... entries for the other English words ...
      zymurgies:true, zymurgy:true, zyzzyva:true, zyzzyvas:true
   };
   let sortedWordList = undefined;
   return { contains, map };

/*
 * Returns true if the word appears in the lexicon.
 */
   function contains(word) {
      return ENGLISH_WORD_MAP[word.toLowerCase()] !== undefined;
   }

/*
 * Goes through the lexicon in alphabetical order, calling fn on each word.
 * For efficiency, this method creates the sorted word only when the client
 * calls map for the first time.  After that call, the sorted list is
 * cached in the sortedWordList array.
 */

   function map(fn) {
      if (sortedWordList === undefined) {
         sortedWordList = [ ];
         for (let key in ENGLISH_WORD_MAP) {
            sortedWordList.push(key);
         }
         sortedWordList.sort();
      }
      for (let i = 0; i < sortedWordList.length; i++) {
         fn(sortedWordList[i]);
      }
   }
}
```

corresponding values are set to **true**, although any defined value would work just as well. All the **contains** method has to do is convert the argument to lower case, look up that key in the map, and check that the value is not **undefined**.

How efficient is the map-based implementation of the **EnglishLexicon** class? Running the **TestLexiconTiming** function together with the implementation of **EnglishLexicon** from Figure 10-5 reveals the following running time:

TestLexiconTiming
Time: 232 milliseconds

The map-based version of the **EnglishLexicon** class runs more than a hundred times faster than the array-based version from Figure 10-4. At the same time, the comparison is not entirely fair. Although **contains** runs dramatically faster when the underlying implementation uses a map, the operation of cycling through the words in alphabetical order takes substantially more time in the map-based implementation than it does in its array-based counterpart. In version 5 of ECMA JavaScript, which this text uses as its standard, the client can make no assumption about the order in which keys are processed using the **for-in** statement. Although more recent versions of JavaScript offer some control over the order, it is unwise to rely on that behavior because programs that do so will fail to work with older browsers. What you need to do instead is store the unordered keys in an array and then use the **sort** method to arrange the keys in alphabetical order.

The implementation of the **map** function checks to see whether the local variable **sortedWordList** has already been defined. If not, the code creates a sorted list of words by running through all the keys in **ENGLISH_WORD_MAP**, adding each key to the **sortedWordList** array, and then sorting that array. Subsequent calls to **map** do not pay this cost. If you run **TestLexiconTiming** a second time with the same lexicon, the time required to look up every word drops substantially, as illustrated in the following console log:

TestLexiconTiming
Time: 21 milliseconds

The process of looking up every word in the lexicon is now more than 1000 times faster with the map-based implementation than it is with the original array-based model. Preparing the sorted list on the first call, however, still takes on the order of a quarter of a second, even though that cost is incurred only once. While a quarter of a second is hardly in the same league as the 36 seconds required to look up the words in the array-based lexicon, it would be nice to avoid this cost, if possible.

The linear and binary search algorithms

The original version of the array-based implementation of **EnglishLexicon** runs slowly primarily because the **indexOf** method uses a strategy called *linear search* that looks at each array element in turn to check for a match. Fortunately, the fact that the array is stored in alphabetical order makes it possible to do much better. The key to improving the efficiency of **contains** is to compare the word you're looking for against the entry in the middle of the array. If your word precedes in alphabetical order the value you find at the center position, you only have to search the first half of the array. Conversely, if your word follows the value in the center position, you only have to search the second half. Repeating this process means that you can throw away half of the values in the array on each cycle of the search loop. This algorithm, which is implemented in Figure 10-6 on the next page, is called *binary search.*

After converting the parameter **word** to lower case to ensure that it matches the words in the lexicon, the binary-search implementation of **contains** begins by setting the variables **min** and **max** to the first and last index positions in the array. The first index, of course, is 0, and the last index is one less than the length of the **ENGLISH_WORDS** array. If **word** is in the lexicon, it must lie somewhere in this range of indices. The rest of the function consists of a loop that successively narrows this range by comparing **word** against the entry in the middle of the index range and using the result of that comparison to decide how to adjust the index bounds. The loop continues until the word is found or until there are no elements left in the range, which means that the word is not in the lexicon.

The binary-search implementation of **contains** is sufficiently important that it makes sense to go through an example. Suppose that you wanted to check whether *lexicon* is really an English word or simply part of a technical vocabulary that computer scientists use. To do so, you could execute the following line, assuming that the variable **english** is defined to be the English lexicon:

```
if (english.contains("lexicon")) ...
```

The **ENGLISH_WORDS** array contains 127145 words, which means that the initial values of **min** and **max** are 0 and 127144. On the first cycle of the loop, the code computes the midpoint of the remaining range by averaging **min** and **max**. The code then stores this position in the variable **mid** after calling **Math.floor** to ensure that the value is an integer. The word at index 63572 is the unfamiliar but nonetheless legitimate word *lightered.* Since *lexicon* comes before *lightered* in lexicographic order, **contains** can narrow the search to the range between **min** and **mid − 1**, which therefore narrows the search range to the indices between 0 and 63571. The process then continues until it either finds the specified word or there are no elements left in the index range.

FIGURE 10-6 Array-based implementation of the English lexicon using binary search

```
/*
 * File: BinarySearchLexicon.js
 * ----------------------------
 * This file implements the EnglishLexicon class using a sorted array to
 * store the words and the binary search algorithm to implement contains.
 */

"use strict";

/*
 * This class implements a lexicon containing all English words.
 */

function EnglishLexicon() {
   const ENGLISH_WORDS = [
      "a", "aa", "aah", "aahed", "aahing", "aahs", "aal", "aalii",
      ... entries for the other English words ...
      "zymosis", "zymotic", "zymurgies", "zymurgy", "zyzzyva", "zyzzyvas"
   ];
   return { contains, map };

/*
 * Returns true if the word appears in the lexicon.
 */

   function contains(word) {
      word = word.toLowerCase();
      let lh = 0;
      let rh = ENGLISH_WORDS.length - 1;
      while (lh <= rh) {
         let mid = Math.floor((lh + rh) / 2);
         if (word === ENGLISH_WORDS[mid]) return true;
         if (word < ENGLISH_WORDS[mid]) {
            rh = mid - 1;
         } else {
            lh = mid + 1;
         }
      }
      return false;
   }

/*
 * Goes through the lexicon in alphabetical order, calling fn on each word.
 */

   function map(fn) {
      for (let i = 0; i < ENGLISH_WORDS.length; i++) {
         fn(ENGLISH_WORDS[i]);
      }
   }
}
```

Calling `english.contains("lexicon")` makes the sequence of comparisons shown in the following console log:

```
TraceBinarySearch
Enter word: lexicon
Searching between min = 0 and max = 127144
Consider word at halfway index 63572 ("lightered")
"lexicon" < "lightered", so set max = mid - 1
Searching between min = 0 and max = 63571
Consider word at halfway index 31785 ("distaining")
"lexicon" > "distaining", so set min = mid + 1
Searching between min = 31786 and max = 63571
Consider word at halfway index 47678 ("gorp")
"lexicon" > "gorp", so set min = mid + 1
Searching between min = 47679 and max = 63571
Consider word at halfway index 55625 ("inconsumably")
"lexicon" > "inconsumably", so set min = mid + 1
Searching between min = 55626 and max = 63571
Consider word at halfway index 59598 ("jin")
"lexicon" > "jin", so set min = mid + 1
Searching between min = 59599 and max = 63571
Consider word at halfway index 61585 ("lability")
"lexicon" > "lability", so set min = mid + 1
Searching between min = 61586 and max = 63571
Consider word at halfway index 62578 ("lax")
"lexicon" > "lax", so set min = mid + 1
Searching between min = 62579 and max = 63571
Consider word at halfway index 63075 ("lensed")
"lexicon" > "lensed", so set min = mid + 1
Searching between min = 63076 and max = 63571
Consider word at halfway index 63323 ("libationary")
"lexicon" < "libationary", so set max = mid - 1
Searching between min = 63076 and max = 63322
Consider word at halfway index 63199 ("leva")
"lexicon" > "leva", so set min = mid + 1
Searching between min = 63200 and max = 63322
Consider word at halfway index 63261 ("levogyre")
"lexicon" > "levogyre", so set min = mid + 1
Searching between min = 63262 and max = 63322
Consider word at halfway index 63292 ("lexicon")
"lexicon" found at index 63292, so return true
```

As you can see from the trace output, `contains` is able to find the word *lexicon* by making just 12 comparisons, even though the lexicon contains 127145 words. Reducing the number of required comparisons speeds up the implementation of the `EnglishLexicon` class considerably, as shown in the following console log for the `TestLexiconTiming` program:

```
TestLexiconTiming
Time: 46 milliseconds
```

The range of running times for the three implementations of `EnglishLexicon` underscores the importance of choosing the right algorithm. The version that uses `indexOf` has to look at every element in the array, which means that its running time is proportional to the number of words in the lexicon. Because of the direct proportionality of lexicon size to running time, computer scientists say that this implementation runs in *linear time.* In the implementation that uses binary search, the running time is proportional to the number of times you can divide the lexicon in half, which is in turn proportional to the logarithm of the lexicon size. This algorithm is therefore said to run in *logarithmic time,* which grows much more slowly than linear time. The internal implementation of maps in JavaScript uses a technique called *hashing,* which is essentially an algorithm that tells the computer where to look for each entry. As you will discover if you go on to a more advanced course on data structures and algorithms, hashing can be made to run in *constant time,* which means that its performance is independent of the lexicon size.

Divide-and-conquer algorithms

The `binarySearch` function in Figure 10-6 solves the problem of searching for a key in a sorted array by dividing the problem in half on each cycle. Strategies that depend on dividing a problem into smaller instances of that problem are often called *divide-and-conquer algorithms.* Because divide-and-conquer algorithms involve solving smaller instances in the same form as the original problem, such algorithms are typically implemented recursively. You can, for example, easily implement the binary search algorithm as a recursive function and will have a chance to do so in exercise 12.

The strategy of divide-and-conquer is sufficiently important for you to look at another example. It is easy, for example, to write a function `raiseToPower(x, n)` that calculates x^n where n is a nonnegative integer by relying on the following recursive formulation:

$$x^n = \begin{cases} 1 & \text{if } n \text{ is } 0 \\ x \times x^{n-1} & \text{otherwise} \end{cases}$$

which looks like this in JavaScript:

```
function raiseToPower(x, n) {
   if (n === 0) {
      return 1;
   } else {
      return x * raiseToPower(x, n - 1);
   }
}
```

This function requires n recursive calls to evaluate `raiseToPower(x, n)` and therefore runs in linear time.

You can, however, adopt a recursive strategy similar to the one used in binary search by taking advantage of the fact that

$$x^n = \left(x^{n/2}\right)^2$$

if n is even and

$$x^n = \left(x^{(n-1)/2}\right)^2 \times x$$

if n is odd. These formulas make it possible to write the following recursive implementation of **raiseToPower**, which runs in logarithmic time:

```
function raiseToPower(x, n) {
    if (n === 0) {
        return 1;
    } else if (n % 2 === 0) {
        return square(raiseToPower(x, n / 2));
    } else {
        return square(raiseToPower(x, (n - 1) / 2)) * x;
    }
}

function square(x) {
    return x * x;
}
```

To get a better sense of how this implementation works, it is useful to trace through the recursive calls required to compute **raiseToPower(2, 11)**. On the first call, n is odd, so the evaluation chooses the last branch of the **if** statement, and evaluates **raiseToPower(2, 5)**. Because n is again odd, the computation again chooses the last branch for which it has to compute **raiseToPower(2, 2)**. In that call, n is even, so **raiseToPower** chooses the middle branch to compute the value of **raiseToPower(2, 1)**, which in turn requires a call to **raiseToPower(2, 0)**. The computation then unwinds through the recursive levels, squaring the result on each cycle and adding in an additional factor of 2 for each level at which n was odd, as illustrated in the following diagram:

$$\texttt{raiseToPower(2, 11)} = 32^2 \times 2 = \boxed{2048}$$
$$\texttt{raiseToPower(2, 5)} = 4^2 \times 2 = \boxed{32}$$
$$\texttt{raiseToPower(2, 2)} = 2^2 = \boxed{4}$$
$$\texttt{raiseToPower(2, 1)} = 1^2 \times 2 = \boxed{2}$$
$$\texttt{raiseToPower(2, 0)} = \boxed{1}$$

10.4 Representing real-world data

One of the most important skills that software developers need to learn is how to represent real-world information in a form that computers can easily manipulate. As a concrete example, let's suppose that you have been hired by a political party to store voting data from past presidential elections on the theory that understanding the historical data may yield important insights that affect elections in the future. As a starting point, it is a useful exercise to design a data structure to represent the information shown in Figure 10-7, which lists the popular vote for the four largest parties in the 2016 presidential election in the United States.

Given the data in Figure 10-7, the important question to ask is how to represent the electoral information in a way that preserves the relationships among the individual data values. In doing so, it is useful to think carefully about those relationships and to avoid jumping to conclusions based on the way in which the information is presented to human readers. For example, the two-dimensional structure of a printed table does not necessarily imply that the best representation is a two-dimensional array, but may simply indicate that this representation is easiest to display on the printed page.

As you design a data structure for the state-by-state electoral tallies—or any data structure, for that matter—it is important to keep in mind that arrays and objects are *tools*. Designing effective data structures requires you to think in a holistic way that focuses on the abstract structures represented by those arrays and objects. Thinking holistically makes it easier to recognize the relationships that define the overall structure.

You have already seen examples of the following abstract data structures:

- *Lists.* A *list* is an abstract data structure in which the individual elements form a logical sequence in which you can identify each element by its position.

- *Records.* A *record* is an abstract data structure in which the elements are part of a logical whole but not in an ordered relationship. Typically, elements of a record are identified by name.

- *Maps.* A *map* is an abstract data structure in which a set of keys is associated with a corresponding set of values.

Choosing which of these structures to use depends on the characteristics of the data values you are trying to model. If the data collection has a first element, a second element, and so on, a list is probably the most appropriate choice. If instead the data collection consists of independent pieces, you presumably want to use a record. Finally, if the data collection contains a set of values each of which is marked with a unique identifier, you are likely to choose a map.

FIGURE 10-7 Votes by state in the 2016 presidential election

	Electoral votes	Democratic	Republican	Libertarian	Green	Other
Alabama	9	729,547	1,318,255	44,467	9,391	21,712
Alaska	3	116,454	163,387	18,725	5,735	14,307
Arizona	11	1,161,167	1,252,401	106,327	34,345	18,925
Arkansas	6	380,494	684,872	29,829	9,473	25,967
California	55	8,753,788	4,483,810	478,500	278,657	186,840
Colorado	9	1,338,870	1,202,484	144,121	38,437	56,335
Connecticut	7	897,572	673,215	48,676	22,841	2,616
Delaware	3	235,603	185,127	14,757	6,103	2,224
District of Columbia	3	282,830	12,723	4,906	4,258	6,551
Florida	29	4,504,975	4,617,886	207,043	64,399	25,736
Georgia	16	1,877,963	2,089,104	125,306	7,674	14,685
Hawaii	4	266,891	128,847	15,954	12,737	4,508
Idaho	4	189,765	409,055	28,331	8,496	54,608
Illinois	20	3,090,729	2,146,015	209,596	76,802	13,282
Indiana	11	1,033,126	1,557,286	133,993	7,841	2,712
Iowa	6	653,669	800,983	59,186	11,479	40,714
Kansas	6	427,005	671,018	55,406	23,506	7,467
Kentucky	8	628,854	1,202,971	53,752	13,913	24,659
Louisiana	8	780,154	1,178,638	37,978	14,031	18,231
Maine	4	357,735	335,593	38,105	14,251	2,243
Maryland	10	1,677,928	943,169	79,605	35,945	44,799
Massachusetts	11	1,995,196	1,090,893	138,018	47,661	53,278
Michigan	16	2,268,839	2,279,543	172,136	51,463	27,303
Minnesota	10	1,367,716	1,322,951	112,972	36,985	104,189
Mississippi	6	485,131	700,714	14,435	3,731	5,346
Missouri	10	1,071,068	1,594,511	97,359	25,419	20,248
Montana	3	177,709	279,240	28,037	7,970	4,191
Nebraska	5	284,494	495,961	38,946	8,775	16,051
Nevada	6	539,260	512,058	37,384		36,683
New Hampshire	4	348,526	345,790	30,777	6,496	12,707
New Jersey	14	2,148,278	1,601,933	72,477	37,772	13,586
New Mexico	5	385,234	319,667	74,541	9,879	8,998
New York	29	4,556,124	2,819,534	176,598	107,934	61,263
North Carolina	15	2,189,316	2,362,631	130,126	12,105	47,386
North Dakota	3	93,758	216,794	21,434	3,780	8,594
Ohio	18	2,394,164	2,841,005	174,498	46,271	40,549
Oklahoma	7	420,375	949,136	83,481		
Oregon	7	1,002,106	782,403	94,231	50,002	72,594
Pennsylvania	20	2,926,441	2,970,733	146,715	49,941	71,648
Rhode Island	4	252,525	180,543	14,746	6,220	10,110
South Carolina	9	855,373	1,155,389	49,204	13,034	30,027
South Dakota	3	117,458	227,721	20,850		4,064
Tennessee	11	870,695	1,522,925	70,397	15,993	28,017
Texas	38	3,877,868	4,685,047	283,492	71,558	51,261
Utah	6	310,676	515,231	39,608	9,438	256,477
Vermont	3	178,573	95,369	10,078	6,758	24,289
Virginia	13	1,981,473	1,769,443	118,274	27,638	87,803
Washington	12	1,742,718	1,221,747	160,879	58,417	133,258
West Virginia	5	188,794	489,371	23,004	8,075	5,179
Wisconsin	10	1,382,536	1,405,284	106,674	31,072	50,584
Wyoming	3	55,973	174,419	13,287	2,515	9,655

There are at least two reasons why a two-dimensional array is probably not the best option for storing the voting data. First, elements of an array are usually of the same type, even though JavaScript does not enforce that restriction. In the table of election results, the rows have the same structure, but the columns do not. The first column in each row is the number of electoral votes assigned to that state, while the other columns list vote totals by party. This distinction suggests that each row is best represented as an object in which one property is the number of electoral votes and a second property is a map that links party names and vote totals.

If you adopt this strategy, you can represent the data from the 2016 presidential election as shown in Figure 10-8. The entire structure is an array with one element

---

FIGURE 10-8 Results of the 2016 presidential election in JSON form

```
/*
 * File: PresidentialElection2016.js
 * ----------------------------------
 * This file exports a constant array named PRESIDENTIAL_ELECTION_2016.
 * Each array element is an object containing the following properties:
 *    name          -- The name of the state
 *    electoralVotes -- The number of electoral votes for the state
 *    popularVote   -- A map from party names to popular vote totals
 */

const PRESIDENTIAL_ELECTION_2016 = [
   {
      "name": "Alabama",
      "electoralVotes": 9,
      "popularVote": {
         "Democratic": 729547,
         "Republican": 1318255,
         "Libertarian": 44467,
         "Green": 9391,
         "Other": 21712
      }
   },
   ... Entries for the other states ...
   {
      "name": "Wyoming",
      "electoralVotes": 3,
      "popularVote": {
         "Democratic": 55973,
         "Republican": 174419,
         "Libertarian": 13287,
         "Green": 2515,
         "Other": 9655
      }
   }
];
```

for each state and one for the District of Columbia. Each element in the array is an object containing the election data for that state: the number of electoral votes and the map from party names to vote totals. The JSON structure is flexible enough to accommodate the missing data values represented by the blank cells in Figure 10-7, but the code used to process the table must allow for the possibility that a field is `undefined`. The `index.html` file can load the entire data structure by including the JSON file in a `<script>` tag, just as if it were a library.

Once you have defined the data structure, you can then write applications that use that structure to generate whatever summary reports you need. For example, the `CountVotes.js` program in Figure 10-9 calculates the overall winner in both electoral and popular votes. The data structure for the election is supplied as an argument to the `countVotes` call in the `index.html` file. Running the program in Figure 10-9 using the `PresidentialElection2016.js` data file produces the following output on the console:

```
                          CountVotes
Popular vote:
   Democratic:  65853516
   Republican:  62984825
   Libertarian:  4489221
   Green: 1457216
   Other: 1884459
Electoral vote:
   Republican: 305
   Democratic: 233
```

The structure of the `CountVotes` application is surprisingly flexible. It is easy to substitute election data for any other year just by changing the parameter to `countVotes` in the `index.html` file. For example, if you were to create a new file containing the data from the 2012 presidential election, load that file using a `<script>` tag in `index.html`, and then change the `<body>` tag to

```
<body onload="CountVotes(PRESIDENTIAL_ELECTION_2012)">
```

you would see the following result:

```
                          CountVotes
Popular vote:
   Democratic:  65915794
   Republican:  60933504
   Libertarian:  1275971
   Green: 469627
   Other: 490510
Electoral vote:
   Democratic: 332
   Republican: 206
```

FIGURE 10-9 Program to count the popular and electoral votes by state

```
/*
 * File: CountVotes.js
 * --------------------
 * This program generates a report showing the popular and electoral vote
 * totals for a presidential election in the United States.
 */

"use strict";

/*
 * This program counts the popular and electoral votes from the structure
 * stored in the data parameter, which is supplied by the index.html file.
 */

function CountVotes(data) {
   console.log("Popular vote:");
   reportVoteTotals(countPopularVotes(data));
   console.log("Electoral vote:");
   reportVoteTotals(countElectoralVotes(data));
}

/*
 * Returns a map in which the keys are the parties and the values
 * are the corresponding popular vote totals.
 */

function countPopularVotes(electionData) {
   let popularVotes = { };
   for (let i = 0; i < electionData.length; i++) {
      let stateData = electionData[i];
      for (let party in stateData.popularVote) {
         if (popularVotes[party] === undefined) popularVotes[party] = 0;
         popularVotes[party] += stateData.popularVote[party];
      }
   }
   return popularVotes;
}

/*
 * Returns a map in which the keys are the parties and the values
 * are the corresponding electoral vote totals.
 */

function countElectoralVotes(electionData) {
   let electoralVotes = { };
   for (let i = 0; i < electionData.length; i++) {
      let stateData = electionData[i];
      let party = determineWinner(stateData.popularVote);
      if (electoralVotes[party] === undefined) electoralVotes[party] = 0;
      electoralVotes[party] += stateData.electoralVotes
   }
   return electoralVotes;
}
```

FIGURE 10-9 Program to count the popular and electoral votes by state (continued)

```
/*
 * Generates a report showing the vote totals for each party contained
 * in votes, which is a record in which the keys are parties and the
 * values are the vote counts. The report is sorted in decreasing order
 * by vote count.
 */

function reportVoteTotals(votes) {
   let array = [ ];
   for (let party in votes) {
      array.push({ party: party, votes: votes[party] });
   }
   array.sort(sortByDecreasingVoteCount);
   for (let i = 0; i < array.length; i++) {
      let entry = array[i];
      console.log("   " + entry.party + ": " + entry.votes);
   }

/*
 * Implementation notes:
 * --------------------
 * This function implements the desired sort order for the displayed data.
 * The parameters are objects with two properties: "party" and "votes".
 * As with any comparison function, the return value is negative if e1 comes
 * before e2, positive if e1 comes after e2, and zero if the two entries are
 * the same.  This function ordinarily compares the vote counts but includes
 * a special check to ensure that a party named "Other" comes at the end.
 */

   function sortByDecreasingVoteCount(e1, e2) {
      if (e1.party === "Other" && e2.party !== "Other") return 1;
      if (e1.party !== "Other" && e2.party === "Other") return -1;
      return e2.votes - e1.votes;
   }

}

/*
 * Determines which party has the largest total in votes.  The argument is
 * a record in which the keys are parties and the values are vote counts.
 */

function determineWinner(votes) {
   let winner = undefined;
   let maxVotes = 0;
   for (let party in votes) {
      if (winner === undefined || votes[party] > maxVotes) {
         winner = party;
         maxVotes = votes[party];
      }
   }
   return winner;
}
```

▄▄ Summary

This chapter continues the discussion of JavaScript objects, focusing on abstract data types that are useful in a variety of applications. Important points in this chapter include the following:

- Classes that implement a set of operations without revealing the internal data structures are called *abstract data types*. Abstract data types offer several advantages over structures whose details are visible, including simplicity, flexibility, and security.

- Separating behavior and representation in an abstract data type allows the implementer to change that representation without adversely affecting clients.

- A sequence of characters that has integrity as a unit is called a *token*. This chapter presents a simple implementation of a **TokenScanner** class that divides a string into tokens consisting of consecutive letters. The libraries included with this text include a **JSTokenScanner** class that offers clients considerably more flexibility. The methods exported by the expanded **JSTokenScanner** class appear in Figure 10-3.

- A *lexicon* is a list of words without associated definitions.

- The underlying representation of an abstract type and the algorithms used to implement its methods can have a profound effect on efficiency. For example, the original array-based implementation of the **EnglishLexicon** class runs 1000 times more slowly than the map-based version.

- The *linear search* algorithm operates by looking at each element of an array in order until it finds the desired element.

- The *binary search* algorithm is more efficient than linear search but requires that the elements of the array be in sorted order. The efficiency advantage of binary search lies in the fact that you can discount half the remaining elements on each cycle of the search loop.

- The class method **Date.now** returns the number of milliseconds that have elapsed since January 1, 1970. By checking the time both before and after an operation, you can determine how long that operation takes, assuming that the operation takes long enough to fit within the precision of a millisecond clock.

- In designing the data structure for an application, it is usually better to think in terms of abstract conceptual models—lists, records, and maps—rather than the concrete structures—arrays and objects—used to represent those models.

- It is important to think carefully about structural relationships and avoid jumping to premature conclusions arising from how information is presented.

Review questions

1. What is an *abstract data type?*

2. True or false: One of advantages of separating the behavior of an abstract data type from its underlying representation is that doing so makes it possible to change that representation without forcing clients to change their programs.

3. In your own words, describe the function of a token scanner.

4. Given the **TokenScanner** class presented in this chapter, what statements would you use to list every token from a string stored in the variable **str**?

5. What is a *lexicon?* How does a lexicon differ from a conventional dictionary?

6. What are the two public methods exported by the **EnglishLexicon** class?

7. What is a *mapping function?*

8. What value is returned by the **Date.now** method? How can you use that value to measure the elapsed time required to execute some segment of code?

9. True or false: The map-based implementation of the **EnglishLexicon** class is more than a thousand times faster than the original array-based implementation in checking whether a string is a legal word.

10. Figure 10-10 shows an array called **STATE_CODES** containing the two-letter abbreviations for the 50 states, arranged in alphabetical order. Show the steps involved if you use the binary search algorithm to search for the code **"OK"**. How many comparisons are required to find this value?

11. How would you describe the binary search algorithm to someone who has little familiarity with computers and programming?

12. Using the diagram at the bottom of page 369 as a model, draw a diagram showing the recursive calls made in evaluating **raiseToPower(3, 9)**.

FIGURE 10-10 **A sorted array containing the two-letter codes for the 50 states**

STATE_CODES

AK	AL	AR	AZ	CA	CO	CT	DE	FL	GA	HI	IA	ID	IL	IN	KS	KY	···
0	1	2	3	4	5	6	7	8	9	10	11	12	13	14	15	16	

LA	MA	MD	ME	MI	MN	MO	MS	MT	NC	ND	NE	NH	NJ	NM	NV	NY	···
17	18	19	20	21	22	23	24	25	26	27	28	29	30	31	32	33	

OH	OK	OR	PA	RI	SC	SD	TN	TX	UT	VA	VT	WA	WI	WV	WY
34	35	36	37	38	39	40	41	42	43	44	45	46	47	48	49

Exercises

1. Write a program that uses the **TokenScanner** class to display the longest word that appears in a file chosen by the user. A word should be defined as any consecutive string of letters and digits, just as it is in the **TokenScanner** class.

2. Write a program called **CountWordFrequencies** that reads a sequence of lines and produces a table showing how many times each word appears. Your program should be able to replicate the following sample run:

```
                     CountWordFrequencies
Enter lines of text, ending with a blank line.
One fish
Two fish
Red fish
Blue fish

blue: 1
fish: 4
one: 1
red: 1
two: 1
```

3. Write a function **elapsedTime** that returns how many milliseconds are required to perform an operation. The **elapsedTime** function takes two parameters. The first is a callback function that implements the operation whose running time you want to measure. The second argument, which is optional and defaults to 1, indicates how many repetitions of the function call should occur between the time measurements. Although it is impossible to use **Date.now** to measure short running times, you can, for example, see how long it takes to call a function 100,000 times and then compute the average running time by dividing the total elapsed time by the number of repetitions. You could therefore see how long it takes for the **Math** library to calculate the square root of 2 by calling

```
elapsedTime(function() { Math.sqrt(2); }, 100000)
```

4. When playing Scrabble, one of the most useful things to memorize is the list of all legal two-letter words. It is easy to use the English lexicon to create a list of two-letter words, but there are at least two strategies for doing so. The most natural one is to iterate through the words in the lexicon and print those whose length is two. A somewhat less obvious strategy is to generate all 26×26 combinations of the letters and see which ones are words. Implement each of these strategies and then use the **elapsedTime** function from the preceding exercise to see which strategy is more efficient.

5. One of the most important strategic principles in Scrabble is to conserve your **S** tiles, because the rules for English plurals mean that many words take an

S-hook at the end. Some words, of course, allow an **S** tile to be added at the beginning, but it turns out that there are 680 words—including, for example, the words *cold* and *hot*—that allow an **S**-hook on both ends. Write a program that uses the `EnglishLexicon` class to display a list of all such words.

6. If you manage to play all seven of your tiles in a single turn, you get a 50-point bonus for what Scrabble players call a **bingo.** To help you find bingos, it would be useful to have a function `listAnagrams` that takes a string of letters you might have in your Scrabble rack and returns all the legal words that can be formed by rearranging those letters in any order. Although the technique for generating all rearrangements of a string requires concepts beyond the scope of this book, you can achieve the same result by going through the English lexicon and printing every word that contains the same set of letters. The following console log shows a few examples:

```
                    JavaScript Console
> listAnagrams ("aeinrst");
anestri
nastier
ratines
retains
retinas
retsina
stainer
stearin
> listAnagrams ("adehrst");
dearths
hardest
hardset
hatreds
threads
trashed
> listAnagrams ("aelqtuz");
quetzal
>
```

If you have trouble figuring out how to implement `listAnagrams`, you might look at exercise 6 from Chapter 8 for an idea.

7. Section 7.5 includes a definition of the function `isPalindrome` that checks whether a word reads identically forward and backward. Use that function together with the `EnglishLexicon` class to display all English palindromes.

8. When you convert English to Pig Latin, most words turn into something that sounds vaguely Latinate but different from conventional English. There are, however, a few words whose Pig Latin equivalents just happen to be English words. For example, the Pig Latin translation of *trash* is *ashtray,* and the translation for *express* is *expressway.* Use the `PigLatin.js` program from Chapter 7 together with the `EnglishLexicon` class to write a program that displays a list of all such words.

9. Write a program that displays a table showing the number of words that appear in the **EnglishLexicon** class, sorted by the length of the word. The output from your program should look like this:

EnglishWordCounts	
1	3
2	94
3	962
4	3862
5	8548
6	14383
7	21729
8	26448
9	18844
10	12308
11	7850
12	5194
13	3275
14	1775
15	954
16	495
17	251
18	89
19	48
20	21
21	6
22	3
24	1
28	1
29	1

10. Write a program to produce a trace of the binary search algorithm of the sort shown on page 367. To give clients the option of generating such a trace, add to the **EnglishLexicon** class a new exported method called **setTraceMode**, which takes a Boolean value indicating whether tracing should occur. If the client calls **setTraceMode(true)** on the lexicon object, calling **contains** should generate a complete trace on the console.

11. The binary search algorithm is useful enough that it makes sense to export it to clients. Define a class method

    EnglishLexicon.binarySearch(key, array, min, max)

    that searches for an occurrence of **key** in **array**, which must be in sorted order. The optional **min** and **max** parameters specify the range of indices included in the search. If these parameters are missing, **binarySearch** should look at every element in the entire array. The **binarySearch** method should return the index at which **key** appears in **array**. If **key** appears more than once in the array, the return value can be any of its index positions. Make sure that you update the code for **contains** to call the **binarySearch** method.

12. Rewrite the **binarySearch** method from the preceding exercise so that it operates recursively rather than iteratively.

13. The fact that it is possible to compute x^n in logarithmic time makes it possible to compute the Fibonacci function **fib(n)** in logarithmic time, as promised in Chapter 5. To do so, you need to rely on the fact that the Fibonacci function is related to a value called the *golden ratio,* which makes its first appearance in classical Greek mathematics. The golden ratio, usually designated by the Greek letter phi (φ), is defined to be the value that satisfies the equation

$$\varphi^2 - \varphi - 1 = 0$$

Because this is a quadratic equation, it actually has two roots. If you apply the quadratic formula, you will discover that these roots are

$$\varphi = \frac{1 + \sqrt{5}}{2}$$

$$\hat{\varphi} = \frac{1 - \sqrt{5}}{2}$$

In 1718, the French mathematician Abraham de Moivre discovered that the nth Fibonacci number can be represented in closed form as

$$\frac{\varphi^n - \hat{\varphi}^n}{\sqrt{5}}$$

Moreover, because $\hat{\varphi}^n$ is always very small, the formula can be simplified to

$$\frac{\varphi^n}{\sqrt{5}}$$

rounded to the nearest integer.

Write a new implementation of the **fib** function that uses de Moivre's formula to compute **fib(n)** in logarithmic time.

14. Use the data from the **PresidentialElection2016.js** to find all states in which the winning candidate got less than 50 percent of the vote. In 2016, seven of these states were won by Democrats and seven by Republicans.

15. Exercise 2 asks you to write a program that counts the number of words in a sequence of lines. Extend that program by making the following changes:

- Read the input from a data file instead of the console.
- Use the strategy from the **CountVotes.js** program to sort the words in decreasing order by the number of times they appear.
- Allow the client to specify a minimum count below which words are not reported. For example, if **text** contains the complete text of Shakespeare's *Hamlet,* calling **sortWordFrequencies(text, 200)** should display a list of the words in *Hamlet* that appear at least 200 times, as follows:

```
┌────────────────────────────────────────────┐
│              SortWordFrequencies            │
├────────────────────────────────────────────┤
│ the: 1084                                   │
│ and: 966                                    │
│ to: 750                                     │
│ of: 671                                     │
│ you: 555                                    │
│ i: 551                                      │
│ a: 550                                      │
│ my: 520                                     │
│ in: 433                                     │
│ it: 419                                     │
│ that: 388                                   │
│ ham: 358                                    │
│ is: 346                                     │
│ not: 314                                    │
│ his: 304                                    │
│ this: 298                                   │
│ with: 278                                   │
│ but: 273                                    │
│ for: 249                                    │
│ your: 242                                   │
│ me: 234                                     │
│ as: 227                                     │
│ be: 223                                     │
│ lord: 223                                   │
│ he: 212                                     │
│ what: 208                                   │
└────────────────────────────────────────────┘
```

16. Suppose that a bank has hired you as a programmer and given you the task of automating the process of converting between different foreign currencies at the prevailing rate of exchange. Every day, the bank receives a file called **ExchangeRates.js** containing the current exchange rates stored in JSON format as shown in Figure 10-11. Each value in the **currencies** map is an object that specifies the name of the currency and its current exchange rate relative to the dollar. For example, the entry

FIGURE 10-11 JavaScript file containing exchange rates expressed as a JSON structure

```javascript
const EXCHANGE_RATES = {
   "date": "13-Sep-2017",
   "currencies": {
      "USD": { "name": "US dollar", "rate": 1.00000 },
      "EUR": { "name": "European Euro", "rate": 1.07397 },
      "JPY": { "name": "Japanese yen", "rate": 0.00889 },
      "GBP": { "name": "Pound sterling", "rate": 1.23586 },
      "AUD": { "name": "Australian dollar", "rate": 0.77300 },
      ... Entries for the other currencies ...

      "THB": { "name": "Thai baht", "rate": 0.02885 },
      "MYR": { "name": "Malaysian ringgit", "rate": 0.22590 }
   }
};
```

```
    "GBP": { "name": "Pound sterling", "rate": 1.23586 }
```

indicates that the three-letter code `"GBP"` has the name `"Pound sterling"` and is currently trading at 1.23586 dollars to the pound.

Your task in this problem is to write a program that reads conversion requests from the user in the form

> *amount* *XXX* `->` *YYY*

where *amount* is the monetary value you want to convert, and *XXX* and *YYY* are the three-letter codes for the old and new currency. Alternatively, the input line may consist of a three-letter currency code, in which case the program should report the full name of that currency. A sample run that illustrates both input forms might look like this:

```
                    JavaScript Console
Conversion: 1.00USD -> JPY
1 USD = 110.11441294928758 JPY
Conversion: 200 GBP -> EUR
200 GBP = 221.82879596017673 EUR
Conversion: MYR
MYR = Malaysian ringgit
Conversion:
```

17. In J. K. Rowling's *Harry Potter* series, the students at Hogwarts School of Witchcraft and Wizardry study many forms of magic. One of the most difficult fields of study is potions, which is taught by Harry's least favorite teacher, Professor Snape. Mastery of potions requires students to memorize complex lists of ingredients for creating the desired magical concoctions. Presumably to protect those of us in the Muggle world, Rowling does not give us a complete ingredient list for most of the potions used in the series, but we do learn about a few, including those shown in Figure 10-12.

FIGURE 10-12 Ingredients used in potions from J. K. Rowling's *Harry Potter* series

Polyjuice Potion
shredded boomslang skin
lacewing flies
leeches
knotgrass
powdered bicorn horn
fluxweed
a bit of the person one wants to become

Shrinking Solution
chopped daisy roots
skinned shrivelfig
sliced caterpillar
rat spleen
leech juice

Wit-Sharpening Potion
ground scarab beetle
ginger root
armadillo bile

Draught of Living Death
asphodel in an infusion of wormwood
valerian roots
sopophorous bean

Design a data structure that encodes the information shown in Figure 10-12 and then create a JavaScript file that stores that information in JSON form. Test your data structure by writing a console-based program that requests a potion name from the user and then displays a list of its ingredients.

18. For certain applications, it is useful to be able to generate a series of names that form a sequential pattern. For example, if you were writing a program to number figures in a paper, having some mechanism to return the sequence of strings `"Figure 1"`, `"Figure 2"`, `"Figure 3"`, and so on, would be very handy. However, you might also need to label points in a geometric diagram, in which case you would want a similar but independent set of labels for points such as `"P0"`, `"P1"`, `"P2"`, and so forth.

    If you think about this problem more generally, the ADT you need is a label generator that allows the client to define arbitrary sequences of labels, each of which consists of a prefix string (`"Figure "` or `"P"` for the examples in the preceding paragraph) coupled with an integer used as a sequence number. Because the client may want different sequences to be active simultaneously, it makes sense to define the label generator as a **LabelGenerator** class. To initialize a new generator, the client provides the prefix string and the initial index as arguments to the **LabelGenerator** factory method. Once the generator has been created, the client can return new labels in the sequence by calling **nextLabel** on the **LabelGenerator** object.

    Design and implement the **LabelGenerator** class along with a suitable program to test your implementation.

19. When text is displayed on the printed page or a computer screen, it usually must be adjusted to fit within fixed margins. Output that is too wide must be broken up and displayed on several lines. If the text is composed of words, divisions between the lines are made at the spaces that mark the word boundaries. As long as an entire word fits on the current line without extending past the right margin, it is placed on that line. If a word would extend past the right margin, the current line is displayed, and the word that caused the overflow is placed at the beginning of the next line. Subsequent words are then added to the newly created line until that line fills up as well. This process is called *filling* and can be repeated as long as there is any text to display or the client specifies a line break.

    Implement a **FilledConsole** class that allows clients to write data to the console in a way that supports filling. The **FilledConsole** factory method takes the margin, which is the number of characters allowed on each console line. For example, the declaration

    ```
    let fc = FilledConsole(55);
    ```

creates a `FilledConsole` object with a line width of 55 characters. Clients then send output to the `FilledConsole` class by calling either of two methods. The `print` method should take any value and add it to the end of the current line, but only display the output if the line overflows the margin. The `println` method operates similarly but forces a line break at the end.

To test your implementation, write a program that displays the integers between 1 and 100 using as few lines as possible for the output. The following sample run shows the output when using a fill margin of 55 characters:

```
                      TestFilledConsole
1,  2,  3,  4,  5,  6,  7,  8,  9,  10,  11,  12,  13,  14,  15,  16,
17,  18,  19,  20,  21,  22,  23,  24,  25,  26,  27,  28,  29,  30,
31,  32,  33,  34,  35,  36,  37,  38,  39,  40,  41,  42,  43,  44,
45,  46,  47,  48,  49,  50,  51,  52,  53,  54,  55,  56,  57,  58,
59,  60,  61,  62,  63,  64,  65,  66,  67,  68,  69,  70,  71,  72,
73,  74,  75,  76,  77,  78,  79,  80,  81,  82,  83,  84,  85,  86,
87,  88,  89,  90,  91,  92,  93,  94,  95,  96,  97,  98,  99,  100
```

20. For some applications, JavaScript's limitation on how many significant digits appear in an integer can be a limitation. For those applications, it is useful to have access to a `BigInteger` class that is capable of storing integers with an arbitrarily large number of digits. Several such packages exist on the web, all of which use techniques whose complexity puts them beyond the scope of this text. Nonetheless, you can get some idea of how such a package might work by writing a simplified `BigInteger` class that supports only addition and multiplication.

The simplest internal representation for a `BigInteger` object is a string of digits, which can, of course, be arbitrarily long. The factory method, which can take either an integer or a string as its argument, can then look like this:

```
function BigInteger(n) {
    let digits = "" + n;
    return { add, mul, toString };
    . . . you fill in the definitions for these methods . . .
}
```

The challenge in this problem is to write the methods that perform the required arithmetic operations. In doing so, you must go back to the rules you learned in elementary school for doing arithmetic by hand.

Addition proceeds digit by digit from the right end of the number, just as when you first learned to add multidigit numbers. To add two `BigInteger` values, you need to select characters from the `digits` string and convert them to numeric form. Once you have obtained the corresponding digits from each number, you can add them, record the single-digit sum, and keep track of the carry. You can then go on to the next digit, moving from right to left.

Multiplication is a little trickier but also follows the rules you learned in school. For each digit in the multiplier, you can form the product of that digit and the multiplicand by repeated addition, since the loop will run at most nine times. You then move on to the next digit and perform a similar calculation, multiplying the result by 10 simply by concatenating a `"0"` to the end of the string. You can then use the **add** method to sum these partial products.

Test your program by using it to generate a table of factorials from 0 to 25 as shown in the following console log:

BigFactorial
0! = 1
1! = 1
2! = 2
3! = 6
4! = 24
5! = 120
6! = 720
7! = 5040
8! = 40320
9! = 362880
10! = 3628800
11! = 39916800
12! = 479001600
13! = 6227020800
14! = 87178291200
15! = 1307674368000
16! = 20922789888000
17! = 355687428096000
18! = 6402373705728000
19! = 121645100408832000
20! = 2432902008176640000
21! = 51090942171709440000
22! = 1124000727777607680000
23! = 25852016738884976640000
24! = 620448401733239439360000
25! = 15511210043330985984000000

CHAPTER 11
Inheritance

[I remember the exact moment] when the concept of "inheritance" (or classes and subclasses) had been created. I realized immediately that this was the solution to a very important problem Ole-Johan Dahl and I had been struggling with for months and weeks. And sure enough, inheritance has become a key concept in object-oriented programming, and thus in programming in general.

—Kristen Nygaard, address at the IRIS 19 conference, 1996

(Courtesy of Eric Roberts)

Kristen Nygaard (1926–2002)

Along with his countryman and colleague Ole-Johan Dahl, Kristen Nygaard formulated the central ideas of object-oriented programming more than 50 years ago in the context of a programming language called SIMULA developed at the Norwegian Computing Center, a state-funded research laboratory focusing on software engineering. Nygaard and Dahl later joined the faculty at the University of Oslo. Interest in object-oriented techniques has grown considerably in recent years, driven by the success of object-oriented languages like C++ and Java. For their contributions, Nygaard and Dahl received both the 2001 Turing Award from the Association for Computing Machinery and the 2001 John von Neumann Medal from the Institute of Electrical and Electronic Engineers. Deeply committed to ensuring that computing benefits society, Kristen Nygaard is the only person to receive both the Turing Award and the Norbert Wiener Award for Social and Professional Responsibility.

Object-oriented languages like JavaScript are characterized by two properties: encapsulation and inheritance. Chapters 9 and 10 cover encapsulation in detail, but you have not as yet had the opportunity to learn about JavaScript's model of *inheritance* in which a class acquires characteristics from other classes at higher levels in the programming analogue of a family tree. This chapter begins by introducing the concept of inheritance in the biological world and then moves on to show how the biological metaphor applies in the programming domain.

11.1 Class hierarchies

Carl Linnaeus

(Gianni Dagli Orti/Shutterstock)

One of the defining properties of object-oriented languages is that they allow you to specify hierarchical relationships among classes. Those hierarchies are reminiscent of the biological classification system developed by the eighteenth-century Swedish botanist Carl Linnaeus as a means of representing the structure of the biological world. In Linnaeus's conception, living things are first subdivided into *kingdoms.* Each kingdom is further broken down into the hierarchical categories of *phylum, class, order, family, genus,* and *species.* Every species belongs not only to its own category at the bottom of the hierarchy but also to a category at each higher level.

This biological classification system is illustrated in Figure 11-1 at the top of the next page, which shows the classification of the common black garden ant, whose scientific name, *Lasius niger,* corresponds to its genus and species. This species of ant, however, is also part of the family *Formicidae,* which is the classification that identifies it as an ant. If you move upward in the hierarchy from there, you discover that *Lasius niger* is also of the order *Hymenoptera* (which includes bees and wasps), the class *Insecta* (which consists of the insects), and the phylum *Arthropoda* (which also includes, for example, shellfish and spiders).

One of the properties that makes this system of biological classification useful is that all living things belong to a category at every level in the hierarchy. Each individual life form therefore belongs to several categories simultaneously and inherits the properties that are characteristic of each one. The species *Lasius niger,* for example, is an ant, an insect, an arthropod, and an animal—all at the same time. Moreover, each individual ant shares the properties that it inherits from each of those categories. One of the defining characteristics of the class *Insecta* is that insects have six legs. All ants must therefore have six legs because ants are members of that class.

The biological metaphor also helps to illustrate the distinction between classes and objects. Although every common black garden ant has the same biological classification, there are many individuals of the common-black-garden-ant variety. In the language of object-oriented programming, *Lasius niger* is a class and each individual ant is an object.

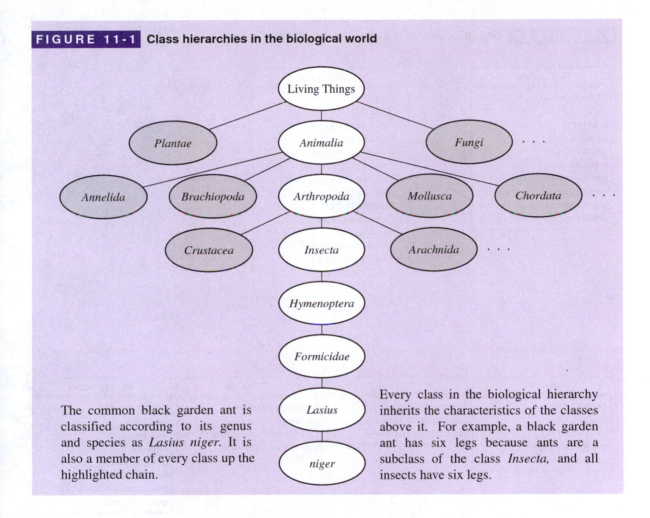

FIGURE 11-1 Class hierarchies in the biological world

The common black garden ant is classified according to its genus and species as *Lasius niger*. It is also a member of every class up the highlighted chain.

Every class in the biological hierarchy inherits the characteristics of the classes above it. For example, a black garden ant has six legs because ants are a subclass of the class *Insecta,* and all insects have six legs.

Class structures in JavaScript follow much the same hierarchical pattern, as illustrated in Figure 11-2 on the next page, which shows the relationships among the classes in the graphics library. The **GWindow** class is in a category by itself. The other class at the top of the diagram is a class called **GObject**, which you have not yet seen but in some sense have been using all along. The **GObject** class forms the top of a hierarchy that encompasses every graphical object that can be displayed in a **GWindow**. The classes that represent graphical objects are all descendants of **GObject**, some directly and some through an intermediate **GFillableObject** class that encompasses the classes that have a fillable interior.

The diagram in Figure 11-2 illustrates several aspects of a standard methodology for illustrating class hierarchies called the **_Universal Modeling Language_** or **_UML._** In a UML diagram, each class appears as a rectangular box whose upper portion

FIGURE 11-2 **UML diagram for the classes in the graphics library**

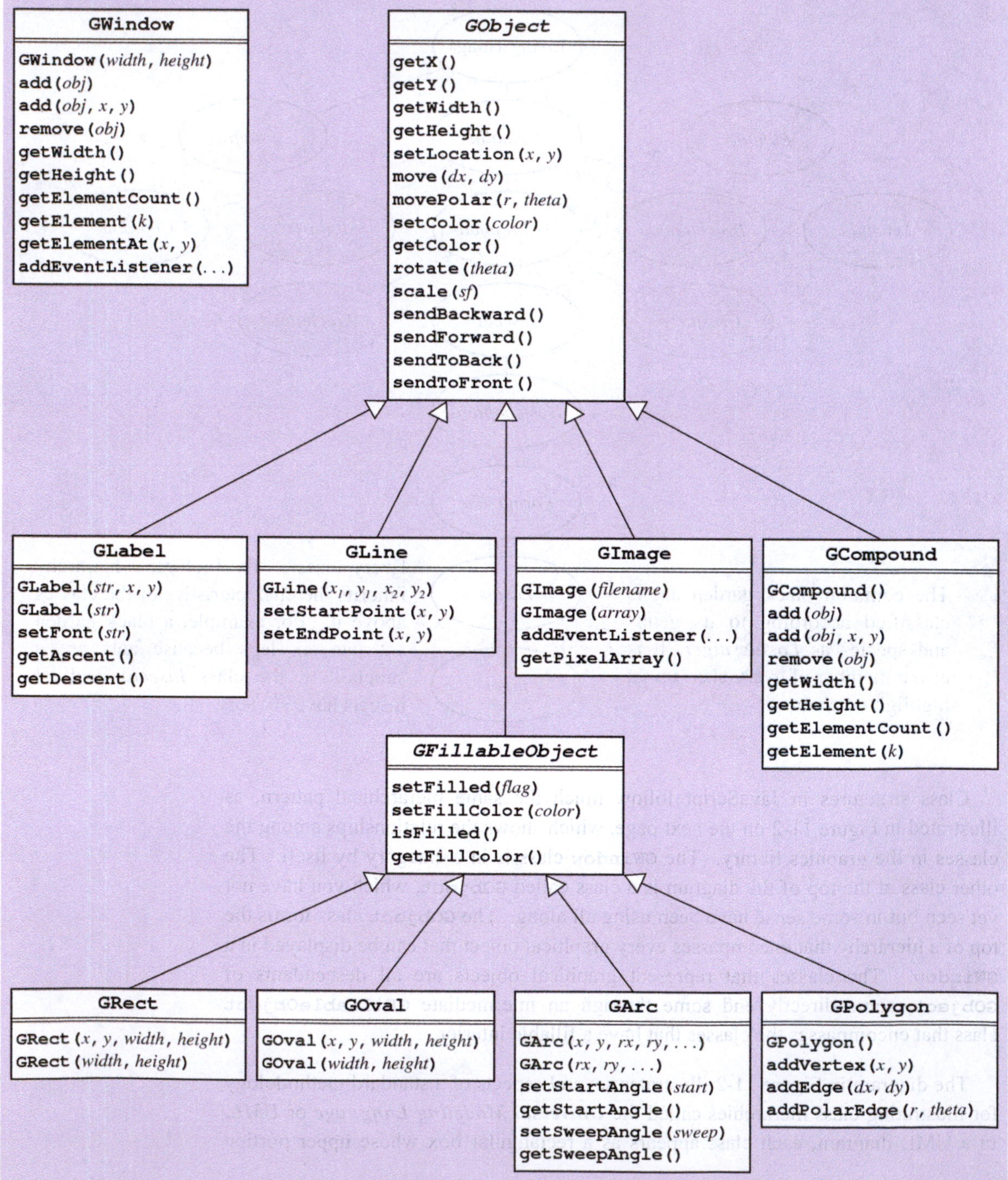

GWindow

GWindow(*width*, *height*)
add(*obj*)
add(*obj*, *x*, *y*)
remove(*obj*)
getWidth()
getHeight()
getElementCount()
getElement(*k*)
getElementAt(*x*, *y*)
addEventListener(...)

GObject

getX()
getY()
getWidth()
getHeight()
setLocation(*x*, *y*)
move(*dx*, *dy*)
movePolar(*r*, *theta*)
setColor(*color*)
getColor()
rotate(*theta*)
scale(*sf*)
sendBackward()
sendForward()
sendToBack()
sendToFront()

GLabel

GLabel(*str*, *x*, *y*)
GLabel(*str*)
setFont(*str*)
getAscent()
getDescent()

GLine

GLine(*x₁*, *y₁*, *x₂*, *y₂*)
setStartPoint(*x*, *y*)
setEndPoint(*x*, *y*)

GImage

GImage(*filename*)
GImage(*array*)
addEventListener(...)
getPixelArray()

GCompound

GCompound()
add(*obj*)
add(*obj*, *x*, *y*)
remove(*obj*)
getWidth()
getHeight()
getElementCount()
getElement(*k*)

GFillableObject

setFilled(*flag*)
setFillColor(*color*)
isFilled()
getFillColor()

GRect

GRect(*x*, *y*, *width*, *height*)
GRect(*width*, *height*)

GOval

GOval(*x*, *y*, *width*, *height*)
GOval(*width*, *height*)

GArc

GArc(*x*, *y*, *rx*, *ry*, ...)
GArc(*rx*, *ry*, ...)
setStartAngle(*start*)
getStartAngle()
setSweepAngle(*sweep*)
getSweepAngle()

GPolygon

GPolygon()
addVertex(*x*, *y*)
addEdge(*dx*, *dy*)
addPolarEdge(*r*, *theta*)

contains the name of the class. The methods implemented by that class appear in the lower portion of the box. The hierarchical relationships among the classes are indicated using arrows with open arrowheads that point from one class to another class at a higher level of the hierarchy. The class that appears lower in the hierarchy is a ***subclass*** of the class to which it points, which is called its ***superclass.***

In an object-oriented language, each subclass ***inherits*** the methods that apply to its superclasses all the way up through the top of the hierarchy. The `GRect` class, for example, inherits all the methods in `GFillableObject`, which in turn inherits all the methods from `GObject`. Given an instance of the `GRect` class, you can call `setFillColor` because that method is defined in `GFillableObject`. Similarly, you can call `setColor`, which is defined two levels up in `GObject`.

In the UML diagram in Figure 11-2, the names of the classes `GObject` and `GFillableObject` appear in italics. This notation is used to define an ***abstract class,*** which is a class that is never used to create an object but instead acts as a common superclass for ***concrete classes*** that appear beneath it in the hierarchy. Because `GObject` is abstract, you never create a `GObject` but instead create one of its concrete subclasses.

In addition to the methods it inherits from its superclass, each class in a hierarchy can implement additional methods that are specific to that class. For example, the idea of a font applies only to the `GLabel` class, which means that the `setFont` method is defined in `GLabel` and not at a higher level of the inheritance hierarchy. By contrast, the `setFilled` method applies only to the classes that descend from `GFillableObject` and not to the other `GObject` subclasses. It therefore makes sense to define `setFilled` in `GFillableObject` so that the definition is inherited by the `GRect`, `GOval`, `GArc`, and `GPolygon` classes.

 11.2 Defining an employee hierarchy

Although the simple model for keeping track of employee data used in Chapter 9 might work for a two-person firm like Scrooge and Marley, large companies have different classes of employees that are similar in some ways but different in others. For example, a company might have hourly, commissioned, and salaried employees. Because those employee categories will share some information, it makes sense to define methods like `getName` and `getJobTitle` that work for all employees. By contrast, calculating the pay for each class of employee differs according to the employee type. A `getPay` method must therefore be implemented separately for each subclass of `Employee`. This model suggests that the class hierarchy used to represent employees might look something like the UML diagram in Figure 11-3 at the top of the next page.

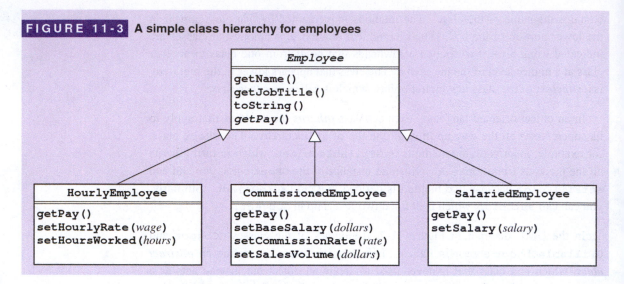

FIGURE 11-3 A simple class hierarchy for employees

The root of this hierarchy is the **Employee** class, which defines the methods that are common to all employees. The **Employee** class therefore exports methods like **getName** and **getJobTitle**, which the other classes simply inherit. Conversely, it is almost certainly necessary to write separate **getPay** methods for each of the subclasses, because the computation is different in each case. The pay of an hourly employee depends on the hourly rate and the number of hours worked. For a commissioned employee, the pay is typically the sum of some base salary plus a commission on the sales volume for which that employee is responsible. At the same time, it is useful to note the fact that every employee has a **getPay** method, even though its implementation differs for each of the subclasses. The UML diagram therefore includes a **getPay** method at the level of the **Employee** class, even though that method is defined at a lower level. The names of the **Employee** class and the **getPay** method within it are set in italic type to indicate that these are abstract entities that act as placeholders for the concrete definitions.

Figures 11-4 and 11-5 on the next two pages define a simple version of the **Employee** class and its **HourlyEmployee** subclass. The factory method for **Employee** takes two parameters, **name** and **title**, and creates an object that contains these fields along with the methods that are common across all subclasses. The factory method for **HourlyEmployee** takes these same two parameters and uses them as arguments to **Employee** to set up the common parts of the structure. The **HourlyEmployee** factory method also defines the local variables required to compute an hourly employee's pay and then adds a definition for **getPay**:

```
function getPay() {
    return hoursWorked * hourlyRate;
}
```

FIGURE 11-4 Definition of the Employee class

```
/*
 * File: Employee.js
 * ------------------
 * This file defines the Employee class, which is the top of a class
 * hierarchy with three subclasses: HourlyEmployee, CommissionedEmployee,
 * and SalariedEmployee.  The HourlyEmployee subclass is defined in a
 * separate file; the other two subclasses are left as exercises.
 */

"use strict";

/*
 * This class represents the superclass of the various categories of
 * employees.  It defines the methods that are common to all employees.
 */
function Employee(name, title) {
   return { getName, getJobTitle, getPay, toString };

/*
 * Returns the name of the Employee object.
 */

   function getName() {
      return name;
   }

/*
 * Returns the job title of the Employee object.
 */

   function getJobTitle() {
      return title;
   }

/*
 * Returns the current pay due to this employee.  This method is specified
 * at this level but implemented only in each Employee subclass.
 */

   function getPay() {
      throw Error("getPay not defined at this level");
   }

/*
 * Converts the Employee object to a string in the form "name (title)".
 */

   function toString() {
      return name + " (" + title + ")";
   }
}
```

FIGURE 11-5 Definition of the `HourlyEmployee` class

```
/*
 * File: HourlyEmployee.js
 * ------------------------
 * This file defines the HourlyEmployee subclass of Employee.
 * The definitions of CommissionedEmployee and SalariedEmployee are
 * left as exercises.
 */

"use strict";

/*
 * This subclass represents an hourly employee whose pay is the
 * product of the hourly rate and the hours worked.  The code for
 * the subclass begins by calling the factory method for the
 * Employee superclass to create the template for the object.
 * It then defines the new variables and methods that the subclass
 * needs and assigns those methods to the original object.
 */

function HourlyEmployee(name, title) {
   let emp = Employee(name, title);
   let hourlyRate = 0;
   let hoursWorked = 0;
   emp.setHourlyRate = setHourlyRate;
   emp.setHoursWorked = setHoursWorked;
   emp.getPay = getPay;
   return emp;

/*
 * Sets the hourly rate for this employee.
 */

   function setHourlyRate(wage) {
      hourlyRate = wage;
   }

/*
 * Sets the number of hours worked in the current pay period.
 */

   function setHoursWorked(hours) {
      hoursWorked = hours;
   }

/*
 * Overrides the getPay method in the Employee superclass.
 */

   function getPay() {
      return hoursWorked * hourlyRate;
   }
}
```

Because the `getPay` method is part of the specification for the `Employee` class itself, the definition of `Employee` in Figure 11-4 also defines a `getPay` method, which looks like this:

```
function getPay() {
    throw Error("getPay not defined at this level");
}
```

The body of this function introduces a new JavaScript statement called `throw`, which is used to signal an unexpected condition called an *exception.* Although a complete treatment of exceptions is beyond the scope of this text, it is important for you as a class designer to report errors in a consistent way. The built-in `Error` class in JavaScript creates an exception value that JavaScript debuggers recognize as an error condition. The factory method for `Error` takes a message string that is displayed either in the debugger, if one is running, or on the system console.

Fortunately, this error condition will never occur as long as the client uses the `Employee` class hierarchy correctly. Because `Employee` is an abstract class, clients will not call its factory method but will instead create one of its concrete subclasses. Each of those subclasses must replace this version of the `getPay` method with one that calculates the employee's pay appropriately. In object-oriented programming, the process of providing a new definition for a method defined at a higher level is called *overriding.*

You will have a chance to implement the other two subclasses of `Employee` in exercise 1.

11.3 Extending graphical classes

As you saw in Figure 11-2, the classes in the graphics library form an inheritance hierarchy in which classes like `GRect`, `GOval`, and `GLabel` extend a more general class called `GObject`. You can easily extend this hierarchy by defining new classes that build on the existing ones.

Extending the `GPolygon` class

In a way, you have already seen examples of programs that create new `GObject` subclasses, although you didn't at the time have the necessary vocabulary to see them in that light. Consider, for example, the `createStar` function, which appears in Figure 6-12 on page 219. That function creates an empty `GPolygon` object and then adds the necessary edges to create a five-pointed star, which is then returned to the client. It is, however, equally reasonable to think of this function as a factory method for a new `GPolygon` subclass that appears on the graphics window as a star.

FIGURE 11-6 Extended class representing a five-pointed star

```
/*
 * File: GStar.js
 * --------------
 * This file illustrates the strategy of subclassing GPolygon by
 * creating a new GObject class depicting a five-pointed star.
 */

"use strict";

/*
 * This class represents a five-pointed star with its reference point
 * at the center.  The size parameter indicates the width of the star
 * at its widest point.
 */
function GStar(size) {
   let poly = GPolygon();
   let dx = size / 2;
   let dy = dx * Math.tan(18 * Math.PI / 180);
   let edge = dx - dy * Math.tan(36 * Math.PI / 180);
   poly.addVertex(-dx, -dy);
   let angle = 0;
   for (let i = 0; i < 5; i++) {
      poly.addPolarEdge(edge, angle);
      poly.addPolarEdge(edge, angle + 72);
      angle -= 72;
   }
   return poly;
}
```

Figure 11-6 contains the same code as Figure 6-12 but defines the operation as creating an instance of a new **GObject** subclass instead of a new graphical object.

As a subclass of **GPolygon**, the **GStar** class implements the **setFilled** and **setFillColor** methods, which makes it possible to display a gold star outlined in black at the center of the graphics window by executing the following function:

```
const STAR_SIZE = 100;

function DrawOutlinedGoldStar() {
   let gw = GWindow(GWINDOW_WIDTH, GWINDOW_HEIGHT);
   let cx = gw.getWidth() / 2;
   let cy = gw.getHeight() / 2;
   let star = GStar(STAR_SIZE);
   star.setFilled(true);
   star.setFillColor("Gold");
   gw.add(star, cx, cy);
}
```

Running this program produces the following output on the graphics window:

Extending the GCompound **class**

The **GCompound** class turns out to be an even more useful platform for designing extended classes than **GPolygon** because it allows you to combine several graphical objects into a single object that acts as an independent unit. As a simple example, you can extend **GCompound** to create a new class called **GTextBox** that consists of a rectangular box that includes a text string centered inside the frame. The factory method for **GTextBox** takes three arguments: the width of the box, the height of the box, and the text to display inside the box. For example, the program

```
const BOX_WIDTH = 80;
const BOX_HEIGHT = 40;

function HelloBox() {
   let gw = GWindow(GWINDOW_WIDTH, GWINDOW_HEIGHT);
   let cx = gw.getWidth() / 2;
   let cy = gw.getHeight() / 2;
   let box = GTextBox(BOX_WIDTH, BOX_HEIGHT, "Hello");
   gw.add(box, cx - box.getWidth() / 2,
               cy - box.getHeight() / 2);
}
```

displays an 80×40 box containing the string **"Hello"** at the center of the window, as follows:

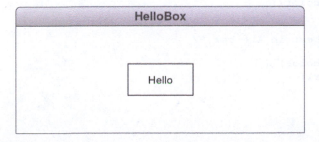

The code for the **GTextBox** class itself appears in Figure 11-7.

FIGURE 11-7 Extended class representing a box containing text

```
/*
 * File: GTextBox.js
 * ------------------
 * This file creates a new GTextBox class that extends GCompound to
 * display text inside a rectangular box.
 */

"use strict";

/*
 * This class represents a compound that displays text in a rectangular
 * box.  The factory method returns a new GTextBox object with the
 * specified width, height, and text.
 */

function GTextBox(width, height, text) {
   const DEFAULT_FONT = "18px 'Helvetica Neue','Arial','Sans-Serif'";
   let box = GCompound();
   let frame = GRect(width, height);
   let label = GLabel(text);
   frame.setFilled(true);
   frame.setFillColor("White");
   label.setFont(DEFAULT_FONT);
   box.add(frame);
   box.add(label, (width - label.getWidth()) / 2,
                  (height + label.getAscent()) / 2);
   box.setLineColor = setLineColor;
   box.setFillColor = setFillColor;
   box.setTextColor = setTextColor;
   return box;

/* Sets the line color of the frame surrounding the text */

   function setLineColor(color) {
      frame.setColor(color);
   }

/* Sets the fill color of the frame surrounding the text */

   function setFillColor(color) {
      frame.setFillColor(color);
   }

/* Sets the color of the text in the box */

   function setTextColor(color) {
      label.setColor(color);
   }

}
```

In addition to the factory method that creates the `GCompound` along with the `GRect` and `GLabel` objects it contains, the `GTextBox` exports three additional methods—`setLineColor`, `setFillColor`, and `setTextColor`—that control the colors of different aspects of the display. Each of these methods redirects the client's request to the graphical object that is responsible for displaying that feature. The `setLineColor` and `setFillColor` methods pass those messages along to the `GRect` object stored in the local variable `frame`, and the `setTextColor` method sends the appropriate message to the `GLabel` stored in the variable `label`. Passing an operation along to a private object stored inside a class is called *forwarding.*

11.4 Decomposition and inheritance

The `DrawHouse.js` program in Figure 4-11 offered an illustration of how to apply the idea of decomposition to drawing a house, by dividing the program into smaller functions to draw the frame, the doors, and the windows. Suppose instead that you wanted to write a graphical program that creates the following picture of a three-car train consisting of a black engine, a green boxcar, and a red caboose:

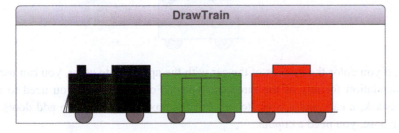

How would you go about designing such a program?

If you followed a decomposition strategy similar to the ones used in Chapter 4, you would implement this program by dividing it up into separate functions such as `drawEngine`, `drawBoxcar`, and `drawCaboose`. Each of these functions could in turn be broken down into functions that draw parts of each car, particularly when the same code can be shared by more than one type of car. That strategy, however, has a serious drawback that was not so serious in drawing a house. While houses tend to stay in one place, trains are designed to *move*. If you wanted to animate the drawing of the train, you would need to have your program change the position of *every* graphical object in the diagram on each time step. It would be much better if the train were a `GCompound` that you could animate as a single unit.

Fortunately, the strategy of decomposition is not limited to functions. In many cases, it is equally useful to decompose a problem by creating a hierarchy of classes whose structure reflects the relationships among the objects. For this application, it makes sense to define a `Train` class as a subclass of `GCompound` so that it acts as a single graphical object. The individual components inside a train can then be objects of a class called `TrainCar`, which is also a subclass of `GCompound`. The three different types of train cars then become subclasses of `TrainCar`.

At this point, it helps to think carefully about the decomposition. In particular, it often makes sense to look for subtasks that recur in multiple subclasses. To see how that strategy might apply in the current problem, it's worth taking another look at the three different types of cars:

If you look at the diagrams for these three cars, you will see that they share a number of common features. The wheels are the same, as are the connectors that link the cars together. In fact, the body of the car itself is the same except for the color. Each type of car shares a common framework that looks like this:

Thus, if you color the interior of the car with the appropriate color, you can use it as the foundation for any of the three car types. For the engine, you need to add a smokestack, a cab, and a cowcatcher. For the boxcar, you need to add doors. For the caboose, you need a cupola.

To make it possible to draw cars in any color, the simplest approach is to have the `TrainCar` factory method take a `color` parameter that specifies the fill color of the gray box shown in the most recent diagram. Individual subclasses can then choose whether to make a specific decision about color, which might be that engines are always black and cabooses are always red, or to pass that choice on to the subclass. The `Boxcar` subclass, for example, can also take a `color` parameter and then pass it along to the `TrainCar` factory method.

The fact that each car has two wheels suggests that defining a `TrainWheel` class will simplify the `TrainCar` class by allowing the code for creating a wheel to be shared. Putting all these ideas together gives rise to the class hierarchy shown in Figure 11-8. Every class in the UML diagram is a `GObject` and can therefore be displayed on the graphics window.

Given this design, you can assemble the three-car train shown at the beginning of this section using the following code:

FIGURE 11-8 UML diagram for the train classes

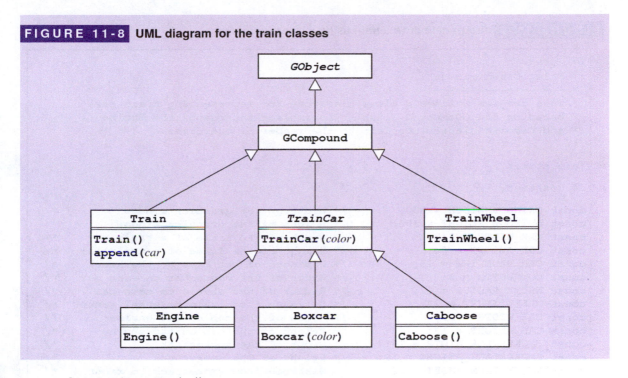

```
let train = Train();
train.append(Engine());
train.append(Boxcar("Green"));
train.append(Caboose());
```

The first line creates an empty train, and the remaining lines add an engine, a green boxcar, and a caboose to the end of the train. To center the train at the base of the window, you can take advantage of the fact that the **Train** class inherits the **getWidth** method from **GObject**. You can therefore simply ask the train how long it is and then subtract half its width from the coordinates of the center of the window.

The **Train** object created in this snippet of code is a **GCompound** that contains every graphical object that appears in the window. If you want the train to move, all you have to do is animate the location of the **GCompound**, since all of its pieces will move together with the top-level compound.

The code to create and animate this train appears in Figure 11-9 on the next three pages. The implementation includes the class definitions for **Train**, **TrainCar**, **TrainWheel**, and **Boxcar**. You will have the chance to implement the **Engine** and **Caboose** subclasses in exercise 8.

FIGURE 11-9 Program to draw a train using a class hierarchy

```
/*
 * File: DrawTrain.js
 * -------------------
 * This program defines a class hierarchy for representing train cars
 * based on the GCompound class.  The implementations of the Engine
 * and Caboose classes are left to the reader as exercises.
 */

"use strict";

/* Constants */

const GWINDOW_WIDTH = 500;        /* Width of the graphics window          */
const GWINDOW_HEIGHT = 300;       /* Height of the graphics window         */
const CAR_WIDTH = 113;            /* Width of the frame of a train car     */
const CAR_HEIGHT = 54;            /* Height of the frame of a train car    */
const CAR_BASELINE = 15;          /* Distance of car base to the track     */
const CONNECTOR = 6;              /* Width of the connector on each car     */
const WHEEL_RADIUS = 12;          /* Radius of the wheels on each car      */
const WHEEL_INSET = 24;           /* Distance from frame to wheel center   */
const CAB_WIDTH = 53;             /* Width of the cab on the engine        */
const CAB_HEIGHT = 12;            /* Height of the cab on the engine       */
const SMOKESTACK_WIDTH = 12;      /* Width of the smokestack               */
const SMOKESTACK_HEIGHT = 12;     /* Height of the smokestack              */
const SMOKESTACK_INSET = 12;      /* Distance from smokestack to front     */
const DOOR_WIDTH = 27;            /* Width of the door on the boxcar       */
const DOOR_HEIGHT = 48;           /* Height of the door on the boxcar      */
const CUPOLA_WIDTH = 53;          /* Width of the cupola on the caboose    */
const CUPOLA_HEIGHT = 12;         /* Height of the cupola on the caboose   */
const TIME_STEP = 20;             /* Time step for the animation           */

function DrawTrain() {
   let gw = GWindow(GWINDOW_WIDTH, GWINDOW_HEIGHT);
   let train = Train();
   train.append(Boxcar("Green"));
   let x = (gw.getWidth() - train.getWidth()) / 2;
   let y = gw.getHeight();
   gw.add(train, x, y);
   let timer = null;
   gw.addEventListener("click", clickAction);

   function clickAction() {
      timer = setInterval(step, TIME_STEP);
   }

   function step() {
      train.move(-1, 0);
      if (train.getX() + train.getWidth() < 0) {
         clearInterval(timer);
      }
   }
}
```

FIGURE 11-9 Program to draw a train using a class hierarchy (continued)

```
/*
 * Creates a new instance of the Train class, which is a subclass of
 * GCompound extended to include an append method.
 */

function Train() {
   let train = GCompound();
   train.append = append;
   return train;

/*
 * Appends the car to the end of the train.
 */

   function append(car) {
      train.add(car, train.getWidth(), 0);
   }
}

/*
 * Creates a new instance of the TrainCar class, which is the common
 * superclass for the concrete subclasses Engine, Boxcar, and Caboose.
 */

function TrainCar(color) {
   let frame = GCompound();
   let x = CONNECTOR;
   let y = -CAR_BASELINE;
   frame.add(GLine(0, y, CAR_WIDTH + 2 * CONNECTOR, y));
   frame.add(TrainWheel(), x + WHEEL_INSET,  -WHEEL_RADIUS);
   frame.add(TrainWheel(), x + CAR_WIDTH - WHEEL_INSET,  -WHEEL_RADIUS);
   let r = GRect(x, y - CAR_HEIGHT, CAR_WIDTH, CAR_HEIGHT);
   r.setFilled(true);
   r.setFillColor(color);
   frame.add(r);
   return frame;
}

/*
 * Creates a new instance of the Boxcar class in the specified color.
 */

function Boxcar(color) {
   let boxcar = TrainCar(color);
   let x = CONNECTOR + CAR_WIDTH / 2;
   let y = -(CAR_BASELINE + DOOR_HEIGHT);
   boxcar.add(GRect(x - DOOR_WIDTH, y, DOOR_WIDTH, DOOR_HEIGHT));
   boxcar.add(GRect(x, y, DOOR_WIDTH, DOOR_HEIGHT));
   return boxcar;
}
```

☞

FIGURE 11-9 Program to draw a train using a class hierarchy (continued)

```
/*
 * Creates a new TrainWheel object whose reference point is the center.
 */
function TrainWheel() {
    let wheel = GCompound();
    let r = WHEEL_RADIUS;
    let circle = GOval(-r, -r, 2 * r, 2 * r);
    circle.setFilled(true);
    circle.setFillColor("Gray");
    wheel.add(circle);
    return wheel;
}
```

■ 11.5 Alternatives to inheritance

Inheritance makes sense when the collection of objects you seek to represent exhibit a clear hierarchical relationship. That relationship is certainly true, for example, of the classes in the graphics library. It also applies to the various element types supported by the Document Object Model you will learn about in Chapter 12, which is implemented as an inheritance hierarchy. Inheritance, however, is often overused in object-oriented languages. The fact that one *can* define one class as a subclass of another does not imply that one *should* do so.

If you look at textbooks for object-oriented languages like Java, you will find no shortage of examples in which inheritance is used without any obvious advantage. Some authors, for example, define a `Pizza` class, which has `PepperoniPizza` and `MushroomPizza` as subclasses. While those classes are arguably specializations of the `Pizza` class, examples of this type do little to illustrate the value of inheritance. If nothing else, the proposed strategy leaves completely unanswered the questions of how to classify a pizza that has both pepperoni and mushrooms or why one would even try to define a class hierarchy with so many independent options. A far better strategy is to store a list of toppings as part of a simple `Pizza` class without any hierarchical structure.

In many cases, extending an existing class to include new operations is less appropriate than the alternative strategy of embedding an object inside a new class that exports the desired set of operations and then implements those operations by forwarding the appropriate methods to the embedded value. This combined strategy of embedding and forwarding often provides the best model for a data structure that uses the behavior of an existing class but does not in any real sense extend it.

 **Summary**

This chapter includes a brief introduction to the idea of inheritance in JavaScript along with some appropriate examples. Important points in this chapter include the following:

- Classes in an object-oriented language form hierarchies in which classes at lower levels *inherit* the methods defined by the classes above them in the hierarchy.

- The immediate descendants of a class are called its *subclasses*. The immediate ancestor of a class is called its *superclass*.

- Classes that form part of the inheritance hierarchy but do not correspond to any actual objects are called *abstract classes*.

- The *Universal Modeling Language* or *UML* provides a notational structure for representing the relationships in a class hierarchy. Each subclass in a UML diagram is connected to its superclass using an arrow with an open arrowhead.

- The graphics library presented in Chapters 4 and 6 uses the class hierarchy shown in the UML diagram in Figure 11-2 on page 390. That hierarchy includes two abstract classes—**GObject** and **GFillableObject**—that serve to unify graphical objects that share a set of common operations.

- You can implement inheritance in JavaScript through a hierarchical invocation of factory methods. The factory method for a subclass calls the factory method for its superclass and then adds any new definitions the subclass requires.

- The conventional way to report an error in the implementation of a class is to throw an error exception using the statement

      throw Error(*message***);**

  where *message* is a string describing the error. This statement stops the program and returns control to the JavaScript debugger. If no debugger is running, the message is displayed on the system console.

- Inheritance allows you to apply the principles of top-down design and stepwise refinement in the data domain.

- The classes in the graphics library, especially **GPolygon** and **GCompound**, offer useful starting points for inheritance relationships as illustrated by the **GStar.js**, **GTextBox.js**, and **DrawTrain.js** programs in Figures 11-6, 11-7, and 11-9.

- Inheritance can easily be overused. In many situations, it is better to embed an existing object inside a new class and then use forwarding to implement the desired operations.

Review questions

1. Choose a favorite animal and add it to the biological hierarchy in Figure 11-1. To find the appropriate place in the hierarchy, you will need to use the web to look up its phylum, class, order, family, genus, and species.

2. Every organism that descends from the class *Insecta* has six legs because that is one of the properties that all insects share. Does this fact mean that all organisms with six legs are insects?

3. Define the terms *subclass* and *superclass*.

4. True or false: A subclass inherits the methods in its superclass along with all of its superclasses in the inheritance hierarchy.

5. What does *UML* stand for?

6. How is the relationship between subclasses and superclasses represented in a UML diagram?

7. Given a class in a UML diagram, how can you determine what methods it supports?

8. What is the difference between an *abstract class* and a *concrete class?*

9. In your own words, explain the purpose of the `GFillableObject` class in the graphics hierarchy shown in Figure 11-2.

10. Does the `GOval` class implement the `rotate` method? Why or why not?

11. The implementation of `getPay` in the `Employee` class signals failure by throwing an error exception. What keeps this error from occurring if the client uses the employee hierarchy correctly?

12. What term is used to describe the process of providing a new definition for a method to replace one defined in a superclass?

13. What is meant by the term *forwarding?*

14. The `Train` class in Figure 11-9 exports a method called `append` to add a car to the end of the train. Would it have worked just as well to use `add` as the name of this method?

15. True or false: Inheritance is often overused in programming applications.

16. What strategies are suggested in the chapter as alternatives to inheritance?

Exercises

1. Complete the definition of the `Employee` hierarchy from Figures 11-4 and 11-5 by defining `CommissionedEmployee` and `SalariedEmployee`.

2. Inheritance comes up naturally in many games. If you were writing a chess program, for example, you could represent the pieces by defining an abstract `ChessPiece` class along with the subclasses `King`, `Queen`, `Rook`, `Bishop`, `Knight`, and `Pawn` for the different piece types. The `ChessPiece` class keeps track of the color and location of the piece. The individual subclasses extend this common framework by implementing the moves for that particular piece.

    Write the code necessary to define the classes shown in the UML diagram in Figure 11-10. The factory methods for the concrete classes each take an argument `bw`, which is either `"B"` or `"W"`, and a designation for the location of the piece composed of the letter indicating the column and a number indicating the row, as shown in the following diagram of the initial chessboard state:

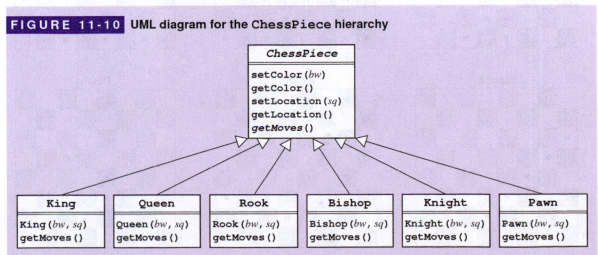

FIGURE 11-10   **UML diagram for the `ChessPiece` hierarchy**

For example, calling `Queen("W", "d1")` would create a white queen on **d1**, which is its initial square.

The interesting challenge in this exercise is to implement the `getMoves` method for each of the concrete subclasses. This method should return an array of all the two-character locations to which that piece could move from its current square, assuming that the rest of the board were empty. Figure 11-11 shows how the different pieces move, in case you are unfamiliar with the rules of chess. The white pieces can move to any of the squares marked with an ✗, and the black pieces can move to any square marked with an ◯. The white pawn in the last diagram can move either one or two squares because it is in its initial position on row 2, but the black pawn can only move one square because it has already moved from its initial position on row 7.

3. Create a new `GRegularPolygon` class that extends `GPolygon` so that it is easy to represent a *regular polygon,* which is a polygon whose sides all have the same length and whose angles are equal. The `GRegularPolygon` factory method should take two parameters: **nSides**, which indicates the number of

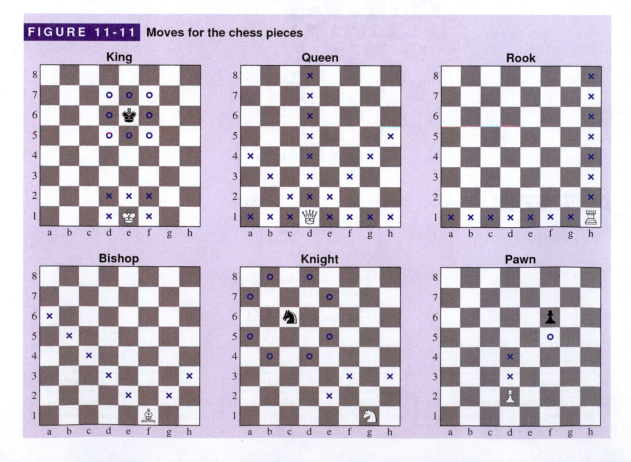

FIGURE 11-11   **Moves for the chess pieces**

sides, and **radius**, which indicates the distance from the reference point at the center to any of its vertices. The polygon should be oriented so that it is flat along the bottom. For example, calling **GRegularPolygon(5, 30)** should create a **GRegularPolygon** object that looks like this:

Similarly, calling **GRegularPolygon(200, 30)** should create a 200-sided polygon whose appearance—at least at the scale of the graphics window—is indistinguishable from that of a circle of radius 30:

4. Use the **GRegularPolygon** class from the preceding exercise to create a **GStopSign** class that extends **GCompound** to create a picture that looks like this when displayed in the center of the window:

5. The factory method for the **GRect** class takes two possible argument forms. Calling **GRect**(*x*, *y*, *width*, *height*) creates a **GRect** object with the specified dimensions. You can also call **GRect**(*width*, *height*), which creates a **GRect** of the specified size initially positioned at the origin. Add this feature to the **GTextBox** class from Figure 11-7.

6. Extend the **GTextBox** class so that it also exports a **setFont** method that resets the font used for the text string. Because changing the font typically changes the dimensions of the label, the implementation of **setFont** will need to adjust the position of the label within the box.

7. Implement a **GCompound** subclass called **GVariable** class that makes it easy to draw box diagrams of variables on the graphics window. The methods implemented for **GVariable** appear in Figure 11-12. The reference point for the **GVariable** should be the upper left corner of the variable box.

8. Complete the implementation of the **DrawTrain.js** program in Figure 11-9 by writing definitions for the **Engine** and **Caboose** classes. Update the main program so that the train includes an engine, a green boxcar, an orange boxcar, and a caboose.

9. In Chapter 6, you had the chance to work with several programs that let you create shapes by dragging the mouse on the graphics window. Using those programs as a starting point, create a more elaborate **DrawShapes** program that displays an onscreen menu of five shapes—a filled rectangle, an outlined rectangle, a filled oval, an outlined oval, and a straight line—along the left side of the window, as shown in the following diagram:

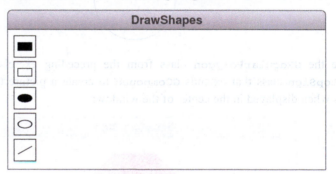

FIGURE 11-12 Methods implemented by the **GVariable** class

GVariable (*name*) **GVariable** (*name*, *width*) **GVariable** (*name*, *width*, *height*)	Creates a new **GVariable** object with the specified name. If either of the *width* and *height* parameters is missing, the implementation should use suitable default values. The initial value of a **GVariable** is **undefined**, which should appear as blank space inside the variable box.
gvar.**getName** ()	Returns the name of the **GVariable**. Once created, the name of the variable cannot be changed.
gvar.**setValue** (*value*)	Sets the value of the variable. The *value* parameter can be of any type, and its string representation should then appear in the center of the variable box.
gvar.**getValue** ()	Returns the most recent value to which the variable was set.
gvar.**setFont** (*font*)	Sets the font of the internal **GLabel** used to display the value of the variable.

Clicking one of the squares in the menu chooses that shape as a drawing tool. Thus, if you click the filled oval in the middle of the menu area, your program should draw filled ovals. Clicking and dragging outside the menu should draw the currently selected shape.

Each of the drawing tools along the left edge of a window should be a **GCompound** that combines the symbol for the tool and the enclosing square. Each tool, moreover, should define additional methods that create the shapes. Your program should check to see whether a mouse click is inside one of the tools and, if so, store that tool in a variable so that the callback functions for the mouse events can perform whatever actions are required to implement that tool.

10. Extend the **DrawShapes** application from the preceding exercise so that the left sidebar also includes a palette of colors. Clicking one of the colors sets the current color for the application, so that subsequent shapes are drawn in that color. Since there is not enough room to display all of JavaScript's predefined colors, you will need to choose a subset that you find aesthetically pleasing.

11. In the 1990s, my Stanford colleague Nick Parlante developed a wonderful simulation game that not only involves inheritance but also pays tribute to the evolutionary metaphor from which the idea of inheritance is derived. The Darwin game operates in a rectangular grid that looks like this:

The sample world on the preceding page is populated with twenty creatures, ten of a species called *Flytrap* and ten of a species called *Rover*. In each case, the creature is identified in the graphics window with the first letter in its name. The orientation is indicated by the figure surrounding the identifying letter; the creature points in the direction of the arrow. Each creature—which you can think of as a simple robot much like Karel—runs a program that is particular to its species. Thus, all Rovers behave in the same way, as do all Flytraps, but the behavior of each species is different from that of the other.

As the simulation proceeds, every creature gets a turn. On its turn, a creature executes one of the actions shown in the first section of Figure 11-13. As soon as one of these actions is completed, the turn for that creature ends, and some other creature gets its turn. When every creature has had a turn, the process begins again with each creature taking a second turn, and so on.

FIGURE 11-13 **Instructions for programming Darwin creatures**

Darwin actions

`move`	The creature moves forward as long as the square it is facing is empty. If the creature is blocked, the `move` instruction does nothing.
`turnLeft`	The creature turns left 90 degrees.
`turnRight`	The creature turns right 90 degrees.
`infect`	If the square in front of this creature is occupied by a different species, that creature is "infected" so that it becomes an instance of this species. The old creature is removed and replaced by a new creature in the same orientation.

Control instructions

`goto` *n*	Take the next instruction from index *n* in the program array. Like all control actions, executing a `goto` instruction does not count as a turn.
`ifEmpty` *n*	If the square in front of this creature is unoccupied, take the next instruction from index *n* in the program array. If not, continue on to the next instruction.
`ifWall` *n*	If this creature is facing one of the border walls, take the next instruction from index *n* in the program array. If not, continue on to the next instruction.
`ifSame` *n*	If the square in front of this creature is occupied by the same species, take the next instruction from index *n* in the program array. If not, continue on to the next instruction.
`ifDifferent` *n*	If the square in front of this creature is occupied by a different species, take the next instruction from index *n* in the program array. If not, continue on to the next instruction.
`ifRandom` *n*	Randomly choose with equal probability whether to take the next instruction from index *n* in the program array or to continue on to the next instruction.

If one creature is facing another creature of a different species in the next square, the first creature can "infect" the second, which turns the infected creature into an instance of the infecting one. The goal for each species in the Darwin game is to infect as many creatures as possible.

The program for each species is represented as an array of strings, each of which is one of the statements in Figure 11-13. The program for the Flytrap creature, for example, consists of the following five-element array:

```
[
    "ifDifferent 3",
    "turnRight",
    "goto 0",
    "infect",
    "goto 0"
]
```

Each creature instance keeps track of the index of the current instruction in this program, which always begins at 0 when a creature is created. On a turn, the creature executes instructions until one of the Darwin actions occurs. The Flytrap creature, for example, begins by executing the `"ifDifferent 3"` instruction at index 0 in the array. If the Flytrap is facing a creature of a different species, it goes to the `"infect"` instruction at index 3 and executes that operation. If the `ifDifferent` instruction does not apply, the creature continues with the `"turnRight"` instruction at index 1. In either case, this creature's turn ends after executing the action. On its next turn, the creature begins by executing one of the `"goto 0"` instructions, which sends the program back to the top. The Flytrap creature therefore rotates clockwise until it sees a creature of a different species, in which case it infects it to make it a Flytrap.

Your job in this exercise is to implement both the `Darwin.js` file that runs the simulation and the `Creature` class, which is the abstract superclass of `Flytrap` and `Rover` as well as any other creatures you design. The definitions of these two subclasses appear in Figure 11-14 on the next page. Your definition of `Creature` must provide the methods that these subclasses need. The `Creature` class is also responsible for managing the display of the creature on the graphics window, which is most easily accomplished by making `Creature` a subclass of `GCompound`.

The main `Darwin` program is responsible for the following actions:

- Setting up the graphics window and drawing the grid
- Initializing the grid by creating 10 creatures of each species and positioning them randomly in the grid facing in randomly chosen directions
- Iterating through the grid giving each creature a turn

FIGURE 11-14 Code for the `Flytrap` and `Rover` subclasses

```
/*
 * This class implements the Flytrap creature.  A Flytrap never moves
 * but instead spins clockwise, infecting any creatures it sees.
 */
function Flytrap() {
   const FLYTRAP_PROGRAM = [
      "ifDifferent 3",    /* 0 */
      "turnRight",        /* 1 */
      "goto 0",           /* 2 */
      "infect",           /* 3 */
      "goto 0"            /* 4 */
   ];
   let flytrap = Creature()
   flytrap.setSymbol("F");
   flytrap.setProgram(FLYTRAP_PROGRAM);
   return flytrap;
}

/*
 * This class implements the Rover creature.  A Rover constantly moves
 * forward.  When it runs into a wall or another Rover, it randomly
 * turns left or right.
 */
function Rover() {
   const ROVER_PROGRAM = [
      "ifDifferent 10",   /*  0 */
      "ifWall 5",         /*  1 */
      "ifSame 5",         /*  2 */
      "move",             /*  3 */
      "goto 0",           /*  4 */
      "ifRandom 9",       /*  5 */
      "turnLeft",         /*  6 */
      "goto 0",           /*  7 */
      "turnRight",        /*  8 */
      "goto 0",           /*  9 */
      "infect",           /* 10 */
      "goto 0"            /* 11 */
   ];
   let rover = Creature()
   rover.setSymbol("R");
   rover.setProgram(ROVER_PROGRAM);
   return rover;
}
```

The most interesting part of this problem is designing new creatures that perform well in the survival-of-the-fittest evolutionary challenge that the Darwin game provides.

CHAPTER 12

JavaScript and the Web

> The Web as I envisaged it, we have not seen it yet. The future is still so much bigger than the past.
>
> — Tim Berners-Lee, 18th World Wide Web Conference, 2009

(Philip Toscano/EMPPL PA Wire/AP Images)

Tim Berners-Lee (1955–)

Tim Berners-Lee graduated from Oxford University with a degree in physics and went on to become a research fellow at CERN, the international nuclear research lab near Geneva, Switzerland. In March 1989, Berners-Lee wrote a proposal for a new set of communication protocols that would allow users to navigate easily through a large collection of data repositories stored on many different computers. That vision became the World Wide Web, now used by billions of people throughout the world. Throughout the web's history, Berners-Lee has campaigned to ensure that access to the web remains free and open, unrestricted by either government or corporate control. For his pioneering contributions, Berners-Lee was knighted by Queen Elizabeth II in 2004 and received the Turing Award, the computing field's highest honor, in 2016.

JavaScript is the most widely used language for implementing interactive content on the web and is likely to remain so for some time to come. After completing the first 11 chapters of this book, you have learned enough about JavaScript to write exciting programs of your own. So far, however, the chapters have focused on JavaScript in isolation without considering its relationship to other programming models that are fundamental to the web. The point of Chapter 12 is to teach you how to combine these models to create more sophisticated applications.

As you learned in Chapter 2, three technologies are responsible for different aspects of a web page, as follows:

1. HTML specifies the structure and contents of the page.
2. CSS controls stylistic aspects of the visual appearance.
3. JavaScript implements interactive behavior.

Although covering HTML and CSS in detail would require another book at least as long as this one, the examples in this chapter will establish the foundation you need to create interesting interactive applications.

12.1 A simple interactive example

Before exploring the interactions between JavaScript and the web environment in detail, it is useful to set the stage by looking at a simple web page that uses buttons to trigger interactions just as most modern applications do. My favorite illustration of this interaction model comes from the following scene in Douglas Adams's 1979 novel, *The Hitchhiker's Guide to the Galaxy,* in which Arthur Dent and Ford Prefect find themselves aboard a marvelous new spaceship:

> Arthur listened for a short while, but being unable to understand the vast majority of what Ford was saying he began to let his mind wander, trailing his fingers along the edge of an incomprehensible computer bank, he reached out and pressed an invitingly large red button on a nearby panel. The panel lit up with the words "Please do not press this button again."

It is easy to simulate this vignette in a web page. The first step is to create a button in the window, which for the moment can be labeled with its color, as follows:

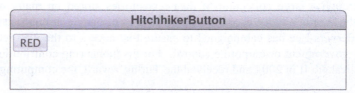

Clicking the button should display a warning message, as follows:

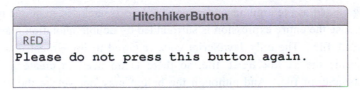

Although Adams's story gives no indication of what consequences accompany pressing the button again, the simplest approach is to repeat the warning:

> HitchhikerButton
>
> RED
> Please do not press this button again.
> Please do not press this button again.

   Implementing this program in a web page is straightforward, particularly if you take advantage of the **JSConsole.js** library you've been using since Chapter 2. HTML includes a **<button>** tag that creates a button in the window. The label for the button appears between the **<button>** tag and the matching **</button>** tag, so that the HTML specification

   <button>RED</button>

displays a button marked with the label **RED**. The action performed by the button is specified in the attributes supplied with the **<button>** tag, as illustrated by the complete **index.html** file shown in Figure 12-1. The **type="button"** attribute is required to indicate that pressing the button will be handled by JavaScript and not by the server supplying the web page. The **onclick** attribute specifies the code to execute when the button is pressed, which in this case is the JavaScript call

---

FIGURE 12-1   The **index.html** file for the **HitchhikerButton** page

```html
<!DOCTYPE html>
<html>
  <head>
    <title>HitchhikerButton</title>
    <script src="JSConsole.js"></script>
  </head>
  <body>
    <button type="button"
            onclick="console.log('Please do not press this button again.')">
      RED
    </button>
  </body>
</html>
```

```
console.log('Please do not press this button again.')
```

The string passed as the argument to **console.log** is enclosed in single quotation marks because the entire expression is surrounded by double quotation marks in the **index.html** file. The only JavaScript code required to implement this program appears inside the **index.html** file, so there is no need to create and load a separate JavaScript file. And although the button may not yet be the "invitingly large red button" the novel describes, you will have a chance to repair that shortcoming in exercise 1.

 ## 12.2 An expanded look at HTML

The **index.html** files you have seen in this book use only a tiny fraction of the features available in HTML. The current version of the HTML standard, which is called *HTML5* written as a single word, defines over 100 different tags. There is no way to cover all those tags in a book focused on JavaScript and, fortunately, no need to do so. As with most programming languages and tools, the best strategy is to learn enough to get started and then build incrementally on that foundation. When you discover that you need a feature beyond what you already know, you can find the necessary documentation on the web. Even so, it is important to learn a few new HTML concepts and tags so that your framework of knowledge is large enough to create interesting web pages.

Figure 12-2 on the next page defines a "starter kit" of 25 HTML tags that are sufficient to implement the examples and exercises appearing in this book. As you know, HTML tags are typically paired, so that the **<body>** tag is matched with a **</body>** tag marking its end. A few tags, however, are standalone and do not require a corresponding closing tag. For example, you can insert a line break by including a **
** tag in the HTML specification. The slash preceding the closing angle bracket indicates that **
** serves as its own closing tag.

You have already used the tags in the first section of Figure 12-2 and the **<title>** and **<script>** tags from the second section. The sections that follow explain how to use the other tags to create more interesting web content.

Displaying text in a web page

When you look at a web page in your browser, much of the content appears in the form of text organized into paragraphs. Those paragraphs typically include text that is styled in various ways along with images and links to other web pages. So far, the **index.html** files in this book have used the **<body>** section only as a placeholder for the output produced by the **JSConsole** and **JSGraphics** libraries. To create a more interesting web page, you need to include other types of content in the body.

FIGURE 12-2 A "starter kit" of HTML tags

Document tags

`<!DOCTYPE html>`	Appears on the first line of an HTML document.
`<html>`	Encloses the HTML content of a page.
`<head>`	Encloses the head section.
`<body>`	Encloses the body section.

Tags that appear in the `<head>` section

`<title>`	Specifies the title for the document, which appears in the browser header.
`<script>`	Loads a script file, which is usually written in JavaScript.
`<style>`	Encloses CSS style definitions.
`<link />`	Links the document to an external resource such as a CSS style sheet.

Block elements

`<div>`	Encloses a section in a document that can be styled as a block.
`<p>`	Encloses a text paragraph.
` `	Inserts a line break. Note that ` ` has no matching end tag.
`<blockquote>`	Encloses an indented quotation.
`<pre>`	Encloses preformatted text such as a program fragment.
`<ol>`	Encloses an ordered list in which elements are numbered.
`<ul>`	Encloses an unordered list in which elements are preceded by a marker.
`<li>`	Encloses a list item that falls within either an ordered or an unordered list.

Inline elements

`<span>`	Defines an inline region that can be styled as a unit.
`<b>`	Sets the text between `<b>` and `</b>` in boldface.
`<i>`	Sets the text between `<i>` and `</i>` in italics.
`<code>`	Sets the text between `<code>` and `</code>` in a monospaced font.
`<a>`	Creates a hyperlink from this page to an external reference.
`<img />`	Inserts an image as specified by the `src` attribute of the tag.

HTML interactors

`<button>`	Inserts a button that triggers a `click` event.
`<input>`	Inserts a text field that triggers an `input` event on any change.

HTML comments

`<!-- ... -->`	Encloses a comment in an HTML file, which is ignored by the browser.

For the most part, the text you see on a web page appears in the `index.html` file in more or less the same form. HTML files, however, are written in plain text. You cannot, for example, set a word in italics simply by changing the font of that word in the `index.html` file the way you would with a word processor. What you need to do instead is specify that formatting information using HTML tags. For instance, to make text appear in italics, you need to enclose it between the paired tags `<i>` and `</i>`. In much the same way, you enclose the text for a paragraph between the tags `<p>` and `</p>`. Thus, if an `index.html` file includes the lines

```
<p>
   This paragraph consists of one sentence and
   includes a word set in <i>italic</i> type.
</p>
```

the corresponding image in the browser window will look something like this:

ItalicsExample
This paragraph consists of one sentence and includes a word set in *italic* type.

Beyond the fact that the word *italic* appears, as expected, in italics, there are other important details to notice about this output. First of all, the text is set in a serif font (typically Times New Roman), which is the standard font used by the browser if no additional style information appears. The word *italic* therefore appears in the italic version of the surrounding serif font. In addition, the line breaks appear in different places in the `index.html` file and in the browser window. By default, the browser displays words in a paragraph on a single line until the next word would no longer fit, at which point the browser advances to the next line. This behavior is called ***filling.*** The filling operation, moreover, occurs dynamically. If you change the size of the window, the line breaks in the paragraph will occur at different places. Finally, the extra spaces that appear at the beginning of each line in the `index.html` file have disappeared in the screen version. With the exception of content enclosed between the `<pre>` and `</pre>` tags, HTML treats all whitespace characters identically and collapses strings of consecutive whitespace characters into a single space.

The `<p>` and `<i>` tags used in this example are representatives of two distinct classes of HTML tags. The `<p>` tag is an example of a ***block element,*** which is a region of the web page that stands alone as a vertical unit. The `<i>` tag is an example of an ***inline element,*** a region of the web page that can exist within a line. Filling, for example, applies to the interior of a block element but not to two block elements that appear consecutively in the HTML file. By contrast, inline elements appearing within a block element are filled just as if they were normal text. Thus, the word *italic,* which is specified by the HTML inline element `<i>italic</i>`, is positioned in the browser display in the same fashion as the rest of the words.

Several of the tags in Figure 12-2 are easy to understand by making the appropriate mental connections to the `<p>` and `<i>` tags. The `<blockquote>` tag, for example, functions similarly to the `<p>` tag except that it also indents the text on both the left and right sides. The inline tags `<b>` and `<code>` are analogous to the `<i>` tag but specify a boldface or monospaced font, respectively. The other tags are somewhat more complicated and are introduced as they are needed.

The fact that HTML encloses tags in angle brackets raises a couple of interesting questions. What happens if you want to include angle brackets in the text of a web page, as you might if you were trying to illustrate HTML code or if you needed to include the less-than and greater-than operators? Similarly, how can you display special characters that don't appear on the standard keyboard but may nonetheless be essential for a web page that includes text in a language with a different alphabet? HTML solves both of these problems by defining symbolic representations for characters that would otherwise be impossible to include in a plain-text HTML file. These symbolic character designations, which are called **character entities,** begin with an ampersand and end with a semicolon. HTML defines a large number of character entities; the ones in Figure 12-3 represent the most common entities used in a typical web page.

As an illustration that includes block elements, inline elements, and character entities, Figure 12-4 on the next page shows both the `index.html` file and the

FIGURE 12-3 Useful character entities in HTML

`&amp;`	The ampersand character (&), which otherwise starts a character entity.
`&lt;`	The less-than character (<), which otherwise starts an HTML tag.
`&gt;`	The greater-than character (>), which otherwise ends an HTML tag.
` `	A nonbreaking space character that will not be split across lines.
`&lsquo;`	A left single quote character (').
`&rsquo;`	A right single quote character ('), also used as an apostrophe.
`&ldquo;`	A left double quote character (").
`&rdquo;`	A right double quote character (").
`&ndash;`	A medium-width dash (–) whose width is 1 en in traditional printing measurements.
`&mdash;`	A wide dash (—) whose width is 1 em in traditional printing measurements.
`&#x`*dddd*`;`	The Unicode character with the hexadecimal value *dddd*.

FIGURE 12-4 Extended `HitchhikerButton` web page and sample run

```html
<!DOCTYPE html>
<html>
  <head>
    <title>HitchhikerButton</title>
    <script src="JSConsole.js"></script>
  </head>
  <body>
    <p>
      Before exploring the interactions between JavaScript and the web
      environment in more detail, it is useful to set the stage by looking
      at a simple web page that uses buttons to trigger interactions just
      as most modern applications do.  My favorite example comes from the
      following scene in Douglas Adams&rsquo;s 1979 novel, <i>The
      Hitchhiker&rsquo;s Guide to the Galaxy,</i> in which Arthur Dent
      and Ford Prefect find themselves aboard a marvelous new spaceship:
    </p>
    <blockquote>
      Arthur listened for a short while, but being unable to understand the
      vast majority of what Ford was saying he began to let his mind wander,
      trailing his fingers along the edge of an incomprehensible computer
      bank, he reached out and pressed an invitingly large red button on a
      nearby panel. The panel lit up with the words &ldquo;Please do not
      press this button again.&rdquo;
    </blockquote>
    <p>
      It is easy to simulate this vignette in a web page.  The first step
      is to create a button in the window, which for the moment can be
      labeled with its color, like this:
    </p>
    <button type="button"
            onclick="console.log('Please do not press this button again.')">
      RED
    </button>
  </body>
</html>
```

HitchhikerButton

Before exploring the interactions between JavaScript and the web environment in more detail, it is useful to set the stage by looking at a simple web page that uses buttons to trigger interactions just as most modern applications do. My favorite example comes from from the following scene in Douglas Adams's 1979 novel, *The Hitchhiker's Guide to the Galaxy,* in which Arthur Dent and Ford Prefect find themselves aboard a marvelous new spaceship:

> Arthur listened for a short while, but being unable to understand the vast majority of what Ford was saying he began to let his mind wander, trailing his fingers along the edge of an incomprehensible computer bank, he reached out and pressed an invitingly large red button on a nearby panel. The panel lit up with the words "Please do not press this button again."

It is easy to simulate this vignette in a web page. The first step is to create a button in the window, which for the moment can be labeled with its color, like this:

RED

resulting screen image for a web page that displays the beginning of section 12.1, which introduces the example from *The Hitchhiker's Guide to the Galaxy*. The `<body>` section includes two `<p>` tags for the text paragraphs, a `<blockquote>` tag for the inset quotation from the novel, and the `<button>` tag from the original example to simulate the operation of the button. The HTML code uses the `<i>` tag to italicize the title along with the character entities `&rsquo;`, `&ldquo;`, and `&rdquo;` to produce the apostrophe and the two double quotation marks. As you can see from the screen image at the bottom of the figure, the line breaks in the text are different from those in the `index.html` file because filling is applied in the `<p>` and `<blockquote>` elements.

Displaying images

The modern web would be unimaginable if it were impossible to display images along with text. Because most web pages include images, it is important for you to know how to include images in the web pages you design.

The idea of integrating images and text in a universally accessible repository is much older than the modern web. The Belgian bibliographer and inventor Paul Otlet envisioned such a system in the 1930s. In his most influential work, *Traité de documentation: le livre sur le livre* (whose English title would be *Treatise on Documentation: The Book on the Book*), Otlet laid out a sophisticated design for a multimedia repository that anticipates many of the ideas we take for granted on the Internet today. Sadly, most of Otlet's work was destroyed when the German Army occupied Brussels during World War II.

If you wanted to create a web page to honor the contributions of this little-known pioneer, it would be useful to include a picture of Otlet along with other biographical information. Fortunately, there are many pictures of Otlet on the web, including several that are in the public domain. If you download one of these images and store it in the file `PaulOtlet.png`, you can display that image (and the citation for its source) as part of a web page by writing an `index.html` file in which the `<body>` section includes the following lines:

```
<img src="PaulOtlet.png" alt="Paul Otlet image" />
<br />(Art Collection 4/Alamy Stock Photo)
```

The `src` attribute of the `<img>` tag tells the browser where to find the image file. The value can be the complete URL of an image on the web, in which case the value begins with the prefix `http:` (or `https:` if you insist on a secure connection as most modern web pages do). More commonly, the `src` attribute specifies the name of a file, which typically appears together with the other files used to display the page. Here, for example, the image file `PaulOtlet.png` must appear in the same directory as the `index.html` file.

The `alt` attribute specifies what the browser should show if it is unable to display the image. In the early days of the web, the primary purpose of using the `alt` attribute was to accommodate browsers that did not support images, but few such tools still exist. The `alt` attribute today fills the important function of providing greater service to users with impaired vision. When users enable the appropriate accessibility options, the text-to-speech synthesis technology that reads the content of the web page can offer a description of what each image contains.

Loading a web page containing this `<img>` tag produces the following browser display:

(Art Collection 4/Alamy Stock Photo)

The size of the image on the screen is the same as the size of the image contained in the file. When you are designing a web page, you will often have occasion to change the size and position of an image. Doing so in a modern way, however, requires the use of CSS styling, as described in section 12.3.

Hyperlinks

One of the fundamental advantages of the web is that pages can include references to other pages that provide additional information. These references to other pages are called *hyperlinks.*

As with Otlet's vision of a universal web of documentation, the idea of linking documents together has a long history. A surprisingly modern conception of the web appears in a 1945 article in *The Atlantic Monthly* entitled "As We May Think," written by Vannevar Bush, who headed the U.S. Office of Scientific Research and Development during World War II. The pioneering information technologist Ted Nelson coined the term *hyperlink* in 1963.

You can add hyperlinks to a web page using the `<a>` tag, which is called an ***anchor tag,*** mostly for historical reasons. In early releases of HTML, the `<a>` tag was used to mark specific locations in a web page and therefore served as an anchor for a specific location. That function is now the responsibility of the `id` attribute, but the `<a>` tag nonetheless retains its name as an abbreviation of its older function. The destination page of an anchor tag appears in an `href` attribute, which uses the URL of the destination page as its value. If, for example, you want to include a hyperlink to the *New York Times* homepage in your `index.html` file, you can include an anchor tag that looks like this:

```
<a href="https://www.nytimes.com">New York Times</a>
```

The text between the `<a>` and `</a>` tags becomes the hyperlink, which appears in a highlighted form in the browser. Clicking the highlighted link asks the browser to show the web page specified by the `href` attribute.

The use of hyperlinks in the context of a complete web page is illustrated in Figure 12-5, which displays the first two paragraphs of this section with hyperlinks to the Wikipedia page for the "As We May Think" article and the pages for the

---

FIGURE 12-5 The `index.html` file for the Hyperlinks page

```html
<!DOCTYPE html>
<html>
  <head>
    <title>Hyperlinks</title>
  </head>
  <body>
    <p>
      One of the fundamental advantages of the web is that pages
      can include references to other pages that provide additional
      information.  These references to other pages are called
      <b><i>hyperlinks.</i></b>
    </p>
    <p>
      As with Otlet&rsquo;s vision of a universal web of documentation,
      the idea of linking documents together has a long history.
      A surprisingly modern conception of the web appears in a 1945
      article in <i>The Atlantic Monthly</i> entitled
      &ldquo;<a href="https://en.wikipedia.org/wiki/As_We_May_Think">As We
      May Think</a>,&rdquo; written by
      <a href="https://en.wikipedia.org/wiki/Vannevar_Bush">Vannevar Bush</a>,
      who headed the U.S. Office of Scientific Research and Development
      during World War II.  The pioneering information technologist
      <a href="https://en.wikipedia.org/wiki/Ted_Nelson">Ted Nelson</a>
      coined the term <i>hyperlink</i> in 1963.
    </p>
  </body>
</html>
```

computing pioneers Vannevar Bush and Ted Nelson. If you load the `index.html` file from Figure 12-5 into a browser, the display will look something like this:

> ### Hyperlinks
>
> One of the fundamental advantages of the web is that pages can include references to other pages that provide additional information. These references to other pages are called *hyperlinks.*
>
> As with Otlet's vision of a universal web of documentation, the idea of linking documents together has a long history. A surprisingly modern conception of the web appears in a 1945 article in *The Atlantic Monthly* entitled "As We May Think," written by Vannevar Bush, who headed the U.S. Office of Scientific Research and Development during World War II. The pioneering information technologist Ted Nelson coined the term *hyperlink* in 1963.

Clicking any of the three underlined hyperlinks on this page will redirect the browser to the page specified in the associated `href` attribute.

12.3 Using CSS

As noted at the beginning of this chapter, HTML is used to define the *structure* of a web page and CSS is used to define its *style.* CSS allows the designer of the web page to control a variety of properties such as fonts, sizes, and colors. While it is impossible to cover the nearly 400 style properties that CSS defines, Figure 12-6 on the next page lists several of the most important ones. If you find you need to control aspects of the presentation style that are not covered by the properties in this list, you can make use of the many websites that describe CSS in more detail.

CSS declarations

Web designers control the style of a page by writing one or more ***CSS declarations,*** each of which consists of a property name, a colon, a value, and a semicolon, like this:

> *name* : *value* ;

The values associated with the CSS properties listed in Figure 12-6 take different forms depending on the property. The following value types are the most common:

- *Keywords.* Many CSS properties define a set of keyword values specific to that property. The `display` property, for example, supports the keywords `block`, `inline`, and `none`. The most common keywords supported by each property are listed in Figure 12-6.

FIGURE 12-6 Selected CSS style properties

Display properties

`display`	Controls how an element is displayed. The default value is `block` for elements like `<p>` and `<div>` that form a separate vertical unit and `inline` for elements that appear within a line of text. Setting `display:none` indicates that the element should not be displayed at all.
`background-color`	Sets the background color. As with all color specifications in CSS tags, the value can be any legal JavaScript/CSS color.

Margin, padding, border, and size properties

`margin`	Sets the size of the margin area outside the border. The `margin` property itself applies to all four sides. You can, however, set individual values by adding the suffix `-left`, `-right`, `-top`, or `-bottom`. The same suffixes apply to `padding` and `border` as well. For block elements, `margin:auto` centers the element in the enclosing context.
`padding`	Sets the size of the *padding*, which is the space between the content area and the border.
`border`	Sets the properties for the border around this element. The corresponding value consists of three components—*style width color*—separated by spaces. Common *style* values are `solid`, `dotted`, `dashed`, and `double`. The *width* component specifies the width of the border and is usually specified in pixels. The *color* component is any JavaScript/CSS color.
`width` `height`	Set the dimensions of the content area. The values are typically specified either in pixels or as a percentage of the size of the enclosing element.

Text properties

`font`	Sets the font properties using a value that supplies the font style, weight, size, and family, as described on page 129. CSS also allows you to change a font component by adding the suffix `-style`, `-weight`, `-size`, or `-family`.
`color`	Sets the color used for text in this element.
`text-align`	Sets the horizontal alignment for text in this element. The acceptable values are `left`, `right`, `center`, and `justify`.
`text-indent`	Sets the indentation of the first line of text in a block element. The indentation value may be negative, in which case the first line is shifted left from the prevailing margin.

List properties

`list-style-type`	Sets the style in which lists are marked or numbered. Unordered lists created using the `<ul>` tag support the values `disc`, `circle`, and `square`. Ordered lists created using the `<ol>` tag support a wider range of property values including `decimal` (1, 2, 3), `lower-alpha` (a, b, c), `upper-alpha` (A, B, C), `lower-roman` (i, ii, iii), and `upper-roman` (I, II, III).
`list-style-image`	Sets the list marker to be an image specified as `url('`*filename*`')`. To cancel a `list-style-image` set by an enclosing list, use the value `none`.

- *Measurements.* CSS properties that control the size or position of an element take values associated with a unit of measurement. The values for these properties consist of a number followed by one of the unit abbreviations shown in Figure 12-7.

- *Colors.* CSS properties that refer to colors can use any of the JavaScript color names defined in Figure 4-5 on page 125. For example, the CSS declaration **background-color:yellow** indicates a yellow background. The color value can also take the form #*rrggbb,* where *rr, gg,* and *bb* are the hexadecimal components of the color.

You have already seen the **font** property in the discussion of the **GLabel** object on page 129. The value of the **font** property consists of four values—the *font style, weight, size,* and *family*—separated by spaces. Each of these values is optional, but any options that appear must be in the specified order. For example, to change the font so that text appears in boldface Times New Roman with a size of 20 pixels, you would use the following CSS declaration:

```
font:bold 20px 'Times New Roman','Serif';
```

As with the font specifications you worked with in Chapter 4, this declaration includes the standard serif font as an alternative in case Times New Roman is not available.

Assigning styles to elements

The combined HTML/CSS model supports several techniques for assigning a style declaration to elements within the HTML document. The easiest—although typically not the best—is to include a **style** attribute as part of a tag. For example, the HTML fragment

---

FIGURE 12-7 CSS units of measurement

px	Absolute size in pixels.
in	Absolute size in inches.
cm	Absolute size in centimeters (**1in = 2.54cm**).
mm	Absolute size in millimeters (**1in = 25.4mm**).
pt	Absolute size in points (**1pt** = 1/72 of **1in**).
pc	Absolute size in picas (**1pc = 12pt**).
em	Relative size as a multiple of the current point size (**2em** is twice the current size.)
%	Relative size as a percentage of the container size (**100%** is the full container size).

```
<p style="font:16px 'Helvetica Neue','Sans-Serif';">
   This paragraph appears in a 16-pixel sans-serif font.
</p>
```

asks the browser to render the contents of this paragraph in a 16-pixel sans-serif font, which is Helvetica Neue if that font is available and the default sans-serif font otherwise. The result in the browser window looks like this:

SansSerifExample
This paragraph appears in a 16-pixel sans-serif font.

The problem with this strategy is that the `style` attribute applies only to the element in which it appears. In most cases, what you want to do is define styles that apply throughout the document. To do so, the conventional approach is to define a set of **CSS rules,** each of which has the following form:

```
selector {
       CSS style declarations separated by semicolons
}
```

The *selector* component of this pattern can take any of the following forms:

- *An HTML tag name.* This selector form applies the associated rule to every tag with the specified name. Thus, the selector `p` applies to all paragraphs marked with the `<p>` tag, and the selector `code` applies to every `<code>` tag.

- *A period followed by a class name.* This selector applies to every element that includes a `class` attribute that matches the specified class. For example, the selector `.example` matches any HTML tag that includes a `class="example"` attribute. This form of the selector makes it possible to apply a set of styles selectively to a set of designated elements.

- *A hashtag symbol followed by an id name.* This selector applies only to the element that has the specified `id` attribute. Thus the selector `#appendix` applies only to an element that includes the attribute `id="appendix"`.

If more than one selector applies to an element, the browser chooses the most specific one, so that selection based on the `id` attribute overrides selection based on the `class` attribute, which in turn overrides selection based on the tag name.

The list of rules for a document can appear in two distinct places. If you want to use a set of rules in a single web page, you can include those rules in a `<style>` tag that appears as part of the `<head>` section. For example, if you want to change all paragraphs in your document so that the text appears in a 16-pixel sans-serif font and the first line of each paragraph is indented half an inch from the left margin, you can add the following `<style>` section to the `index.html` file:

```
<style>
    p {
        text-font: 16px 'Helvetica Neue','Sans-Serif';
        text-indent: 0.5in;
    }
</style>
```

If you insert this `<style>` section into the `index.html` file for the hyperlinks example shown in Figure 12-5 on page 425, the output will look like this:

> **Hyperlinks**
>
> One of the fundamental advantages of the web is that pages can include references to other pages that provide additional information. These references to other pages are called *hyperlinks.*
>
> As with Otlet's vision of a universal web of documentation, the idea of linking documents together has a long history. A surprisingly modern conception of the web appears in a 1945 article in *The Atlantic Monthly* entitled "As We May Think," written by Vannevar Bush, who headed the U.S. Office of Scientific Research and Development during World War II. The pioneering information technologist Ted Nelson coined the term *hyperlink* in 1963.

The list of CSS rules can also be stored in a file, which makes it possible to share the same rule set among many different pages. If, for example, you create a file called `SansSerifRules.css` containing the rule shown at the top of this page, you can then import these rules, which in the file-based model are usually referred to as a *style sheet,* by including the following `<link>` tag in the `<head>` section:

```
<link type="text/css" href="SansSerifRules.css"
      rel="stylesheet" />
```

Styles defined in a style sheet can be overridden either by defining additional local styles for the document or by including a `style` attribute for specific elements.

Controlling margins, borders, padding, and sizes

The style properties in the second section of Figure 12-6 make it possible to set the size of an element, add borders, and adjust the space that surrounds it. Although these properties are likely to seem confusing at first, the diagram in Figure 12-8 illustrates precisely what each of the keywords mean in the context of what web designers call the *CSS box model.* The `width` and `height` properties adjust the size of the *content area,* which is the region of the window in which the contents of an element are displayed. The `border` property controls the style, width, and color of the border surrounding the element, and the `padding` and `margin` properties add extra space inside the border and outside the border, respectively.

FIGURE 12-8 **The CSS box model**

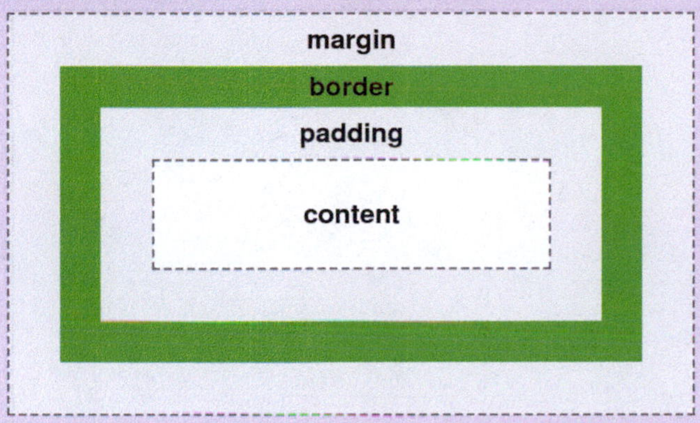

margin

border

padding

content

The **margin** property sets the width of the transparent margin outside the border.

The **border** property sets the width of the border.

The **padding** property sets the width of the transparent padding inside the border.

The **width** and **height** properties set the size of the content area.

The **border**, **padding**, and **margin** properties apply by default to all four sides of the content area. For example, the CSS style declaration

```
border:solid 1px blue;
```

draws a solid blue border with a width of one pixel just outside the content and padding areas on all four sides. You can, however, control the properties of the individual sides by adding **-left**, **-right**, **-top**, and **-bottom** to any of these property names. As an example, the declaration

```
border-right:solid 3px black; padding-right:10px;
```

draws a three-pixel black border down the right side of the content area that is separated from the text by 10 pixels of space. You could use this style of border to create what editors call a ***change bar,*** which is a solid black line in the right margin used to indicate parts of a document that have changed since the preceding version.

The **index.html** file in Figure 12-9 at the top of the next page illustrates each of these properties that apply to the CSS box model in the context of a page that produces the following screen display:

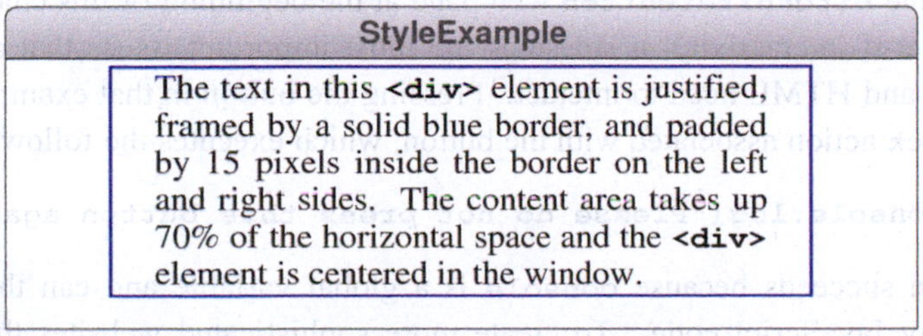

StyleExample

The text in this **<div>** element is justified, framed by a solid blue border, and padded by 15 pixels inside the border on the left and right sides. The content area takes up 70% of the horizontal space and the **<div>** element is centered in the window.

The CSS rule marked by the selector **#example** applies to the **<div>** element that includes the attribute **id="example"**. The declarations in this rule define the

FIGURE 12-9 The `index.html` file for the `StyleExample` page

```html
<!DOCTYPE html>
<html>
  <head>
    <title>StyleExample</title>
    <style>
      code {
        font-weight: bold;
      }
      #example {
        text-align: justify;
        border: solid 1px blue;
        padding-left: 15px;
        padding-right: 15px;
        width: 70%;
        margin: auto;
      }
    </style>
  </head>
  <body>
    <div id="example">
      The text in this <code>&lt;div&gt;</code> element is justified,
      framed by a solid blue border, and padded by 15 pixels inside
      the border on the left and right sides.  The content area takes
      up 70% of the horizontal space, and the <code>&lt;div&gt;</code>
      element is centered in the window.
    </div>
  </body>
</html>
```

properties for that element in the order in which those properties are described in the text. The CSS rule for the **code** tag ensures that the text within a **<code>** tag is set in boldface, which makes it stand out more clearly on the page.

12.4 Connecting JavaScript and HTML

Although the **HitchhikerButton** web page at the beginning of this chapter offers an example of interactivity, it sidesteps the most important issues that arise when JavaScript and HTML need to interact. Pressing the button in that example triggers the **onclick** action associated with the button, which executes the following code:

```
console.log("Please do not press this button again.");
```

This action succeeds because **console** is a global variable and can therefore be used in any JavaScript code. To create more sophisticated websites that support interactivity, you need to learn how HTML entities can interact with other code.

The Document Object Model

The key to forging a connection between the HTML description of a web page and JavaScript is the fact that the browser reads the contents of the `index.html` file into an internal data structure. Like the inheritance-based structures described in Chapter 11, the internal form of a web page uses a hierarchical framework called the ***Document Object Model,*** usually abbreviated to the acronym ***DOM.***

In its entirety, the DOM is extremely complex and difficult to understand. Part of the complexity arises from the fact that the DOM must support obsolete features that still appear in some web pages. As a result, the DOM is an assemblage of old and new features that resists all attempts to describe it in a coherent, integrated way. Fortunately, you can use much of the DOM without having to master its intricacies. The examples in this text limit themselves to classes, fields, and methods that make sense if you view the DOM as a conventional class hierarchy.

A simplified UML diagram for the DOM classes appears in Figure 12-10. To make this diagram as easy to understand as possible, several classes have been

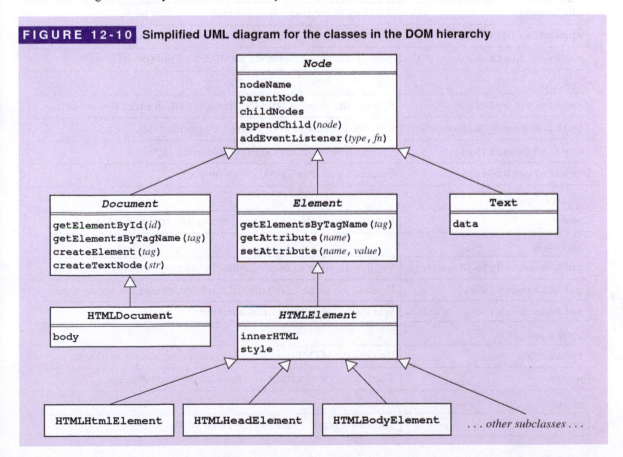

FIGURE 12-10 Simplified UML diagram for the classes in the DOM hierarchy

eliminated from the hierarchy and a few of the fields and methods have been moved into the classes in which someone writing JavaScript code would be most likely to expect them. The fields and methods shown in the concrete classes at the bottom of the hierarchy are precisely the ones you would want to use, even if they are defined at slightly different levels than the diagram suggests.

Figure 12-11 offers one-line descriptions for each of the fields and methods shown in Figure 12-10. More complete details for these methods—and a listing of the many fields and methods that are omitted from this simplified description—are easy to find on the web.

FIGURE 12-11   Field and method summaries for the DOM classes

Node

`nodeName`	The uppercase tag name for this node, as in **DIV** or **P**.
`parentNode`	The parent of this node.
`childNodes`	An array of the nodes that are children of this node.
`appendChild`(*node*)	Appends the specified node as the last child of this node.
`addEventListener`(*type*, *fn*)	Adds a listener to this node for events of the specified type.

Document

`getElementById`(*id*)	Returns the element with the specified **id**, or **null** if none exists.
`getElementsByTagName`(*tag*)	Returns an array of nodes with the specified tag.
`createElement`(*tag*)	Creates a new element with the specified tag.
`createTextNode`(*str*)	Creates a new **Text** node containing *str*.

HTMLDocument

`body`	Returns the DOM element corresponding to the **<body>** tag.

Element

`getElementsByTagName`(*tag*)	Returns an array of nodes inside this element that match the tag.
`getAttribute`(*name*)	Returns the value of the named attribute, or **null** if none exists.
`setAttribute`(*name*, *value*)	Sets the value of the named attribute.

HTMLElement

`innerHTML`	Returns the HTML text for this element, including any tags.
`style`	The CSS style structure as a record with named fields.

Text

`data`	The string represented by this **Text** node.

When you load a web page, the browser sets the global variable **document** so that it holds the data structure for that page. JavaScript code can then call methods on the **document** object, which gives it complete access to the contents. Those methods allow you to analyze or modify the structure of the page, change the style of existing elements by supplying new CSS declarations, and attach callback functions to elements in order to make them interactive.

The **document** variable contains an instance of the class **HTMLDocument**, which means that it has a field named **body**. That field, in turn, holds the DOM object corresponding to the **<body>** tag in the **index.html** file. Moreover, because **HTMLDocument** is a **Document** subclass, it inherits the methods **getElementById**, **getElementsByTagName**, **createElement**, and **createTextNode** defined in the parent class. Similarly, the **document** variable also supports the fields and methods defined for the **Node** class.

The value stored in **document.body** is an object of type **HTMLBodyElement**, which defines no fields and methods of its own. Since **HTMLBodyElement** inherits behavior from its ancestor classes **HTMLElement**, **Element**, and **Node**, code that works with **document.body** can use the fields and methods defined at any of those levels. Each of the **HTML** tags is associated with its own **HTMLElement** subclass, but none of the classes that appear in this book add any new fields or methods beyond those already available from the abstract classes that appear closer to the root of the DOM hierarchy.

Attaching event listeners to HTML elements

As an illustration of how to make connections between HTML elements and JavaScript code, this section walks through the implementation of a simple web application that converts temperatures in either direction between Fahrenheit and Celsius, using the formulas introduced in Chapter 2. The **index.html** file for the temperature converter appears in Figure 12-12.

FIGURE 12-12 The **index.html** file for the **TemperatureConverter** page

```html
<!DOCTYPE html>
<html>
  <head>
    <title>TemperatureConverter</title>
    <script src="TemperatureConverter.js"></script>
  </head>
  <body onload="TemperatureConverter()">
    <input id="Fahrenheit" value="32" />Fahrenheit<br />
    <input id="Celsius" value="0" />Celsius
  </body>
</html>
```

The only new HTML tag in this example is `<input>`, which creates an input field that allows the user to enter text. Each of the `<input>` fields includes an `id` attribute, which makes it possible for JavaScript code to refer to that element, and a `value` attribute, which indicates the initial value of the field. The `index.html` file includes all the information that allows the browser to display the following page:

TemperatureConverter	
32	Fahrenheit
0	Celsius

The `index.html` file also loads the `TemperatureConverter.js` file, which appears in Figure 12-13 on the next page. The `onload` attribute in the `<body>` tag causes the browser to call the `TemperatureConverter` function, which begins with the following statements:

```
let fahrenheit = document.getElementById("Fahrenheit");
let celsius = document.getElementById("Celsius");
fahrenheit.addEventListener("input", convertFToC);
celsius.addEventListener("input", convertCToF);
```

The first two lines use the `getElementById` method to store references to DOM elements to the variables `fahrenheit` and `celsius`. The next two lines assign callback functions that are triggered whenever an `"input"` event occurs. Typing a character into the `<input>` element stored in `fahrenheit`, for example, generates an `input` event, which calls the function `convertFToC`. This function reads the `value` field of the `fahrenheit` element, converts that string to a number, applies the formula for converting Fahrenheit to Celsius, and then uses the result of that calculation to set the `value` field of the `celsius` element. For example, if the user enters 212 in the `fahrenheit` field, the callback function stores the corresponding Celsius temperature in the `celsius` field, like this:

TemperatureConverter	
212	Fahrenheit
100	Celsius

The conversion operation is triggered on every keystroke, so the user would see the Celsius equivalents of 2°F and 21°F before seeing the Celsius equivalent of 212°F.

The `convertCToF` function operates in a similar fashion but performs the conversion in the opposite direction. Before displaying the converted result, each of the callback functions calls `roundedString` to ensure that the value contains no more than two digits after the decimal point.

FIGURE 12-13 Interactive program to convert temperatures between Fahrenheit and Celsius

```javascript
/*
 * File: TemperatureConverter.js
 * -----------------------------
 * This program implements an interactive Fahrenheit-to-Celsius converter.
 */

"use strict";

/* Constants */

const DIGITS_AFTER_DECIMAL_POINT = 2;

/* Main program */

function TemperatureConverter() {
   let fahrenheit = document.getElementById("Fahrenheit");
   let celsius = document.getElementById("Celsius");
   fahrenheit.addEventListener("input", convertFToC);
   celsius.addEventListener("input", convertCToF);

/* Converts the value in the Fahrenheit box to Celsius */

   function convertFToC() {
      if (fahrenheit.value === "") {
         celsius.value = "";
      } else {
         let f = Number(fahrenheit.value);
         let c = 5 / 9 * (f - 32);
         celsius.value = roundedString(c);
      }
   }

/* Converts the value in the Celsius box to Fahrenheit */

   function convertCToF() {
      if (celsius.value === "") {
         fahrenheit.value = "";
      } else {
         let c = Number(celsius.value);
         let f = 9 / 5 * c + 32;
         fahrenheit.value = roundedString(f);
      }
   }

/* Converts n to a string, limiting the digits after the decimal point */

   function roundedString(n) {
      let str = n.toFixed(DIGITS_AFTER_DECIMAL_POINT);
      while (str.endsWith("0")) {
         str = str.substring(0, str.length - 1);
      }
      if (str.endsWith(".")) str = str.substring(0, str.length - 1);
      return str;
   }
}
```

Collapsible lists

The `<ul>` and `<ol>` tags support the display of formatted lists in HTML. The `<ul>` tag generates **unordered lists** in which a marker character precedes each element in the list. The `<ol>` tag generates **ordered lists,** in which the elements are numbered consecutively as determined by the `list-style-type` property. The individual elements in either type of list appear in `<li>` tags inside the enclosing element.

Lists may be nested inside other lists. For example, the HTML specification

```
<ul>
  <li>Item 1</li>
  <li>
    Item 2
    <ul>
      <li>Item 2.1</li>
      <li>Item 2.2</li>
      <li>Item 2.3</li>
    </ul>
  </li>
  <li>Item 3</li>
</ul>
```

generates a two-level list that looks like this when it is displayed in the browser:

NestedList
• Item 1
• Item 2
◦ Item 2.1
◦ Item 2.2
◦ Item 2.3
• Item 3

The default formatting for lists works well if a list is small but is hard to read if a list is large or deeply nested. In such cases, users find it much more convenient if the list shows only part of the detail. At the beginning, the browser shows only the top-level elements of the list. Each element, however, is marked with a clickable triangle that opens that item to reveal its internal structure. Lists that support this sort of selective viewing are called **collapsible lists.**

As an example, the following screen display shows the chapter-level entries in a collapsible list that displays the table of contents for this book, eliding the information for the individual sections and subsections that occupy lower levels of the hierarchy:

Table of Contents

▶ Chapter 1. A Gentle Introduction
▶ Chapter 2. Introducing JavaScript
▶ Chapter 3. Control Statements
▶ Chapter 4. Simple Graphics
▶ Chapter 5. Functions
▶ Chapter 6. Writing Interactive Programs
▶ Chapter 7. Strings
▶ Chapter 8. Arrays
▶ Chapter 9. Objects
▶ Chapter 10. Designing Data Structures
▶ Chapter 11. Inheritance
▶ Chapter 12. JavaScript and the Web

Clicking the triangle preceding the entry for Chapter 1 expands that item to reveal the next level of detail, as follows:

Table of Contents

▼ Chapter 1. A Gentle Introduction
   ▶ 1.1 Introducing Karel
   ▶ 1.2 Teaching Karel to solve problems
   ▶ 1.3 Control statements
   ▶ 1.4 Stepwise refinement
     1.5 Algorithms in Karel's world
▶ Chapter 2. Introducing JavaScript
▶ Chapter 3. Control Statements
▶ Chapter 4. Simple Graphics
▶ Chapter 5. Functions
▶ Chapter 6. Writing Interactive Programs
▶ Chapter 7. Strings
▶ Chapter 8. Arrays
▶ Chapter 9. Objects
▶ Chapter 10. Designing Data Structures
▶ Chapter 11. Inheritance
▶ Chapter 12. JavaScript and the Web

Clicking the triangle again collapses the item and hides its contents. Computer scientists use the verb *toggle* to describe the operation of switching back and forth between two states. In this case, clicking the triangle toggles between the collapsed and expanded state of an item. The state of each list item is indicated by the orientation of the triangle that serves as the list marker. A collapsed element is marked with a triangle pointing to the right. An expanded element is marked with a triangle pointing down.

When you expand the list for Chapter 1, the entries for sections 1.1 through 1.4 are marked with rightward-facing triangles indicating that they contain additional data at a further level of nesting. Section 1.5, by contrast, contains no subsections and therefore appears without a marker. You can expand any of the first four sections by clicking the triangle that precedes the list item. For example, if you click the triangle before the list item for section 1.3, that item will expand, revealing the following three-level list:

```
┌─────────────────────────────────────────────────────┐
│                 Table of Contents                   │
├─────────────────────────────────────────────────────┤
│   ▼ Chapter 1. A Gentle Introduction                │
│         ▶ 1.1 Introducing Karel                     │
│         ▶ 1.2 Teaching Karel to solve problems      │
│         ▼ 1.3 Control statements                    │
│                 Conditional statements              │
│                 Iterative statements                │
│                 Solving general problems            │
│         ▶ 1.4 Stepwise refinement                   │
│           1.5 Algorithms in Karel's world           │
│     ▶ Chapter 2. Introducing JavaScript             │
│     ▶ Chapter 3. Control Statements                 │
│     ▶ Chapter 4. Simple Graphics                    │
│     ▶ Chapter 5. Functions                          │
│     ▶ Chapter 6. Writing Interactive Programs       │
│     ▶ Chapter 7. Strings                            │
│     ▶ Chapter 8. Arrays                             │
│     ▶ Chapter 9. Objects                            │
│     ▶ Chapter 10. Designing Data Structures         │
│     ▶ Chapter 11. Inheritance                       │
│     ▶ Chapter 12. JavaScript and the Web            │
└─────────────────────────────────────────────────────┘
```

Amazingly, the code to convert a conventional HTML list into the far more useful form of a collapsible list fits on a single page of JavaScript code, as shown in Figure 12-14 on the next page. The `onload` attribute in the `<body>` tag calls the `collapseAll` function, which goes through every `<li>` tag and performs the following operations on the corresponding DOM element:

- Call `setDisplayState` to ensure that the element starts out collapsed.

- Add an event listener that responds to click events by invoking a callback function that toggles between the expanded and collapsed states.

The `setDisplayState` function loops through the children of the list node looking for nested `<ul>` elements. If it finds them, it changes the `display` field in the `style` field of the node to `"none"` or `"block"` depending on whether the element is collapsed or expanded. It also records the display state in a field called `isCollapsed`, which is then used to check the current state in the callback function that toggles the element between collapsed and expanded. Finally, the code for `setDisplayState` changes the marker at the beginning of each list item either to the URL for an image file (`TriangleRight.png` or `TriangleDown.png`) for lists containing nested sublists or to `"none"` for list items without nested children.

FIGURE 12-14 Code to replace a standard HTML list with a collapsible one

```javascript
/*
 * File: CollapsibleList.js
 * -------------------------
 * This file contains code for converting HTML lists into collapsible lists.
 */

"use strict";

/*
 * Collapses all <li> elements and adds a listener for click events.
 */

function collapseAll() {
   let nodes = document.getElementsByTagName("li");
   for (let i = 0; i < nodes.length; i++) {
      initListItem(nodes[i]);
   }

/* Initializes a list item and marks it as collapsed */

   function initListItem(listItem) {
      setDisplayState(listItem, true);
      listItem.addEventListener("click", clickAction);

      function clickAction(e) {
         e.stopPropagation();
         setDisplayState(listItem, !listItem.isCollapsed);
      }
   }

/* Sets the display state of the specified list item */

   function setDisplayState(listItem, isCollapsed) {
      let containsNestedLists = false;
      for (let i = 0; i < listItem.childNodes.length; i++) {
         let node = listItem.childNodes[i];
         if (node.nodeName.toLowerCase() === "ul") {
            containsNestedLists = true;
            node.style.display = (isCollapsed) ? "none" : "block";
         }
      }
      if (containsNestedLists) {
         let marker = (isCollapsed) ? "TriangleRight.png"
                                    : "TriangleDown.png";
         listItem.style.listStyleImage = "url('" + marker + "')";
         listItem.isCollapsed = isCollapsed;
      } else {
         listItem.style.listStyleImage = "none";
         listItem.style.listStyleType = "none";
      }
   }
}
```

There are a few aspects of the `CollapsibleList.js` code in Figure 12-14 that are worth looking at in more detail. First, the code for `setDisplayState` makes the necessary changes to the list style by assigning new values to individual fields inside the record returned by `listItem.style`. The names of the subfields in the `style` component of an `HTMLElement` are chosen to be as close as possible to the names of the corresponding CSS properties. In many cases the names are exactly the same, as in the assignment

```
listItem.style.display = "none";
```

which has the same effect as the CSS style declaration

```
display:none;
```

The names, however, need to change if the CSS property names contain hyphens, which are illegal in JavaScript identifiers. The solution used by the DOM is to remove the hyphens and then capitalize the letter that follows each one, creating a camel-case field name consistent with JavaScript's rules. Thus, the assignment

```
listItem.style.listStyleImage = "none";
```

is equivalent to the CSS style declaration

```
list-style-image:none;
```

At first glance, it's probably not immediately clear why it is necessary to set the `listStyleImage` field to `"none"` in the case of list elements that have no nested children. By default, list items inherit the behavior from any enclosing list, which means that leaving out the explicit assignment of `"none"` would cause the list to inherit the image of its parent, which is not the desired behavior in this case.

The one other feature that requires further explanation is the line

```
e.stopPropagation();
```

in the callback function. The purpose of this line is to ensure that the click event affects only the list item on which it was invoked. If a list is nested, a click will typically occur inside more than one list node. A click on a particular triangle is located within the list node that the triangle marks, but it is also inside the list node at every higher level. When JavaScript delivers events to DOM objects, it begins by invoking the event listener at the lowest level but, by default, continues to call event listeners for every higher-level node that contains the current node. This process is called **bubbling.** Each event bubbles up through every level of the hierarchy to give each node a chance to respond. Calling `stopPropogation` prevents any further bubbling and ensures that only the current node is toggled.

12.5 Storing data in the `index.html` file

The existence of the Document Object Model described in section 12.4 opens up a new way of storing data for a web application. Although the security restrictions imposed on JavaScript make it impossible to read an arbitrary data file, all JavaScript programs running in a browser have access to the data contained in the `index.html` file. That information, moreover, has already been interpreted by the browser and stored in the DOM hierarchy. If you can find a way to encode the data you need for your application in a form that is compatible with the `index.html` file, you can then use the methods available in the DOM to gain access to that information.

Representing data using XML

As you know from Chapter 2, the `index.html` file is written in a language called HTML. HTML is a specialization of a more general language called **XML,** which stands for **Extensible Markup Language.** XML is easily read by both humans and machines and is flexible enough to use in many different applications. Over the last decade or so, commercial applications have increasingly used XML to store information that used to be represented in proprietary binary forms. In the Microsoft Office collection of tools, for example, the `x` in the file types `.docx` and `.pptx` signifies that these files are stored using XML format.

Both XML and HTML represent structured data in the form of sections bounded by tags enclosed in angle brackets. These tags are typically paired, so that the `<body>` tag that marks the start of the body of the web page is matched with a `</body>` tag that marks its end. Tags that have no closing tag like the `<br />` tag in HTML *must* include the slash before the closing angle bracket when used in XML, even though that slash is optional in HTML. Tags in both XML and HTML may specify additional information in the form of attributes, which have the same form in both languages.

The essential idea behind using XML to represent the application data is that all modern browsers allow the `index.html` file to include XML code beyond the HTML tags that drive the browser. The browser, moreover, scans the entire contents of the `index.html` file and assembles it into a hierarchical data structure that includes all the tags and their attributes, even if those tags and attributes are not defined in HTML. As a result, it is perfectly legal to invent new XML tags for a specific application and then include those tags in the `index.html` file.

Creating a teaching machine

As with most programming concepts, the idea of including XML data in the `index.html` file is easiest to illustrate by example. The goal of this section is to create a "teaching machine" that uses a strategy called *programmed instruction* in which a computerized teaching tool asks a series of questions so that previous answers determine the order of subsequent questions. As long as a student is getting the right answers, the programmed instruction process skips the easy questions and moves on to more challenging topics. For the student who is having trouble, the process moves more slowly, leaving time for repetition and review. Although the idea of programmed instruction was quite the rage some 40 years ago, it didn't live up to the potential its proponents claimed. Even so, building a simple teaching machine based on the programmed-instruction model offers a useful illustration of the general technique of storing application data in HTML form.

To make the idea of a teaching-machine application more concrete, it helps to imagine how the student might use it. When the program starts, it begins by asking the student a question. For example, a programmed-instruction course on simple JavaScript might begin like this:

```
TeachingMachine

True or false: Numbers in JavaScript may contain a
decimal point.
>
```

The program then waits for the student to enter an answer. Depending on the response, the program will choose the next question either to provide more review or to let the student move ahead more quickly. For example, if the student enters an incorrect answer, the program will continue with another question about numbers, which might look like this:

```
TeachingMachine

True or false: Numbers in JavaScript may contain a
decimal point.
> false
True or false: Numbers can be negative.
>
```

If the student instead supplies the correct response, the program moves on to a more advanced question, such as the one shown in the following console log, which asks the student a question about the remainder operator:

```
TeachingMachine

True or false: Numbers in JavaScript may contain a
decimal point.
> true
What is the value of 7 % 4?
>
```

The text of each question, the list of possible answers, and the appropriate next question to ask are stored in XML format in the `index.html` file. For example, the first question in the simple JavaScript course is represented in the `index.html` file in the following form:

```
<question id="Numbers1">
   True or false: Numbers can have fractional parts.
   <answer response="true" nextQuestion="Remainders1" />
   <answer response="false" nextQuestion="Numbers2" />
</question>
```

The `<question>` tag encloses both the text of the question and the list of possible responses, each of which appears in the form of an `<answer>` tag with two attributes. The `response` attribute indicates a possible response from the user, and the corresponding `nextQuestion` attribute provides the identifying key for the next question to ask if the user gives that response. Here, for example, entering the answer `true` sends the teaching machine to a question whose `id` attribute is `"Remainders1"`, which is the first question on the topic of the remainder operator. Conversely, entering the answer `false` sends the teaching machine to the question whose `id` attribute is `"Numbers2"` on the theory that the student needs more practice with this topic.

The `index.html` file for a tiny JavaScript course with seven questions appears in Figure 12-15 on the next page. The `<question>` tags for those seven questions are included in the `index.html` file enclosed within the following tag:

```
<div style="display:none;">
```

The CSS declaration `style="display:none;"` ensures that the browser does not display the embedded text within the `<question>` tags.

The code for the `TeachingMachine` application itself appears in Figure 12-16 on page 447. The program begins by setting the variable `questionXML` to the DOM object that corresponds to the first question in the `index.html` file, which appears at index 0 in the array of all `<question>` tags. The program then calls `askQuestion` to display the text of the current question. It does so by calling a new method exported by the `console` object. The `console.write` method is similar to `console.log` in that it sends output to the console. The difference is that `console.write` interprets its argument as HTML rather than a simple string, which means that course designers can include HTML formatting tags in their questions. The argument to `console.write` is the entire HTML content enclosed within the `<question>` tag concatenated with the string `"<br />"`, thereby ensuring that the question ends with a line break.

FIGURE 12-15 HTML file for a tiny Javascript course

```html
<!DOCTYPE html>
<html>
  <head>
    <title>Simple JavaScript</title>
    <script src="JSConsole.js"></script>
    <script src="TeachingMachine.js"></script>
  </head>
  <body onload="TeachingMachine()">
    <div style="display:none;">
      <question id="Numbers1">
        True or false: Numbers in JavaScript may contain a decimal point.
        <answer response="true" nextQuestion="Remainders1" />
        <answer response="false" nextQuestion="Numbers2" />
      </question>
      <question id="Numbers2">
        True or false: Numbers can be negative.
        <answer response="true" nextQuestion="Remainders1" />
        <answer response="false" nextQuestion="Numbers1" />
      </question>
      <question id="Remainders1">
        What is the value of 7 % 4?
        <answer response="3" nextQuestion="Boolean1" />
        <answer response="*" nextQuestion="Remainders2" />
      </question>
      <question id="Remainders2">
        What is the value of 4 % 7?
        <answer response="4" nextQuestion="Boolean1" />
        <answer response="*" nextQuestion="Remainders1" />
      </question>
      <question id="Boolean1">
        How many values are there of Boolean type?
        <answer response="2" nextQuestion="Finish" />
        <answer response="two" nextQuestion="Finish" />
        <answer response="*" nextQuestion="Boolean2" />
      </question>
      <question id="Boolean2">
        What JavaScript operator best represents the English word "and"?
        <answer response="&&" nextQuestion="Finish" />
        <answer response="*" nextQuestion="Boolean1" />
      </question>
      <question id="Finish">
        You seem to have mastered JavaScript. Start over?
        <answer response="yes" nextQuestion="Numbers1" />
        <answer response="no" nextQuestion="EXIT" />
      </question>
    </div>
  </body>
</html>
```

FIGURE 12-16 JavaScript code for the teaching machine

```
/*
 * File: TeachingMachine.js
 * --------------------------
 * This program executes a programmed instruction course.  The questions
 * and answers appear in the index.html file in the following form:
 *
 *    <div style="display:none;">
 *       <question id="...">
 *          . . . text of the question . . .
 *          <answer response="..." nextQuestion="..." />
 *          . . . more <answer> tags . . .
 *       </question>
 *       . . . more <question> tags . . .
 *    </div>
 */

"use strict";

/* Main program */

function TeachingMachine() {
   let questionXML = document.getElementsByTagName("question")[0];
   askQuestion();

   function askQuestion() {
      console.write(questionXML.innerHTML + "<br />");
      console.requestInput("> ", checkAnswer);
   }

   function checkAnswer(str) {
      let answerXML = getAnswerXML(str.toLowerCase());
      if (answerXML === null) {
         console.log("I don't understand that response.");
      } else {
         let nextQuestionId = answerXML.getAttribute("nextQuestion");
         if (nextQuestionId === "EXIT") return;
         questionXML = document.getElementById(nextQuestionId);
      }
      askQuestion();
   }

   function getAnswerXML(str) {
      let answers = questionXML.getElementsByTagName("answer");
      for (let i = 0; i < answers.length; i++) {
         let answerXML = answers[i];
         let response = answerXML.getAttribute("response").toLowerCase();
         if (response === str || response === "*") return answerXML;
      }
      return null;
   }
}
```

Once the text of the question has been written to the console, `askQuestion` calls `requestInput` to get a line from the user. When the user completes the line, the console invokes the callback function `checkAnswer` to process the user's response. The `checkAnswer` function calls `getAnswerXML` to look up the string entered by the user to see whether it matches any of the responses expected for this question. If not, `getAnswerXML` returns `null`, which allows `checkAnswer` to display a message asking the user to try again. If it finds a match, `getAnswerXML` returns the DOM object for the corresponding `<answer>` tag. In this case, `checkAnswer` can retrieve the `nextQuestion` attribute from that object and ask the next question.

The `TeachingMachine` application includes a couple of special features that are worth noting:

- If the `response` attribute in an `<answer>` tag is the string `"*"`, it matches any answer that the user enters. The `getAnswerXML` function checks the `<answer>` tags in order, so it makes sense to use the `"*"` option only as the final option.

- If the `nextQuestion` attribute is the string `"EXIT"`, the `TeachingMachine` interprets that value as a request to end the course.

Changing the application domain

The fact that the `TeachingMachine` application takes all of its data from the `index.html` file makes it possible to use the program in entirely different contexts. For example, if you change the XML entries that define the course content as shown in Figure 12-17 at the top of the next page, the same `TeachingMachine` program will play a game reminiscent of the Adventure program created by Willie Crowther in the early 1970s.

As a player in Crowther's Adventure game, you assume the role of an adventurer wandering through a world. The individual locations in the game are generically called *rooms,* even though they might be outside. You move from room to room by typing simple commands, as shown in the following sample session:

```
                         Adventure!
You are standing at the end of a road before a
small brick building.  A small stream flows out
of the building and down a gully to the south.
A road runs up a small hill to the west.
> south
You are in a valley in the forest beside a stream
tumbling along a rocky bed.  The stream is flowing
to the south.
> south
At your feet all the water of the stream splashes
down a two-inch slit in the rock.  To the south,
the streambed is bare rock.
>
```

FIGURE 12-17 XML definitions for a text-based adventure game

```
<div style="display:none;">
  <question id="OutsideBuilding">
    You are standing at the end of a road before a small brick
    building.  A small stream flows out of the building and down
    a gully to the south.  A road runs up a small hill to the west.
    <answer response="south" nextQuestion="Valley" />
    <answer response="in" nextQuestion="InsideBuilding" />
    <answer response="west" nextQuestion="EndOfRoad" />
  </question>
  <question id="Valley">
    You are in a valley in the forest beside a stream tumbling along
    a rocky bed.  The stream is flowing to the south.
    <answer response="south" nextQuestion="SlitInRock" />
    <answer response="north" nextQuestion="OutsideBuilding" />
  </question>
  <question id="SlitInRock">
    At your feet all the water of the stream splashes down a two-inch
    slit in the rock.  To the south, the streambed is bare rock.
    <answer response="north" nextQuestion="Valley" />
    <answer response="south" nextQuestion="OutsideGrate" />
  </question>
  . . . entries for the other rooms . . .
</div>
```

Summary

This chapter gives you a taste of how to use JavaScript together with HTML and CSS to create interactive web pages. Although a complete discussion of these facilities would require another book, the examples in this chapter are sufficient to get you started. Important points in this chapter include the following:

- HTML includes a `<button>` tag that displays an onscreen button. Clicking the button runs the JavaScript code associated with the `onclick` attribute.

- The `<button>` tag is only one of many new HTML tags introduced in this chapter. Figure 12-2 on page 419 summarizes the tags used in this chapter.

- Most tags in HTML are paired so that they have both a start and an end tag; a few tags are standalone. In keeping with conventional practice, standalone tags in this book all include a slash before the closing angle bracket, as in `<br />`.

- Tags that create the elements displayed on a web page fall into two classes. *Block elements* represent a region of text that has its own vertical space. *Inline elements* occur within a line and are subject to filling, just like standard text.

- HTML supports a wide selection of *character entities* used to display characters that do not appear on a standard keyboard or that have special significance in HTML. Figure 12-3 on page 421 lists the most important character entities.

- The `<img>` tag makes it possible to display an image in a web page. The `src` attribute specifies the source of the image, and the `alt` attribute provides an alternative text description that offers greater accessibility.

- HTML files use the `<a>` tag to define a *hyperlink,* which is an active link from one page to another.

- HTML defines the *structure* of the elements that make up a web page; CSS defines the *style* of those elements.

- CSS specifications are composed of a set of *CSS rules,* each of which associates a *selector* with a set of *CSS declarations* that define a relationship between a *property* and its corresponding *value.* Figure 12-6 on page 427 lists some of the most important style properties available in CSS.

- The selector in a CSS rule can be a tag name, a `class` name preceded by a period, or a specific `id` name preceded by a hashtag symbol.

- CSS properties that refer to lengths use a variety of suffixes to specify the unit of measurement. These suffixes are listed in Figure 12-7 on page 428.

- CSS specifications can appear in the `style` attribute of a single element, within a `<style>` section in the `index.html` file, or in a separate *stylesheet* loaded using the `<link>` tag.

- Spacing and borders for block elements adhere to the rules of the *CSS box model,* which appears in Figure 12-8 on page 431.

- The browser reads the entire contents of the HTML file into a hierarchical data structure called the *Document Object Model* or *DOM.* Each level of the DOM hierarchy defines fields and methods inherited by any subclasses. Descriptions of the DOM hierarchy appear in Figures 12-10 and 12-11. The `HTMLDocument` object for the current page is stored in the global `document` variable.

- The `addEventListener` method in the `Node` class makes it possible to specify a callback function for events that occur in any HTML element. Those callback functions typically refer to private data for the application through its closure. Events are passed to all enclosing elements unless `stopPropagation` is called.

- The DOM allows JavaScript programs to refer to attributes and properties defined by CSS. CSS names containing hyphens are written in camel case, so that the CSS property `font-size` becomes `fontSize` in JavaScript.

- JavaScript applications can store data in the `index.html` file by encoding it in *XML,* which stands for *Extensible Markup Language.*

Review questions

1. What attribute in the `<button>` tag makes it possible to associate JavaScript code with an HTML button?

2. What is the standard convention for marking a standalone tag in HTML?

3. In your own words, describe the differences between a *block element* and an *inline element*.

4. What is a *character entity?*

5. How do you represent each of the following characters in a web page: an ampersand character (`&`), a less-than sign (`<`), a greater-than sign (`>`), and a space that will not be broken across a line boundary?

6. Why is it still important to include the `alt` attribute in an `<img>` tag even though all modern browsers make it possible to display images?

7. Who coined the term *hyperlink?* Which two individuals does this chapter recognize for having come up with a similar idea earlier in the 20th century?

8. What CSS rule would you use to justify the text in all paragraphs on a page?

9. What are the three forms for a CSS selector listed in this chapter?

10. What are the three places in which CSS style rules may appear?

11. Describe the relationship between the *border, margin, padding,* and *content* components used in the CSS box model.

12. What does the acronym *DOM* stand for?

13. What reason does the chapter offer for the complexity of the *DOM?*

14. Does the `HTMLBodyElement` class support the method `addEventListener`?

15. The `TemperatureConverter.js` program includes no code to guard against the possibility that the user might enter something other than a number in the input box. What does the program do if that situation occurs?

16. Why is there no triangle in front of the line for section 1.5 in the second table of contents listing on page 439?

17. In the implementation of `clickAction` shown in Figure 12-14 on page 441, what is the purpose of the call to `stopPropagation`? Describe the situations in which omitting this call would lead to incorrect behavior.

18. How does JavaScript handle the fact that the names of many CSS properties contain hyphens, which are not legal in JavaScript identifiers?

19. What JavaScript code would you use to double the font size of an HTML element stored in the variable **node**?

20. What does the **x** stand for in the Microsoft file types **.docx** and **.pptx**?

21. True or false: Browsers report an error when they encounter an unrecognized tag in an HTML file.

22. Describe the differences between **console.log** and **console.write**.

 ## Exercises

1. As noted in the chapter, the button displayed by the **HitchhikerButton** page is not the "invitingly large red button" that Douglas Adams describes. Use CSS styles to change the font size, text color, background color, and alignment of the button so that it looks like this, horizontally centered in the window:

2. Starting with the version you wrote for the preceding exercise, rewrite the **HitchhikerButton** page so that the messages become increasingly strident the first three times the button is pressed, as follows:

After the user presses the button a third time, it should stop responding. To make this change, you will need to create a **HitchhikerButton.js** file that contains the code to implement the callback function for the button.

3. Add a **Clear** button to the **DrawDots.js** program from Figure 6-1 on page 199. Pressing the **Clear** button should erase all the dots previously drawn in the graphics window.

4. Add the necessary CSS styles to the `index.html` file for the web page that displays a picture of Paul Otlet so that the image is centered in the window and dynamically resized so that its width is a third of the window size. Center the caption and credits under the picture so that the screen image looks like this:

5. Write a program to play the game of Concentration. The layout for Concentration consists of a shuffled deck of cards arranged face down in four rows of thirteen cards each. The player then turns over any two cards. If those cards match in rank, both cards are removed from the layout. If they don't match, the cards are turned face down again, and the player has a chance to pick new cards. The purpose of the game is to sharpen your memory for where you have seen cards in earlier rounds. The screen image in Figure 12-18 shows the state of a game after the player has turned over two matching queens, which

FIGURE 12-18 Screen image from the middle of a game of Concentration

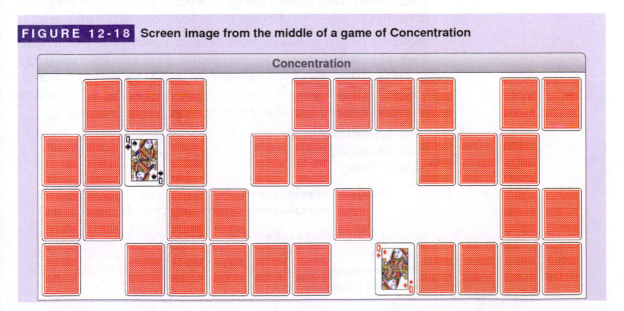

will be removed from the layout. Your program should pause two seconds before removing or turning over the cards so that the player can remember their location.

The challenge in this problem is to implement Concentration without using the graphics library. The cards should be displayed using `<img>` tags, and your program should update the image on the screen by changing the `src` attribute to the name of the appropriate image file. The website for this book includes image files for a standard deck of cards.

6. As written, the `TeachingMachine.js` program provides no feedback when the user gives an incorrect answer. Add the necessary code to allow an optional `msg` attribute in the `<answer>` tag. If this attribute exists, the program should display that message before asking the next question.

7. Modify and extend the `TeachingMachine.js` program so that it plays a more interesting Adventure game. The changes you need to make include:

   • Update the XML structure so that the names of the new tags are appropriate to the Adventure context. For example, it seems better to use the tag names `<room>` and `<passage>` than the tag names `<question>` and `<answer>`.

   • Add objects to the game by introducing a new XML `<object>` tag that looks something like this:

     ```
     <object name="keys" description="a set of keys"
             room="InsideBuilding" />
     ```

     The attributes in this example specify the name of the object, the string used to describe the object, and the room in which the object is initially placed.

   • Implement the user commands **TAKE**, **DROP**, and **INVENTORY** that allow the player to work with objects. For example, the command **TAKE KEYS** should take the keys from the current room and add them to the player's collection, **DROP KEYS** should leave the keys in the current room, and **INVENTORY** should display the descriptions of the objects the player is carrying.

   • Make it possible to create interesting puzzles by allowing the player to move through a passage only if the player is carrying some object. For example, the tag

     ```
     <passage direction="down" key="keys"
              destination="BeneathGrate" />
     ```

     indicates that the player can move down to the room whose `id` attribute is `"BeneathGrate"` if the object named `"keys"` is in the player's inventory. Later `<passage>` tags can specify what action to take if the player tries to move down without the keys.

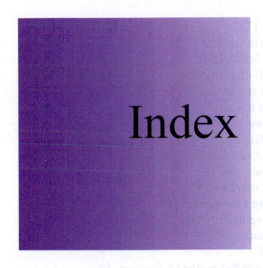

Index